D1083074

Fulk Nerra,
the Neo-Roman Consul

Fulk Nerra, the Neo-Roman Consul, 987–1040

A Political Biography
of the Angevin Count

Bernard S. Bachrach

UNIVERSITY OF CALIFORNIA PRESS

Berkeley / Los Angeles / London

University of California Press
Berkeley and Los Angeles, California

University of California Press
London, England

Copyright © 1993 by The Regents of the University of California

Printed in the United States of America

1 2 3 4 5 6 7 8 9

Library of Congress Cataloging-in-Publication Data
Bachrach, Bernard S., 1939–
    Fulk Nerra, the neo-Roman consul, 987–1040: a political
biography of the Angevin count / Bernard S. Bachrach.
      p.   cm.
    Includes bibliographical references and index.
    ISBN 0-520-07996-5
    1. Fulk III Nerra, Count of Anjou, ca. 970–1040. 2. Anjou
(France)—History.   3. France—Civilization—Roman influences.
4. France—Kings and rulers—Biography.   5. Anjou, House of.
I. Title.
DC611.A606B23   1993
944'.021'092—dc20   93–13891
[B]   CIP

For Jacques Boussard *in memoriam*
and for Olivier Guillot

Contents

Preface

When the political unity of *Francia Occidentalis* finally succumbed to the dual burdens of endemic civil war and foreign invasions during the late ninth century, the realm gradually fragmented into a congeries of smaller states.[1] Many of these polities were based on the old Roman *civitates*, that is, the fundamental local political structures that first had coalesced into a Romano-German *regnum* ruled by the Merovingian dynasty and later into the Carolingian state west of the Rhine.[2] The new small states that developed at the dissolution of the Carolingian empire exhibited a political dynamic in which a plethora of dynasties, many with family connections to the house of Charlemagne, vied to absorb their neighbors' lands and rights in an ongoing effort to aggrandize their territorial holdings and assure the legitimacy of their positions for themselves and their descendants.[3]

During the course of the tenth, eleventh, and twelfth centuries the major powers in the west of the French kingdom—and the position of the Capetian kings was not negligible[4]—were the counts of Rouen who became dukes of Normandy,[5] the counts of Poitou who became dukes of Aquitaine,[6] the counts of Blois–Chartres whose interests were diverted east into Champagne,[7] and the counts of Anjou, whose capital was at Angers, the erstwhile fortified Roman *urbs* of *Juliomagus* at the confluence of the Mayenne and Loire rivers about a hundred kilometers from the Atlantic coast at Nantes.[8] In an ongoing struggle for land and power the dynasty of Angevin counts gradually emerged as the leading power. Indeed, when Count Henry of Anjou conquered England in

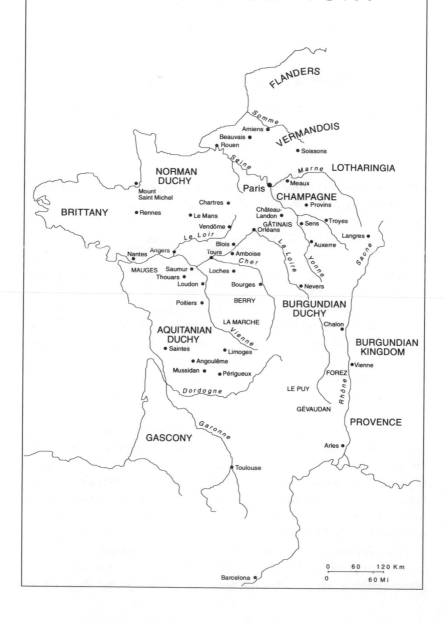

FRANCIA
in the
ELEVENTH CENTURY

FLANDERS

Somme

VERMANDOIS

Amiens •
Beauvais •
• Rouen

• Soissons

Marne   LOTHARINGIA

NORMAN
DUCHY

Seine

Paris

• Meaux

CHAMPAGNE

Mount
Saint Michel •

Chartres •

• Provins

BRITTANY

• Rennes

• Le Mans

Château-
Landon •

• Sens   • Troyes

Vendôme •

GÂTINAIS
Orléans •

• Langres

Le Loir

Blois •

• Auxerre

Nantes •

Angers •

Tours •

• Amboise

Saône

Cher

Saumur •

La Loire

MAUGES
Thouars •

Loches •

Yonne

Loudon •

Bourges •

• Nevers

Poitiers •

BERRY

BURGUNDIAN
DUCHY

LA MARCHE

Vienne

Chalon •

AQUITANIAN
DUCHY

BURGUNDIAN
KINGDOM

• Saintes

• Limoges

• Vienne

Mussidan •

• Angoulême

• Périgueux

FOREZ

LE PUY

Dordogne

GÉVAUDAN

Rhône

PROVENCE

Garonne

GASCONY

Arles •

• Toulouse

0   60   120 Km
0   60 Mi

Barcelona •

1154, he created an empire stretching from the Pyrenees in the south to Scotland in the north; this empire included two kingdoms, the *regnum Aquitanorum* and the *regnum Anglorum*.[9] The key figure in this Angevin success story, recognized both by his contemporaries during the Middle Ages and by modern scholars, was Fulk Nerra, count of the Angevins, 987–1040 (see genealogy 1).[10]

The purpose of this book is to explain how Fulk Nerra, after coming to power as a teenager, rose to be master in the west and in the process built the state upon which his descendants would create the Angevin empire.[11] My thesis is that Fulk built the Angevin state in a physical sense, on the ground, by gradually fortifying his lines of communication between important population centers eastward from his capital at Angers to Amboise, Loches, and Vendôme. This process resulted both in fortified frontiers, which where possible followed natural barriers such as le Loir river, and a defense in depth which protected communication and transportation along the old Roman roads and navigable waterways. These efforts not only made the Angevin state militarily defensible but enabled Fulk to isolate and take control of lands and fortifications held by his adversaries within the frontiers.[12] Fulk's strategy and indeed also his tactics were informed by Roman military science, most likely Vegetian in inspiration, which he modified according to his needs.[13] In addition, Fulk employed a highly eclectic collection of techniques, images, and ideas, which in a broad sense can be traced to the Roman past and which were of the utmost importance in legitimizing his exercise of political power within the Angevin state.[14]

This political biography is not an effort to revivify the argument over "the hero in history." Indeed, Fulk cannot be credited with having begun his state building *de novo*. Rather, prior to his accession in 987, his ancestors had come to control the greater part of the Angevin *civitas* and much of value beyond its frontiers.[15] Both Geoffrey Greymantle (d. 987) and Fulk the Good (d. 960), Fulk's father and grandfather, respectively, played a substantial role in developing the economic, political, and human resources that made possible his success.[16] Of equal importance, however, was the Angevin family network, an extensive system of marriage alliances built up over several generations, the component parts of which in large part saw their interests linked to the success of the Angevin count.[17]

That Fulk's state-building techniques were overwhelmingly successful and unique among the great magnates of Francia Occidentalis, especially in contrast to his major adversaries, Odo II of Blois-Champagne and Duke William of Aquitaine, will emerge in the course of this study. Indeed, the leader with whom comparisons are best made in terms of stature and worthiness of study is Fulk Nerra's younger contemporary, Count William of Rouen, prior to 1066, who came to dominate the Norman duchy before he conquered England.

Fulk Nerra may seem the more unique and his accomplishments outstanding because in the post-World War II era there has been a signal dearth of comprehensive political biographies dedicated to important French secular figures of the pre-Crusade era.[18] This vast lacuna in the literature has resulted largely from a dubious focus in medieval French history on static depersonalized "structures," a version of the "institutional" approach once favored by Anglo-American medievalists, now, however, cluttered with social science jargon and putatively informed by *mentalités* which in essence are so generalized that they appear disembodied.[19] Thus, *Fulk Nerra, the Neo-Roman Consul* is intended primarily as a political biography, a narrative that unfolds the political process from the perspective of those making the major policy decisions and the important members of their entourage who participated in the process at the highest levels. Although my approach not only firmly breaks with the current French *Tendenz,* especially history from the bottom up, and is critical of that trend, at least by implication, I do not ignore such areas of importance as economics, religion, demography, climate, and even art and architecture. They are deployed however, only to further the political narrative, not as stories of their own.[20]

Several other matters potentially vexing to contemporary specialists in French medieval history require some clarification before I move on to the telling of Fulk's story. The title of a work serves as an initial signal of sorts, and undoubtedly my characterization of Fulk Nerra as "neo-Roman consul" will wave a red flag in front of some readers only lately engaged in struggles over the "feudal" construct.[21] Scholars recognize that all constructs, such as neo-Roman and feudal, are developed in a circular manner and at best have limited heuristic value; this point is too obvious to belabor here.[22] But in a competition of constructs, I emphasize that Fulk Nerra and his contemporaries did not know that they were "feudal." Indeed, they did not even know that they were "medieval." More than three centuries would pass following Fulk Nerra's death before the "Middle Age" would be invented[23] and yet another two centuries would pass before a feudal system was conceptualized.[24]

Fulk and those around him saw themselves as neither medieval nor feudal but living *tempore moderno*.[25] When they sought information about how to govern, they had two basic models. One came to them from classical antiquity and was thoroughly heterogeneous in its composition. There were some classical sources gleaned from surviving texts; others were mediated by and through the later Roman Empire and the Romano-German kingdoms of Gaul. These likely reached Anjou through Carolingian conduits, and there they were merged with contemporary Byzantine, ecclesiastical, and Western secular influences to create a corpus of information available to Fulk Nerra and his contemporaries. For want of a more felicitous locution I have used the label "neo-Roman" to describe these sources.[26] The other model was provided by the Holy Scriptures with the vast body of commentary which had been developing for almost a millennium.[27] These two sources were not hermetically sealed categories, and thus, for example, Charlemagne, whose life and legend served as a model to posterity, cultivated his image both as *imperator Romanorum* and as King David.[28] Indeed, he apparently also wanted to be associated in the minds of his subjects with both Constantine and Christ.[29]

In this context of images and labels, it is worth pointing out that Sir Ronald Syme in characterizing the *nobiles,* who dominated the Roman Republic, observed: "As in its beginning, so in its last generation, the Roman Commonwealth, *res publica populi Romani,* was a name; a feudal order of society still survived in the city-state and governed an empire."[30] Only two years later Sir Richard Southern, Syme's Oxford colleague, chose to characterize Fulk Nerra as "a pioneer in feudal government."[31] We do not know whether Southern saw Fulk in light of Syme's Julius Caesar. But twelfth-century writers at the Angevin court, working with eleventh-century materials, did make the connection. Southern was not unaware of this but considered it the result of "the romantic prejudices of that period."[32] *Au fond,* it seems that Syme and Southern got their constructs backward.[33]

In a practical sense it is impossible to adduce sufficient quantity and/or quality of information in this volume to validate the application of the "neo-Roman" label to Fulk Nerra. That is not how labels work in history. In the final analysis the contours and content of any construct rest with the individual who conceptualizes it, whether author or reader.[34] Convincing the reader that Fulk is perhaps somewhat better understood in the long term as the living heir of the Roman world rather than as a model developed during the second half of the twentieth century and fitted into a construct developed by seventeenth-century legal scholars may be useful in establishing proper historical priorities.[35] This question of constructs, however, is likely less important than raising some questions about the relative value of modern ways of thinking about the creation of the Angevin state compared to those generated a thousand or so years ago by Fulk and his posterity.

I maintain that Fulk Nerra's success was due not only to his creative use of *romanitas* but to a well-developed family network. The "family," however, has become an overheated subject these days, a result in part of the explosive growth of a relatively new field, the history of women, which its practitioners not unreasonably have sought to develop and perhaps exploit with regard to the family, its area of greatest advantage.[36] Yet this social science–oriented hypertrophy in family studies has resulted among medievalists an unnecessary atrophy of more traditional approaches, especially a relative inattention to the political family.[37] Thus, it is not without some sense of irony that in trying to cast light, by analogy, on what is intended by the phrase "family network," I turn to Sir Ronald Syme who cogently observed that the great families of the Roman Republic wielded three weapons: the family, money, and the political alliance. "The *nobiles* were dynasts, their daughters princesses. Marriage with a well-connected heiress therefore became an act of policy and an alliance of power, more important than a magistracy, more binding than any compact of oath or interest."[38] Syme observes: "The family was older than the State," and "Loyalty to the ties of kinship in politics was a supreme obligation."[39] Of course, the family network did not always work as was hoped, either among the Romans or the Angevins.

Traditionally, political biographies are organized chronologically, and *Fulk Nerra, the Neo-Roman Consul* is no exception. I open with a discussion of Fulk's family background and childhood with a focus on marriage connections, education, and personality development; the subsequent nine chapters detail his career, with an emphasis on his policies, both domestic and foreign. Where necessary this analysis includes an examination of Fulk's administration, military organization, economic development, and religious activities and policies.

The substantial corpus of diplomatic and narrative sources as well as the physical artifacts used in this study pose a number of technical problems for the writing of a political biography. During the past decade and a half I have examined a great many of these technical questions in a lengthy series of articles. As a result, I have not rehearsed these arguments here but have often referred the reader to the relevant article.

Personal names may perhaps present a problem to readers since there is no basic guiding principle. I have in general used the form of the name with which I am most comfortable, whether English, French, or Latin. Thus, for example, Fulk is never Foulques or Fulco in the narrative, but I have rendered a relatively obscure *miles* Rainaldus, the historian Raoul Glaber as Raoul, and the bishop of Angers as Renaud. I have made every effort to maintain consistency in form when discussing the same individual throughout the narrative. Obviously, my comfort will undoubtedly cause discomfort to one or another reviewer who if sufficiently annoyed may well be able to propose a generally acceptable solution to this irksome situation. Place-names, by contrast, generally appear in the modern French form with the occasional exception of a common English usage or a German locality.

It remains now only to acknowledge the debts I have incurred to individuals and institutions during the years that I have worked on this book. Thus, I take this opportunity to offer thanks while at the same time absolving one and all from the responsibility for any advice I may have used in a wrongheaded manner. From a financial perspective my research in France would have been impossible without timely grants from the American Council of Learned Societies and the University of Minnesota. In France I owe particular thanks to the staffs of the Bibliothèque Nationale, the Centre des Etudes Médiévales at Poitiers, where I spent a very productive year, and the Archives de Maine-et-Loire. At the latter Madam Poirier-Countansais, director of the archives, has earned my deepest gratitude for her efforts on my behalf. The staff of the German Historical Institute in Paris was also particularly helpful. Professor-Doctor Karl Ferdinand Werner (now director emeritus), Dr. Martin Heinzelmann, and Dr. Hartmut Atsma made available the excellent resources of the institute and have been good friends. Also in Paris Col. Jacques Lablancherie, former president of La Société des Amis du Pays Lochois, was very helpful with my work on Belli Locus. Here in the United States, Drs. Steven Fanning, Richard Hogan, William Ziezulewicz, and W. Scott Jessee, all former students, repaid their teacher by publishing useful studies often cited in my notes. I particularly want to thank Professor Fanning, who read several drafts of this work and provided invaluable advice. Special thanks is also due my friend and frequent collaborator, Dr. Jerome Kroll, professor of psychiatry at the University of Minnesota, for his valuable advice and discussion regarding contemporary views on personality formation and the methodological basis, from a scientific perspective, of the value of historical evidence. Finally, I owe thanks to the anonymous scholars who read the manuscript for the University of California Press and thereby contributed in various ways to its improvement. They likely will be able to identify the impact of their own contributions.

Anyone who works extensively in a foreign country knows how important it is to have at least one friend to provide help in getting through the system. I have been fortunate to have had two such good friends. The late Jacques Boussard, professor at Poitiers and director in the Ecole des Hautes Etudes, gave me the benefit of his lengthy experience in the history of the west of France, sent me difficult-to-obtain publications, eased my path in dealing with local specialists, and consistently gave me his warm encouragement. Olivier Guillot, professor of the history of law in the University of Paris IV (the old Sorbonne), who is the acknowledged master of medieval Angevin history, provided the kind of support one could normally expect only from a very old friend. His graciousness, despite the fact that we have not always agreed, is a model from which we all can learn. It is my privilege to dedicate *Fulk Nerra, the Neo-Roman Consul* to Jacques Boussard (*in memoriam*) and to Olivier Guillot.

CHAPTER ONE

Family Background
and Childhood

For more than a half-century prior to Fulk Nerra's accession to the comital title, his father, grandfather, and great grandfather—Geoffrey Greymantle, Fulk the Good, and Fulk the Red, respectively—had been styled "count of the Angevins."[1] The earlier generations of Fulk's family, both in the male and female lines, were described in some detail during the early twelfth century by the authors of the *Gesta Consulum* who were working at the Angevin court.[2] These writers had at their disposal a collection of genealogies which are no longer extant but likely date, at least in part, from the late ninth or early tenth centuries and which make it possible for us to trace the Angevin comital lineage in the male line back to the mid-ninth century.[3]

These genealogies, used by Angevin historians in concert with various other documents, some of which are still extant, make it clear that Fulk Nerra's most ancient forbears in the male line can be traced to a soldier of fortune named Tortulfus who operated in the environs of Rennes on the Breton-Angevin frontier (see genealogies 1 and 2).[4] Tortulfus came to the attention of Charles the Bald, ruler of the West Frankish kingdom (840–877), early in his reign, ca. 843, and he was given a position as a royal forester at Limelle near the *urbs* of Angers.[5]

Tertullus, Tortulfus's son, also appears to have impressed King Charles in a positive manner and was recruited for the *clientela regis* in 851.[6] Shortly thereafter, as the great Burgundian magnate Hugh the Abbot became a prominent figure in King Charles's entourage, the former arranged for one of his relatives, a noble lady named Petronilla,

1

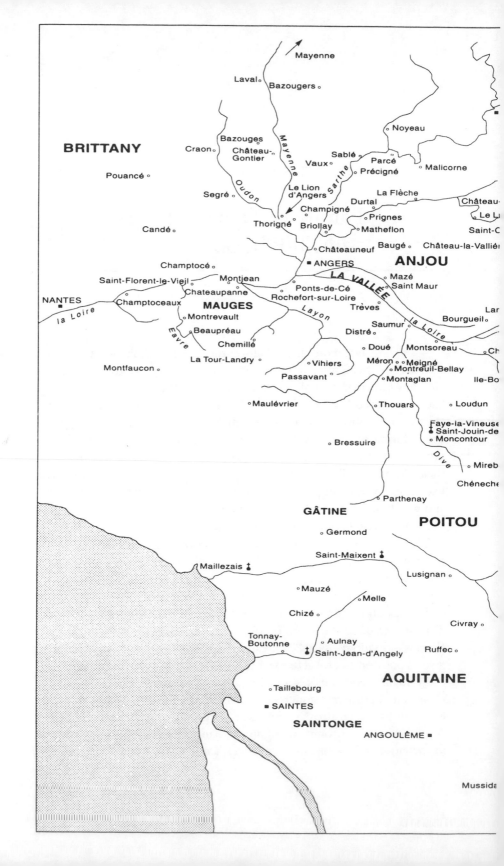

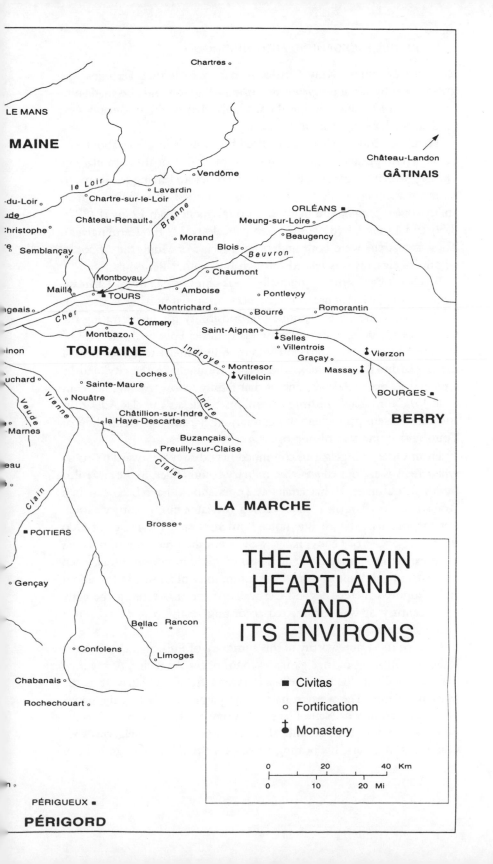

THE ANGEVIN
HEARTLAND
AND
ITS ENVIRONS

■ Civitas

○ Fortification

☦ Monastery

| 0 | | 20 | | 40 | Km |
| 0 | 10 | | 20 | | Mi |

to marry Tertullus.[7] King Charles then saw to it that Tertullus was granted a substantial *beneficium* at Château-Landon and also made him *casatus* both in Francia and in the Gâtinais, that is, the wasteland west of Château-Landon as far as Orléans.[8]

Tertullus's son Ingelgarius inherited his father's holdings about 877 under what appears to have been the stipulations of the capitulary of Quierzy which Charles the Bald had issued before leaving for Rome to receive the imperial title.[9] Ingelgarius is described as a soldier of great ability, *miles optimus,* and he received preferment from Louis II (877–879) and Louis III (879–882) (see genealogy 11, the Carolingians). These monarchs were both under the tutelage of Hugh the Abbot to whom Ingelgarius was related through his mother Petronilla.[10]

Ingelgarius's fortunes gradually took him west from Château-Landon, with what appears to have been an initial posting as viscount at Orléans. There he had primary responsibility for orchestrating the defense of the urbs, which was essentially under episcopal rule. At Orléans Ingelgarius came into close and friendly contact with members of the Adelardus-Raino family, who were prominent in the city, and he arranged to marry Adelais, one of that family whose grandfather controlled the formidable *castrum* of Amboise. Adelais's uncles Adelardus and Raino were prominent churchmen; Adelardus was archbishop of Tours and Raino was bishop of Angers.[11]

From Orléans Ingelgarius continued his odyssey westward to Tours where he was appointed *prefectus,* military commander, in the city ruled by his wife's uncle.[12] That affairs at Tours should have been cast in a Roman or neo-Roman manner during the later ninth century should not surprise us. At least one noted contemporary, the father of Odo the future abbot of Cluny, had a well-established reputation in Tours as an expert in Roman law.[13] It is also of some importance that when the castrum was built to defend the community of Saint-Martin, about eight hundred meters beyond the walls of the urbs during the early tenth century, it was constructed according to the plan of a Roman legionary camp.[14]

Perhaps most noteworthy in this summary of Fulk Nerra's ancestors is the appointment of Ingelgarius as count of the Angevins. At the time that he obtained this title the *pagus* extended only as far west as the Mayenne River. The western half of the pagus was first in the hands of Count Lambert of Nantes (see genealogy 9) and then passed to the Bretons Salomon, Erispoë, and Alan the Great.[15] Like Ingelgarius's advancement at Tours, his posting to Angers should be seen in light of the influence of his wife's family, for her uncle Raino was bishop of Angers.

Ingelgarius's preferment can be seen as the result of the propitious combination of his military talents with his relation through his mother to Hugh the Abbot and through his wife to a family of major importance in the west from Orléans to Angers. A sense of how high Ingelgarius and Adelais had risen in the estimation of powerful contemporaries can be gauged by the marriage of their son Fulk the Red to Roscilla, daughter of Warnerius, a magnate who controlled the important strongholds of Loches, Villentrois, and la Haye in the southern Touraine (see genealogy 3).[16] This Warnerius has been identified as a son of Count Adalhard, the seneschal of Louis the Pious who was king of the Franks and emperor (814–840).[17] Irmentrude, who became Charles the Bald's queen, was the niece of Adalhard and a cousin of Warnerius.[18] Thus Roscilla, Fulk the Red's wife, was a not-too-distant cousin of the royal family.

While this connection to the family of the Carolingian monarch surely brought the Fulconians prestige and status, Roscilla's maternal lineage was also important to her young husband's success and to that of their descendants. Roscilla's mother was either the daughter or the granddaughter of the Widonian lords of the Breton march in whose family were to be found the counts of Nantes. These Widonians intermittently bore the responsibility for the defense of the western frontier of Francia Occidentalis as far east as the Angevin pagus.[19] This responsibility brought Roscilla's maternal relatives into close contact with members of Fulk the Red's maternal lineage as led by his uncle, Bishop Raino of Angers.

Fulk the Red's family connections enabled him to expand his interests and acquisition of lands and titles westward from the Gâtinais as Amboise, Loches, Villentrois, and la Haye came to form the nucleus of Fulconian holdings in the Touraine.[20] At Tours itself, where his maternal uncle Adalhard had been archbishop, Fulk obtained the title of viscount no later than 898 with military responsibility for the defense of the urbs.[21] In addition, he garnered the key position of treasurer of the prestigious and rich church of Saint-Martin located in its own castrum only eight hundred meters from the walled city. As treasurer of Saint-Martin, Fulk controlled the fisc and used its resources to reward his supporters. Among those who benefited from Fulk's largess was a youth named Odo, the future abbot of Cluny. Odo (d. 942) maintained warm and friendly relations with the Fulconians throughout his career and influenced his friend and successor Maiolus in the same direction.[22] In addition, Fulk saw to it that two of his own sons, Fulk the Good and Guy, were made canons of Saint-Martin at Tours; Guy was to become bishop of Soissons.[23]

The influence of Roscilla's maternal relatives combined with recognition of Fulk the Red's skill as a military administrator seems to have won him preferment far to the west of Tours. By 914 at the latest he has the title count of Nantes.[24] The combination of Roscilla's Widonian relatives and Fulk's maternal connections also made it possible to bring the Fulconians back to Angers. The Widonians had been abbots and more precisely the lay archabbots of the monasteries of Saint-Aubin and Saint-Lézin, and Raino had held the episcopal see. First, Fulk the Red was made viscount of Angers and soon after that he took the abbatial titles that his in-laws had held earlier.[25] By 929–930 he obtained the title *comes Andegavorum* from the Robertian duke of Paris.[26] Why there was a hiatus between Ingelgarius and Fulk the Red as Angevin counts remains obscure.

As one result of their new western holdings and responsibilities, the Fulconians were particularly troubled by the Normans and their Viking allies who frequently penetrated the Breton frontier and found the Loire River an inviting entrée into Anjou itself.[27] Ingelgarius, Fulk the Red's eldest son, was killed while fighting the Normans in one of the many conflicts that saw the ravaging and depopulation of the Angevin countryside during the first third of the tenth century.[28] Indeed, William Longsword, the Norman count of Rouen, issued coinage bearing the title "William Duke of the Bretons," and claims were generated, which are noted in later sources, that he had been granted "the land of the Bretons on the sea-coast" in 933 by King Raoul, the West Frankish monarch.[29]

From a strategic perspective, one of Fulk the Red's more enduring responses to the Norman threat was to arrange the marriage of his daughter Adelaide (see genealogy 4) to Count Walter, who held the counties of Vexin, Valois, and Amiens, positioned to the east of William Longsword's territories.[30] The Angevin-Vexin alliance constituted a containment strategy that had a modicum of royal support as evidenced by the appointment of Guy, Fulk the Red's younger son, as bishop of Soissons, where he exercised substantial secular as well as episcopal power and served as one of the king's close advisors.[31] Indeed, it should be emphasized that the Valois with Soissons in the north and Amiens to the northwest formed a strategic triangle with the Vexin that stood between the Vermandois and Normandy. William Longsword's earlier marriage to Leutgarde, a daughter of the count of Vermandois, highlights these opposed systems of military alliance.[32]

Although Fulk the Red had more than enough to occupy his attention in the west of France, his ambitions for family aggrandizement were not limited to the region. Thus, for example, when the time came to secure a wife for Fulk the Good, his son and heir, Fulk the Red appears to have taken advantage of his friendship with Odo of Cluny and also perhaps with the support of his mother's noble relatives to arrange an alliance with the viscomital house of Vienne.[33] At first glance this marriage would seem to have been a foolish move since it certainly was a step down for the heir to a *comté* to marry the daughter of a mere viscount, in any case a viscount whose base of power was so distant from Anjou and the Fulconians' main interests.

It might be a bit rash to suggest that as early as the 930s Fulk the Red had intuited that Cluny would become a dominant force in the region and that he intended to utilize his close ties with Odo to follow such a farsighted policy in the east. In a rather more practical vein, however, it was likely that a grandson of Viscount Ratburnus I of Vienne, in accordance with a widely developed custom of episcopal succession, had a good chance to succeed his maternal uncle Hector as count-bishop of le Puy (see genealogy 14).[34] Thus, it is perhaps not surprising that Guy, the younger son of Fulk the Good and his wife Gerberga, became bishop of le Puy.[35] In addition, and perhaps even more important, both Viscount Ratburnus I and his wife Gerberga appear to have had Carolingian royal blood in their veins, and Adelaide, their granddaughter, was considered to have sufficiently distinguished ancestry to marry the Carolingian Louis V.[36]

When Gerberga of Vienne died sometime before 952, Fulk the Good, who had held the Angevin comital title for a decade, continued the family tradition of searching out politically productive marriage connections and arranged to wed the widow of Count Alan of Nantes. She was the sister of Count Theobald I of Blois (see genealogy 7), and her marriage to Alan had sealed a Blésois alliance with Nantes which also likely assured to her brother the domination of Rennes.[37] Theobald, until the marriage of his sister to Fulk, was the Angevins' most persistent adversary in the west of France. Both Fulk and Theobald were *fideles* of the Robertian house (see genealogy 12), and Hugh the Great honored each of them generously in order to keep their support while maintaining the balance of power in the west. Theobald, however, had tilted the balance by his alliance with Alan; this gave him control of Rennes in addition to his titles as count of Tours, Chartres, and Châteaudun.[38]

Relative latecomers to the upper echelons of the powerful in the west of France, the Fulconians, whose lands were widely scattered, were not in a position to compete against the counts of Blois on equal terms. The situation changed suddenly and dramatically, however, with the premature death of Alan of Nantes, which left eastern Brittany in a disorganized state and more open than before both to Angevin and Norman penetration. Theobald was thus in a position either to lean toward the Angevins or toward the Normans. Despite his earlier rivalry with the Fulconians he chose the former.[39] The key to Theobald's decision may well have been his wife Leutegarde, who earlier had been married to the Norman ruler William Longsword. When William was assassinated in 942, his son Richard by a Breton concubine succeeded, and Leutegarde left the court at Rouen. She thereafter became a sworn enemy of the new Norman ruler.[40]

The deal struck by Fulk and Theobald saw transferred to Blois the stronghold of Saumur, which dominated the frontier of the Angevin pagus with the Touraine along the Loire River and the Roman road to Tours. In addition, the newly reestablished monastery of Saint-Florent, located within the walls of the castrum at Saumur, went in the bargain.[41] In return, Fulk obtained Theobald's sister as his wife, domination of Nantes, and a free hand to push Fulconian interests into southeastern Brittany.[42] Fulk moved quickly to secure his position. First, he eliminated Alan's heirs and then installed a count of his own choosing at Nantes.[43] No appeal to Fulk's sobriquet "the good" or acknowledgment of the peaceful character (by contemporary standards) of the greater part of his eighteen-year reign—that peace probably a result of his alliance with Theobald—should mislead us concerning the brutality of dynastic policy, even when guided by the count reputed to be most pious among the Angevins.[44]

The satisfactory progress of the alliance between Fulk and Theobald was demonstrated no later than 955 when a marriage was arranged between Fulk's elder son Geoffrey Greymantle, the heir apparent to the Fulconian lands and titles, and Adele, the younger sister of Leutegarde.[45] Thus, it was probably no accident that as part of the dowry that Adele of Vermandois brought to Geoffrey were lands in the Beauvais region, which bordered on Normandy and on the comté of Vexin.[46] The latter region was ruled by Geoffrey's uncle Walter. The general anti-Norman thrust of the Angevin-Blésois connection reached a peak in 960 when, with Leutegarde's encouragement, Theobald and Geoffrey Greymantle allied with King Lothair against Count Richard of Rouen and his Norman supporters.[47]

Like Fulk the Red, Fulk the Good was unwilling to concentrate his full efforts toward dynastic aggrandizement in the west of France. At about the same time that he arranged for Geoffrey Greymantle to marry Adele of Vermandois, he sent his daughter Adelaide-Blanche (see genealogy 5), who could not have been much more than fifteen years of age at the time, to be the wife of Stephen, count of Forez and of Gévaudan and the second most powerful magnate in the eastern reaches of Aquitaine.[48] This marriage, which is likely to have been attractive to Stephen because of Adelaide-Blanche's family connections with Cluny and at Vienne, seems from Fulk the Good's perspective to have been a continuation of the initiative begun earlier by his own father in arranging the marriage to Gerberga.[49]

Nonetheless, it may be emphasized at this point that Fulk the Good's younger son Guy had been named with the thought that he would find a career in the church as a bishop.[50] With Angevin interests strongly represented in Forez and Gévaudan, Guy's chances to succeed to the nearby bishopric of le Puy would certainly be enhanced, even though his maternal uncle Hector, who had held the see earlier in the century, had died prematurely and the succession would not be direct.[51] Indeed, as the situation ultimately developed, Guy was to require the intervention of armed forces from Gévaudan and Forez in order to secure his position as count-bishop of le Puy, an office to which he was appointed by King Lothair only in 975.[52]

The reign of Geoffrey Greymantle (960–987) links the two main themes of this chapter: the family background and the childhood of Fulk Nerra. Geoffrey married Adele of Vermandois, a direct descendant of Charlemagne through her father Count Herbert and a granddaughter of King Robert I on her mother's side (see genealogy 13). Hugh Capet was her first cousin.[53] Indeed, by the mid-950s, when Geoffrey and Adele were wed, the Fulconians had through marriage become part of the highest nobility of the West Frankish kingdom.

Geoffrey was one of three siblings who lived to adulthood, and his wife Adele had seven brothers and sisters who survived beyond the age of thirty.[54] This certainly may be considered a healthy background by the standards of pre-Crusade Europe.[55] When Adele gave birth to a daughter no later than 956 a sense of optimism for the survival of the dynasty and the success of the alliance is likely to have pervaded the court at Angers as well as among the Vermandois. The infant was named Hermengarde-Gerberga in honor of Geoffrey's mother, grandmother, and great grandmother; this was double recognition of the Angevin count's Carolingian ancestry through his own mother Gerberga.[56]

How long the good feeling lasted following Hermengarde-Gerberga's birth is impossible to know. Surely, however, Geoffrey and Adele began to suffer some strain in the long years before Fulk was born, a decade and a half after his sister.[57] Curiously, none of the few surviving documents issued by Geoffrey show concern for a male heir. This is in contrast, for example, to the act issued by his son Fulk Nerra, who put the matter of his concern for a male heir into a grant to Marmoutier only a few years after his own marriage:

I, Fulk count of the Angevins by the will of God . . . as much for the remedy of my soul and the soul of my wife Elizabeth and so that almighty God through the intercession of the most pious Confessor Martin would bestow sons on us, who would be able to inherit after us. . . . I give and bestow all fishing rights at Bessé . . . to Marmoutier.[58]

Indeed, although Geoffrey does make reference to his daughter while strengthening an act in favor of Saint-Aubin, he expresses no sentiment that he seeks a son. In these same types of documents Geoffrey acts in favor of one or another saint for the health of the souls of his parents and of the soul of his *dominus,* Hugh Capet, and even for the health of the souls of the latter's parents, but he does not mention his own wife, nor does she act with him in any surviving document issued during the first decade of his reign. On one occasion Adele's brother, Count Robert of Troyes, attended the comital court at Angers and supported Count Geoffrey's act, but his sister, the Angevin countess, appears nowhere on the scene.[59]

During the first decade of his reign Geoffrey appears to have been considerably less active than he was to become during the last seventeen years.[60] In addition, his brother Guy, who was named in anticipation of a career in the church, did not become a priest during this period when Geoffrey lacked a direct male heir. This delay presumably was to keep Guy available as a potential successor to Geoffrey should no son be born. Guy remained unconsecrated but played the major role in administering Geoffrey's ecclesiastical policies.[61] We cannot ascertain whether Geoffrey was the victim of a lengthy illness or perhaps had been wounded seriously in the war against the Normans in 960 or in some later combat; we do not know whether Adele was sickly. In short, there are many possible reasons for the absence of a record of Adele's giving birth or even being pregnant during the fifteen years after Hermengarde-Gerberga's birth, but there is no evidence to sustain even speculation.[62]

When Adele became pregnant with Fulk in 970 after a decade and a half without issue, we can imagine much surprise at Angers.[63] Even greater probably was the surprise about a year after Fulk Nerra was born when Adele again became pregnant and gave birth to a second son, this one named Geoffrey.[64] Thus, after bearing her first child in her teens, Adele gave birth to two additional children in her early thirties.[65] All that can be said is that the pattern is unusual.

There can be little doubt that Fulk was a much desired and long-awaited child. He was named for his grandfather Fulk the Good and clearly intended to succeed to the comital *officium*.[66] Young Fulk's uncle Guy was no doubt cheered by the birth of his nephew insofar as he could look forward with some sense of security to his long-desired ecclesiastical career.[67] Adele, whatever her feelings may have been about pregnancy and childbirth—both of which were not without great danger in the Middle Ages—surely was relieved of the worry that her husband, in a panic to produce a male heir, would put her aside and take a new wife.[68] Fulk's sister (see genealogy 6) had little time to get to know her little brother since she was sent off to Rennes as the wife of Conan before her sibling was a year old.[69] As later events would show, either she formed a close attachment to Fulk during the year they spent together at Angers or her loyalty to her patrilineage was very strong.[70]

Fulk's early years were somewhat hectic. His sister left for Rennes before his first birthday, and not long after, his mother was again pregnant. The timing of this pregnancy may well permit the inference that Adele either did not nurse Fulk or was not regularly involved in the nursing for very long.[71] Before Fulk was three years old he had a new brother named Geoffrey. Arguably, Geoffrey's appearance on the scene drew away some of the attention that heretofore had been lavished on Fulk. Fulk's situation, however, was greatly worsened when his mother took ill, either as a result of childbirth or shortly thereafter. She never recovered. Adele of Vermandois was dead by the spring of 974.[72]

Count Geoffrey, Fulk, and young Geoffrey attended the reading of Adele's testament and they all are recorded as "confirming" her bequests to the monastery of Saint-Aubin of Angers where she was buried; Hermengarde-Gerberga, however, did not attest[73] and it is likely that she was not there.[74] This may have been a result of the exceptionally bad winter of 974–975,[75] for Adele's sister Leutegarde and her family also apparently missed the funeral and the reading of the will. Leutegarde apparently had an interest in the testament because her son Odo I subsequently challenged a part of the will.[76] From what is known of the will—the original document does not survive—the monastery of Saint-Aubin was a major beneficiary, but Fulk received some lands that apparently had come to Adele as her bridal gift. He still remembered this bequest almost a half-century later.[77]

The loss of a mother early in childhood often causes problems for normal children; deep feelings of loss, rejection, and even guilt can develop. Sometimes there is anger and a tendency to blame one's father or even one's self.[78] Such reactions are known even in pre-Crusade Europe.[79] Fulk's problems, however, were to be greatly compounded during the next few years. Within a year of Adele's death, Fulk's uncle Guy, who for both personal and dynastic reasons had been solicitous of his nephew's welfare, finally got his bishopric and went off to take over the see of le Puy as count-bishop; this had been "promised" almost forty years earlier when Fulk the Good married Gerberga.[80] Two years later Fulk's younger brother Geoffrey died, and the future Angevin count was thus very much alone at the impressionable age of six.[81]

Fulk's situation seems to have been partially ameliorated by his father's actions. As early as the summer of 976, following the death of Adele and the departure of Guy, Fulk is found traveling with his father and appearing at the court of Hugh Capet in Orléans. During the next several years Fulk appears to have accompanied Count Geoffrey rather regularly, for we find the boy in his father's entourage in the Touraine and in various settings in the Angevin pagus but outside the city of Angers itself.[82] Fulk is conspicuously absent from Geoffrey's entourage only during the early spring of 976 when the Angevin count campaigned in the Poitou.[83]

Parental love for children and concern for their well-being is extensively documented for the Early Middle Ages. We therefore cannot rule out the possibility that Geoffrey Greymantle took Fulk with him for emotional reasons. It may even be that he appreciated his son's sense of loss and tried to compensate.[84] Of course, we cannot affirm that Geoffrey acted from such insights or feelings. Whatever may have been the norms of the age, at a remove of a thousand years we are far from understanding Geoffrey's emotional makeup.

Perhaps it is safer to ascribe the Angevin count's behavior to tradition. Important noblemen often took at least some of their children with them when they traveled on the business of government. For example, Einhard reports in the *Vita Karoli* that Charlemagne followed this practice. He even leads us to believe that the Frankish emperor loved his children.[85] In this context it should not be ignored that the *Vita Karoli* provided a model of sorts to later generations on many topics, including the raising of children. Indeed, William the Conqueror, Fulk Nerra's later contemporary, kept his sons with him when he traveled.[86] Whether tradition or parental love is at issue here, or more likely some combination of the two, Geoffrey Greymantle's actions in keeping Fulk at his side were likely to have had a positive impact on the development of the child's personality in light of his losses.[87]

At the various courts he attended, Fulk met relatives like his great-uncle Walter, count of Amiens, Vexin, and Valois, along with the latter's two sons Walter and Radulf. Fulk also had the opportunity to meet his cousin Odo I, who succeeded Theobald as count of Blois.[88] Fulk's sense of importance and personal worth is likely to have been reinforced when on occasion during the excitement and pageantry that accompanied the gathering of these nobles he was permitted, though only six or seven years of age, to play an official role alongside his father and the others at the court by attesting documents.[89]

The death of young Geoffrey, or more accurately Geoffrey Greymantle's response to the loss of the boy, was to have important repercussions for the Fulconian dynasty. With Fulk Nerra left as the sole heir to the countship before the age of eight, Count Geoffrey acted to provide a "backup" for his only son. Probably with the help of King Lothair, Geoffrey arranged to wed Adele, the recently widowed countess of Chalon. Her husband Lambert earlier had been established there as count by the monarch.[90] This *comté*, over which Geoffrey was to exercise comital power for the remainder of his life, was strategically located to the north of his sister Adelaide-Blanche's holdings in Gévaudan and Forez and not far from his brother Guy's power base at le Puy, where he had been established with the help of King Lothair in 975. Indeed, Chalon was close to Vienne, where Geoffrey's cousin was viscount. Clearly, from a purely political perspective this marriage was important in helping the Angevins to develop an enclave in eastern Aquitaine on the borders of Burgundy. With the aid of King Lothair, Geoffrey was following a policy that seems to have been foreshadowed two generations earlier when Fulk the Red arranged for his son Fulk the Good to marry Gerberga.

From a personal as well as a political perspective, Geoffrey's marriage to Adele of Chalon proved a success when the countess gave birth to a son whom the couple named Maurice. How this turn of events affected Fulk is not clear. By naming the child Maurice after the famous saint, Geoffrey was signaling that his newly born son was not to be considered a competitor for the Angevin comital title.[91] Geoffrey may have tried to forestall problems in this area by never having Adele of Chalon styled as "Angevin countess." On the negative side, Adele already had a son, Hugh, by her first marriage to Count Lambert, and thus it would not be an easy matter to provide for Maurice at Chalon.[92]

Whatever Fulk's early feelings may have been about his stepmother and new half-brother, it is clear that by the time Maurice reached his teenage years he enjoyed very good relations with his elder Angevin sibling.[93] It is perhaps of some importance in this context that Fulk appears never to have accompanied Geoffrey Greymantle when he brought his court east. We have no reason to believe that Fulk ever met his stepmother, Adele of Chalon.[94] Fulk's first recorded meeting with Maurice probably took place around 985 at Loches in the Touraine when Geoffrey's court met to support the foundation of a church dedicated to Saint-Mary. At this court none of Geoffrey's fideles from the east attended or at least none are attested in the surviving acta.[95]

In a personal sense Fulk's position as Geoffrey Greymantle's heir to the Angevin comté may have been more seriously threatened by events that took place in the west. A year or so before Maurice was born, but after the death of young Geoffrey, Fulk's sister Hermengarde-Gerberga gave birth to a son, who was named Geoffrey-Berengar in honor of his maternal and paternal grandfathers. That the first of the two names was the Angevin name Geoffrey, in spite of the boy's position as heir to the comté of Rennes, may well suggest that Hermengarde-Gerberga and her husband Conan saw their son also as a potential heir ro the Angevin comté should anything happen to Fulk.[96]

The significance of the birth and naming of Geoffrey-Berengar should also be seen in light of the radical realignment of forces in the west of France that followed the death of Count Theobald I of Blois in 977 and the marriage of Geoffrey Greymantle to Adele of Chalon in the following year. The family ties that had bound the Fulconians and the Blésois for a quarter-century were broken.[97] Odo I, Theobald's successor, chafed under the earlier arrangements that limited Blésois western expansion at Angevin expense, and in this he was joined by Conan who resented his father-in-law's Breton policy that reserved control of the Nantes region to the Angevins.[98] In addition, Geoffrey had treated Count William Iron Arm of the Poitou very roughly, and he was the husband of Odo's sister Emma.[99] In short, Conan of Rennes had substantial support to oppose Geoffrey and in 982 he went to war with the Angevin count. Geoffrey, however, was victorious at what has come to be called the first battle of Conquereuil, and the threat from Rennes was blunted for the time being.[100]

The cooling of Angevin-Blésois relations and the Breton threat were followed shortly by a falling out between Geoffrey Greymantle and the Carolingian king Lothair. In 982 Louis V, Lothair's son and heir, had married Geoffrey's widowed sister Adelaide-Blanche, who controlled the counties of Forez and Gévaudan. The couple were crowned king and queen of Aquitaine at Brioude by Bishop Guy of le Puy. But the marriage lasted little more than a year as Geoffrey's plans to gain the dominant position in Aquitaine through control of young Louis foundered on the inability of the fifteen-year-old monarch and his wife, who was about forty, to live together peacefully.[101]

The failure of Geoffrey's Aquitanian policy and the concurrent breakdown of the Blésois entente prompted the Angevin count to seek closer ties with Hugh Capet. This led Geoffrey to focus more narrowly on affairs in the west of France. Many of the policy decisions that Geoffrey was to make during the last two years of his life, given the new circumstances of the early 980s, were to have a profound effect on Fulk Nerra's future. In essence, Geoffrey Greymantle set in motion a process by which the scattered lands of the Angevin counts in the west of France would take on the characteristics of a territorial principality defined in part by natural and defensible frontiers that were made necessary largely as a result of military problems.

The western frontier of this Angevin state ran north along the river Eavre through the Mauges region to la Loire, then east along the river to the stronghold at Rochefort-sur-Loire and Morin to Angers, and finally north along the Oudon to the strongholds of Segré and Craon. From Craon the northern frontier ran east to Sablé and then south along the valley of the Sarthe to le Loir. The northern frontier continued east along the valley of le Loir to Vendôme and then south through Morand and the important fortifications at Amboise to Buzan-çais. From this anchor in the southeast, the southern frontier ran west to Preuilly-sur-Claise and then northwest to la Haye-Descartes on the Claise to Nouâtre on the Vienne, then west to Loudun, Méron, Mon-taglan, Vihiers, and the upper valley of the Eavre on the southwestern frontier.[102]

Among the more important steps taken by Geoffrey Greymantle to carry out his territorial ambitions was to begin the process by which the Angevins would come to dominate the Vendômois with its formi-dable castrum at Vendôme. To this end Geoffrey acquired Viscount Fulcradus of Vendôme as his fidelis, or client, and arranged for Fulk Nerra to marry Elizabeth, daughter and heiress of Count Bouchard of Vendôme. Elizabeth's brother Renaud, Bouchard's immediate heir to the comté, was a cleric pointed toward high church office and therefore was unlikely to have legitimate offspring of his own. Thus through Elizabeth either Fulk or his heir would rule the Vendômois sometime in the future if Geoffrey's plan proved successful.[103]

During the summer of 985 Geoffrey Greymantle, Fulk Nerra, Count Bouchard, Viscount Fulcradus, and Count Guerech, who held Nantes from the Angevin count, toured many of the lands that one day would come under the political control of Elizabeth's husband-to-be. With a substantial entourage this group traveled through the southern reaches of the Touraine where they visited the strongholds of Angevin fideles, such as that of Guenno of Nouâtre. Finally, on 20 August a court was held at Angers. Either at this court or shortly thereafter the final ar-rangements were made for Fulk's marriage to Elizabeth, and Fulk was associated in the countship with his father so as to assure his accession to the comital office. This precaution proved wise indeed, for Geoffrey died unexpectedly on 21 July 987 while besieging the stronghold of Marçon on le Loir.[104]

Fulk Nerra thus experienced another serious loss in his short life. Yet even though he was less than seventeen years of age, he had been given some preparation to assume the responsibility of ruling the Angevin state. From youth he had frequently accompanied his father when Geoffrey Greymantle was on the road governing the Angevins. In this way Fulk not only became acquainted with many of his well-placed rel-atives but he also attended the court of Hugh Capet from whom Geof-frey recognized that he held the comté. Moreover, Bouchard, Fulk's father-in-law, was a close associate of the man who was to become rex Francorum less than three months after Geoffrey's death. Hugh and

Geoffrey were also well acquainted and the future Capetian monarch was at the Angevin count's side when he took ill and breathed his last during the siege of Marçon.[105]

Fulk's acquaintance with these important men and his participation in the courts they attended was a vital part of his education. No less important were his relations with Geoffrey's *fideles*. In fact, this point was forcefully made in Fulk's presence at Loches in 985 when Geoffrey insisted that he was powerfully positioned as count of the Angevins because of the "*generositas* [bravery, ability] of his *milites*." Geoffrey went on to emphasize how he worked closely with his *optimates*. One can almost hear an echo of Septimius Severus's advice to his sons regarding the importance of the army.[106] Indeed, while traveling with Geoffrey and visiting various outlying strongholds like Nouâtre on the frontiers of the Angevin state, Fulk surely came to know many of these *fideles* who served as castellans as well as those who served in his father's military household and moved around with the count. Men such as Ascelinus of Braine, Cadilo of Blaison, Joscelin of Rennes, and Walter, who would be made castellan of Montsoreau, are only a few of those who served Geoffrey loyally and then his son Fulk as well.[107]

Through his official documents Geoffrey Greymantle expressed his personal views on a wide variety of important issues, which like the advice concerning the *generositas* of the *milites* could be vital to the young count.[108] These documents and indeed many other *acta* that were either never recorded or have subsequently disappeared were no doubt first expressed orally in the vernacular in the count's court so that all who attended could understand what had transpired and so that those who attested knew what they had supported.[109]

The nature of the surviving documents makes it clear that Geoffrey worried about his own salvation and the salvation of his close relatives. He showed particular interest in the souls of his mother and father. He emphasized his belief in God's mercy and in the importance of being charitable to the church. He expressed the view "It is good work to endow the competent churches of powerful saints," and he emphasized in his grants that the monks or canons who served these saints regularly were to render prayers for his soul and for the souls of those in whose names he was generous. Geoffrey also encouraged his *fideles* to be generous to the church.[110]

Geoffrey's charity to churches in his patronage was unlikely to undermine the resources of the comital fisc. For example, while in his "reforming" efforts Geoffrey required that all those who held lands belonging to the monastery of Saint-Aubin at Angers return these to the saint, Geoffrey himself continued to use the resources of Saint-Aubin and the cathedral chapter and all the other religious establishments in the Angevin state to reward his supporters or clients *ex rebus ecclesiae*. He made it clear in his act "reforming" Saint-Aubin that he expected the monks to provide *auxilium* from their resources (*ops*) when "secularium bellorum turbinibus occupato."[111]

When Geoffrey made gifts to religious foundations he was careful not to alienate vast estates and he never granted immunity from comital jurisdiction over high justice, such as homicide, robbery, and arson. Such alienations would not only have weakened the government's direct control over peacekeeping but would also have cost substantial revenues to the fisc accruing from the *freda,* the count's share of the fines.[112]

Geoffrey's dealings with the church made clear to those who heard or read his *acta* the importance of comital control. He always indicated in the so-called election charters of abbots that he had chosen the new abbot.[113] He clearly chose the bishop of Angers. In that case he obtained a substantial reward for the appointment of Renaud II in 973; this reward was to add much of the Mauges region directly to the comital fisc.[114]

Geoffrey nevertheless knew well the problem of simony and was careful to arrange matters to avoid such a charge. In a document of 985 by which he regulated the selection of canons for his newly refounded church of Notre-Dame at Loches, Geoffrey revealed his thinking on this delicate topic. He stipulated that each candidate to become a canon at Saint-Mary's must give the count a present of twenty solidi. The count then went on to point out that if charges of simony were to be avoided "the money is to be considered a gift because the resources of the place [Saint-Mary's] are slight. . . . The twenty solidi are to be given to the count so that the canons' community and their resources may be defended by the count."[115]

In a more purely secular vein Geoffrey stressed the *strenuitas* of his Fulconian ancestors, as though by calling attention to their history of military and political success he legitimized his own right to rule. He also noted how important it was for the count to obtain counsel from his fideles, rely on the support of his *milites,* and work closely with his *optimates.*[116]

Geoffrey also demonstrated in his *acta* a commitment to economic development and recognized that the Vikings had done a great deal of damage during the previous century: "The sword of the barbarians spared neither the young nor the old, orphan or widow . . . they stripped the land of almost everything that was edible and left it uninhabitable. . . . The strongholds where kings, dukes, and princes were established, alas, lack garrisons and are the habitation of wild beasts."[117] In response, Geoffrey built strongholds of his own, drove out the "wild beasts" (perhaps a metaphor here for bandits or robbers), and went about the process of restoration by supporting the assarting of wooded lands and the building of aqueducts for irrigation and mills for grinding grain.[118] In the environs of Angers itself he supported Abbot Albert of Saint-Aubin in building a burg that on one side backed up against the wall of the urbs and on the other three sides had access to the public road. The burg was afforded easy access to protection and transportation and thus was likely to attract the merchants who were needed to make the project a financial success.[119]

As a member of Geoffrey Greymantle's entourage, Fulk, in his early life, had the opportunity for important educational experiences that would prepare him to assume the responsibilities of government, in which he was formally associated during his sixteenth year.[120] This process, for want of a better term, may be characterized as Fulk's informal education. There was much, however, that he could learn were he disposed to benefit from what today we would consider a formal education. For example, did he find congenial the idea that "the use of the mind to obtain knowledge from books provides a way for one man to gain victory over another" and did he have the training to take advantage of such opportunities?[121]

Since the time of Charlemagne, nobles were encouraged to give their sons a formal education. The Frankish kings made provision for such efforts at the royal court, and the *Gesta Karoli*, which was written toward the end of the ninth century but remained popular thereafter, emphasized in no uncertain terms Charlemagne's censure of those who were slackers:

You young nobles, [who] have neglected the pursuit of learning and have wasted your time . . . I have no regard for your nobility . . . and know for certain that unless you immediately make up for your earlier time-wasting by serious study, you will never get anything worthwhile from Charlemagne.[122]

But how effective was this thunderous warning, attributed to Charlemagne, through a century of foreign invasions and civil wars during which much of what the great emperor had built was destroyed. To bring matters closer to the Fulconians, it is clear that twelfth-century writers at the court of Henry II, working with oral traditions and earlier written sources that for the most part are no longer extant, depict the king's Angevin ancestors as well educated. Thus, for example, one story went so far as to describe Fulk the Good writing a note to the Carolingian king Louis IV after the monarch had laughed at the Angevin count for singing in the choir of Saint-Martin's at Tours. The note is alleged to have said: "You should know my lord that a *rex illiteratus* is a crowned ass."[123]

That Fulk the Good wrote such a note is doubtful. But perhaps more important is the definition of *illiteratus,* which in this context does not mean unable to read and write or even unable to read and write Latin but rather unable to read and to write Latin in the classical style.[124] Although late sources describe Fulk the Good as "worthy in God," "an adept *miles,*" and "literatus" we cannot be sure that he could either read or write in any style. Fulk, however, was raised with a career in the church in mind and he did become a canon of Saint-Martin's at Tours. This upbringing may provide some basis for his later literate reputation.[125]

We are much better informed about Geoffrey Plantagenet, who succeeded as Angevin count less than a century after Fulk Nerra's death. Geoffrey is known to have read Vegetius's *De re militari* while on campaign.[126] He was not only *literatus* but he used books "to gain victory over another." Fulk le Réchin, Fulk Nerra's grandson and Geoffrey Plantagenet's grandfather, was given his early education under the direction of his grandmother, Countess Hildegarde, at the comital court in Angers.[127] Late in life Fulk wrote the *History of the Angevin Counts* in Latin; a fragment of this work still survives.[128]

As we draw closer to Fulk Nerra, we can speculate on literacy in the Angevin environment in which he was raised. His grandfather Fulk the Good, who was slated originally for a career in the church, probably was taught to read and write. Similarly, Fulk the Good's brother Guy, who had a distinguished career as bishop of Soissons after serving as a canon of Saint-Martin's at Tours, was probably literate.[129] Geoffrey Greymantle's brother Guy, who was also originally marked for a career in the church and ended his life as count-bishop of le Puy, is reported not only to have been literate but well educated, and we have documentary evidence that he could at the least write his name.[130]

With the likelihood that Geoffrey Greymantle's father, uncle, and younger brother were literate, it seems fair to suggest that the Angevin court in the tenth century was in harmony with Charlemagne's warning not to neglect education. As to Geoffrey himself, we have no evidence of any formal education. But it is clear that Fulk Nerra's father did place a high value on the written word and expressed that sentiment in his son's presence: "Because the memory of things done rightly slips away from the senses . . . I make clear through the writing down of this charter that . . ."[131] Geoffrey was consistent in this regard. For example, he tried to assure the perpetuity of a significant concession by the abbess of Sainte-Croix with a charter (963–975) introduced in the following manner: "The shrewdness of the holy ancient fathers was that whatever agreements or decrees one would wish to have endure in force should not so much be supported by worthy men but be placed in an enduring form by means of writing."[132] Geoffrey's emphasis on the importance of the written word also extended beyond the concerns of law and politics, for the rule he instituted for the canons of the church of Notre-Dame at Loches insisted that the canons appointed "know how to read and to sing properly."[133]

The environment at the Angevin court in which Fulk Nerra was raised and the nobility with which it had close contact evidence an interest in books and learning. Fulk Nerra's neighbor, Count William of the Poitou, received a fine education and is said, perhaps with some exaggeration, to have traveled everywhere, even on military campaigns, with his books.[134] Geoffrey Greymantle's close friend Hugh Capet saw to it that his son and heir Robert was given a good education. This was done before Hugh became king, but perhaps he was merely imitating royal practice.[135]

The households of the upper nobility in Francia Occidentalis during the late tenth century seem to have been disposed to follow Charlemagne's admonition concerning the importance of education.[136] During *infantia* (childhood prior to the age of seven) children were exposed, at least minimally, to the basics of religious education, which included the memorization of the Lord's Prayer and the Creed, both in Latin.[137] In Fulk Nerra's case, the Creed is of particular interest because it was his custom "to swear by the souls of God"; this seems to hint at a habit developed early in life and based on some childish perversion of the creed.[138] Whether the loss of Fulk's mother during his early years encouraged this type of asocial behavior, which was likely to attract the attention of his elders, is possible given what we know about the way in which children who suffer such losses often react.[139] We cannot know whether Fulk emerged from infancy with the normal education of someone of his social status; this phase of child rearing was traditionally left to the mother, and Adele of Vermandois died when Fulk was no more than four years of age. What is clear, however, is that the nature of Fulk's formal education once he entered *pueritia* (the period beginning at age seven and ending at fourteen) would be much different from what he had experienced earlier.[140] The well-known Frankish proverb to the effect that "a mounted fighting man can be made in childhood but hardly ever or never at a more advanced age" played an important role in educating boys of aristocratic birth during the late tenth century.[141] This part of the education was usually supervised by the father or a close male relative. Fulk's travels with Geoffrey, whose martial abilities were the stuff of legends, likely gave the Angevin count substantial opportunity to monitor his son's education for the hunt and more especially for war.[142]

If the boy is father to the man, as both common wisdom in the Middle Ages and modern developmental psychology aver, an examination of some of Fulk's later behavior patterns will cast light not only on his childhood and youth in general but on his education in particular. From a substantial body of sources, some contemporary and others redacted after Fulk's death, we can discern an outline of the Angevin count's attitude toward education and perhaps his views on the notion of learning things of practical value from books. Perhaps most significant here is the strong probability that Fulk was acquainted with the advice presented in the *De re militari* by Vegetius, the Roman military writer, and that he used this information throughout his career in making both tactical and strategic decisions. Early in his reign, before he could fully consolidate the forces of the Angevin state, Fulk is reported by a contemporary to have used hit-and-run tactics against his enemies. These are exactly the tactics advocated by Vegetius for someone whose army is considerably inferior to that of his adversary. In his first major battle in the field at Conquereuil in 992, Fulk employed a tactical reserve, a major point in Vegetian thought, and arguably the young Angevin count won the victory because of it.[143]

As Angevin count, Fulk supported Bishop Hubert in the foundation of the cathedral school at Angers and encouraged him to bring able scholars such as Bernard, Renaud, and Berengar from Chartres to serve there. Several of these well-educated men are seen from time to time drawing up documents for Fulk. Fulk's efforts to combat ignorance were praised by later writers.[144] Like his father Geoffrey, Fulk frequently recognized in his official documents the importance and advantages of the written word.[145] Fulk was considered a *vir prudens* whose *probitas* was worthy of praise[146]—this at a time when in the vernacular culture, Olivier, Roland's companion in the famous *Chanson* and the contemporary symbol of prudence and wisdom contrasted with rash courage, enjoyed immense popularity. In the scholarly culture the Roman notion of *gravitas* complemented *prudentia*.[147]

These observations on Fulk's education and interest in the subject lead us toward an analysis of his personality, or perhaps more accurately an understanding of his contemporaries' and near contemporaries' interpretation of his behavior and their characterization of the man. At a remove of a millennium we may be more accurate in speaking of Fulk's *persona*, the image he projected by word and deed, rather than of his personality.[148]

If, indeed, Fulk was the kind of man who saw a practical value for education, we cannot prove that he was formally educated. The few extant letters in his name are in Latin but survive only in copies of various kinds, and there is no reason to believe that Fulk wrote the originals himself.[149] In one letter that survives only in a slightly altered form, Fulk exposed his personal feelings in a particularly revealing manner: he exhibited a sense of interiority not generally regarded as usual among lay nobles during the early eleventh century. This may simply mean that he personally dictated the letter in question, perhaps even in the vernacular, to his scribe.[150] Fulk did not sign his own documents but confirmed them with a *signum* in the form of a cross; this suggests that he could not write his own name.[151]

As Einhard made clear in the *Vita Karoli*, learning to write Latin was far more difficult than learning to read it; Charlemagne, who certainly was thought a worthy model by posterity, was credited with having mastered reading but he failed at writing.[152] There is no firm evidence that Fulk could read Latin or that he even could understand it when read or spoken. But Fulk's acquaintance with a broad spectrum of Vegetian military ideas does require some explanation. This may perhaps be found in the medieval tradition that "princes should be instructed in moral principles (ethics) and political wisdom." Such instruction, Frank Barlow speculates in the case of William Rufus, "probably took the form of learning by heart a number of maxims read out . . ." Alfred the Great, for example, whose literary achievements were celebrated, appears to have gained his early education through the process of memorization.[153]

The likelihood that an intelligent youth exposed to such a method would come to understand some Latin during the process should not be ignored. This could have been the case regarding the reading aloud of Latin documents, probably with a local French accent and Romance syntax. Such reading was done at the Angevin court.[154] With the ability to understand documentary Latin encouraged through this process, understanding maxims was but another short step. Indeed, one military maxim that Fulk seems to have learned well was that *prudentia* was basic "for the policy of a soldier who uses trickery to crush an enemy." This came by way of late antique military science and was a favorite of Odo of Cluny, who was a close friend of Fulk the Red.[155]

Fulk entered *adolescentia* at age fourteen, but he was not destined to remain long in this dependent status, when the skills and maxims learned in *pueritia* were sharpened and applied under the guidance of those with greater experience. Before his seventeenth birthday, Fulk had been associated in the countship, married, and succeeded his father as sole ruler of the Angevin state. During this period Fulk also became a father.[156] In short, while most noble youths of his age could look forward to perhaps another decade or more of tutelage, Fulk faced a struggle for political survival, and he shouldered the full responsibility for preserving all that his ancestors had so carefully built up during the preceding century.[157]

Great losses in childhood and a foreshortened youth may well have taken their toll in the development of Fulk's personality. The Angevin count throughout his life appears to have been an angry man whose violent rages were well known to contemporaries and widely feared.[158] Fulk's sobriquet Nerra, that is, "the black," however, which might well lead us to think that he acquired it for his black temper or black moods of depression, cannot be shown to have been given him during his lifetime.[159] This lacuna in the evidence is curious because both Geoffrey "Greymantle" and Geoffrey "Martel" can be shown to have obtained their sobriquets while living.[160] We should note that Greymantle and Martel are either neutral or positive nicknames whereas Nerra may have been so negative that contemporaries feared to put it in writing. Fulk surely did not use the epithet himself.

Fulk's sense of individuality and personal self-awareness did not depend on a nickname, whether Nerra referred to dark moods or a swarthy complexion. During his life he often expressed his innermost feelings. He made clear that he was terrified of Hell. Remarks in charters and letters, such as: "I Fulk . . . mindful of human weakness and fearing the day of judgment . . ." or "[I] was terrified by the fear of Gehenna . . . ," are quite expressive.[161] There may also be a certain sense of balance or a quid pro quo in Fulk's thoughts and feelings that may recall Jacob's bargaining with God: "I Fulk . . . for the cure of my soul and for penance for the very great massacre of Christians which was made in the plain of Conquereuil, and so that the blessed Virgin Mary . . . and the bishop Saint Maurilius might intercede with our Lord Jesus Christ for me a sinner . . . give . . . ," and so on.[162]

Fulk's legalistic sense of balance and his processes of ratiocination on the emotional subject of salvation are more fully exposed in the following text that he subscribed:

Since the fragility of the human race thoroughly fears that the last moment of life may come to an end in a very sudden manner, it is prudent to do enough with care so that one is not found wholly unprepared and so that one does not migrate from this world without having provided any good works. As long as it is within one's *jus* and *potestas,* it is helpful to prepare oneself for attaining salvation in some way. Therefore, I, Count Fulk . . . for the health of [my soul] and the remission of our sins and so that we would merit to gain forgiveness for these sins, cede . . .[163]

For a commander who saw the trickery of *insidiae* (ambushes) as crucial to victory, Fulk was not one to be ambushed by the devil without having taken appropriate precautions.

Such precautions seemed necessary, for throughout his career Fulk's sins and crimes were great. On four separate occasions he made pilgrimages to the Holy Land, in an age when few people made one and even fewer returned home to tell about it.[164] In a letter written shortly after returning from the first of these efforts, Fulk recounts his feelings: "As a result of this pilgrimage, [I] was in high spirits and returned to Anjou exultant." He goes on to say that his "ferocity was replaced by a certain sweetness for a time" and continuing this "published" introspection, Fulk observes a cause-and-effect relationship with the conclusion: "Thus [I] conceived in [my] mind the idea of constructing a church on the best site among the lands that [I] held by [my] own legal right so that monks would be joined there and pray day and night for the redemption of [my] soul."[165]

What is of some special interest here is Fulk's awareness of his anger as an abiding characteristic, perhaps even the dominant element of his character. This ferocity appears not to have been merely a pattern of behavior projected by Fulk and shaped into a politically usable tool, although contemporaries responded to his anger or potential for anger and made accommodations, but a "devil" in his heart or mind that could be calmed "for a time" by the deep spiritual experience of his first pilgrimage. If Fulk's inner rage was brought about, at least in part, by feelings of abandonment after the premature death of mother, father, and brother, combined with the departure of his sister and uncle Guy and exacerbated by the anxieties of meeting the responsibilities of government thrust on him by Geoffrey Greymantle's death, then the youth's response can hardly be considered abnormal.[166]

What is important about Fulk's personality development is that a balance seems to have been maintained in a highly rationalized manner. Indeed, Fulk was prudent in using his *jus* and *potestas* to prepare the way for salvation so that he would not be surprised by sudden death. Here Saint Augustine's teaching (*De Trin.* 14.9, 12) for the man and soldier alike—"prudentia in praecavendis insidiis"—served as the *locus classicus* among scholars and perhaps among some laymen like Fulk as well.[167]

In his letter concerning the building of the church at *Belli Locus* Fulk mentions that he "never takes anything of importance lightly" and goes on to indicate that he took counsel with his advisors.[168] Here Fulk not only affirms the characteristic Roman virtue of *gravitas* but echoes a theme—the importance of taking counsel—that his father Geoffrey thought so worthy of emphasis.[169] Fulk also makes clear that he has no use for *levitas,* even the *levitas* of youth.[170] Among those from whom Fulk sought counsel was his wife. On one occasion he makes clear that he had no time to attend to the important task of allocating largess to the church and thus he delegated this job to the countess.[171]

Although Fulk had received a modicum of preparation for the tasks thrust upon him, only time would tell whether he was suited to fill the cloak of Geoffrey Greymantle.[172] Fulk was provided with the opportunity to make effective use of the power, wealth, and authority that Geoffrey had so competently wielded for more than a quarter-century. Geoffrey presided over the disposition of a broad spectrum of judicial matters that provided him with income and with power over people and land. He collected taxes, imposed new ones (*consuetudines*), carried out administrative innovations, sponsored the development of economic resources, commanded the military, carefully controlled the rewards of his fideles, and dominated the church. In short, Geoffrey ruled the Angevin state, a complex of delicately balanced interests, a living organism of human relationships with the greymantled count at its heart. The survival of what Geoffrey had so successfully crafted from the legacy provided by his predecessors depended above all on the talents of the new count, Fulk Nerra.

CHAPTER TWO

The Struggle for
Survival: 987–996

The succession of an untried youth to sole power and responsibility in a position that previously had been held by a vigorous and successful leader, especially during the fluid circumstances that prevailed during the Early Middle Ages, frequently provoked trouble and uncertainty.[1] We should therefore not be surprised that medieval chroniclers recognized this phenomenon of political instability. The authors of the twelfth-century *Gesta Consulum,* one of the more important narrative sources for Fulk Nerra's reign, put it succinctly: "Fulk Nerra . . . who had the enthusiasm of youth, most bravely set out to defend the *comté* from many enemies. For new wars always break out quickly against new rulers."[2]

Fulk's survival would depend on far more than youthful enthusiasm and personal bravery. Odo I (d. 996), count of Blois, Tours, Chartres, Châteaudun, and Meaux, was Fulk's most dangerous adversary. Odo commanded vast resources and was allied with powerful magnates who had good reason to try to reduce Fulk Nerra's holdings and power before he could assume the position in the political arena that his father, Geoffrey Greymantle, had held. Odo's policy in the west of France was one of expansion in the Loire valley at Angevin expense.[3] William Iron Arm, Odo's brother-in-law, was count of the Poitou and duke of Aquitaine. He also had good reason to go to war against Fulk in order to retake lands that he had lost to the Angevins during Geoffrey Greymantle's reign.[4] Count Conan of Rennes, whom Geoffrey had defeated only five years earlier, still coveted Nantes.[5] Conan was a supporter of Odo, and in addition he was friendly with the Normans, longtime enemies of the Angevins, whose Scandinavian allies possessed the naval capability to penetrate the heart of Anjou.[6]

At the start of Fulk's reign, however, a combination of fortunate circumstances over which he had little control saved him from the full force of his enemies' military potential. Odo of Blois was unable to muster his resources to attack the new count because of preoccupations in eastern France. After Hugh Capet became king in October 987, Odo had attached himself to the Carolingian claimant to the throne, Charles of Lorraine, whereas the Angevins had supported and received the support of the Capetians.[7] It was also Fulk's good fortune that William Iron Arm, Odo's most powerful potential ally on Anjou's southern border, was at that crucial time estranged from his wife, Emma of Blois.[8] Moreover, Anjou's allies in the Poitou, such as the viscount of Thouars, and in Aquitaine, such as the counts of Périgord, la Marche, Forez, Gévaudan, and the count-bishop of le Puy, were likely perceived by William Iron Arm as deterrents to any plans he might have entertained for immediate hostilities against Fulk.[9] Finally, the premature death of Odo's brother Hugh, archbishop of Bourges, in 985 had permitted the Capetian-Angevin allies to secure this important base of ecclesiastical power for one of their own supporters. Archbishop Dagobert cooperated closely with Fulk's uncle, Bishop Guy of le Puy, in advancing Angevin interests at le Puy.[10]

Since a massive coordinated campaign against Fulk was not an immediate alternative for Odo, he left to Count Conan of Rennes, Abbot Robert of Saint-Florent de Saumur, and Gelduin of Saumur the task of bringing down the youthful and inexperienced Angevin count. Conan concentrated his efforts in campaigning against Count Guerech, Fulk's man at Nantes, with the aim of capturing the city and establishing himself as duke of Brittany.[11] While Conan threatened Fulk's western frontier, Abbot Robert and Gelduin undertook to isolate Fulk's eastern strongholds at Amboise and Loches.[12] To this end Gelduin's horsemen ranged through the Saumurois in an effort to interdict Fulk's communications with his eastern lands. As a later chronicler working with hostile sources that are no longer extant observed somewhat rhetorically: "How many times Fulk, count of the Angevins, as he was crossing through this neighborhood [the Saumurois] would say in terror, 'Let us get away from the devil of Saumur, I always seem to see him in front of me.'"[13]

With Gelduin's troops busy blocking the roads, harassing communications, and raiding the estates of the Angevin count and his supporters, Abbot Robert labored on the diplomatic front to isolate Fulk. By midsummer of 987 Abbot Robert had set in motion plans to obtain the defection of Viscount Renaud of Angers from Fulk's entourage by securing his services to protect the possessions of Saint-Florent in the Saumurois from raids by the Angevin count and his fideles. After what were probably delicate negotiations—defection by the most powerful magnate in Anjou after the count can hardly be considered a decision taken lightly—Robert obtained Viscount Renaud's word that he would protect Saint-Florent's interests in the region. This would bring Renaud into a confrontation with Fulk, and the viscount was handsomely rewarded with the villas of Saint-Georges-sur-Layon, Denezé, Distré, and Ulmes in the southwestern regions of the Saumurois.[14]

Winning the support of Viscount Renaud was only part of Robert's plan. In the summer of 987 Abbot Robert may have had a hint that Bishop Renaud of Angers, the viscount's son, was not unwilling to use the power and prestige of his episcopal office against Fulk's interests. Shortly after Fulk succeeded to sole possession of the countship, a dispute between the monks of Saint-Florent and the monks of Saint-Maur concerning the tithes of Saint-Pierre-de-Meigné was adjudicated by Bishop Renaud who found in favor of Abbot Robert. The interest of the Angevin count at this time was in seeing Saint-Maur prevail.[15]

The willingness of Viscount Renaud and his son the bishop to deal with Abbot Robert may even have provided some encouragement to the pious Abbot Guntarius of Saint-Aubin to oppose the new count. Although we know of no actions taken by Guntarius, two issues frequently placed Fulk at odds with reform-minded ecclesiastics. One was the continuance of Geoffrey Greymantle's policy of using church estates or the income provided by these lands to reward members of the comital entourage, and the other was the requirement that churchmen meet the military obligations imposed upon them and their dependents by the state. Fulk's obvious need following Geoffrey's death for both economic resources and military support permits the inference that at least one or perhaps both of these issues caused friction with Abbot Guntarius, whose subsequent pilgrimage to Jerusalem seems to indicate an inclination toward piety.[16] Indeed, Fulk's demands on the resources of the church early in his reign were condemned by both Abbot Abbo of Fleury[17] and Bishop Renaud of Angers.[18]

Not only was political stability in the Angevin heartland endangered both from within and without but the complex family network nurtured by Geoffrey Greymantle and on which much Fulconian influence in the broader political arena traditionally rested also was at risk. For example, could Aldebert, count of both Périgord and la Marche and Fulk Nerra's cousin-in-law, be relied upon to act as a restraining influence to deter William Iron Arm from attacking Anjou now that a man of Geoffrey Greymantle's reputation and charisma no longer led the Angevin family network?[19] Farther east, would Geoffrey's widow Adele of Chalon and perhaps Abbot Maiolus of Cluny be willing to act to ensure that Maurice, Fulk's half-brother who was no more than nine years of age and probably much younger, would have a role at Chalon? Maurice's maternal half-brother Hugh had already reached his majority and, although a cleric, had supporters who wanted to see him become count of Chalon.[20]

In the northeast the Angevins' long-standing alliance with Walter, count of Amiens, Valois, and Vexin, might seem less attractive in the third generation now that a man of Geoffrey's stature had been replaced by a teenaged youth. With the threat to Normandy from the Vexin perhaps lessened by a probable weakening of Vexin-Angevin ties, would the Normans be more eager to support Conan of Rennes in going beyond Nantes to Angers itself, as Viking forces had done so successfully in 843?[21] We should note here that Conan's son Geoffrey-Berengar was Geoffrey Greymantle's grandson, and the youth may have been thought by some to have a claim to succeed his grandfather should Fulk Nerra meet an early end.[22]

Clearly, at this crucial time, Fulk Nerra was not in a position, either on the basis of experience or personal prestige, to lead the Angevin family network. Yet the spirit of cooperation that the men and women of the Angevin comital family had shared for at least three generations was not lost.[23] Guy, count-bishop of le Puy, acted quickly on learning of his brother's death. His first and closest concern appears to have been to try to secure his nephew Maurice's position at Chalon and to preserve the integrity of the Angevin enclave in the east. Thus on 11 August, just three weeks after Geoffrey's death, and probably not much more than two weeks after Guy received the news, the count-bishop is to be found in close touch with the authorities at Cluny.[24] It seems reasonable to suggest that Guy conferred with Maiolus, the single most influential man in the region from a moral perspective and also a close friend of Hugh Capet, about the situation at Chalon. Whatever may have been the dynamics, and the details are obscured, the situation at Chalon was stabilized for the time being. It was arranged that the half-brothers Hugh, who was a cleric, and Maurice, who was a young boy, jointly assume the title of count under the watchful eye of their mother Adele, who retained the title *comitissa*.[25]

The influence of Abbot Maiolus and of the Angevin family network should not be discounted in the settlement that saw young Maurice share in the comital title. Maiolus had succeeded Odo, Fulk the Red's friend, in 942 and was a close friend of both Hugh Capet and Count William of Arles. The latter had saved Maiolus from Muslim captivity at le Freinet and subsequently rescued Countess Adelaide-Blanche of Forez and Gévaudan from the wrath of King Lothair. William then married Adelaide-Blanche, who was Geoffrey Greymantle's sister.[26] Her daughter Adalmode, by her first husband, was the wife of Aldebert, count of Périgord and la Marche, at this time.[27] In addition, Guy of le Puy, Adelaide-Blanche's brother, was close to Odilo, Maiolus's confidant and ultimately his successor as abbot of Cluny.[28] Adelaide's sons Stephen and Pons were counts of Forez and Gévaudan, which were not very distant from Chalon. In short, moral support from Cluny and the spectre of an "Angevin" army led by relatives of the late Geoffrey Greymantle seem to have been sufficient to deter those of Hugh of Chalon's supporters who might have flirted with the idea of depriving Maurice of a share in the comital title. Indeed, the memory of such an "Angevin" army supporting Guy at le Puy only twelve years earlier can hardly have faded completely.[29]

After attending to affairs in the east, Guy went to Angers. There he acted quickly to sustain the monks of Saint-Maur in their conflict with Saint-Florent. With Guy's support the Saint-Maur monks rejected Bishop Renaud's decision against them in favor of Saint-Florent. They used force to hold on to their tithes at Meigné and drove out Robert's men.[30] Guy's action placed him squarely in opposition to Bishop Renaud, but the bishop of Angers seems to have tried to avoid a confrontation. In part, Bishop Renaud's reluctance to support Saint-Florent at this time may have been a result of Viscount Renaud's failure to honor his agreement with Abbot Robert. The viscount not only refused to defend the Saumurois against Fulk's incursions but he was required by the Angevin count to dispose of the lands that had been entrusted to his care by Abbot Robert. Renaud handed over these estates to Alberic of Vihiers and Roger of Loudun, two of Fulk's most trusted fideles.[31]

It seems that when the agreement between Viscount Renaud and Abbot Robert became known to Fulk, the count obtained help from King Hugh. Viscount Renaud was made treasurer of Saint-Martin at

Tours through the intervention of Fulk's Capetian ally, who opposed the expansionist policies of the house of Blois. Thus with the aid of Hugh Capet, Fulk seems to have been able to outbid Abbot Robert and Odo I for Viscount Renaud's support.[32] In addition, Fulk put pressure on Count Guerech of Nantes to hand over to Viscount Renaud the stronghold of Champtoceaux on the left bank of the Loire in the northern part of the Mauges region.[33]

At home, Fulk took severe measures against Abbot Guntarius and the monks of Saint-Aubin. The abbot resigned and went on a pilgrimage to the Holy Land. Fulk, with the help of his uncle Guy, saw to it that Guntarius was replaced by a monk named Renaud.[34] Some sense of the strength of Fulk's reaction against both the monks of Saint-Aubin and against Bishop Renaud can be gained from the *Carta de electione Rainaldi abbatis* (988). The custom under Geoffrey Greymantle had been to grant, or actually to "regrant," a new abbot of Saint-Aubin control over the lesser vicarial powers in the lands of the monastic fisc.[35] This concession provided the monastery with partial immunity from the interference of government officials and was of substantial economic value since the one-third of the fines that normally went to the *vicarius* and probably the one-third that normally were kept by the count went instead into the coffers of Saint-Aubin. Geoffrey traditionally retained for himself jurisdiction over major crimes, such as theft, arson, and homicide.[36]

By contrast, in the election charter of 988 Fulk did not grant any judicial rights at all to the monks of Saint-Aubin. This meant that the count's vicarii would hear all cases on the lands belonging to the monastery and all revenues due to the count or to his agents would be duly collected by them. In addition, whereas the monks of Saint-Aubin traditionally had been permitted to show support for the election of a new abbot either with their *signa* or with their signatures on the election charters, in abbot Renaud's election charter the monks played no juridical role. Furthermore, although the bishop of Angers usually played both an advisory role and a juridical role in the election of the abbot of Saint-Aubin, Bishop Renaud was permitted no role at all in the election of 988. Finally, Bishop Guy of le Puy, Fulk's uncle, signed this charter and the Angevin count affixed his *signum* in the form of a cross. None of the monks, who in the body of the document are said to have "consented" to the choice of Abbot Renaud, attested.[37]

The important role that Bishop Guy played in providing counsel to young Fulk cannot be underestimated, but we must be careful not to generalize from the behavior of Viscount Renaud and Bishop Renaud

in order to posit widespread defections by Geoffrey Greymantle's fideles after his death. In the earliest surviving charters with witness lists
in the new count's reign, the names of the men who made their *signa*
in support of Fulk's acts are in most cases the same as those who supported Geoffrey's charters during the last decade of his reign.[38] We may
perhaps account for this support by noting that Geoffrey had cultivated
the loyalty of a cadre of magnates: men like Alberic of Vihiers, Cadilo
of Blaison, Roger I (the Old) of Loudun, Joscelin of Rennes (castellan
of Baugé), Suhard I (the Old) of Craon, and the several leaders of the
Bouchard family as well as Robert of Buzançais and later his two sons,
Archembaud and Sulpicius.[39] As we have seen, Geoffrey had involved
Fulk in a process of interacting with the comital fideles, and he was the
first count in the west of France to associate his heir in the comital
title.[40]

Once Viscount Renaud returned to the comital entourage, Fulk was
in a position to look after Anjou's defensive interests in a more systematic manner. Thus Count Guerech of Nantes, who needed Angevin
support against Conan of Rennes, was prevailed upon to hand over
the stronghold of Champtoceaux to Viscount Renaud. This stronghold, only twenty kilometers up the Loire from Nantes, strengthened
Angevin control of the left bank of the river west of Angers and thereby
placed another formidable defensive barrier to a Norse naval incursion
into the Angevin heartland. Viscount Renaud, who seems to have envisioned expanding his dominions east of the Mauges region into the
Saumurois when he made his short-lived treaty with Abbot Robert,
apparently resigned himself to a less grandiose enclave when he surrendered to Fulk Nerra's fideles the lands entrusted to him by the abbot of Saint-Florent.

The *quartae* of Dacea which were given to Roger, Fulk's castellan
at Loudun, and Saint-Georges-sur-Layon, which was given to Alberic,
the Angevin count's castellan at Vihiers, along with Méron, which
served as a base for several of the count's fideles, and Meigné, which
the monks of Saint-Maur and Bishop Guy fought to keep out of the
hands of Saint-Florent—all constituted a formidable point d'appui in
the Saumurois from which Angevin troops could be provided logistic
support for operations against Odo I's economic and military assets in
the region. In addition, this strategic matrix served defensively as a
shield on the Angevin count's southern line of communications from
Angers to Loches which Geoffrey Greymantle had hastily established
and which ran through Vihiers, Montaglan, Loudun, and Nouâtre.[41]

At the time these lands were taken from Saint-Florent and brought under Angevin jurisdiction, the full range of taxes, that is, *consuetudines*, owed to the state were imposed on the people living on these estates and on their resources.[42] From the military perspective the *commendiciae* was most important. According to the *commendiciae*, all landholders, free and unfree alike, were responsible for the *bidamnum*, which required fifteen days of work each year for the building or repair of fortifications located within the Angevin state or on its frontiers. This was in addition to the more general *corvadae* required to support public works such as road repair. Furthermore, all those who produced agricultural products were responsible for the *fodrum*, the tax used to feed the army; the *angaria* was imposed on those with animals and wagons or carts to haul supplies for the army. Finally, every able-bodied man had to answer the count's *submonitio* or summons to war, that is, *bellum publicum* or *expeditio publica*. *Satellites* serving in the military households of Fulk's fideles were directly responsible to the count for military service; their position was not mediated by their domini.[43]

Fulk's efforts to follow his father's advice and example by assuring the support and loyalty of his fideles, upon whose *generositas* comital strength was regarded as resting, while at the same time building up the defenses of the Angevin state to obviate the threat posed by Odo I and his allies is amply illustrated in the Angevin count's relations with Alberic of Vihiers. Alberic was a relative of the Fulconians whom Geoffrey Greymantle had recruited for service in Anjou around 981 and established at Vihiers. Fulk arranged for Alberic to be rewarded with the villa of Saint-Georges-sur-Layon, which also strengthened the strategic position of the castrum at Vihiers.[44] Shortly thereafter Fulk entrusted to Alberic the very large and rich *curtis* of Champigné-sur-Sarthe, which dominated the region between the Sarthe and Mayenne only twenty kilometers north of Angers.[45] Although this curtis was distant from Vihiers, it did have the capacity to support many garrison troops, *vasvassores*, and thus it gave Alberic the opportunity and resources to reward his own fideles with advancement in the northwest while at the same time aiding Fulk in the defense of the Angevin state.[46]

Before Fulk could hand Champigné-sur-Sarthe over to Alberic, however, he had to regain possession of the curtis from Alberic of Orléans, who had received it many years earlier from Geoffrey Greymantle as part of an effort to strengthen the Fulconian position among the magnates of the Orléanais and Gâtinais.[47] Thus Fulk arranged a *scambium* that provided Alberic of Orléans with lands in Francia and granted the curtis as a *beneficium* to Alberic of Vihiers.[48] The latter then divided the holding into two parts and honored two of his *milites* from the Touraine, Odo Brisahasta and Hardredus, each with a half of the curtis.[49] Hardredus, whose obligations in the Touraine apparently precluded his active participation in the defense of the northwest, granted his half of the curtis as a dowry to his daughter when she married Dodo of Bazouges, a local *miles* from just north of Champigné-sur-Sarthe.[50]

The detailed record of land transfers just described accounts for only a small part of the complicated tenurial history of this curtis of Champigné-sur-Sarthe during the reigns of Geoffrey Greymantle and Fulk Nerra. This record and many similar ones attract immediate attention to the administrative underpinnings of the Angevin state during this period. Just as the cathedral of Saint Maurice and the monastery of Saint-Aubin, both at Angers, maintained archival chests, *scrinia,* so too did the Angevin count. Of particular interest in the present context are the *tabulae fiscorum,* the lists of fiscal lands and resources that were under the count's control whether directly in his possession or in the hands of his supporters.[51]

Who kept these documents for the count or even where they were kept is not known. But an educated guess would have to give serious attention to the Bouchard family, which for decades played a major role in the administration of the cathedral of Saint Maurice. Members of this group not only wrote documents for Geoffrey and Fulk Nerra but from time to time they controlled the office of treasurer of the cathedral. Fulk rewarded secular members of this clan with substantial beneficia and also entrusted at least two different Bouchards with the office of castellan. Geoffrey Greymantle chose as the first abbot of the reformed monastery of Saint-Aubin a member of the Bouchard family, who then cooperated closely with the count in the exploitation of the house's resources.[52]

While the government administration kept the records, Fulk was occupied on the diplomatic front with making his position in Anjou more secure and in maintaining his communications with the important centers of power at Amboise and Loches. Nevertheless, he had time personally to lead at least one *expeditio* and several smaller raids through the Saumurois which were to the detriment of Saint-Florent. Fulk even seems to have raided Odo's holdings on the lower reaches of the Vienne in the neighborhood of Ile-Bouchard and Chinon.[53]

Fulk's military organization at this time appears to have been traditional. He had a military household that traveled with him. There were also garrison troops (*vasvassores*) based in strategic locations under the command of castellans such as Roger of Loudun and Alberic of Vihiers. Throughout the Angevin state all able-bodied men were eligible for military service when the count went to war.[54]

The Angevin *exercitus* at this time was composed of both mounted troops and foot soldiers (*equites* and *pedites*). The army as a whole appears to have been formed, for organizational purposes, into four groups, perhaps reflecting the regions where they were raised, and these likely were known in the old French vernacular as *legiones,* following the traditional Latin *legio* used by contemporary writers. It is possible that the term *phalange* was also used either for an army group, as a whole, or for a part of a *legio.* These army groups at full strength were probably intended to have been about a thousand men each, as was the case in other parts of the erstwhile Frankish empire. Sobriquets such as *Mille Clipei, Chiliarchus,* and *Tribunus* carried by important men in the entourage of the Angevin counts tend to support the possibility that thousand-man divisions were at least a *desideratum.*[55]

The observations of the contemporary chronicler Richer permit the inference that Fulk Nerra had four army groups at his disposal but nevertheless lacked sufficient manpower under arms to challenge Odo of Blois and his allies in the field.[56] It is likely that because of the difficulties he faced on his accession Fulk was unable to bring his field forces up to full strength. This would probably have been the case especially on his eastern frontiers in the regions around Amboise and Loches, which were farthest from Angers. Fulk responded by using hit-and-run raids to strike his enemies' resources without risking a confrontation. This tactic of avoiding combat is exactly what the Roman military authority Vegetius advised in his popular handbook, *De re militari,* for someone in the Angevin count's disadvantaged position.[57]

While Fulk executed raids to keep the Blésois and their allies on the defensive and to prevent them from developing significant offensive operations against Anjou itself, Odo's men, apparently led by Gelduin of Saumur, pursued a strategy intended to isolate Amboise by placing a ring of fortifications around it. A stronghold was built at Chaumont less than twenty kilometers upriver from Amboise. At about the same time Odo's forces also fortified Montsoreau from which the confluence of the Vienne and Loire rivers could be dominated. In addition, Odo's supporters completed and garrisoned the stronghold of Saint-Aignan on the Cher only thirty kilometers south-southeast of Amboise.[58] These fortifications not only could be used to put pressure on Amboise, Fulk's major base in the middle Loire valley and the most important Fulconian stronghold that stood between Odo's centers of power at Blois and Tours, but also threatened the Angevin count's economic resources. Amboise had grown substantially during the peace of Fulk the Good's reign, and Geoffrey Greymantle had fortified its most prosperous suburb, which he called Châteauneuf.[59] In general, the Fulconians benefited substantially from the river tolls their agents collected.[60]

Despite the support of his fideles within Anjou and his efforts in the field, Fulk's position gradually deteriorated. Conan of Rennes killed Count Guerech of Nantes in 988 and harassed the latter's young son Alan ceaselessly. Without help from Fulk, Nantes was likely to fall to Conan.[61] The only question was how long it would take. With the enemy exerting great pressure both in the east on Amboise and in the west on Nantes, Fulk was not in a position to provide the vigorous diplomatic and military support to Hugh Capet in his contest with Charles of Lorraine which the new king would have reason to expect, indeed, to have required, from the successor of Geoffrey Greymantle. To King Hugh, moreover, the Fulconian enclave in the Gâtinais, with its great stronghold of Château-Landon, was of crucial strategic importance as a buffer between the Capetian's western frontier based on the fortress of Melun and Blésois interests that stretched eastward toward Orléans and beyond the Gâtinais toward Provins.[62] Because of Fulk's difficulties, it was arranged, likely by Hugh Capet, that possession of Château-Landon be transferred from the Angevin count to his cousin, Geoffrey, the son of Adelaide, Fulk the Good's sister who had married Walter I, the count of Amiens, Vexin, and Valois. Geoffrey was then given the new title of count of the Gâtinais.[63]

This "reorganization" provides an additional perspective from which to view Fulk Nerra's scambium with Alberic of Orléans through which the latter returned the curtis of Champigné-sur-Sarthe and received in exchange lands located in Francia.[64] By this arrangement Fulk obtained the presence of one of his prominent supporters where he could more easily aid Hugh Capet and thus fulfill the new count's obligation to his king. In addition, and probably for the same reason, Fulk virtually stripped the fisc of the monastery of Saint-Pierre-en-Gâtinais so as to provide beneficia to his *vassali* in this region.[65]

The new count of the Gâtinais was chosen from among Fulk's relatives—indeed, he was a relative with an Angevin *Leitname*; this selection indicates the enduring importance of family interests and their recognition even in an extended sense, when arrangements were made among friends.[66] In this context royal support for Angevin allies can also be seen in Hugh Capet's selection of Bouchard of Vendôme, Fulk's father-in-law, as count of Melun.[67] Parenthetically we may note here another indicator of Fulk's difficulties, for the Fulconians' traditional role as an ally and protector of the viscomital family of le Mans, which also controlled the bishopric, was ceded at least temporarily to Bouchard of Vendôme.[68] In short, Fulk Nerra's relatives and friends can be seen sustaining some of the obligations that Geoffrey Greymantle had previously undertaken but which the new Angevin count could not maintain in the wake of his father's death.

Fulk was to receive a respite of sorts from his military problems when during the winter of 990 Hugh Capet and Odo I arranged a truce.[69] As far as Fulk was concerned, however, the war was on again in the spring of 990 when Conan of Rennes attacked Nantes, killed Count Alan, and assumed the title "duke of Brittany."[70] Fulk entered the field again but still focused his activities in the east. He raided as far as the suburbs of Blois itself and burned the monastery of Saint-Lomer.[71] During the summer of 991, the next regular campaigning season, Fulk participated with Hugh Capet, Bouchard of Vendôme, and Richard of Normandy in retaking the stronghold of Melun, which Odo had seized in June of that year.[72] Fulk seems to have followed up the advantage gained at Melun and, perhaps with the support of Bouchard of Vendôme, carried out a raid in force against Châteaudun.[73]

Hugh Capet had gathered a formidable array of powers—Vendôme, Anjou, and Normandy—for the campaign to retake Melun, but he was unable to hold this alliance together in order to deliver a more decisive blow against Odo I because of a threat from the north. Robert, Hugh's son, repudiated his wife Rozala-Suzanne of Flanders at this time; when she attempted to reclaim her dowry, the Capetians refused to relinquish possession of the stronghold of Montreuil-sur-Canche. The Flemish then built a stronghold at Montreuil to block Capetian use of the river, so Hugh mustered his forces for a campaign in Flanders.[74] The Normans, however, were apparently persuaded by Conan of Rennes that the road to Angers lay open—Nantes was already in the new Breton duke's hands—and an alliance was forged with Duke Richard to provide a Norse naval force.[75] Odo of Blois clearly benefited from the fragmentation of the royal alliance and it hardly seems unreasonable to suspect, although it cannot be proven, that he played a role in encouraging the Flemish in their resistance to Hugh Capet and in supporting Conan's plans in the west.

When Fulk Nerra learned that Conan was massing his forces in Brittany and that he had made an alliance with the Normans, the Angevin count realized he could no longer risk remaining in the middle Loire region to maneuver against Odo I and his supporters.[76] Conan could not be permitted to join forces with his allies at Nantes and then move up the Loire valley toward Angers with a secure base at his back and Norse ships to supply the campaign with food and siege equipment. Fulk understood that he would have to capture Nantes in order to deprive the Bretons and their allies of their base and the use of the river.

Nantes, however, was a formidable fortified urbs with a perimeter wall of some 1,600 meters dating from Roman times. These walls were strengthened with some thirty towers. In addition, there was also an internal citadel (arx) originally constructed during the later Roman era. When Conan took the city, he built yet another tower, which in the vernacular was called "le Bouffay."[77] This impressive defensive complex could be supplied by both land and water. Thus, a successful siege could not be undertaken without a fleet.[78] Conan also garrisoned both the circuit walls and the old Roman citadel, the former with custodes, who likely were drawn in large part from the able-bodied male inhabitants of the city, and the latter with milites, elite troops probably posted from the Breton count's military household.[79] The defensive thinking that prevailed in this period calculated the number of defenders required to hold a fortification in relation to the available technology. Given these circumstances Conan needed approximately 1,450 custodes armed either with bows or crossbows in order to establish a credible deterrent to a force large enough to contemplate storming the circuit walls.[80]

Despite what seemed to be great odds, Fulk gambled that he could retake Nantes before Conan and his allies arrived with a relief force. By mid-May at the latest Fulk had mustered an army, advanced to Nantes, deployed his forces, and established a landward siege.[81] But lacking both a fleet and the time for a siege, the Angevin count's only hope was to win a quick victory. Obviously, this precluded reducing the defenders by starvation or by undermining the walls. The city had to be taken either by storm or by subversion. According to one contemporary, Fulk was able through the judicious use of bribes and promises to convince those elements of Conan's garrison (custodes) in the urbs that surrender was preferable to resistance.[82]

The rapid surrender of the urbs suggests that the defenders were intimidated by the size of Fulk's forces and judged the Angevins capable of taking the city by storm. The lex deditionis, or law of surrender, protected those defenders who gave up without resistance while it permitted successful attackers to treat the defeated garrison troops who had fought in vain as the victors saw fit.[83] During the previous year Fulk had played a major role in two successful and bloody attacks on fortifications, Melun and Châteaudun, where elements of the defeated defending force were treated brutally.[84]

If the Nantes garrison was intimidated and surrendered in fear of a successful assault on the walls of the urbs, then the Angevin count's forces must have been at least twice as numerous as those who defended the circuit.[85] With a minimum force of about 3,000, Fulk would have had a good chance of taking the walls, for the technology was available for building assault towers on site and the attacking force would not have had to rely solely on the use of ladders.[86] Without assault towers, Fulk would have required perhaps as many as 5,000 men to storm a properly defended walled urbs the size of Nantes.[87]

After Fulk entered the city, he took hostages from among the citizens (*cives*) and secured an oath of faithfulness from the adult males, the armsworthy segment of the society.[88] The Angevin count then turned his attention to the citadel within the walls of the city; these fortifications, garrisoned by Conan's *milites*, who likely were bound by strong personal oaths to the Breton leader, refused to surrender.[89] Fulk recognized that time was growing short; he may even have received intelligence that Conan was approaching with an army too large to meet in the field, for after having sustained operations at Nantes for a total of three weeks, time enough to build assault towers and to intimidate the garrison, the Angevin count withdrew his forces and marched back to Angers.[90] Fulk's intention was to raise additional troops for the purpose of meeting Conan and either relieving the siege of Nantes, which he assumed the Breton count would mount, or retaking the city if it fell to the enemy before his return.[91]

While Fulk was returning home in order to recruit reinforcements, Conan did reach Nantes with a large army of Bretons. He was supported by a naval force of Norsemen which was deployed on the river. The *urbani*, who had sworn an oath to Fulk and given hostages to the Angevin count, defended the city's perimeter walls. They were caught in a cross fire between the besiegers outside the urbs and Conan's *milites*, who held the citadel. As a contemporary chronicler reported the situation: "The garrison in the citadel and the besiegers worked for Conan's victory whereas the inhabitants of the city worked for Fulk's victory."[92]

On his return to Anjou, Fulk reinforced his army with men called up from the Poitou and from Maine. The men of Poitou were under the command of Viscount Aimery of Thouars and those of Maine likely were led either by Viscount Radulf of le Mans or his brother Geoffrey of Sablé. These men were longtime allies who had been brought into the Angevin *mouvance* by Geoffrey Greymantle.[93] Fulk also recruited mercenaries who were probably military specialists of some type— engineers and crossbowmen are the most likely possibilities.[94]

With this large force, Fulk now made his way west once again to Nantes and a confrontation with his brother-in-law Conan of Rennes. It seems clear that Fulk's army was sufficiently superior in size to the forces commanded by Conan that the Breton abandoned his plans to recapture Nantes by siege and began to withdraw. Fulk, however, challenged Conan to do battle at Conquereuil, a large grassy plain about fifty-five kilometers north of Nantes where Geoffrey Greymantle had defeated his son-in-law a decade earlier.[95]

Conan apparently agreed to do battle—an arranged combat that contemporaries and near contemporaries depicted as a judicial dual between two armies in contrast to the more traditional confrontation of individuals often orchestrated in similar circumstances.[96] Conan thus withdrew to Conquereuil and Fulk followed. The accounts are in accord that Conan, who arrived at Conquereuil several days before Fulk, prepared the field with pits and ditches, which he covered with sod in order to disguise them so that if and when the forces of the Angevin count charged across the plain they would fall into the traps. Finally, Conan had an earthwork constructed across the width of the field, which was bordered to the left and right with impassable swamps. Some of the water from the swamps was also directed into the ditches.[97]

Commentators on the conflict between Fulk and Conan present different points of view on the rest of the action. For example, the contemporary chronicler Richer, whose sympathies lay with Conan, depicts the Breton count as taking a purely defensive position and as having no intention of initiating combat. Richer describes the count of Rennes' situation as if he had learned about it from someone who had been privy to Conan's thinking:

If the enemy attacked him, he would defend his life. It is not a question of fear [that led him to prepare traps and go on the defensive], but if they [the Angevins] seek him out and attack, they act contrary to the law [*contra jus*]. Thus their defeat would result more easily because they had the rashness to attack peaceful and inoffensive men who were defensively deployed.[98]

By contrast, Raoul Glaber, though not partial to Fulk, was overtly hostile to the Bretons in general and to Conan in particular. He describes the Bretons as uncivilized and hotheaded and pronounces their customs boorish and their language a stupid gibberish. Raoul asserts that after Conan married Fulk Nerra's sister Hermengarde-Gerberga, the Breton count was the most insolent of *principes*. He says that Conan had himself crowned like a king and that he subjected his people to "open tyranny."[99]

A third source, the chronicler of Nantes, makes the legitimacy of Angevin action clearer when he asserts that Conan was the murderer of several counts of Nantes and that Fulk was merely taking vengeance against the man who had killed them. This chronicler, however, who is committed to emphasizing the independence of the counts of Nantes from the Angevin count, pointedly omits mention of the fact that Fulk was avenging the murder of men he had put in office, an office the Angevins controlled.[100]

When Fulk arrived in the environs of Conquereuil, the *Chronique de Nantes* describes him as commanding that the boy Judicaël, the young illegitimate son of Hoël the murdered count of Nantes, be brought before the assembled troops. Then "taking the boy in his hands," the Angevin count raised him up to show him to the men who were about to go into battle. Fulk is said to have proclaimed that this boy was the legitimate count of Nantes and that he had a better right to the *civitas* than anyone else.[101]

The obvious symbolism of this act—raising up an individual to office—was probably not lost on the troops.[102] But Fulk's assertion of the boy's legitimate right to Nantes despite his status as the son of a concubine requires some attention. We might hazard that the ceremony of raising the boy up had a second significance, a legitimation of his birth. In this context, we recall the traditional and well-known ceremony, associated among the Romans with the goddess Levana, by which the father picks up the newborn son from the ground and presents the child to those assembled in order to signal that he accepts the baby as legitimate.[103] Thus, Fulk as Hoël's erstwhile dominus legitimates the son of his fidelis.[104] Fulk followed this impressive ceremony with yet another, calling forth from the assemblage of fighting men Viscount Aimo, the maternal uncle of young Judicaël, and presenting him with the standard.[105] By awarding this particular honor to Aimo, Fulk not only indicated his confidence in the loyalty and ability of the viscount but signified that the battle was being fought to free Nantes from Conan of Rennes and not merely as part of a larger Angevin program.[106]

Fulk then moved his forces to the field of Conquereuil, probably just beyond arrow range of Conan's archers. He deployed his troops "wisely," according to the Nantes chronicler,[107] in two units, an *exercitus prior* and an *exercitus posterior*, a lead unit and a backup or reserve unit, according to Richer.[108]

As Fulk deliberately proceeded through the ceremonies described above and then judiciously deployed his forces, Conan apparently became worried that the Angevins and their allies would not initiate the pell-mell attack he needed if the Breton traps were to succeed. Indeed, if Fulk and his men proceeded carefully, they might discover the traps that had been dug. As a result, the Breton count ordered a feigned retreat in order to draw Fulk's troops into a precipitous charge that would founder in the water-logged pits and ditches scattered throughout the field. If the plan worked, the Bretons could then wheel their horses and deliver a crushing counterattack to the disordered enemy forces.[109]

Conan's ruse worked, but only partially. Fulk's lead squadron charged, "seeing an easy victory," according to Raoul Glaber. Fulk himself apparently did not give the order, but having lost immediate command and control of his designated attack force, the prior exercitus, the Angevin count joined the charge himself.[110] Fulk's lead unit was thrown into confusion as men and horses sprawled into the ditches. The Breton counterattack was furious, and many of Fulk's troops, especially those who had been unhorsed, were killed or wounded. The Angevin count was unhorsed, but apparently his heavy coat of mail saved him from serious injury. Aimo, the viscount of Nantes and standard bearer, was cut down. With the count unhorsed and his standard lowered, the latter being the traditional signal for retreat, Fulk's forces withdrew from the field.[111]

The Bretons also disengaged, apparently deterred from hot pursuit of the defeated and disorganized enemy by Fulk's reserve unit, the posterior exercitus, which had held its position. Fulk reached his own lines and rapidly reassessed the situation. Almost immediately he led his intact and alerted reserve against the now disorganized Bretons, who undoubtedly thought that the field of battle was theirs. The counterattack caught the Bretons by surprise. They were driven from the field with great losses. The number of Bretons killed was put at about a thousand. The Angevins no doubt suffered many casualties as well.[112]

Although contemporaries and near contemporaries who speak directly of Conan's fate agree that he was killed at Conquereuil, there is some doubt about the circumstances. Richer, who was consistently sympathetic to Conan, claims that the Breton count was murdered by one of his enemies while resting without his armor following the failure of Fulk's charge and his own successful counterattack. Richer goes on to say that this murder gave the victory to Fulk even though the Angevin count had fled the battlefield in fear when his forces were routed.[113]

Raoul Glaber, in contrast, though hardly a partisan of Fulk Nerra, whom he vigorously criticizes in his *Histories,* was hostile to Conan and tells a very different story. Raoul not only credits Fulk's bravery but gives us reason to believe that the Breton count was taken alive. After describing Conan's tricks in a negative manner, as if to intimate that these were a violation of the rules of judicial combat (Richer seems to defend the tricks), Raoul adds that the Breton count's right hand was cut off, that he was taken to Fulk, and that the Angevin count "had the victory." Finally, without indicating that Conan had been killed and thus leaving his readers to believe that only mutilation had taken place, Raoul emphasizes that Fulk never again was bothered by the Bretons.[114]

Raoul may perhaps be describing, in a somewhat confused manner, part of a Roman triumphal ceremony. Cutting off the right hand was one element of the ritual in which a victor celebrated his triumph over a defeated usurper.[115] Raoul's initial description of Conan as an insolent *princeps* "who had himself crowned in the manner of a king" hints at the idea of usurpation. The chronicler's following observation that Conan "subjected his lands to open tyranny" makes the idea of usurpation explicit insofar as a tyrant, in the intellectual tradition in which Raoul wrote, was considered a usurper and vice versa.[116] Raoul's concluding remark that Fulk "potitia victoria" may perhaps be thought to indicate that he was using *victoria* as a synonym for *triumphus.*[117]

We cannot insist that Raoul is providing the correct sequence of events or that he is not telescoping the period of time between the cutting off of Raoul's right hand or arm and Fulk's *victoria*. Indeed, Raoul was less than explicit about Conan's death. Whether these problems are a result of Raoul's normally sloppy handling of his information or the bias of his sources, who likely were the monks of Fulk Nerra's monastery Belli Locus, founded later as the Angevin count's own "Battle Abbey," cannot be ascertained, and there is likely enough blame to go around.[118] What is clear, however, is that sometime after the victory at Conquereuil, Fulk celebrated a triumph at Angers, renaming the old Roman road from Nantes to Angers along which his troops had to march the *Via Triumphalis*.[119]

Once the field of Conquereuil was in Angevin hands, the enemy forces routed, and Conan eliminated (one way or another), Fulk ordered his troops back to Nantes. He occupied the city and laid siege to the citadel, which was still in the hands of Conan's *milites*. After a short time, those who had held out so bravely when relief was possible capitulated, now that the Breton army had been defeated and there was no reasonable chance of rescue. As part of the terms of surrender, Conan's *milites* promised to be faithful to Fulk.[120] The Angevin count then concluded arrangements for the administration and established a garrison of his own men in the city. Fulk passed over, at least for the time being, Judicaël, who was still a minor, and established Geoffrey Greymantle's longtime ally Viscount Aimery of Thouars as count of Nantes.[121]

The victory at Conquereuil earned Fulk Nerra more than prestige and confidence. Several immediate consequences stand out. With Nantes firmly in Angevin hands, the western frontier could once again be considered secure. Conan's death, whether murder or execution, left the situation at Rennes unstable. Fulk perhaps could hope for some immediate relief from the policy of consistent hostility that his brother-in-law had pursued.[122] Fulk's sister, Countess Hermengarde-Gerberga of Rennes, appears to have exercised some considerable influence over her son Geoffrey-Berengar, who was still a minor, for the latter went to Paris and there repudiated Odo I's overlordship of Rennes in favor of King Hugh's.[123]

Great battles in the open field involving large numbers of men, such as the engagement at Conquereuil, were infrequent in pre-Crusade Europe, and Fulk, in an active military career of fifty-three years, fought only two such battles.[124] In this era of epic, however, the victor of such a highly publicized but rare battle might well have his reputation established in song and story. Conquereuil was Fulk Nerra's first great test. He succeeded and thereafter could no longer be regarded as the struggling heir of a great man. Though barely out of his teens, he was now a military commander of note.[125]

If we can correctly conclude that Fulk Nerra orchestrated elements of a Roman triumph in the wake of his victory at Conquereuil, then we can also view his effort as part of a process both to legitimize and to publicize his actions. We have already noted that the partisan Richer worked to diminish Fulk's accomplishment. Indeed, Richer depicts Conan as taking the position that an attack by the Angevin count was *contra jus*—and perhaps within the legal framework understood by Richer, Conan, and Odo I this was true.[126] Raoul Glaber presented Fulk's side of the story—probably from information provided by the monks of Belli Locus during the decade after the Angevin count's death—and he pictures Conan as a "usurper" who was treated as such within what may be construed as the framework of vulgar Roman law in the west of the regnum Francorum at this time.[127]

Contemporaries and near contemporaries raised questions regarding the legitimacy of Conan's rule and the legality of Fulk's victory. The Angevin count, however, made his position clear by carrying out a victory celebration along a section of the old Roman road which he had newly named *Via Triumphalis*. The crushing of Conan's "tyranny" and "usurpation" thus was highlighted in a neo-Roman setting while at the same time Fulk's victory was publicized. In using a Roman model, Fulk was likely following a pattern of behavior at which his father's activities hint. For example, Geoffrey Greymantle had used honorifics such as *illustrissimus, fortissimus,* and *noblissimus*. These appellations, like those used by Carolingians and Merovingians earlier, either actually indicated the holding of the consulship or were considered indicators of consulship by contemporary advisors, even though they might not have been as knowledgeable about the intitulation of the *cursus honorum* as perhaps they supposed.[128] Geoffrey also seems at times to have worn a red cloak, the consular *trabea*, in Anjou, although his image as a greymantled count won the day in French royal epic.[129]

This apparent dabbling in neo-Roman image-making can also be seen among Geoffrey's and Fulk's contemporaries. For example, Count Richard I of Rouen (d. 996) was styled *consul* by his publicist, Dudo of Saint-Quentin. Indeed, Dudo went so far as to cast the *gesta* of the Norman ruling family, *De moribus et actis primorum Normanniae ducum,* in the framework of the *Aeneid* of Virgil, the father of state-building epics in Western civilization.[130] Fulk Nerra's southern neighbor, Duke William of Aquitaine, is said by a contemporary panegyrist, the chronicler Adémar of Chabannes, to have been welcomed by the popes "so reverently when he visited Rome that it was as if he were their *augustus* and the entire Roman senate acclaimed him as its father . . ." In addition, Adémar compared William to the *imperator* Louis the Pious, to Magnus Karolus, to Theodosius ("victor augustus") and even to "Octavianus Cesar Augustus."[131] The scholar Fulbert, another contemporary, who first headed the cathedral school at Chartres and then guided its development as bishop, was an expert in Roman law. Throughout his career he pressed the importance of the *leges Romanorum* and Roman tradition, striving to use and teach literary texts such as Livy's *Histories*.[132]

Roman remains were all around a man such as Fulk Nerra, who himself operated with Vegetian maxims to guide his military tactics and strategy. Indeed, Fulk's uncle Guy had used a version of the Roman *adventus* ceremony when he took control as count-bishop of le Puy in 975. A local chronicle describes the ceremony in an abbreviated form which nevertheless would have easily been recognized by a late Roman observer:

Guy set out for le Puy . . . Having heard this, his nephews, Pons and Bertrand, the most distinguished consuls [*clarissimi consules*] of Aquitaine, along with their mother Adelaide, his sister, came to meet him. . . . When he entered le Puy a great procession [*processio*] of clerics was made for him [and] a great *exultatio* of lay people was made for him because God had given them a [worthy] *defensor*.[133]

Later in his career, Fulk too would use the *adventus* ceremony within the framework of a late antique model and would again use various elements of the Roman triumph.[134]

This digression regarding the development of a neo-Roman patina, perhaps to help establish political legitimacy independent of the newly crowned Capetian kings and very likely to help in publicizing Fulk's victory at Conquereuil, should not lead us to give all the credit to the young Angevin count. We must note the important role played by Viscount Aimery of Thouars in leading a contingent from the Poitou and credit the performance of troops from Maine; furthermore we must acknowledge the careful work of Geoffrey Greymantle in establishing the close relations with these men that bound them to the Angevins. Similarly, Fulk's ability to hire mercenaries no doubt depended on the health of the Angevin treasury, which appears to have been left well stocked by Geoffrey.[135] Add to these legacies the protection of Fulk's eastern frontiers at this time by his father-in-law, Bouchard of Vendôme, who with the support of the Angevin count's cousin Geoffrey, count of the Gâtinais, engaged and defeated an army of Odo I of Blois at Orsay.[136] This Vendôme connection had been secured by Geoffrey Greymantle by 985, while the Angevin alliance with the family of Geoffrey of the

Gâtinais can be traced as far back as the reign of Fulk the Red. Finally, if one were to look for an éminence grise to advise Fulk on the value of employing Roman or neo-Roman ritual and ceremony, then his uncle Guy, count-bishop of le Puy, who came north to advise the young count, is a possible candidate.

Following the victory at Conquereuil, which temporarily secured the Angevin position in the west, Fulk turned his attention to the eastern part of his territory, more particularly to the problem of strengthening his lines of communication with Amboise, which was in danger of being isolated by Odo I's strongholds. The first apparent step in this effort was to bolster his position at Bourgueil on the border between the Touraine and Anjou about twenty kilometers upriver from Saumur and only twelve kilometers northeast of Odo's stronghold at Mont-soreau. Fulk already enjoyed a point d'appui in this region in the person of a *miles* named Renaud, one of the Angevin count's fideles who possessed allods near Bourgueil.[137] The town itself, however, appears to have been dominated by the monastery of Saint-Peter, which had been founded by Emma of Blois, Odo I's sister, and which was administered by their cousin, Abbot Gauzbert.[138]

Viscount Aimery of Thouars, to whom Fulk had given the title count of Nantes during the summer of 992 following the victory at Conquereuil, appears to have played a leading role in trying to help the Angevin count improve relations with Saint-Peter. Aimery, who in his capacity as count of Nantes held from Fulk the right to collect tolls on ships and their cargoes leaving and entering the city along the Loire, conceded to Saint-Peter freedom from these taxes for one of their ships each year.[139] Fulk's required confirmation of this act, which conveyed to Saint-Peter a valuable exemption in monetary terms, probably was intended to win some sort of quid pro quo from the monastery.[140] It is perhaps of some importance to note that riverboats such as those serving the monastery of Bourgueil had logistic value for the transportation of men and supplies in this era of poor roads and unreliable vehicles.[141]

At about the same time that overtures were being made to Saint-Peter, Fulk took much more aggressive steps to improve his position in this area. In the woodlands between Bourgueil and Langeais farther to the east, Fulk ordered the construction of a wooden stronghold. This installation was on land that evidently belonged to the Angevin count but it was located in the Touraine and therefore under Odo's jurisdiction. The structure was built at Fulk's orders to resemble an innocent resting place intended to serve as a hunting lodge. When Odo learned that Fulk had built this somewhat ambiguous structure that was obviously defensible, the count of Blois ordered its destruction. His men in the area were levied and they attacked the position but were driven off by the garrison Fulk had placed there.[142] A monkish chronicler who noted the strategic significance of this stronghold reported that Fulk had it built because "he had no resting place between Bourgueil and Amboise along the Loire river."[143]

When Fulk learned that Odo's local forces had failed to take this small woodland fortification east of Bourgueil, he set out to build a major military installation at Langeais only twenty-four kilometers downriver from Tours. In order to keep the enemy from interfering with construction of this new stronghold, Fulk acted in accordance with Vegetian military thinking and had various of his forces engage in diversionary hit-and-run operations against Odo's assets throughout the region.[144] Thus, no later than the spring of 994, Fulk's men had built a stronghold at Langeais on a narrow spur of land separating the Roumer and Loire rivers. According to the chronicler Richer, who discusses this work in more detail than any of his contemporaries, Fulk's fortifications at Langeais consisted of a tower (*oppidum*) around which the count built (*munit*) a perimeter wall for defensive purposes.[145] In the technical terminology of the period in this region such a defensive military complex, a tower (or several towers) almost invariably built of stone surrounded by a perimeter wall, was considered a castrum. By contrast a *castellum* was merely a defensive walled enclosure. Although some writers of the time seem to have been committed to using the technical definitions, most unfortunately were not.[146]

Archaeological remains establish the nature of the castrum at Langeais. It is clear that Fulk's tower was a stone structure that at one time stood about 15 meters in height and about 17 by 10 meters at its rectangular base. (The original measurement was probably made by the Roman foot of 11.5 inches.) The walls average about 1.55 meters in thickness; the west wall was the most formidable, nearing 2 meters at points at the base. In its earliest phase of construction (992–994), this structure was not reinforced by contreforts and no moat was dug. The stronghold was not built on an artificially constructed hill or motte but rested on a natural rise of little consequence. It was, however, the first "romanesque" stone tower in the region.[147]

Many of the technical architectural features of the tower at Langeais—the shallow foundation, the relatively limited height, and the arguably thin walls—distinguish it from Fulk's later efforts while providing vivid physical evidence that the design or perhaps more precisely the actual construction was conditioned by haste.[148] Indeed, Fulk's construction crews worked under various constraints, for the project was undertaken in enemy territory and materials could not easily be transported to the building site by water because Odo I controlled the Loire River in the immediate region both east and west.[149] Despite these difficulties, the Angevins were able to build a respectable defensive complex that included both the stone tower and a circuit wall of about 250 meters in circumference which at crucial places was strengthened by formidable ditches.[150] The entire operation required a period of no more than twenty-two months but likely was accomplished somewhat more quickly.[151]

We can gain some insight into the social and institutional resources that Fulk commanded through an analysis of the basic costs incurred in building the stronghold at Langeais. For example, just for building the tower an average of 140 workers was required on the site each day; some days many more were needed and on other days fewer.[152] These workers were probably levied through the *bidamnum,* a tax in labor owed by all subjects of the Angevin count to work fifteen days each year building or repairing fortifications.[153] To feed these workers on a minimal regimen of wheat-equivalent calories required each year the surplus produced by more than 450 agricultural workers from more than 2,700 hectares of average arable.[154] Fulk is likely to have levied these resources and the means to haul them to Langeais through the *fodrum,* the *angaria,* and allied taxes.[155]

The organization of these men and resources undoubtedly required the efforts of many of the *agentes, servientes,* and *ministeriales* who served in Fulk's government. That some efficiency was gained through the use of written records denoting who owed various levies in kind, services, and equipment is also likely.[156] In addition, it seems clear that lists of workers on the site and their assignments were also kept.[157] In short, it seems that the Angevin count possessed a government or perhaps more accurately a military bureaucracy of the order of magnitude which enabled Fulk Nerra's younger contemporary, William the Conqueror, to launch his invasion of England.[158]

While Fulk was busy constructing his strongholds between Bourgueil and Tours, Odo I was engaged in a conspiracy which, if successful, would completely alter the balance of power in Francia Occidentalis. With the help of Bishop Adalbero of Laon, Odo conspired with

the advisors of the German emperor Otto III to overthrow the Capetians and place a Carolingian on the West Frankish throne. The elimination of the Capetians would then enable Odo to become duke of
the Franks. A meeting was arranged for April-May 993 at Metz to
which Hugh Capet and his son Robert were both invited; the plan was
to capture them there. The Capetians learned of the plot, however,
avoided the meeting, and imprisoned the Carolingian pretender.[159]

In preparation for this usurpation of the dukedom of the Franks,
Odo I had negotiated a series of military alliances. He arranged a pact
with the count of Flanders, who was still angered over the loss in property and honor that he suffered as a result of King Robert's repudiation
of Rozala-Suzanne. Odo also secured the support of Duke Richard of
Normandy, who had been allied with Conan of Rennes in 992 and
probably was eager to despoil Anjou.[160] In addition, Odo arranged an
alliance with his brother-in-law, William Iron Arm, count of the Poitou
and duke of Aquitaine. William had just at that very time reconciled
with his estranged wife, Emma of Blois, and established their son William as coruler of his dominions.[161]

While Odo organized a military alliance of the greater powers,
Abbot Robert of Saint-Florent again worked in the west of France to
undermine the Angevin position. At this time Fulk Nerra honored his
promise to the people of Nantes before the battle of Conquereuil and
replaced Aimery of Thouars as count with Judicaël, who was probably
still too young to rule.[162] Aimery, as Fulk should have expected, was
not happy at this turn of events. So when the viscount of Thouars was
approached by Abbot Robert, he allowed himself to be convinced to
become a friend of that wealthy and strategically located monastery in
return for the possession of various estates belonging to Saint-Florent.
In fact, Aimery found this connection so rewarding that he and William
Iron Arm together became involved in the protection of Saint-Florent's
holdings.[163] This break between Fulk and Aimery and Aimery's rapprochement with William Iron Arm may also be seen as strengthening
the threat against Anjou from Aquitaine.

Fulk responded to the potential threat of an attack from the Poitou
by calling upon Aldebert, count of la Marche and Périgord, to provide
a diversion that would keep the Aquitanian Williams, father and son,
from aiding Odo I of Blois. Although Aldebert was Fulk's cousin-in-
law (through Fulk's aunt Adelaide-Blanche) and may have been motivated in part by a feeling of family interest, he also had sound political
reasons of his own for moving against the Williams. The reconciliation

of William Iron Arm and Emma and the association of their son in the comital title made it clear that young William's succession would not be disputed within the family and that Odo I could be relied upon to place his great power and influence behind this settlement.[164] Aldebert's efforts to aggrandize his own position, perhaps by taking the title "duke of Aquitaine," were surely limited by the alliance between William and Odo. Thus Aldebert opened an offensive in the Poitou, and when Odo I called on William Iron Arm for aid in attacking Anjou the latter was unable to respond in force but sent his son to represent him.[165]

Fulk's position was further complicated by the establishment at Nantes of Judicaël, an inexperienced youth of about fifteen years of age. As events were to prove, the boy lacked talent as a military leader. When Count Geoffrey-Berengar, Conan's son, assumed full control of affairs at Rennes, he launched a series of campaigns against Nantes and its region.[166] Clearly, by the early part of 994, Fulk's sister Hermengarde-Gerberga had lost whatever influence over her son that she had exercised immediately following Conan's death in June 992. Thus Geoffrey-Berengar's repudiation—or perhaps more accurately his attempted repudiation—of Odo's overlordship had proved only a temporary gain for Fulk after his victory at Conquereuil, Conan's death, and the establishment of Hermengarde-Gerberga as regent for her minor son.[167]

In early 994 Odo decided it was time to take the offensive and drive Fulk from Langeais. Thus he called upon his Norman, Flemish, and Aquitanian allies to join him in an concerted campaign against Anjou. Odo also levied forces from his own lands, both in the east and in the west; among the former, for example, were levies from the Verdunois.[168] By 20 May 994 Odo was encamped at Tours, joined by some of his most important followers in the west, including Gelduin of Saumur, Alo of Chinon, and Corbo of Rochecorbon.[169] The exercise of patience, however, was not part of Odo's general pattern of behavior, and he decided to lay siege to Langeais before most of his allies had arrived.[170] When the siege began, Fulk, who was already at Langeais in personal command of the defense, sent to Hugh Capet for aid. The Capetian, however, was in the Auvergne, apparently ill and on his way to participate in the rites following the burial of the late abbot of Cluny, Maiolus. Nonetheless, Hugh sent a message promising to help Fulk. The Angevin count's father-in-law, Bouchard of Vendôme, who had given Fulk vital assistance by defeating Odo at Orsay, was accompanying Hugh on the journey south.[171]

Before Fulk departed Angers for the defense of Langeais, he took several actions that from a diplomatic perspective might have been intended to strengthen his position at home. For example, in March 994 at Angers Fulk exempted the cloister of Saint-Maurilius, which belonged to the cathedral of Angers, from all comital right to the requisition of hospitality and logistic support. This tax exemption provided the public forum for Fulk's announcement that he was trying to expiate whatever sins he may have committed in the course of the battle of Conquereuil, where he acknowledged that a great many Christians on both sides had been killed. From a political point of view, this act provided Fulk with the opportunity to present Bishop Renaud, whose loyalty had earlier been suspect, with valuable relief from costly burdens that weighed heavily on church revenues. In addition, Fulcoius, the new viscount of Angers (he had recently succeeded his father Viscount Renaud) who held the stronghold of Rochefort on the frontier with Brittany, and the brother of Bishop Renaud appeared with Count Fulk in support of this act.[172] As the successor of Viscount Renaud, Fulcoius had an important role to play in the defense of Anjou's western frontier. With the accession of Judicaël as count of Nantes and the hostility of Aimery of Thouars, it was vital that Fulk maintain Fulcoius's loyalty.

By late spring the siege of Langeais was under way, and through the summer of 994 the *milites* of Fulk's military household and the *castrenses* who garrisoned the stronghold served under the personal command of the Angevin count. As the siege wore on, small groups of supporters continued to join the Blésois besiegers and it seemed that the allies of the count of Blois would eventually mass in such great force that they would be able to overwhelm the defenders by the sheer weight of numbers before Hugh Capet would arrive with help.[173]

As the summer progressed Fulk understandably became anxious about continuing to hold out and apparently discussed terms of surrender with Odo's legates. According to Blois supporter Richer, Fulk accepted Odo's terms but later repudiated them. Whether this was the case or not is far less important than the terms themselves, which illuminate Odo's immediate thinking regarding Fulk Nerra and the Angevins.

Odo appears to have stipulated the following terms:

1. Fulk must destroy the stronghold of Langeais and withdraw the garrison.
2. Fulk must surrender the urbs of Nantes and withdraw his troops.
3. Fulk must pay a sum of one hundred pounds of silver to Odo for having killed Conan of Rennes.

4. Fulk must take an oath of faithfulness to Odo in his hands. By these acts Fulk must swear to serve Odo in all matters except those in which the Angevin count has a prior obligation to his own son, brother, nephews (grandsons?), or the king.
5. Fulk personally must serve the count of Blois in a military capacity to compensate the latter for his loss of Conan's services.
6. Fulk must take an oath of faithfulness to Odo's son.
7. Fulk, in person, must do military service for the son of Count Odo.
8. Fulk's son [should there be one] is to take an oath of faithfulness to Odo's son.
9. Fulk's son, in person, is to do military service for the son of the count of Blois in place of the service lost through the death of Conan of Rennes.[174]

Odo's stipulations are in some cases obvious in relation to the campaign at hand, the evacuation and destruction of the stronghold of Langeais. Others, such as the wergild to be paid for Conan of Rennes, are quite surprising.[175] It is clear that aside from driving Fulk from Langeais, Odo had two major goals in mind. First, he wanted to severely weaken Fulk's position on the western frontier of Anjou. Concomitantly, Odo sought to strengthen his own relations with Conan's son, Count Geoffrey-Berengar of Rennes, who was also Fulk's estranged nephew. Geoffrey-Berengar's earlier repudiation of Odo, likely at the urging of Hermengarde-Gerberga, may well have led the count of Blois to realize that his dominance over the count of Rennes could not be taken for granted. Indeed, we might speculate that close relations between Odo and Geoffrey-Berengar depended on the ability of the former to assure the possession of Nantes to the latter.

Odo's second major goal was the subordination of the Angevin counts to the counts of Blois not only for the present generation but for the next as well. Odo demanded that Fulk and his son—Fulk had no son yet—swear faithfulness to him and to his son. This promise thus covered a future contingency, as did Fulk's promise reserving support in cases involving his son and grandsons. The demand on both Fulk and his son for personal military service further emphasizes the extent of dependence that Odo wanted to impose on the Angevin comital family.[176]

This draft treaty casts some light on Richer's earlier discussion of the conflict between Fulk and Conan. The requirement that the Angevin count pay his victim's wergild (not to the dead man's next of kin but to his dominus) reveals the Blésois interest in seeing Fulk condemned for having attacked Conan *contra jus* and sustains the view that Nantes was held by the Angevins through deceit. In short, Richer works diligently to provide a quasilegal brief for Odo's position.

Fortunately for the Angevin count, Odo did not have the opportunity to impose these terms. Before Fulk found it necessary to surrender, Hugh Capet arrived with an army to relieve Langeais. Odo sought a truce with the king. A treaty was arranged by which Odo promised to abandon the campaign against Fulk and to surrender hostages to the king as evidence of good faith. Hugh then moved to Paris with his army; Odo accompanied him and continued east to Meaux with his army.[177]

While Fulk had been defending Langeais, two important developments took place that weakened his position on the western frontier. Count Geoffrey-Berengar, who had begun to campaign against Nantes, pursued his military efforts in Fulk's absence and reduced Count Judicaël to a position of personal dependence. Judicaël was forced to recognize the overlordship of Geoffrey-Berengar, thereby repudiating his allegiance to Fulk Nerra, who made him count. Although Nantes was not yet in Geoffrey-Berengar's hands and Fulk's troops still garrisoned the urbs and presumably the arx, the western frontier of Anjou was somewhat less secure than it had been after Fulk's victory at Conquereuil less than two years earlier.[178]

To complicate Fulk's problems in defending the western frontier, Abbot Robert of Saint-Florent took up an earlier initiative with Bishop Renaud of Angers. In June 994 Abbot Robert again brought a complaint to Bishop Renaud's court concerning a church belonging to the monks of Saint-Maur. Renaud accepted jurisdiction in the case, found in favor of Saint-Florent, and thus reverted to the policy he had pursued in 988 which was against the interest of the Angevin count. In an addendum to his decision in favor of Saint-Florent, Bishop Renaud went well beyond the limits of the case in question and supported Abbot Robert's general effort to eliminate proprietary churches under the control of laymen, which were seen to siphon income needed for God's work.[179] These proprietary churches in Anjou were widely recognized as valuable resources and were often used by Fulk Nerra to support his followers.[180]

Following Odo's withdrawal to Meaux in the east, Fulk was left free to deal with Bishop Renaud, who seems to have been intent upon pursuing an independent policy. Fulk, not unnaturally, was worried that the new viscount Fulcoius would support his brother, Bishop Renaud, in cooperating with Abbot Robert. Fulcoius, who controlled the Mauges region, had good reason beyond sustaining family solidarity to work with Robert. The religious house of Saint-Florent-le-Vieil, a dependency of Saint-Florent at Saumur, was located in the Mauges and had long-standing claims to substantial property in the region. In pressing Saint-Florent's claims with Abbot Robert's support, Fulcoius could enrich himself substantially.[181] This situation in the west was made even more dismal by the alliance of Viscount Aimery of Thouars, whose lands bordered the Mauges region, with Abbot Robert. Indeed, both Aimery and Robert enjoyed good relations with William Iron Arm, who over the years had lost substantial territory to the Angevins and was eager to take it back. Bishop Renaud and Fulcoius, based in part on their family's longtime association with the monastery of Saint-Jouin-de-Marnes, located in the western Poitou on the borders of Thouars, might well have been persuaded to join a broadly based coalition including William, Aimery, and Robert.[182] The potential defection of the whole Renaud family, seen in light of Count Geoffrey-Berengar of Rennes' success against Judicaël of Nantes, seriously threatened to undo Fulk's efforts to secure Anjou's western frontier.

Although the formation of such a dangerous coalition must have loomed as a distinct possibility, the Angevin count seems to have taken only small steps to deal with this potential problem. He launched no massive campaign against his nephew Geoffrey-Berengar of Rennes, nor did he punish Bishop Renaud for supporting Saint-Florent and trying to undermine comital exploitation of monastic resources. Fulk had already sought and continued to receive the help of his cousin-in-law Aldebert, count of la Marche and Périgord, so the latter's militant presence as an ally of the Angevin count was unmistakably clear to the now ailing William Iron Arm.[183] In addition, it is in these circumstances that Fulk seems to have visited his stronghold at Loudun in the Poitou where he met with Viscount Acfredus of Châtellerault, Bishop Gislebert of Poitiers, Abbot Frotgarius of Saint-Michel-en-le-Herm, Abbot Berengarius of Saint-Jouin-de-Marnes, and other important magnates of the northern Poitou.[184] All of these men were major political figures who controlled substantial resources, and it is probably not unfair to hypothesize that they were at Loudun to confer with Fulk concerning the protection of their lands in a region where the Angevin count exercised considerable influence and sought to obtain even greater power.

Fulk's only noteworthy action with regard to the Breton situation seems to have been the reinforcement of the Angevin position on the northwestern frontier. Aremberga, a relative of the Angevin comital family, had been married to Hubert of Aulnay. Fulk had given the newly married couple the strategically located land of Baugé, which they could presumably be relied upon to defend both in their own self-interest and in the interest of the count. Hubert, however, died early in the 990s and left only a young son, also named Hubert, who was not yet able to provide the kind of military support that Fulk had expected from his father. Thus Fulk and Geoffrey of Sablé, brother of the viscount of le Mans and the major Angevin fidelis in the northwest, joined to arrange a suitable marriage for the count's widowed relative. Herveus of Sablé, one of Geoffrey's supporters, was chosen to marry Aremberga, and Fulk arranged that the couple would receive from Alberic of Vihiers, another of the Angevin count's relatives, half of the strategically located curtis of Champigné-sur-Sarthe, which previously had been in the hands of the *miles* Odo Brisahasta and the latter's son-in-law, Dodo of Bazouges. This holding had reverted to Alberic when Dodo died without offspring.[185]

Alberic never played a personal role at Champigné-sur-Sarthe in the defense of the northwestern frontier. His assignment continued to be to serve Fulk's interests south of the Loire by harassing the lands of Saint-Florent and by maintaining the stronghold of Vihiers as a key position in the Angevin communications network connecting Angers with the southeastern strongholds of Loches, la Haye, and Villentrois.[186] Fulk kept loyal castellans in specifically established districts and permitted them to develop a knowledge of their areas so that they could defend the region effectively. Alberic was one such castellan.

Why Fulk refrained from taking more forceful steps against Renaud, Fulcoius, Aimery, and William Iron Arm in the west is perhaps too easily explained in the first instance by their failure to join forces actively in an offensive alliance against Anjou. Fulk certainly had no interest in precipitating the formation of an enemy alliance by acting rashly while Odo was still capable of serious damage in the east. Fulk's caution in this matter as well as in avoiding a full-scale war against Geoffrey-Berengar may well have been conditioned in part by the actions of Odo, who, despite his treaty with Hugh Capet, moved an army westward and established a military camp at Châteaudun. By this maneuver, Odo positioned his forces so that if Fulk launched an attack either into Brittany or into Aquitaine, the Blésois forces could invade Anjou or reinvest Langeais.[187]

Odo apparently was greatly vexed by Angevin possession of the stronghold at Langeais and by his own previous failure to capture it. Now the count of Blois tried to assure himself of the support of the duke of Aquitaine, who would coordinate his invasion of Anjou from the south with Odo's attack on Langeais. William, son of William Iron Arm, who had recently succeeded his father, was faced with a clearly defined dilemma in his relations with the count of Anjou. Would he support his uncle Odo, avenge Angevin depredation in the Poitou, and assert leadership in his new position, or would he pursue the cautious and perhaps even humiliating policy pursued by his father, who was living out his last years in a monastery? If youthful enthusiasm and a determination to prove himself as a leader among men were not sufficient to determine young William's course of action, then family pressures would probably have tipped the balance toward the Blésois initiative. William had a very close relationship with his mother, Odo's sister, and for many years had been estranged from his father. Thus while Odo had failed to obtain the cooperation of William Iron Arm in the campaign of 994, he apparently believed that he could rely upon the support of young William for the coming offensive.[188]

Fulk, however, had taken precautions to thwart Odo's plans to subject Anjou to a two-front war. The Angevin count looked to his relatives in Aquitaine for support. Aldebert responded to Fulk's request for aid and moved his forces against William. The count of la Marche and Périgord had little trouble in capturing and destroying the Poitevin frontier stronghold at Gençay and then moving his forces against the urbs of Poitiers itself. He established a fortified camp outside of the city and placed it under siege. William's forces sallied forth to do battle and were decisively defeated. Aldebert continued the siege and ultimately captured Poitiers. This campaign by Fulk's cousin-in-law effectively kept William from aiding Odo.[189]

The count of Blois established his second siege at Langeais probably during the second half of 995, shortly before Aldebert launched his offensive against the Poitou. Odo's forces were still emplaced at Langeais as late as 12 February 996 by which time an impressive group of magnates under the count of Blois' direct command had been assembled. These included, among others, two young counts from the east, Manassas of Dammartin and Roger I (later bishop of Chalons [-sur-Marne]?), Viscount Hugh of Châteaudun, Alo his brother, and Gelduin of Saumur. Early in March, however, Odo became ill and was carried to the monastery of Marmoutier at Tours where he took the monastic habit and died on 12 March 996. With Odo's death, the siege of Langeais was abandoned. The vast collection of lands he had pieced together was leaderless and his supporters were in disarray, at least for the moment.[190]

The siege of Langeais broken, Fulk moved his army eastward toward Tours and joined forces with Count Aldebert, who only a short time earlier had defeated William's troops and had taken Poitiers. A decision was made by the two counts to lay siege both to Tours and to the fortified suburb of Châteauneuf, which had been built to protect the church of Saint-Martin and its burg. Aldebert devoted his efforts to the capture of the urbs while Fulk concentrated his forces on taking the castrum. Both were successful. Aldebert then turned possession of Tours over to Fulk, who saw to the garrisoning of both strongholds. The combined forces of Aldebert and Fulk were apparently so large and formidable that there was no need for a siege. The defenders surrendered without significant opposition. Despite this capitulation, Fulk's men caused substantial damage to the internal fortifications that protected the cloister of Saint-Martin at Châteauneuf.[191]

This campaign in the Touraine by Fulk Nerra—it is likely that he captured the stronghold of Montsoreau[192] from Odo's men following the victory at Tours—which came hard upon the death of the count of Blois was the first purely offensive operation undertaken by the Angevin count in the decade following his succession. For ten years Fulk had been in a precarious strategic position which saw him virtually surrounded by powerful enemies. Odo, who aspired to the title *dux Francorum,* held the counties of Blois, Chartres, Tours, and Châteaudun in the west. In addition, at one time or another Fulk faced forces of Bretons, Normans, and Aquitanians. Fulk responded to his strategic difficulties by pursuing the long-term Angevin policies of trying to maintain control of the urbs of Nantes and by securing communications with the main eastern strongholds at Amboise and Loches.

Fulk's defensive strategy made it impossible for him to participate in the greater struggles of Francia Occidentalis and its eastern frontiers as Geoffrey Greymantle had done. But we note that the Angevin family network that Geoffrey had so ably led and that had been a major force on the political stage ceased during the first decade of Fulk's reign to be the great power it once had been. Fulk's field of military involvement was far more limited than that of his father and he was unable or perhaps unwilling to provide Hugh Capet with the kind of military support in the east that the king would have expected from Geoffrey

Greymantle. Fulk's preoccupation with Anjou's vital interests in the west led him to withdraw from any major personal participation in the affairs of the Orléanais and the Gâtinais. The great Angevin stronghold of Château-Landon was turned over to Fulk's cousin Geoffrey, who was given the title count of the Gâtinais by Hugh Capet. Fulk also withdrew from major participation in the affairs of Maine, and the traditional Angevin role there was assumed by his father-in-law, Bouchard of Vendôme.

Nonetheless, Geoffrey Greymantle's work was not destroyed as a result of his untimely death. The crucial role played by Bishop Guy of le Puy, Fulk's uncle, during the period of transition at both Chalon and at Angers can be seen as a legacy of the spirit of family cohesiveness and cooperation that the Angevins had fostered for several generations and that was fundamental to their success during the tenth century. Equally, the dominant role played by Count Aldebert of la Marche and Périgord in the campaigns from 994 through 996 had its base in work done by Geoffrey Greymantle to develop the Angevin family network. Furthermore, the matrix of Angevin family alliances that Geoffrey and his father had established throughout Aquitaine seem to have deterred William Iron Arm from becoming a full participant in the efforts of Odo of Blois and Conan of Rennes to crush Fulk Nerra. Finally, Count Bouchard of Vendôme, Fulk's father-in-law, played a key role in defending both the Vendômois and Anjou when he defeated Odo I at Orsay in 992.

While Geoffrey Greymantle's work in strengthening the Angevin family network evidently served Fulk well, the new count also clearly benefited from other alliances his father had arranged or strengthened. Hugh Capet supported Fulk most effectively by relieving the siege of Langeais in the autumn of 994 and several years earlier by making the office of treasurer of Saint-Martin available to Renaud of Thorigné, so that the support of the viscount might be retained for the Angevin cause. In addition, Hugh's establishment of Fulk's cousin as count of the Gâtinais may well be attributed to the king's respect for the system of family alliances and interests the Angevin counts had developed from the early tenth century. Other allies Geoffrey had secured, such as Viscount Radulf of le Mans, Viscount Aimery of Thouars, and Geoffrey of Sablé, also provided support for Fulk at critical moments in the first decade of his reign.

Although various forces from outside of Anjou evidently played key roles in securing Fulk's survival against powerful odds during the period 987–996, the new count enjoyed and benefited from the support of Geoffrey Greymantle's *comitatus*. Men like Alberic of Vihiers, Roger of Loudun, and Cadilo of Blaison who had been well treated by Geoffrey saw their interests as tied to the success and prosperity of the Angevin comital house. Fulk did nothing to undermine this perception and by following Geoffrey's policies he tended to strengthen it. The opportunistic policy pursued by the Renaud family was the exception rather than the rule.

Any evaluation of the circumstances that contributed to Fulk's survival cannot be complete without some discussion of conditions over which the Angevin count had no control. Two of these developments were exceptionally important. Emma of Blois' lengthy estrangement from her husband William Iron Arm made it less likely that there would be cooperation between the duke of Aquitaine and his brother-in-law, Count Odo I of Blois. The premature death of Odo I, apparently of natural causes, eliminated the central figure in the drive against Fulk.

In a somewhat different vein, we should note that Fulk proved to be a leader of no mean ability. He clearly possessed considerable military talent, courage, and energy. He showed patience in not overreaching his resources, a willingness to accept prudent counsel from Bishop Guy, and an interest in learning from books, either directly or more likely indirectly, as his employment of Vegetian strategies suggests. On the whole as a youth and as a young man in his early twenties, Fulk appears to have been more careful and conservative than his years led his adversaries to expect. Fulk seems to have valued and possessed *gravitas*.

CHAPTER THREE

The First Capetian-Blésois Axis

The political landscape late in the summer of 996 surely looked brighter than ever before in Fulk Nerra's short reign. Odo I was dead, Conan of Rennes was dead, and William of Aquitaine had been defeated. Tours, Châteauneuf, Montsoreau, and Langeais were in Angevin hands. At about this time, however, Fulk probably learned that his valued ally Count Aldebert of la Marche and Périgord had been killed after taking the Poitevin stronghold of Gençay for a second time.[1] Shortly thereafter, Hugh Capet became ill and Robert broke with his ailing father. Hugh died in late October 996, and King Robert II married Bertha of Blois, Odo I's widow.[2] These events may have dimmed Fulk's prospects considerably.

Robert II's alliance with the house of Blois created a formidable combination, and the new king wasted little time in moving against Fulk's newly established position in the Touraine. Whereas Hugh Capet had used his control of the office of treasurer of Saint-Martin to place one of Fulk Nerra's men in that important position, Robert appointed a magnate named Walter from a family closely allied with the house of Blois to that lucrative and prestigious office.[3] Moreover, Fulk's situation at the castrum of Saint-Martin was also seriously undermined by the rough treatment he had meted out to the canons when Châteauneuf was captured. The canons charged that Fulk had "violently entered the cloister . . . with an armed band" and "although he was not resisted, he unjustly had the defenses . . . destroyed." The canons retaliated by severely limiting access to the shrine; almost everyone was denied entrance, even the inhabitants of the castrum. They enforced this ban by "humiliating" the relics—the bodies of the saints and the crucifix were spread out on the ground and thorns were placed around these and on the sepulchre of Saint-Martin.[4]

After intricate negotiations, a ceremony was arranged by which Fulk would make peace with Saint-Martin. Thus the Angevin count went to Châteauneuf to announce his repentance for what had been done and sought forgiveness. He took off his shoes and went barefoot to the *domus* of Sicardus, the *magister scholarum* of Saint-Martin. After meeting with Sicardus and receiving a dispensation from the ban on visitors imposed by the canons, Fulk and an entourage of his more important supporters (*proceres*) went to the church. There, in front of the tomb of Saint-Martin, Fulk took the hand of Bishop Renaud of Angers and of the bishop of Oca, a visitor from Spain, and promised that he would never do anything of this kind again. Then Fulk "fecit satisfactionem" before the sepulchres of the saints and finally did the same before the crucifix.[5]

Saint-Martin had always been important for the Fulconian house. Fulk the Red had been treasurer, Fulk the Good and his brother Guy were canons there, and the Angevin counts traditionally were generous in support of the saint.[6] Fulk's purpose in the well-orchestrated program of repentance and absolution described above may be evaluated on several levels, but from a political perspective his actions were necessary to restore good relations with Saint-Martin if the Angevins were to exercise control over Châteauneuf. In addition, the reopening of the shrine to business as usual must surely have pleased the inhabitants of the castrum, whose spiritual and economic livelihood likely were damaged by the turmoil that surrounded the "humiliation."[7]

No historian can presume to know Fulk's personal religious feelings in this matter. But by participating in a publicized ceremony in which respect for the sacred was affirmed in a memorable way, Fulk was not breaking new ground or establishing a new policy. Fulk the Red, while ill, had prostrated himself to gain the forgiveness of Saint-Martin and had promised never again to loot the saint's possessions. Thereafter, he is reported to have been returned to good physical and spiritual health.[8] In a similar rite, at least from a functional perspective, Geoffrey Greymantle participated in an elaborate program at Rome in 969. The Angevin count made clear in a document published at Loches that he "set out for Rome . . . to seek forgiveness." After a week of discussion, fasts, prayers, vigils, and alms giving, he confessed to the pope "each and every sin" and states: "While I spoke, tears burst forth from his eyes and from mine." This process combined with a generous gift to the church, Geoffrey emphasizes, were accomplished "so that He would wipe away the stains of my sins."[9]

The canons of Saint-Martin who made peace with Fulk and helped to prepare the ceremony to reestablish good relations with their patron represented many of the influential families in the Touraine. Some of these families such as the Buzançais branch of the Robert-Archembaud group and the Hatto-Hardradus family had been supporters of Hugh Capet as well as of the Fulconians and had opposed the expansionist policy of the Blésois. The alliance of the new Capetian king Robert II with the house of Blois, however, upset this balance of power in the Touraine and threatened the position of those who had benefited from Hugh Capet's efforts to restrain Odo I's policies.[10]

Once Fulk Nerra had been restored to the favor of Saint-Martin, the canons could support the efforts of the Angevin count as the focus of secular opposition to King Robert and his new allies in the Touraine. Although the choice of Walter as treasurer of Saint-Martin had been imposed upon the canons by King Robert, the canons retained the right to elect their leader, the canon-*presul* of Saint-Martin. Thus when Gerardus died the canons chose to succeed him Peter,[11] a choice contrary to the interests of the Capetian-Blésois axis. As a result, Archbishop Archembaud of Tours, who had earlier performed Robert's marriage to Bertha contrary to church law (by reason of consanguinity) and who was one of the king's closest advisors, acted with royal support to refuse to recognize Peter as the new canon-*presul*.[12]

Thus, despite Fulk's rapprochement with Saint-Martin and the canons' stand against the Capetian-Blésois axis, the Angevin position at Tours deteriorated. Fulk was also opposed by Viscount Walter of Tours within the urbs itself and by substantial elements of the populace. Walter's relative, also named Walter, who held the title of treasurer of Saint-Martin, undoubtedly had allies in Châteauneuf and supported Fulk's adversaries. Some time before 25 July 997 the Angevin garrisons were driven from both Tours and Châteauneuf. The castrum, however, was severely damaged by fire, which suggests that Saint-Martin's enclave did not fall to the king without resistance.[13] With the fortifications at Tours and Châteauneuf secure, Robert advanced southward across the Loire to aid young Count William of Poitiers against his adversaries in Aquitaine.[14]

Although Fulk could not have been pleased by this radical shift in

Capetian policy, it is unlikely that the new alignment took him completely by surprise. King Robert had begun his dalliance with Bertha of Blois even before Odo I's death, and this affair had precipitated a breach between Hugh Capet and his son.[15] So, while Fulk was unable to keep Robert's forces from retaking Tours and Châteauneuf, the Angevin count's allies in Aquitaine were not unprepared for the king's push south of the Loire to aid William of Poitou. When Robert's army joined with the forces of Count William to attack Bellac, a stronghold of key importance to Count Boso, Aldebert's successor at la Marche, they found it well prepared to hold out against a lengthy siege and ably defended by Abbo Drutus. After besieging Bellac unsuccessfully for many days, Robert and William abandoned their effort. The king left William to fend for himself and returned to the north where he had many problems of his own.[16]

Fulk responded to Robert's thrust into Aquitaine by strengthening his ties with Walter, count of Valois, Vexin, and Amiens, who earlier had been closely allied with the Capetians and Angevins but now was threatened by King Robert's union with the house of Blois. This was especially a problem for Walter's son Geoffrey, Fulk's cousin, who had been made count of Gâtinais by Hugh Capet and had been given control of Château-Landon. Geoffrey, however, died before 997, and his brother Walter II, guided the affairs of the Gâtinais.[17] Count Walter II ravaged lands belonging to Saint-Benoît-sur-Loire, one of King Robert's most important and wealthy supporters. Fulk acted in concert with Walter and used his control of the fisc of Saint-Pierre-en-Gâtinais to support numerous vassali and to provide them with beneficia in the region. Fulk, in fact, virtually stripped the monastery of Saint-Pierre of the means to sustain itself in order to accomplish his political policy of undermining King Robert's control of the area.[18]

Soon after Fulk lost Tours and while operating in the Gâtinais and its environs with his allies, he saw to the beginning of construction of a major stronghold at Montbazon on the lower reaches of the Indre only thirteen kilometers from its junction with the Loire. This fortification was built on lands belonging to the monastery of Cormery and shows how Fulk used his taxing powers to levy the workers and other resources required to sustain his strategy of building strategically located fortifications. The purpose of building the castrum at Montbazon was to secure Fulk's lines of communication with Amboise in the Loire valley and with his strongholds in the southern part of the Touraine and in northern Berry.[19]

As part of his defensive measures in the Touraine, Fulk also built a stronghold at Montrésor on the east bank of the Indroye River only sixteen kilometers east-northeast of Loches. From a tactical perspective, Montrésor, where Fulk established Roger the Devil as castellan, was positioned so that troops sent west from the Blésois stronghold of Saint-Aignan into the region between Loches and Amboise could be outflanked and cut off by men stationed in this new stronghold at Montrésor.[20]

Fulk complemented his efforts in the Touraine and the Gâtinais during the last three years of the first millennium with initiatives in the Poitou and Aquitaine. After King Robert found it necessary to return north of the Loire, young William, the new count of the Poitou and duke of Aquitaine, continued for a time to pursue an aggressive policy against the count of la Marche and to struggle against what seems to have been general opposition to a new ruler who had neither proven himself as a general nor as a diplomat. William failed miserably against Viscount Guy of Limoges, who successfully routed the count's forces when they tried to take the stronghold of Brosse.[21] At Rochemeaux, however, where William left the execution of the siege and the military planning to his more experienced supporters, the stronghold was taken and Aldebert's widow, Adalmode, was made a prisoner.[22]

This piece of good fortune ultimately helped lead to a rapprochement between William and Fulk. Some very useful information concerning this process is provided by Pierre de Maillezais, who wrote his *Relatio* around 1060 with a strong Aquitanian bias similar to that which permeated the work of Adémar of Chabannes a generation earlier. According to Pierre, William released Adalmode shortly after she had been taken prisoner and sent her to her mother, the countess of Arles. As a result of what is portrayed as a kindly and chivalrous act, Adalmode's mother is said to have recognized that the duke of Aquitaine's rights extended as far east as the Rhône River. Pierre completes this little romance by noting that Emma of Blois, William's mother, sent representatives to Adalmode's mother to arrange the marriage of their respective offspring. Thus Pierre concludes that William's duchy was increased and he was recognized throughout his *regnum* as duke.[23]

Although Pierre confuses many details, he does record two indisputable facts: Adalmode and William were married and Adalmode's brothers, who ruled Gévaudan and Forez on Aquitaine's eastern frontier, recognized William as duke.[24] It is likely that Pierre is correct in attributing to Emma a role in arranging the marriage. But Pierre's representation of the sequence of events and his depiction of the relative strengths and weaknesses of the several parties involved are far less plausible. For example, it is highly unlikely that William or for that matter any late tenth-century magnate would have released a valuable captive without first arranging some kind of quid pro quo. More important is Pierre's failure to portray the broader stage on which the events he describes were taking place. Fulk Nerra had taken the opportunity afforded by William's conflict with the count of la Marche and the viscount of Limoges to pursue the policy that Geoffrey Greymantle had followed: encroachment on the northern part of the Poitou.[25] Not only were the fortifications at Loudun securely in Fulk's hands but he had construction begun on a stronghold at Mirebeau only twenty-five kilometers north of Poitiers itself. This fortification was an Angevin "frontier" post built on lands adjoining estates that belonged to the monastery of Cormery from which Fulk could levy taxes in both labor and materiel for building the stronghold and for logistic support. From Mirebeau, Fulk's mounted troops could raid to the environs of Poitiers.[26]

To appreciate fully the political situation in Aquitaine that led to the marriage of William and Adalmode we must understand the course of events as they developed from 994. William Iron Arm, dispirited and ill, made a final reconciliation with his estranged wife Emma of Blois and associated their son William with him as count of Poitou and duke of Aquitaine. This brought about a new Poitevin alliance with Odo I of Blois, who after failing to usurp the title *dux Francorum*, launched an offensive against Fulk Nerra's castrum at Langeais. Fulk had responded to Odo's threat by obtaining the support of Aldebert, count of la Marche and Périgord, who sought to extend his own power in Aquitaine at the expense of young William. For two years Aldebert kept the Poitevins on the defensive. He caused the defection of many of William's fideles, captured his strongholds, and even took the urbs of Poitiers after a siege. Following the death of Odo I, Aldebert helped Fulk capture Tours and Châteauneuf. These successes placed William in a very difficult position. Aldebert, through his Angevin ties, could call upon the support of Adalmode's brothers who ruled Forez and Gévaudan, of her mother the countess of Arles, and perhaps of her uncle, who was count-bishop of le Puy. Of course, Fulk Nerra could also be relied upon to do his part. Thus, following the death of Odo I, William's uncle and potential protector, one might visualize that the stage was being set for Aldebert to "usurp" the title *dux Aquitanorum*.[27]

When Aldebert was killed unexpectedly at Gençay, the situation changed fundamentally. Aldebert was succeeded by his brother Boso, who continued the conflict against the count of Poitou, but the new count of la Marche's ties with the Angevins were not as strong as his brother's had been. In addition, the marriage of King Robert to Odo's widow Bertha and the monarch's success in retaking Tours can be seen to have encouraged William to confront his adversaries. When the king came south to support the Poitevins against Boso, William's prospects looked brighter than they had in two years. Nonetheless, the failure of the combined forces of Robert and William to take Bellac, the king's hasty return to Francia, and the major defeat inflicted on the Poitevins by viscount Guy of Limoges at Brosse demonstrated to both the duke and the magnates of the region the weakness of William's position, if not his outright lack of ability.[28]

Thus, William's capture of the stronghold of Rochemeaux and of the countess Adalmode provided him with a new opportunity, which his mother Emma appears to have appreciated. Adalmode was a potentially valuable bargaining counter which if used wisely might make William's position considerably less difficult, at least in the short term. Clearly, William could have offered to trade Adalmode to her brother-in-law, Count Boso, perhaps for a castrum such as Bellac or perhaps even in return for an alliance and recognition as duke of Aquitaine. Boso's interest in Adalmode, however, was problematical. Adalmode's son, who was a minor, had temporarily been displaced as heir to his father's lands and titles by Boso, who if successful might well have wanted to have his own sons succeed him and thus deprive his nephew of his rightful inheritance. In this as yet unresolved state of affairs, Adalmode, with her Angevin family ties, was a potential source of danger to Boso. Fulk and his relatives would no doubt have wanted to see Adalmode's children obtain their inheritance, at the least when they came of age.

Whether William understood the potential danger that Adalmode and her Angevin family network posed to Boso cannot be ascertained. It is clear, however, that William and Emma sought to bargain with the Angevins. Adalmode was a widow and William was unmarried.[29] Their marriage could win the recognition of her brothers, who ruled Gévaudan and Forez, her mother, the countess of Arles, and the count-bishop of le Puy. With this alliance, William could curb the pretensions of Boso of la Marche and of Guy of Limoges. He would, however, have to pay a heavy price. Not only would William find himself dependent on various relations of his wife for his security but he would also have to establish a modus vivendi with his bellicose and greedy neighbor, Fulk Nerra, who seemed intent upon gaining control of the northern part of the Poitou.[30]

William came to an agreement with the Angevins which was sealed by his marriage to Adalmode no later than the year 1000 (and probably a short time earlier).[31] The "Angevin" counties of Gévaudan and Forez on the eastern frontier of Aquitaine recognized William as duke. William's arrangements with Fulk Nerra are described by Adémar of Chabannes, a contemporary chronicler whose bias in favor of the count of Poitou often amounts to panegyric: "And when he [William] had Fulk, the Angevin count, commend himself into his hands, he conceded to him as a beneficium Loudun and several other strongholds in the Poitou and also Saintes with certain fortified places in the region."[32] In broad outline this arrangement may have given William some juridical protection and some rather hollow dignity as a result of the ceremony. Fulk, however, gained legal recognition for Angevin conquests in the northern Poitou and major concessions in the Saintonge.[33]

Fulk pursued the advantage that had been grasped by the Angevins in Aquitaine and arranged for his sister Hermengarde-Gerberga, the widow of Conan of Rennes, to marry the new count of Angoulême, William Taillefer.[34] With William of Angoulême drawn into the Angevin family network, William of Poitou had in all of Aquitaine no potential non-Angevin allies of major status other than his two very recent adversaries, Boso of la Marche and Guy of Limoges. Fulk's alliance with William Taillefer also provided the Angevin count with a supporter on the borders of his newly acquired holdings in the Saintonge which included the great walled urbs of Saintes and its noted internal citadel, the Capitolium. William of Angoulême very probably saw the value in having a powerful brother-in-law such as Fulk Nerra who would be in a position to further their mutual interests at the expense of the young and inept William, count of Poitou and duke of Aquitaine.[35]

Despite royal intervention, Fulk had been able to take effective action and to pursue a successful policy in Aquitaine. This was made possible, at least in part, by the network of alliances that Fulk's father and grandfather had established. Indeed, Geoffrey Greymantle had taken various strongholds in the Poitou from William Iron Arm and the Angevin count had supported his sister and her sons, who came to dominate much of the eastern frontier of Aquitaine.[36] Following the loss of Tours, Fulk had been able to maintain a strong position in the

Loire valley by holding on at Langeais and Montsoreau, which were newly acquired, and by building fortifications at Montrésor and Montbazon. These successes helped him to maintain his communication links with his eastern holdings at Amboise and Loches. With the help of Count Walter, an ally whose family had become tied to the Angevins by marriage during the reign of Fulk the Red, Fulk Nerra was able to disrupt King Robert's supporters in the Orléanais and its environs.

A little farther west in the Loire valley at Bourgeuil we catch a glimpse of Fulk's maneuvering to control this strategically located town and to undermine Capetian-Blésois influence at the monastery of Saint-Peter, which had been founded by Emma of Blois and was led by her cousin. In 992 Fulk's fidelis Aimery of Thouars had been encouraged to give Saint-Peter a valuable exemption from river tolls for one of the monastery's ships. Four years later, after Fulk had gained control of the nearby stronghold of Montsoreau and established his fidelis Walter there, the new castellan was encouraged by prevailing circumstances to impose new taxes (*malae consuetudines*) on the lands and dependents of Saint-Peter in the region in order to sustain the logistic requirements of Angevin military operations.[37] Just at the time that Walter was imposing vicarial exactions on Saint-Peter, however, Fulk encouraged a longtime Angevin supporter, a *miles* named Renaud, to make a major gift to the monastery.[38] When Saint-Peter's monks complained to Fulk about Walter's excessive demands, the Angevin count acted to limit some of his castellan's heavier exactions.[39] Thus, through the judicious use of positive and negative reinforcement, Fulk demonstrated to Saint-Peter just how dependent the monastery was on his good will.

These activities notwithstanding, Fulk still faced considerable difficulties because King Robert had overturned the balance of power in the west of France by his marriage to Bertha. Fulk's father-in-law, Count Bouchard of Vendôme, had been Hugh Capet's closest friend and most loyal ally. Bouchard had benefited greatly from this relationship and had secured the countships of Corbeil, Melun, and Paris as a result. Renaud, Bouchard's son, had become bishop of Paris.[40] Thus the aging ruler of the Vendômois faced a difficult choice. Would he support his new lord and king, Robert, the son of his closest friend and benefactor, or would he permit dynastic interests to prevail and lean toward Fulk?

Bouchard's decision was made especially difficult because he was an intensely religious man. Thus he could not lightly regard his oath of faithfulness to Robert. Yet Robert's marriage to Bertha was clearly contrary to the canons; the pope had ordered the couple to separate, and by 999 Robert and Bertha were both excommunicated.[41] Nevertheless, Bishop Renaud of Paris, Bouchard's son and immediate heir of the Vendômois, supported the king.[42] In addition, Robert was well received at Cluny and was supported by many bishops as well as by leading monastic figures like Abbo of Fleury and Robert of Blois, who was abbot of both Saint-Florent de Saumur and Saint-Mesmin-de-Micy in the Orléanais.[43]

In contrast, the advantages of alliance with Fulk were less obvious. The Angevin count was a less than ideal son-in-law. He was not satisfied with his wife Elizabeth, Bouchard's daughter, who after more than a decade of marriage had failed to produce a male heir.[44] Moreover, Fulk had thus far in his career desecrated the monastic enclave of Saint-Martin at Châteauneuf, expropriated the lands of Saint-Pierre-en-Gâtinais, ravaged the territory of Saint-Florent, exploited the holdings of Saint-Peter at Bourgeuil, and burned Saint-Lomer. Although Fulk had occasionally done penance for one or another of his transgressions or granted a privilege or immunity to an ecclesiastical establishment for one or another of these outrages, the pious Bouchard had little reason to believe that his son-in-law, who habitually swore by the souls of God, was prepared to behave in a Christian manner.[45] Meanwhile, although Robert's marriage was something of a scandal, negotiations were under way with the pope to resolve the problem.[46]

Ultimately, Bouchard chose to follow his king and to withdraw active support for Fulk.[47] The count of Vendôme's adherence to Robert and the Capetian-Blésois axis, however, did not lead him to take direct military action against his son-in-law. Still, the end of Bouchard's active support, which had been so important to Fulk's survival during the period 987–996, could not be lightly dismissed. Indeed, Fulk's position north of the Loire was compromised by this loss, Amboise was further exposed to enemy harassment, and Angevin interests in the Gâtinais were placed in greater jeopardy. In addition, efforts to pursue the policy developed by Geoffrey Greymantle of establishing the Loir River as the northern frontier of the Angevin state were undermined and initiatives leading to Angevin penetration of Maine were blunted.

Despite Bouchard's loyalty to King Robert, Fulk knew that he himself was likely to control the destiny of the county of Vendôme. Bouchard was a pious and aged widower and he could not be expected to father any more children. His son and immediate heir to the Vendômois, Bishop Renaud of Paris, could have no legitimate issue. Thus

Fulk had good reason to believe that in the normal course of events he would control the region either through his wife Elizabeth or their daughter Adele, the respective heiresses to the Vendômois after Bishop Renaud of Paris. Control over Adele's marriage was thus of great value to Fulk, and it is probably to the period around A.D. 1000, when Adele was nearing her fifteenth birthday, that we can date the Angevin count's efforts to secure Bodo of Nevers, son of Count Landry of Nevers, as a son-in-law.[48] Like Geoffrey Greymantle and Bouchard of Vendôme, Landry of Nevers had been a strong supporter of Hugh Capet. Landry, however, had sided with Robert in the latter's conflict with his father and strongly supported the young king's proposed marriage to the countess of Blois. Bertha had purchased Landry's support in this matter by promising to give him the town of Provins. After the marriage, however, Bertha refused to honor her promise to Landry, who then defected from the royal cause. This set the stage for an alliance between Fulk and Landry which ultimately would be sealed by the marriage of Adele to Bodo of Nevers.[49]

Fulk's and Landry's mutual interest in opposing King Robert II was multifaceted. In Burgundy a struggle was developing to determine who would succeed the aging Duke Henry, King Robert's uncle. Henry had no legitimate offspring and had designated as his successor Otto-William, son of his second wife Gerberga by her first marriage. The Capetian king opposed this settlement and vigorously pressed his own claim to the duchy of Burgundy. Among Otto-William's staunchest supporters was his brother-in-law (the husband of his sister Mathilda) Landry, count of Nevers.[50]

The leader of the faction that supported King Robert was Count Hugh of Chalon. Although Hugh was Otto-William's uncle, the count of Chalon decided to support the king and oppose his close relative.[51] Here we should recall that Hugh's mother Adele had married Geoffrey Greymantle about 979 and that they had a son named Maurice who by the late 990s had reached adulthood (fifteen years of age). In the eyes of his half-brother Hugh and his mother Adele, Maurice might well have had a supportable claim to the position that Fulk Nerra had inherited from Geoffrey Greymantle. Clearly, Maurice's claims might be pursued to advantage with royal support against those of his niece Adele, should her father Fulk be removed from the scene.

Through the efforts of Maurice's uncle, the Angevin bishop Guy of le Puy, we saw the former receive a share in the comital title of Chalon with his half-brother Hugh in 987–988, that is, shortly after the death of Geoffrey Greymantle. But during the early 990s, as Angevin influence diminished in Chalon, Maurice ceased to be styled count. Nonetheless, sometime before March 999, Hugh of Chalon, perhaps with the aim of pressing a claim for Maurice to be count of the Angevins and heir of Geoffrey Greymantle, once again saw to it that Maurice was styled count of Chalon in official documents. Adele of Chalon confirmed this in a charter which incorporated this intitulation.[52]

In these circumstances Count Hugh may well have lent his support to King Robert, in part at least to encourage the monarch to recognize Maurice either as Angevin count or as heir to Fulk's position. Thus, in May 999 King Robert confirmed a charter issued by Hugh in which Maurice is styled count of Chalon. In addition and equally important, Bishop Renaud of Paris, the maternal uncle of Fulk Nerra's daughter Adele, subscribed this act.[53] Hugh and Robert's alliance was secured when the king established the older count of Chalon, who already was a cleric, as bishop of Auxerre and permitted him to hold both titles simultaneously.[54]

At this time Robert II had been engineering another attack on Fulk Nerra. Working through Abbo of Fleury, Robert sought to have the pope condemn Fulk Nerra for his attacks on the church.[55] If Pope Gregory V excommunicated Fulk and placed his lands under interdict, King Robert would be in a strong position to lead an army against the Angevin count, deprive him of his lands and titles, and establish Maurice, who was also a son of Geoffrey Greymantle, as the possessor of at least a portion of what his half-brother held.[56]

The mutual interest of Fulk Nerra and Landry of Nevers can be dated from 997 when Queen Bertha failed to honor her promise to give the town of Provins to the count of Nevers. The desirability of such an alliance was strengthened by the Capetian rapprochement in Burgundy-Chalon, which became unmistakably clear in March 999 when King Robert affirmed his alliance with Hugh of Chalon and made him bishop of Auxerre. Fulk might also have benefited by Landry's ambition to extend his influence northward toward Provins, in Champagne, only forty kilometers from Melun, Bouchard of Vendôme's stronghold, and slightly farther from Château-Landon. From a strategic perspective, the confluence of Angevin interests with those of the count of the Gâtinais and the count of Nevers in this area could cause serious problems for Blésois communications along an east-west axis and disturb Capetian interests along a north-south one.

Fulk's alliance with Landry established the northern link in a line of friendly powers that dominated the eastern frontier of Aquitaine along the border with Burgundy. Fulk's cousins controlled Forez and Gévaudan and his uncle was count-bishop of le Puy. Together these powers virtually surrounded Chalon, where Fulk's half-brother Maurice shared the comital title and if given proper support might be inclined to take full control of the holdings of his half-brother Hugh. The latter would remain bishop of Auxerre.

Collaboration between Nevers and Angevin interests can be seen to have matured fruitfully at le Puy, where the elderly bishop Guy seems to have been unable to continue the vigorous pace he had once pursued. With the help of Archbishop Dagobert of Bourges and Bishop Roclen of Nevers, Guy arranged to have his grand-nephew Stephen associated with him as bishop of le Puy. It is important to emphasize that Landry's man, Bishop Roclen of Nevers, participated in this effort, which was manifestly contrary to the canons and for which he and his colleagues were condemned at Rome.[57] The important role played by Archbishop Dagobert in the uncanonical elevation of Stephen to the see of le Puy highlights the long-standing and close working relationship he enjoyed with Fulk's uncle as well as his support for Angevin policies. For example, in the early 990s Archbishop Dagobert lent his aid to Bishop Guy when the latter, after putting down opposition to his rule at le Puy with the aid of his nephews from Gévaudan and Forez, imposed a "truce of God" in the region. This enforced peace was secured by the local levy as the bishop was able to draw forces from the countryside.[58]

Dagobert had been made archbishop of Bourges in 987 and was the Capetian-Angevin candidate who succeeded after two successive Blésois prelates had held the see.[59] When the Capetian-Blésois axis was formed, Dagobert sided with the Angevins, probably because the monastery of Fleury and its powerful abbot Abbo were firmly entrenched in King Robert's entourage. Abbo was no friend of bishops, especially when they were in a position to exercise power over his monastery. In a highly propagandistic vein the *Vita Abbonis* condemns Dagobert for refusing consecration to properly elected bishops without first receiving a large payment for doing so.[60]

During the period of the Capetian-Blésois axis Fulk Nerra's relations with Archbishop Dagobert were close and the Angevin count made substantial gains in Berry. The southeastern frontier of the Angevin state was the upper Indre valley. Fulk controlled the valley from Buzançais in the south through Châtillion-sur-Indre, Loches, and the monastery of Cormery to Montbazon in the north, where he built an impor-

tant stronghold at this time.[61] The valuable agricultural region between
the upper Cher valley and the upper Indre valley seems to have been
considered by Fulk as an area for potential Angevin expansion. Due east
of Loches on the road to Bourges, the Angevins already played an important role at the monastery of Villeloin. At Montrésor, nearby Villeloin, the Angevins were also in control, and Fulk had had this place
fortified. Renaud II, the *senior* of Graçay, whose lands were situated east
of Montrésor along the route to Bourges, was one of Fulk's allies.
About 999 Archbishop Dagobert, Viscount Geoffrey of Bourges, and
Fulk lent their support to Renaud's foundation of the church of the
Holy Cross at Graçay.[62]

King Robert and his young stepson, Count Theobald II of Blois,
were surely discomforted by Fulk's encroachment into an area where
both the Blésois and the Capetians had vital interests. The count of
Blois, for example, controlled the monastery of Vierzon,[63] and the king
controlled the monastery of Massay, from which he obtained substantial material support.[64] Fulk built a stronghold near Massay, which enabled him to protect his access route to Bourges along the road from
Loches through Montrésor (and Villeloin) and Graçay. This stronghold also gave the Angevin count a base near the monastery from which
he could more easily extort labor service and material resources much
in the same way that he used the fortifications at Mirebeau, Montrésor,
Montbazon, Montsoreau, and Loudun. By contrast, King Robert took
the doctrinaire position, much favored by his monastic advisors and
supporters, that strongholds should not be constructed in the environs
of monasteries. In 999 Robert managed to destroy the Angevin fortifications at Massay.[65]

Although King Robert II was able to protect the monastery at Massay, he did not attempt to keep the stronghold in his own possession
in order to block the Angevin route from Loches to Bourges. Fulk
seems to have been able to maintain and indeed strengthen the Angevin
position in northwestern Berry. In this context it is important that
King Robert and Count Theobald of Blois took the initiative and laid
siege to Bourges. But they failed to force it to surrender.[66] Fulk's ally,
Archbishop Dagobert, probably with the support of the viscount of
Bourges, succeeded in keeping the Capetian-Blésois axis from seizing
control of the most important stronghold in Berry as well as the center
of the region's religious and economic life.

The struggle to gain an advantage in Berry during this period had
a tit-for-tat aspect. For example, Fulk put considerable pressure on the

monastery of Selles-sur-Cher, located on rich agricultural land only ten kilometers from the Angevin stronghold at Villentrois and twenty kilometers from Graçay, where Fulk's ally Renaud had his main base. Theobald, however, had a stronghold only ten kilometers from Selles at Saint-Aignan, under the command of Geoffrey de Bonzy.[67] One Angevin expedition against the monastery is described in some detail by a hostile contemporary, Letaldus of Micy, more as a foraging expedition or at best as an effort to loot Selles than as an attempted conquest. But Letaldus's description of Fulk's forces as a *hostis* with at least two *phalanges,* one of *equites* and the other of *pedites,* suggests a major campaign.[68] The identification of a unit of foot soldiers seems to preclude a mere raiding party, and if a foraging effort was under way then the forces detached for this operation would have been part of an even larger army.

It is of considerable importance to note that Count Theobald II apparently found it necessary to attack Selles some time before his death in 1004. This permits the inference that Selles or at least some of its estates had fallen into Angevin hands and that Letaldus's claim that Fulk's forces were frightened off by Saint Eusicius's defense of his monks may not be the whole story. The stylistic similarities of sculptures at Selles and at Fulk's church at Belli Locus may also support the idea of Angevin influence at Selles.[69]

While Fulk's fortunes prospered on the diplomatic front, his domestic situation revealed a major difficulty. Countess Elizabeth of Vendôme, after almost fifteen years of marriage, had failed to produce a male heir, and the couple's prayers supported by gifts to powerful saints had been in vain.[70] Moreover, Elizabeth seems to have taken a lover. Whether she was simply trying to produce the required son or had become alienated from Fulk is not clear. In any event, when Elizabeth realized that Fulk had learned of her activities, she seized control of the citadel at Angers with a handful of supporters and held it against her husband. (This seizure may perhaps indicate a conspiracy involving her brother or her father.) Fulk established a siege in the course of which Elizabeth fell from the high walls and was captured. Fulk had her immediately burned for adultery, and a few days later he tried to dislodge the remainder of her supporters by setting the citadel on fire. Although the fire spread throughout the city, Fulk emerged in control. As one somewhat later chronicler of Saint-Florent laconically reported: "Fulk, the hot-tempered one, killed his wife Elizabeth at Angers after she had survived an enormous fall. Then Fulk burned with fiery flames the same city which was defended only by a few men." The account continues: "He burned Elizabeth because she had committed adultery."[71]

Fulk nonetheless strove to maintain a foothold at Vendôme despite Elizabeth's death and the political leanings of both Bouchard and Renaud toward the Capetian-Blésois axis. Since the reign of Geoffrey Greymantle, the Angevins had sought the support of the viscomital family of Vendôme by granting them beneficia. Viscount Fulcradus of Vendôme had been a fidelis of Geoffrey's, and Viscount Hubert, Fulcradus's son-in-law and successor, held the curtis and the church of Mazé from Fulk Nerra. In 1001 Fulk appointed as abbot of Saint-Aubin a certain Hubert, who it has been suggested was a relative of Viscount Hubert. Finally, Fulk named Viscount Hubert's son, also named Hubert, to the bishopric of Angers.[72]

Elizabeth's death, which gave Fulk the opportunity to seek a new wife, may well have increased his chances of fathering a male heir, but the Angevin count's immediate prospects for securing the position of his dynasty were not propitious. Fulk's daughter Adele (by Elizabeth) stood to inherit his lands and titles, but if this inheritance took place sooner rather than later, her policies would probably have been influenced, if not dictated, by her uncle and grandfather in the interests of Vendôme and the Capetian-Blésois axis. Such an eventuality would seriously damage the position of the families that supported Fulk. They understood that their success was closely linked to the success of the Angevin counts. Many of Fulk's supporters had gained greatly in wealth and power as a result of Geoffrey Greymantle's victories. Should the Capetian-Blésois axis gain control in Anjou through the accession of Adele, Fulk's fideles would be seriously disadvantaged through the loss of lands and offices.[73]

Adele's lonely position as Fulk's sole heir was a danger not only to the complex of lands, titles, and alliances her father and his predecessors had built up during the tenth century but it also threatened the investments of a broad spectrum of her paternal relatives, local Angevin magnates, and important families in the west of France, such as the viscounts of le Mans and Vendôme. In these difficult circumstances Fulk acted boldly and perhaps somewhat unconventionally to diminish the risk of Adele's vulnerable position. He brought his half-brother Maurice from Chalon to Angers.[74] Thus, a legitimate son of Geoffrey Greymantle was given hospitality by his brother, and a male adult of the Fulconian dynasty was at Angers to protect the family's traditional interests. The manner in which Fulk's most prominent magnates sustained the count's half-brother shows that Maurice was received as a supporter of traditional Angevin policy and not as a tool of the Capetian-Blésois axis tied to Hugh of Chalon's efforts on behalf of King Robert in Burgundy.[75]

Neither Elizabeth's "execution" nor Maurice's establishment at Angers seems to have had a profound effect on Fulk's dealings with Bishop Renaud of Angers and his brother, Viscount Fulcoius. Following Renaud's participation in the program at Châteauneuf by which Fulk was reconciled with Saint-Martin early in 997, Fulk's relations with the prelate seem to have improved. Thus, for example, on 17 January in the year 1000, just before Elizabeth's death, Fulk acted at Renaud's request to provide the cathedral of Angers with the income from half of the tolls collected at the bridge that crossed the Mayenne at Angers. In addition, Fulk agreed to put an end to new taxes (*malae consuetudines*) he had imposed on lands belonging to the cathedral.[76] In September 1001, not long after his wife's death, Fulk chose a new abbot for Saint-Aubin and this time, unlike in the elections of 988 and 996, he permitted Bishop Renaud to play a role in the process.[77] At the death of Abbot Bouchard of Saint-Serge, a longtime fidelis of the Angevin count, Fulk permitted Renaud to send monks there under a reform-minded abbot.[78]

Bishop Renaud, however, seems to have felt compelled, perhaps by some inner spiritual imperative, to oppose Fulk's utilization of church lands for secular affairs. Thus in 1001 the prelate proclaimed that the *maxima pars* of land in this world "was handed over into the hereditary possession of God's saints." But because of evil and greed, Renaud continued: "Kings . . . sell bishoprics to bishops and monasteries to abbots. These bishops and abbots then hand them over to laymen as hereditary possessions. As a result of this alienation it is seen today that the custom continues and that the possessions of the saints are held in hereditary right by laymen."[79]

That Renaud himself had obtained the bishopric of Angers through a simoniacal transaction is an important fact. His father, Viscount Renaud of Angers, had made a *conventum* with Geoffrey Greymantle as a result of which young Renaud received the bishopric and the allods belonging to the Renaud family in the Mauges region would go to the comital fisc after the death of the prelate.[80] Renaud's lengthy tenure began in 972, but by the beginning of the new millennium he seems to have arrived at a point in his spiritual development when he objected to the *conventum*. Thus at about the same time as he condemned simony and lay possession of church lands he made a *testamentum* by which he alienated the allods in the Mauges region to various religious houses during his own lifetime, thus unilaterally attempting to abrogate the *conventum* his father had made.[81]

At about this time another attack on Fulk's treatment of church offices and wealth materialized. Letaldus, prior of Saint-Florent and of Saint-Mesmin-de-Micy and a member of the entourage of Fulk Nerra's longtime adversary Abbot Robert, was commissioned to "revise" the *Miracula* of Saint Martin of Vertou for the monks of Saint-Jouin-de-Marnes.[82] Bishop Renaud, who had on occasion worked closely with Abbot Robert of Saint-Florent against Fulk's interests, was a major patron of Saint-Jouin-de-Marnes and his family is copiously praised in the version of the *Miracula* drafted by Letaldus. In one of these *Miracula* Letaldus levied a vigorous attack against the secular use of church lands and particularly against the innovative practice of listing half of each monastery's *facultates* (resources) on the *tabulae* of the governmental fisc to meet secular needs. Special condemnation is reserved for the idea that *milites* and *servientes* rather than monks should enjoy the *facultates* that had been dedicated to the saints.[83]

Although Letaldus set this story in the reign of King Dagobert I and had the administrator of the *divisio* die a nasty death at the hands of Saint John and Saint Martin, it is clear from a broad spectrum of evidence, including terminology, that the target of criticism was not an otherwise unknown Merovingian fiscal innovation but Fulk Nerra's systematic efforts to utilize half or perhaps even more of monastic wealth for secular purposes. Letaldus was circumspect in placing the fiscal innovations he condemned in the distant Merovingian era, for he could easily be connected to Bishop Renaud and is likely to have been little more than the prelate's amanuensis in this matter.[84]

Bishop Renaud was also cautious, as we can see from his generalized attack on the secular use of church property and his decision not to publicize his *testamentum*. Fulk Nerra's reputation for a violent temper made him difficult to oppose directly, as the bishop undoubtedly had come to understand during his decade and a half of dealings with the Angevin count. That these criticisms had little effect on Fulk's division of church lands seems clear from various subsequent texts showing the count using halves of various monastic estates for secular purposes.[85]

Fulk seems to have been in control of the domestic situation despite the death of Elizabeth and Bishop Renaud's thinly veiled attacks on the use of church property for governmental needs. The external threat posed as a result of the Capetian-Blésois axis was substantially diminished following the death of Duke Henry of Burgundy in October 1002, for the attention of the Capetian king Robert II was diverted by his ambition to succeed his uncle as duke. To this end he had enlisted the aid of Hugh of Chalon, giving him the bishopric of Auxerre. The king's opponent for the honor of Burgundy, Henry's stepson Otto-William, had the support of Landry of Nevers. War began between the two factions, and Landry was able to capture the heavily fortified urbs of Auxerre. In the spring of 1003 King Robert laid siege to Auxerre with a large force, including a contingent led by Duke Richard of Normandy. The siege lasted into the summer of 1003, but the stronghold did not fall. Robert returned to the north with his forces but remained committed to making good his claim to Burgundy.[86]

Clearly, Fulk Nerra was able to deal effectively with the new political configuration created by King Robert's marriage to Bertha. As long as the king remained allied with the house of Blois, however, the situation on Anjou's western frontier was made more difficult, Fulk's relations with Vendôme were complicated, and Angevin expansion into the Touraine was seriously slowed. Fulk had managed to hold his own at Vendôme through strengthening his relations with the viscomital house, and to the east, with the help of Walter of Montsoreau, he continued to deal with the abbot of Bourgueil. In the west Count Geoffrey-Berengar of Rennes was drawn into Norman affairs after his marriage to the daughter of Duke Richard I, but perhaps for this reason he remained satisfied, at least for the moment, with nominal recognition of his title as duke of Brittany by Count Judicaël of Nantes.[87] The situation on Anjou's western frontier, however, was likely to become more difficult as a result of the marriage of Mathilda, daughter of Richard I of Normandy, to Odo, second son of Odo I of Blois by Bertha, who would soon replace his elder brother Theobald as count of Blois.[88] Thus viewed from the vantage point of 1003, King Robert's involvement in Burgundy could be seen only as temporarily relieving pressure on Anjou. The increased intertwining of the interests of the king, the house of Blois, the duke of Normandy, and Count Geoffrey-Berengar of Rennes surely continued to pose a formidable threat to Fulk Nerra.

If King Robert II abandoned the Blésois alliance, however, Fulk's position obviously would be strengthened. Indeed, great ecclesiastical pressure had been exerted on the king to separate from Bertha. Not only had they both been excommunicated, but Pope Sylvester II, Robert's former tutor, had refused to take steps to legalize the marriage that Pope Gregory V and his council had condemned.[89] Robert had sustained his position for seven years (996–1003) despite ecclesiastical censure. Even though Bertha had failed to provide the king with a male heir (in fact she had borne him no children), probably a source of some consternation, as late as the end of August 1003 Robert designated Bertha's eldest son Theobald as bishop of Chartres. Publicly, at least, the Capetian-Blésois axis was still intact.[90]

Nonetheless, in September 1003, when Fulk announced that he had decided to make a pilgrimage to the Holy Land, we must suspect that the Angevin count knew or believed that the Capetian-Blésois axis was on the verge of dissolution. It is difficult for us to believe that a careful and cautious planner like Fulk would have committed himself publicly to leaving the Angevin state in the hands of his untried brother Maurice without the assurance that a combined Capetian-Blésois-Norman military attack was unlikely.[91] It is of particular importance that when King Robert finally separated from Bertha and took a new wife late in 1003 or very early in 1004, he chose Constance of Arles, Fulk Nerra's first cousin.[92] The arrangements that ultimately brought Constance to Paris were doubtless the subject of delicate and confidential negotiations for some time before Robert actually separated from Bertha. Fulk may very well have been privy to these negotiations. In this light Fulk's decision to leave for the Holy Land was probably the result of firsthand knowledge that his cousin would soon displace Bertha of Blois as queen of France.

Fulk Nerra departed for the Holy Land before the end of 1003, leaving Maurice to rule the Angevin state with the insignia and the title of count.[93] Although the narrative sources that treat Maurice's reign were redacted during the century after his death and are greatly confused on many important details, they do reveal several themes consistent with contemporary circumstances as reflected in documents known to be more reliable.[94] The *Gesta Consulum* depicts Maurice as a learned and well-spoken "lover of peace" (*pacis amator*) who sought to rule "more through wisdom than through war." He is said to have rewarded his relatives and friends with many *beneficia*, to have endeavored to raise up *inferiores* to high *dignitates,* and to have provided them with great *honores.* Yet despite these attributes and policies deemed positive and praiseworthy by the redactor of the *Gesta,* Maurice emerges as beleaguered by external enemies and betrayed by some traditional Angevin supporters who had been expected to remain faithful because of rewards they had received in the past. Finally, the *Gesta* focuses on the Angevin count's loyal supporters who were able to sustain the comital position until Fulk Nerra, *fortissimus miles,* reassumed the reins of government. This section of the *Gesta* ends by echoing the family theme explicit in Geoffrey Greymantle's advice (ca. 985) to both Fulk and Maurice: "No house is weak that has many friends. Therefore I admonish you to hold dear those fideles who have been friends."[95]

The theme of defection vies with the theme of loyalty, in both cases heavily larded with allusions from classical literature, for prominence in the account of Maurice's reign that is developed in the *Gesta Consulum.* It is made clear that Count Odo II of Blois was the major stimulus for the disloyalty of the Angevin count's fideles.[96] During Fulk's first pilgrimage to the Holy Land the most damaging defectors from the Angevin cause were Bishop Renaud of Angers and his brother Viscount Fulcoius. Bishop Renaud, who had developed a close personal relationship with young Count Odo II, granted the youth favors and is found in his entourage very shortly after Fulk departed for Jerusalem.[97] In addition, the prelate acted decisively to undermine the Angevin position in the strategically crucial Mauges region by making public his *testamentum* by which the allods promised to the comital fisc were alienated. Renaud had sought royal approval for these acts and during the period of Fulk's absence he sought papal confirmation for the abrogation of the *conventum* that Viscount Renaud had made with Geoffrey Greymantle.[98] Renaud also moved to undermine Fulk's position in the Angevin heartland as well. The bishop acted to exempt the *burgus* of Saint-Serge, in the environs of Angers, from all taxes normally owed to the count. Bishop Renaud made particular mention in this exemption of the count's right to obtain fodder for his horses and beds for his men. Since Saint-Serge belonged to the cathedral of Angers, Renaud clearly had the right to exempt the burgus from what it owed the bishop. But the bishop's effort to deprive Fulk of the traditional *consuetudines* owed to the state was clearly illegal.[99] This act, given Renaud's presence in the entourage of Odo II, whom the bishop addressed in affectionate terms, assumes a sinister regard. Nor was Renaud alone in acting to deprive the Angevin count of valuable logistic support and other resources, for he handed over this document for strengthening by his own fideles and *amici.*[100] One of these amici was Odericus Silvaticus, who held the curtis and church of Saint-Saturnin from Fulk. Odericus was from Champtocé, which is on the Loire River only twenty kilometers downriver from Rochfort-sur-Loire and thirty kilometers east of Champtoceaux; both of these strongholds were controlled by Viscount Fulcoius, the bishop's brother.[101]

A further glimpse of the pattern of Bishop Renaud's behavior during Maurice's reign can be gained from the prelate's relations with Abbot Robert of Saint-Florent, who had spearheaded the Blésois diplomatic initiative against Fulk since 987. For instance, Renaud agreed with Robert to exempt Saint-Florent from all disturbances and investigations concerning those structures that had been built or would be built in the future which were in the jurisdiction of Saint-Florent but within the diocese of Angers.[102] On another occasion the bishop acted at the abbot's request to curb the activities of Fulk's vassalus Walter, the castellan of Montsoreau, who was harassing Saint-Florent's dependents and lands. Renaud ordered Walter to surrender what he had seized from Saint-Florent and threatened anyone who violated this order with excommunication.[103]

Abbot Robert also acted on his own to punish Fulk's vassali who had been able to obtain beneficia from Saint-Florent because of the Angevin count's "persuasiveness." For example, Count Maurice, *pacis amator*, was apparently unable to force Abbot Robert to ensure that Fulk's *vassalus* Drogo, the son of Roho, be given possession of his late father's holdings at Meigné and Distré. Roho had received these beneficia from Abbot Robert at the intervention of his lord the *fortissimus miles* Fulk Nerra.[104]

The collusion of Bishop Renaud, Abbot Robert, and the Blésois count Odo II is perhaps most clearly illustrated by their combined efforts in weakening Anjou's western frontier. Bishop Renaud worked effectively to undermine the Angevin position in the Mauges region on the border with Nantes by alienating his allods there and thus making them unavailable to Fulk to use as rewards for his supporters. Viscount Fulcoius, who had the major responsibility for defending Anjou's western frontier from the strongholds he commanded at Rochefort-sur-Loire and Champtoceaux, because of his very close ties with his brother Bishop Renaud, clearly could not be relied upon to stop Fulk's enemies from moving eastward into the Loire valley and attacking Angers itself.[105] The breakdown of Angevin defenses in this sector and the weakening of Fulk's position in the Mauges region benefited Abbot Robert, who was also abbot of Saint-Florent-le-Vieil and was intent on recovering lands of that monastery's fisc held by supporters of the Angevin count.[106]

Also dangerous to Anjou were the ambitions of Count Geoffrey-Berengar, who held Rennes from Odo II and who took advantage of Maurice's lack of martial effectiveness to do away with Count Judicaël of Nantes. Judicaël's position had been severely undermined by the defection of Bishop Herveus of Nantes, who made frequent appearances in the entourage of Odo II.[107] The close ties by marriage of both Geoffrey-Berengar and Odo II to the ducal house of Normandy set the stage for a grand alliance against the Angevins which could be at least as great a threat as that posed by the recently dissolved Capetian-Blésois axis.

By mid-1004 Anjou appeared in great peril. Budic, the ten-year-old son and successor of Judicaël, was a prisoner at Nantes. This strategically located stronghold was in effect ruled by Bishop Walter of Nantes, Herveus's successor, who was Count Geoffrey-Berengar's man and had been raised as a *miles* in the comital court at Rennes.[108] With Nantes in Geoffrey-Berengar's hands and the Mauges defenses in disarray, it remained only for Count Odo II to arrange with his brother-in-law, Richard of Normandy, for a coordinated attack on Anjou from both the west and the east.

Such a major offensive never materialized, even though the Angevin state at that time was under the sole leadership of the ineffectual Count Maurice. We can only suggest that in consideration of the vital interests of his new queen's family, King Robert II acted or was perceived by the count of Blois and the duke of Normandy to have acted in support of the Angevins. For example, the king's support for the Angevins can be read into his establishment of Herveus of Buzançais as treasurer of Saint-Martin of Tours. Herveus was the brother of Geoffrey Greymantle's longtime supporter, Robert of Buzançais, and the uncle of Fulk's loyal castellans at Amboise. He was selected as the successor to Walter, who had been in the *mouvance* of the count of Blois.[109] King Robert's abandonment of Queen Bertha and the rupture of the Capetian-Blésois axis gave Bishop Renaud of Paris, Count Bouchard of Vendôme's son, no politically compelling reason to remain aloof from his erstwhile brother-in-law.[110] The resumption of diplomatic relations between Anjou and Vendôme under the leadership of the aged Count Bouchard greatly strengthened the northeastern region of the Angevin state and clearly was a strategic deterrent to any effort Odo II might make against Fulk's interests. The memory of the defeat of Odo I by the counts of Vendôme and the Gâtinais at Orsay a little more than a decade earlier in similar strategic circumstances may well have influenced the decision of Odo II and his advisors not to attack Anjou.

Despite the defection of the powerful Renaud family and of some of the bishop's amici, it is clear that the great majority of Fulk's fideles remained loyal to the comital house. Men such as Alberic of Vihiers, Roger of Loudun, Walter of Montsoreau, Roger the Devil of Mon- trésor, Sulpicius and Archembaud of Buzançais, Cadilo of Blaison, and Suhard of Craon continued to support the Angevin count during this crisis and appear as prominent members of Fulk's entourage after his re- turn from the Holy Land. This continued loyalty gives us no reason to doubt the observation in the *Gesta Consulum* that Maurice was gener- ous in rewarding relatives, men like Alberic, and *fideles* like Roger, Cadilo, and their confreres with beneficia.[111]

Fulk returned from Jerusalem in 1004 and on his way north at- tended the Christmas court held by his cousin Adalmode and her hus- band Duke William of Aquitaine at the monastery of Maillezais.[112] Probably at this time Fulk began negotiations with Bishop Islo of Saintes which appear to have culminated not long afterward in the mar- riage of the Angevin count's half-brother Maurice to the prelate's sister. Islo's family were hereditary viscounts with close connections to the counts of Périgord and Toulouse. One of Islo's brothers held the vis- county of Mussidan and another was abbot of Brantôme and of Saint- Cybard and bishop of Angoulême. The former, Aimery, had succeeded his father while the latter, Grimoard, had been favored by Fulk Nerra's cousin-in-law, Aldebert of Périgord, with the monastery of Brantôme and by the Angevin count's brother-in-law, William Taillefer, count of Angoulême, with the monastery of Saint-Cybard and the bishopric of Angoulême. It seems that Fulk harbored some idea of giving Maurice responsibilities at Saintes where the Angevin family network was well positioned to help him.[113]

During the eight years that King Robert's Blésois-connection had deprived Fulk of royal support, the Angevin count had learned a valu- able lesson: he could survive and even succeed on occasion with the monarch as his adversary. The balance sheet at the end of 1004 seems to have favored Fulk, despite the disastrous weakening of Anjou's west- ern frontier, which was in greater peril than it had ever been in Fulk's reign. Geoffrey-Berengar controlled Nantes and was a loyal supporter of the count of Blois. Both men were closely allied with the Normans, who traditionally had been enemies of the Angevin count.

In the Angevin heartland the Renaud clan, which intermittently had caused trouble for Fulk since Geoffrey Greymantle's death, defected and at least in the short run deprived the Angevin count of valuable and strategically located lands in the Mauges region. This defection also seriously weakened the defenses of Anjou's western frontier by undermining comital authority over the strongholds at Rochefort-sur-Loire and Champtoceaux. Bishop Renaud alienated comital resources under the control of Saint-Serge and renewed his public attack on the use of church property for secular purposes. The prelate's willingness to sustain this radical position by excommunicating offenders threatened the count's use of church *faculatates* to reward his fideles. Finally, Bishop Renaud's support for Abbot Robert against Fulk's men enabled Saint-Florent, a Blésois house, to encroach further on Angevin interests.

On the broader political stage Angevin penetration of Maine was halted and advance into the Touraine blunted. In addition, Fulk was not able to recover earlier losses in the Gâtinais and at Château-Landon. In addition, the Angevin family network also suffered. The pope's attack on Bishop Stephen, Guy's successor at le Puy and Fulk's cousin, weakened the Angevin position there too. Then the Angevins suffered a setback at Chalon where Maurice lost out to his half-brother Hugh. With Aldebert's death, the Angevin connections with both la Marche and Périgord were virtually severed.

On the positive side, the enemy did not succeed in launching a coordinated invasion of Angevin territory. In the Angevin heartland the overwhelming majority of the count's fideles remained loyal, and Fulk retained control of the monastery of Saint-Aubin, which had been hostile at his accession in 987. The execution of Countess Elizabeth and the "revolt" at Angers seem to have had no noteworthy effect, except for the damage caused by the fire. The results for Fulk, in fact, were positive rather than negative. Fulk's daughter remained the heiress to the Vendômois. Fulk was free to marry again, and Maurice, who at one time may have been a pawn in a Capetian-Chalonais plot to displace Fulk, was made a valuable member of the Angevin count's entourage.

Throughout the Angevin state Fulk Nerra's men continued loyally to hold the older Angevin strongholds such as Loudun, Amboise, Loches, la Haye, and Villentrois. Newly built or newly acquired strongholds such as the great fortified urbs of Saintes and lesser ones such as Montbazon, Mirebeau, Vihiers, Montsoreau, and Nouâtre were also loyally held by Fulk's men. These strongholds, which protected Fulk's resources and lines of communication between Angers in the west and his holdings in the east, also helped to outline the frontiers of the Angevin state while revealing a strategic system of defense in depth which would prove a formidable obstacle to potential adversaries.[114]

The Angevin family network, though it suffered some setbacks, also won several remarkable victories. Through the use of the family's broadly based power in Aquitaine and north of the Loire, the Angevins maneuvered Duke William of Aquitaine into a marriage with Fulk's cousin Adalmode. As part of this settlement, Fulk received Saintes and numerous strongholds in both the Saintonge and Loudunais. In order to strengthen further the Angevin position in Aquitaine, Fulk arranged for his sister to marry Count William of Angoulême. Fulk's alliances with Archbishop Dagobert of Bourges and with the counts of Nevers and the Gâtinais also supported the Angevin cause. Finally, the Angevins won a major diplomatic victory when the Capetian-Blésois axis dissolved and Fulk Nerra's cousin Constance married King Robert II. An "Angevin" queen had replaced a Blésois queen on the throne of the French kingdom.

CHAPTER FOUR

Fulk Nerra's Rapprochement with King Robert II

Fulk Nerra's pilgrimage to the Holy Land had a positive effect on his state of mind. In a letter to the archbishop of Tours he explained that he had quieted the "fear of Gehenna" that had terrified him after the vast quantities of Christian blood he had shed in various battles. He observed that he returned from the pilgrimage "in high spirits" and that he was "exultant." As a result, Fulk said, his "ferocity was replaced by a certain sweetness for a time." He continued: "Thus, [I] conceived in my mind the idea of constructing a church on the best site among the lands that [I] held by [my] own legal right so that monks would be joined together there and pray day and night for the redemption of [my] soul."[1]

Fulk's plan to build a new monastery from the ground up was a complete departure from his previous policy of restoring older houses. The latter policy Fulk had inherited from his father, Geoffrey Greymantle, who had done much restoration but had made no new foundations.[2] Indeed, less than a decade before his pilgrimage, Fulk had sought papal support for a policy of restoring "ancient and destroyed monasteries rather than building new ones from the foundations." In hopes of getting Pope Gregory V to sustain this Angevin policy, Fulk gave a *mandatum* to Abbo of Fleury to plead the case in Rome. Although Abbo did not support Fulk's policy, the abbot of Fleury nevertheless presented it to the pope.[3]

For how long Fulk restrained his "normal ferocity" is not clear. When he returned to Anjou early in 1005 after having been away for more than a year, we may assume that he was appraised of the state of both domestic and foreign affairs in considerable detail. (He probably had not received regular dispatches from home while he was traveling or while in the Holy Land.) High on Fulk's immediate agenda was Bishop Renaud's *testamentum* by which the prelate had alienated to Saint-Serge and to Saint Maurice his allods in the Mauges region which, according to the *conventum* agreed upon by Viscount Renaud, his father, and Geoffrey Greymantle, around 972, were to pass into the comital fisc after the younger Renaud's death.[4] According to Bishop Renaud, "Count Fulk and his brother Maurice harassed me with a *calumnia*," and despite the prelate's efforts to make clear to the count and his brother that he was free to dispose of the allods in question however he saw fit, "they persisted in this stubborn behavior." Renaud felt forced into a confrontation with the count and sought by public demonstration to undermine Fulk's claims. The bishop set in motion a trial by ordeal in which he freed a *servus* belonging to the disputed allods and sent him into the forest without protection; his fate would make clear to everyone God's judgment in the affair.[5] The bishop then reported the controversy and his efforts to resolve it: "This *servus*, by the grace of God, was freed on the third day as is the custom, and when he was recalled it was clear to all who were standing nearby that he was *salvus*."[6] As a result of the safe emergence of the *servus* from the customary three-day ordeal—revealing God's judgment in favor of the bishop—Renaud declared:

If anyone, influenced by diabolical instigation, from this day onwards dares to claim anything or introduce a *calumnia*, by the power of God the Omnipotent Father and the Son and the Holy Ghost and of Mary the holy mother of God and of Peter, the first of the apostles, and of all the saints of God, by our authority may he be damned and excommunicated and cut off from all of the faithful eternally.[7]

A careful reading of the threats employed in this act reveals the bishop's inflexibility. Any perpetrator of a violation of God's judgment would find it difficult to "buy" himself out of trouble with money and/or penance. Renaud left no basis for compromise.[8]

Before Bishop Renaud orchestrated the ordeal, the argument with Fulk had been over property. Problems of this type were frequently worked out with *convenientiae* without declaring a winner.[9] Renaud, however, by carrying out the *judicium Dei*, created an impasse. Fulk Nerra needed the Mauges allods to support the *milites* who were to be used to protect Anjou's western frontier and to strengthen Angevin control of Nantes. Renaud, who had been pursuing a reform policy, needed the Mauges allods to sustain the reconstruction of Saint-Serge. No less important, moreover, appears to have been the bishop's need to demonstrate to the community and perhaps even to himself that he was not guilty of simony. By demonstrating in a trial by ordeal the "falsity" of Fulk's claims about the conventum, Bishop Renaud was no doubt trying to "prove," as may be inferred from his account of the ordeal that Viscount Renaud had not purchased the see of Angers for his son from Geoffrey Greymantle.[10]

The impasse between Fulk and the bishop was broken late in May or perhaps very early in June 1005, only a few months after the Angevin count's return home, when the prelate departed Anjou on a pilgrimage to the Holy Land in the company of his brother Viscount Fulcoius.[11] Though it might be illuminating to speculate on the interplay of spiritual and political motives that brought the aging prelate to decide that a pilgrimage, which amounted to "holy exile," was preferable to a continued struggle with the Angevin count, we can merely emphasize that from a political perspective two major figures whose loyalty to Fulk had been questionable for many years suddenly disappeared from the scene.[12]

Fulk was now in a position to seize the Mauges allods without serious opposition and to confiscate the viscomital beneficium that extended over much rich and strategically located land to the west of the urbs of Angers.[13] In addition, Fulk could regain possession of the strongholds at Rochefort-sur-Loire and Champtoceaux from Fulcoius and take control of the viscomital office. Furthermore, without a bishop to protect the canons of the cathedral church of Angers, Fulk was well positioned to manipulate them to gain greater access to the facultates of Saint Maurice and its dependencies. Finally, the very extensive lands as well as the other resources of the Renaud family were open to intensive comital exploitation.[14]

Fulk's rather easy and apparently decisive victory over the Renauds, which was accomplished no later than early June 1005, may be explained in part by a complex of developments over which neither the Angevin count nor the bishop had any direct control but which the count was alertly prepared to exploit. Bishop Renaud had during Fulk's absence established a close personal relationship with Odo II of Blois, and the prelate's collaboration with Abbot Robert of Saint-Florent had the effect of strengthening the Blésois position at Angevin expense.

After Fulk's return from the Holy Land, however, Odo was unable to provide support to the Renauds in their conflict with the Angevin count because the count of Blois was engaged in hostilities with his former brother-in-law, Duke Richard II of Normandy. Odo had married Mathilda, Richard's sister in 1004, but she died shortly thereafter without having given birth to a child. Odo hastily remarried but refused to return Mathilda's dowry, which included part of the stronghold of Dreux.[15]

In order to sustain its position against Fulk, the Renaud clan needed not only the active support of Count Odo II of Blois but also, because of holdings in the Mauges region, the cooperation of Count Geoffrey-Berengar of Rennes, who continued to struggle against the Angevins for control of Nantes. But Geoffrey-Berengar, who held Rennes from Odo, was married to Duke Richard's sister and he sided with his Norman brother-in-law.[16] Thus, the involvement of Odo, Richard, and Geoffrey-Berengar in hostilities made it unnecessary for Fulk to worry about the threat of invasion that for much of his reign had absorbed his attention, particularly opposition to Angevin control of Nantes.

The Blésois-Norman conflict, however, is only part of the story. Odo II, as we have seen, lost the support of King Robert II when the king married Fulk's cousin, Constance, thereby realigning the Capetians with the Angevins. Robert, moreover, maintained a firm alliance with Duke Richard during this period, who not only was able to sustain hostilities against Odo II through much of 1005 and 1006 but also mobilized his resources to support the French king in Burgundy and in Flanders.[17] The break between Odo II and King Robert also had significance at Tours. When Robert's man Archbishop Archembaud died late in 1004, Odo acted quickly and filled the vacancy with his loyal supporter Hugh, viscount of Châteaudun. The king, however, appears not to have recognized Odo's candidate until late in the summer of 1007.[18]

Bishop Renaud died at Embrun in southeastern France on 12 June 1005,[19] and Fulk moved decisively to take advantage of this political good luck. He seized the Mauges allods pursuant to the *conventum* made by Geoffrey Greymantle and Viscount Renaud more than three decades earlier and thereby deprived both Saint Maurice and Saint-Serge of the lands willed to them by Bishop Renaud. Both the prelate's *testamentum* and the results of the trial by ordeal were in effect nullified.[20] Fulk undertook to build a stronghold at Montrevault and to distribute the allods to his supporters as beneficia so that as *milites casati* they would have the means for their support while serving to defend Anjou's western frontier. Fulk then established his fidelis, the *miles* Roger the Old, who commanded the count's stronghold at Loudun, as castellan at Montrevault.[21]

Among those to whom Fulk appears to have given beneficia in the Mauges region at about this time were Stephen, the son-in-law of Viscount Hubert of Vendôme, and Fulcherius, who is likely to have been a relative by marriage of Hubert. Fulcherius replaced Fulcoius as castellan of Rochefort-sur-Loire.[22] Also about this time Fulk apparently established Sigebrannus at the newly constructed stronghold of Chemillé on the eastern limits of the Mauges region.[23]

In July 1005 Fulk resumed personal diplomatic relations with his former brother-in-law, Bishop Renaud of Paris, at a *placitum* held at an important stronghold on the Loir called Chartre-sur-le-Loir. Also in attendance at this important meeting was another of Fulk's erstwhile brothers-in-law, Abbot Theobald of Cormery, as well as Fulk's half-brother Maurice, Viscount Hubert of Vendôme, plus many other important Angevin and Vendômois magnates.[24] The presence of Abbot Theobald along with Bishop Renaud of Paris clearly indicates a family reconciliation, which seems to have ended the divisions caused by King Robert's pro-Blésois policy and perhaps exacerbated by the scandal surrounding the death of Countess Elizabeth. It is also likely that at this time the marriage of Fulk's daughter Adele to Bodo of Nevers, the son of Count Landry, was finally given the support of her uncle, Bishop Renaud of Paris. King Robert also arranged for his infant daughter to marry Bodo's brother.[25]

A second and equally important reason for this meeting was the working out of details for the appointment of Hubert, son of Viscount Hubert of Vendôme, as bishop of Angers. In return for the bishopric of Angers, Hubert's father agreed to surrender to Fulk the beneficium at Mazé that he held from the Angevin count. By choosing Hubert as bishop of Angers, however, Fulk did more than strengthen the Angevin position at Vendôme. This position was already strong since Viscount Hubert was Fulk's fidelis and indeed the viscount's father-in-law, Viscount Fulcradus of Vendôme, had been Geoffrey Greymantle's fidelis. This appointment, which tied the vicomital family of Vendôme more closely to Fulk, had the additional benefit of strengthening the Angevin count's ties with the viscomital family of le Mans and with the house of Bellême. Indeed, Viscount Hubert belonged to that viscomital family which along with the Bellêmes had a role in disposing of the see of le Mans. Geoffrey Greymantle had extended Angevin power in this direction in 971 when he helped the viscomital house of le Mans and the lords of Bellême put their relative in the episcopal chair at le Mans. Finally, Geoffrey who was the lord of the strategically located stronghold of Sablé on the Anjou-Maine frontier and a longtime supporter of both Geoffrey Greymantle and Fulk Nerra was the brother of the viscount of le Mans. The choice of Hubert as bishop of Angers placed at Fulk's side a man whose extended family network provided ready access to the power structure in Maine and furthered the long-term goals of making the Loir River the northern frontier of the Angevin state and establishing Angevin control over the count of Maine.[26]

Also at this *placitum* Fulk apparently promised Abbot Theobald of Cormery that he would not permit his garrisons at the newly constructed strongholds of Montbazon and Mirebeau to exploit illegally the monastery's human and material resources that were within easy reach of these strategically located fortifications. Well before 1 May 1006 Fulk had King Robert confirm this promise concerning Cormery, making clear a public reconciliation between the monarch and the Angevin count.[27] On 13 June 1006, a year and a day after Bishop Renaud's death, Hubert of Vendôme was consecrated bishop of Angers. Hubert demonstrated his support by making no claim on behalf of either Saint Maurice or Saint-Serge to the allods given them by his predecessor but seized by Fulk and granted to his *milites*.[28]

The year 1005-1006 also saw another assertive act by Fulk, but this time on the far eastern frontier of the Angevin state and to the south of the Loire. Seventeen kilometers east-southeast of Amboise, Fulk seized lands held by Gelduin of Saumur from the archiepiscopal fisc of Tours; there he built a stronghold that he named Montrichard.[29] Command of this new fortification, which dominated the lower valley of the Cher, Fulk entrusted to Roger the Devil. Roger was already established at the stronghold of Montrésor, so these two fortifications organized under a unified command virtually nullified the offensive capability of troops based at the Blésois stronghold of Saint-Aignan, eighteen kilometers to the southeast, to challenge Angevin communications between Amboise and Loches from the east.[30] Five years earlier Fulk had constructed the stronghold of Montbazon to protect the route from Amboise to Loches against attack from the west.[31]

Fulk also tried to avoid the communications problems that could result from Odo II's possession of Tours by fortifying in the Touraine a northerly route between Amboise and Angers that ran through Morand

and Semblançay. At Morand Fulk fortified a *domus* on one of his estates where he knew provisions would be available.[32] Semblançay, where Fulk also built a stronghold, was thirty-three kilometers to the west and was linked to the stronghold of Château-la-Vallière, twenty-three kilometers farther to the west. The latter was held by Fulk's *homo,* Hugh of Alluyes, who also held the fortification at Saint-Christophe.[33]

These expenditures of extensive resources to build fortifications throw into high relief Fulk's strategic thinking. Prior to the capture of Tours in 996, Fulk had gained a measure of success by avoiding battle when possible and by building strongholds like Langeais that did not pose an overt challenge to an enemy position. Fulk took this indirect strategy so seriously that the first stronghold he built, albeit a minor one to the east of Bourgueil, was constructed in secret. When Fulk shifted to a direct strategy and captured Tours, he soon learned that the overt approach galvanized enemy opposition. Perhaps in reaction, Fulk returned to an indirect strategy and after 997 abandoned for almost twenty years any effort to pose a direct challenge to Tours.

As the siting of the strongholds at Montbazon, Montrichard, Montrésor, Morand, and Semblançay indicate, the maintenance of secure communications was a primary consideration for Fulk. The Angevins already had substantial communication problems along the chain of strongholds at Buzançais, Châtillion-sur-Indre, and Loches, which dominated the middle reaches of the Indre valley, and those at Preuilly-sur-Claise, la Haye-Descartes, and Nouâtre, which dominated the middle stretch of the Claise-Vienne river chain. Fulk's route from Angers to the east first went thirty-eight kilometers south to the stronghold at Vihiers, then turned east-southeast fifty kilometers to Loudun. From Loudun the route continued thirty-seven kilometers to Nouâtre, and from there it was only thirty-six kilometers to Loches, which was located thirty-one kilometers south of Amboise.

This route had serious flaws, particularly along the fifty-kilometer stretch between Vihiers and Loudun. A horse could not be expected to travel much in excess of thirty-five kilometers during the course of a day and remain battle-ready. At distances of about fifty kilometers, the horses would not have been able to continue the journey or to fight on the following day. Thus it would be necessary to camp in the open for the night. But neither exhausting the horses nor camping in the open were viable alternatives. Moreover, for a relief force to cover ground quickly, it could not be encumbered with the *impedimenta* required to establish a fortified encampment; ox carts could make no more than fifteen kilometers per day, and the Angevins did not use horses for draught purposes.[34]

The fortified western links of the Angevin route to Loches, Buzançais, and even Montrésor, Villentrois, and Graçay had been forged rather hastily by Geoffrey Greymantle in the wake of Odo I's change of policy toward the Angevins. Geoffrey established his relative Alberic at Vihiers in the early 980s, Guenno of Nouâtre first appears in the Angevin entourage in the summer of 985, and the tower at Loudun had been built earlier for different purposes. The weakest part of Geoffrey's route was that problematical fifty-kilometer stretch between Vihiers and Loudun. When Geoffrey established Alberic at Vihiers, the Angevin count was a close ally of Viscount Aimery, whose stronghold at Thouars was twenty-two kilometers west of Loudun and twenty-eight kilometers southeast of Vihiers.[35] But when Viscount Aimery of Thouars defected from the Angevin cause in 994, Fulk found the southern route seriously endangered. The distance between Vihiers and Loudun was too long to be negotiated safely in a day by a relief column that could also remain battle-ready. The region was easily penetrated by the newly hostile men of Thouars from the south and by the men of the Saumurois, who were led by Odo's loyal supporter Gelduin, from the north. Under the pressure of this dual threat, Fulk was apparently willing to abandon his indirect strategy and seize the opportunity offered by Odo I's death to attack Tours in 996. If Fulk could control the Loire valley from Montsoreau to Tours, he would not have to bypass the Saumurois along the newly endangered southern route; instead, he could travel to Langeais and Tours by the northern route through Baugé (without having to go so far out of his way to the east as Amboise) and then turn south toward the valley of the Indre and Loches.

When Fulk lost Tours in 997, he needed to find another safe way to reach Loudun from Vihiers. Fulk compensated for the problem posed by the hostility of the viscount of Thouars by building the stronghold at Passavant to the east of Vihiers where he placed as castellan Bouchard, a member of the Bouchard family of Angers; he also relied for protection on the old *confugium* and fosse at Montaglan only twenty-five kilometers west of Loudun and eighteen kilometers east of Passavant.[36]

A policy of castle building that was primarily defensive during the period of the first Capetian-Blésois axis now developed an offensive and indeed an aggressive character during the period of Fulk's rapprochement with King Robert. For example, the strongholds of Semblançay and Morand undoubtedly were part of a defended route between Angers and Amboise. Morand, however, was located seventeen kilometers north of Amboise. If Fulk had wanted only to provide a secure position north of Amboise and on the direct route to Semblançay, he probably would not have built at Morand but somewhere roughly eight kilometers farther south. His choice of Morand was quite likely influenced by the location of Vendôme, only twenty-eight kilometers north of Morand. Thus the fortification at Morand helped to secure this north-south route between Amboise and Vendôme as well as provide a fortified step in his east-west link between Amboise and Angers.

Choosing to fortify Morand, Fulk also may have taken into consideration the short distance—less than a half day's travel—between this new stronghold and Amboise. Defensively, Morand could serve as a base from which any enemy siege emplacements around Amboise could be harassed, and similarly any effort to besiege Morand could be relieved from Amboise. Offensively, the fortification at Morand was positioned so that forces established there could harass communications and supply lines between Odo II's strongholds of Blois and Château-Renault. Morand sat only nine kilometers east of the Blésois stronghold at Château-Renault, and Fulk may well have considered Morand a useful base camp for a siege of Château-Renault. Troops and supplies could easily be moved north from Amboise and, with slightly greater difficulty, south from Vendôme to Morand; the stronghold could also serve as a shelter for a prepositioned reserve to cut off any force sent from Blois to relieve Château-Renault.

Just as Fulk probably built the tower at Montbazon to strengthen Angevin control of Cormery, he probably built Montrésor at about the same time to protect his interest in the monastery of Villeloin five kilometers to the southeast on the Indroye. Villeloin, whose fisc Fulk controlled, lay only eighteen kilometers southwest of Odo's stronghold at Saint-Aignan, a stronghold that helped give the count of Blois control of the middle reaches of the Cher valley east to the monastery at Vierzon. The garrison at Saint-Aignan was clearly in a position to despoil Villeloin and its lands. Looking at a map suggests that troops from the Angevin stronghold at Villentrois, ten kilometers southeast of Saint-Aignan and nineteen kilometers northeast of Villeloin, were in a position to interdict enemy raiders. But the route between Saint-Aignan and Villeloin passed through the great forest of Brouard. The terrain therefore favored invaders, who could choose the time and place for their attack; defenders stationed at Villentrois would be hampered by the terrain in their efforts to hunt down the enemy. By building a stronghold at Montrésor, Fulk provided direct protection for the monastery and lands of Villeloin.

The essentially defensive nature of Montrésor received an added offensive dimension a few years later in 1005–1006 when Fulk built the stronghold of Montrichard on the Cher only twenty kilometers downriver from Saint-Aignan. With Villentrois, Montrésor, and Montrichard all in place, Saint-Aignan was cut off on three sides; its only open line of communication was north to Blois, thirty-eight kilometers away. When construction at Montrichard was complete, Fulk placed it under the command of Roger the Devil, who already was castellan of Montrésor. This posting suggests that Fulk may have been trying to coordinate Angevin strategy in the region, perhaps specifically against Saint-Aignan.[37]

The suggestion that Fulk's policies in the period of rapprochement with King Robert were more aggressive than they had been earlier is given some support by the recruitment of Lancelinus of Beaugency. Lancelinus, a fidelis of Count Odo II, held the important and strategic stronghold of Beaugency only thirty kilometers up the Loire River from Blois. When Viscount Hubert of Vendôme returned the lands of Mazé that he held from Fulk in return for the bishopric of Angers for young Hubert, the Angevin count gave the curtis at Mazé to Lancelinus. Clearly, if Lancelinus were to move firmly into Fulk's *mouvance*, Odo's position would be greatly weakened at Blois itself.[38]

Fulk's offensives following his return from the Holy Land also affected the policies of Abbot Robert of Saint-Florent, who found himself in a particularly difficult position. Fulk's supporters, led by Alberic of Vihiers and his fideles, ravaged the lands of Saint-Florent and imposed various new taxes (*malae constuetudines* and *exactiones*) on the dependents of Saint-Florent. Without the active support of Odo II, who as we have seen was occupied with the duke of Normandy, Abbot Robert was unable to stop the Angevins. Nor could Robert rely on the help of Gelduin of Saumur who coveted the resources of Saint-Florent for himself.[39]

Three documents issued before the end of the Blésois-Norman conflict reveal a significant policy change undertaken by Abbot Robert in an effort to preserve the lands of Saint-Florent. According to one of these documents, Robert requested that Fulk Nerra put an end to the *pervasiones* and *malae consuetudines* that his *homines* had imposed on lands that were either under the jurisdiction or in the possession of Saint-Florent. In response to Abbot Robert's request, Fulk issued a charter making known to a group of his fideles, in their presence, that they were to give up the said *pervasiones* and *malae consuetudines* and in addition that they were to make a solemn promise (*sponsio*) to God and to Fulk that they would on no occasion, whether *in hoste* or *sine hoste,* carry off any property or attack any of the homines of Saint-Florent or bring any false claims against the monastery or its holdings. Fulk then indicated that if any of his fideles ignored this promise and raised "old false claims" or developed "new false claims," not only would the offender incur the wrath of God but comital punishment would also be meted out.[40]

The second document makes clear that the abbot complained to the count that his fidelis Alberic of Vihiers was oppressing homines under Saint-Florent's jurisdiction and under the pretext of implementing the *commendisia,* the complex of military-related imposts levied on the men and resources within a particular jurisdiction, by the officials of the Angevin count, imposing new *exactiones, consuetudines,* and unjust *leges.* Fulk then ordered that Alberic's wife, his son, and his fideles (Alberic had apparently died during the course of the negotiations or perhaps a short time earlier) to give up the *malae consuetudines* imposed and, for the health of the soul of their lord (*senior*) Alberic, make amends to Saint-Florent.[41]

An obvious question is prompted by these two documents: how did Abbot Robert, despite his weakened political position, manage to convince a traditionally hostile Fulk Nerra to make this impressive effort to control the depredation of Saint-Florent's resources by the count's fideles? The third charter in the group suggests an answer. Here we learn that Abbot Robert had received a request from Drogo, vassalus of Fulk, for the church located at Meigné and a mill located at Distré. Drogo's father, Roho, had held this church and the mill from Saint-Florent, but while Maurice had ruled in Anjou during Fulk's pilgrimage to the Holy Land, Abbot Robert had not passed these beneficia on to the son after the death of the father. Therefore, sometime later Drogo appeared with his *senior,* "the most noble Count Fulk," to convince Abbot Robert that the grant should be made. Abbot Robert apparently recognized the good sense of making the grant to Drogo. In the charter confirming this grant Abbot Robert makes the startling admission that Fulk Nerra is also his *senior.*[42]

Some time between about mid-1005 and the peace between Odo II and Duke Richard of Normandy, which was achieved in 1007,[43] Abbot Robert seems to have concluded that Saint-Florent's interests could best be served by recognition of Fulk Nerra as his *senior*. Thus the abbots of Saint-Florent abandoned—for the moment, at least—a sixty-year tradition of adherence to the counts of Blois who appointed them. The radical changes so recently manifested in the political climate— the breakup of the Capetian-Blésois axis, the death of Bishop Renaud, and above all Odo II's involvement in a conflict with the Normans— made Abbot Robert's course of action a reasonable one.[44]

For Fulk Nerra the recognition accorded him by Abbot Robert meant that control of the richest monastery in the west of France between Marmoutier to the east and Saint-Aubin to the west was within his grasp. Fulk wasted little time in taking advantage of this opportunity and saw to it that Abbot Robert granted to Drogo the beneficia at Meigné and at Distré south of the Loire in the strategic border region between Anjou, Poitou, and the Mauges. In addition, Robert was compelled to recognize Drogo's possession of the stronghold of Châteaupanne and he also found it necessary to give to this vassalus of Fulk in beneficium those lands belonging to Saint-Florent that were adjacent to the important castellum at Châteaupanne.[45]

Like the fortifications at Montrevault, Châteaupanne strengthened the Angevin position in the Mauges region. These two strongholds viewed together may be seen to have initiated Fulk's plans to dominate the remains of Saint-Florent le-Vieil, whose well-endowed fisc had been thoroughly disorganized by the Viking invasions.[46] Finally, Châteaupanne, which was on the west bank of the Loire only thirteen kilometers downriver from Rochefort-sur-Loire, provided another link in the defense of Anjou's western frontier while at the same time it strengthened Fulk's line of communication in the lower Loire valley with Nantes, over which he claimed ultimate control as dominus.

The recruitment of Lancelinus of Beaugency and Abbot Robert of Saint-Florent appears to have been part of a general policy on Fulk's part of trying to win away some of Odo II's most important fideles. Indeed, about this time a certain Renaud, a member of the Plastulfus family traditionally dependent on the counts of Blois, accepted lands from Fulk at Saint-Saturnin just to the west of Angers itself.[47] It is interesting that the lands Fulk granted to both Lancelinus and Renaud were close to Angers while the principal holdings of these men were well beyond the frontiers of the Angevin pagus. Fulk seems to have been acting cautiously so that if either of these new fideles should not perform as expected he could easily repossess the beneficia he had granted them.

Fulk's vigorous activities following his return from the Holy Land were highlighted by his marriage to Hildegarde, an *illustra puella* from Lorraine who was descended from royalty.[48] Although no contemporary source indicates why Fulk chose as his wife a woman from so far to the east rather than one from closer to home, a review of the political circumstances permits some reasonable hypotheses. In either late 1005 or early 1006 (before 1 May), Fulk and King Robert II were publicly reconciled, and the king referred to the Angevin count as his *fidelissimus* supporter.[49] The king's reconciliation with Fulk, as we have seen, coincided with a period in which relations between Robert and Odo II of Blois were poor. At this time the king met on the banks of the Meuse with Henry II, the German emperor, to discuss issues of mutual interest.[50] It is likely that one of these issues concerned Odo II's holdings in the Verdunois region of upper Lorraine which he had inherited from Odo I and from which the latter had levied a conspicuous force of fighting men in 994.[51]

King Robert's diplomatic exchanges with the Germans, of which the Meuse meeting is the best documented, are likely to have brought Fulk Nerra to Lorraine and to have prompted his interest in Hildegarde. More to the point, Fulk needed a wife who could provide a male heir and his choice of a woman from a prominent family in Lorraine might perhaps be seen to have had a diplomatic and strategic purpose as well, especially because of the Blésois holdings in the Verdunois, which could be threatened by Fulk's in-laws if the count of Blois chose to mount military operation against the Angevin count in the west.[52] This type of long-range strategic thinking was not foreign to the Angevin counts, who as early as the 940s had maintained an alliance with the house of Amiens-Vexin-Valois, which was in a position to threaten the eastern frontiers of Normandy if the Norman duke committed himself too vigorously against Anjou in the west.[53]

Fulk's marriage to Hildegarde was consummated no later than mid-January 1006 and is very likely to have taken place in the context of a festive Christmas court in December 1005,[54] when the count began seriously to explore the particulars of building a church where monks would be joined together in order to pray day and night for the redemption of his soul. The "high spirits" and "exultant" feeling that replaced his "ferocity" after he returned from the Holy Land seem to have returned at the time of his marriage.[55]

Fulk's decision to depart from traditional Angevin policy by building new religious houses was set in motion by a series of experiences beginning on 27 June 992 when he won a decisive and crucial victory over Conan of Rennes at the battle of Conquereuil. Following this battle Fulk did penance for "the great slaughter of Christians which occurred on the plain at Conquereuil."[56] Early in the winter of 1003 Fulk made his first pilgrimage to the Holy Land because, as he later put it in a letter, "[I] had shed so much blood in many battles in many places, [I] was terrified by the fear of Gehenna [and] went to the sepulchre of the Savior in Jerusalem."[57]

When Fulk decided to build a monastery, he chose as the site a broad plain about a mile from the castrum of Loches in the southeastern part of the Touraine. This land Fulk held in allodial tenure, and it was called *Belli Locus,* place of battle. Belli Locus was the designated area where trial by battle traditionally was carried out for the judicial district administered by the Angevin praepositus based in the castrum of Loches.[58] It seems that Fulk selected Belli Locus for the site of his new monastery because in pre-Crusade Europe a tradition had developed that the conversion of a field of battle to religious purposes evoked the principle that a *judicium Dei* had been rendered which justified the cause of the victor in spilling blood, even Christian blood.[59] Since Fulk could not express the complex of sentiments inherent in the building of a "battle abbey" at Conquereuil because the battlefield was in territory under control of the count of Rennes, the Angevin count chose another belli locus where God was well known to render his judgment in favor of the righteous.

It is of particular importance that contemporaries of the battle of Conquereuil, including Conan of Rennes himself, saw this encounter as a judicial duel or trial by combat between two armies, much in the same way William of Poitiers depicts the battle of Hastings between the Norman duke, Fulk's younger contemporary, and King Harold in 1066.[60] Indeed, the battle of Conquereuil itself was arranged as to place and time by Fulk's and Conan's representatives, and there was even some contemporary discussion as to whether before the armies met the Breton count had violated the rules to which the parties previously had agreed.[61] The battle of Conquereuil, at least in its initial stage, was in no sense a traditional military engagement resulting from the tactical maneuverings of two armies.

Discussing the planning of Belli Locus, Fulk recounted how he took seriously the matter of the dedication:

Because [I] always make decisions carefully, [I] consulted religious persons concerning the memory of which of the most powerful saints [I] should honor when [I] establish this church so that they might pray to the Lord for the salvation of [my] soul. [I] was advised by [my] wife, among others, a woman of good counsel. It was suggested that to fulfill my oath the church be dedicated in honor and memory of the Heavenly Virtues which Holy Authority testifies to be more sublime than the Cherubim and Seraphim.[62]

The attention given in this letter to the Cherubim and Seraphim marks Fulk's personal interest in them. This is strongly reinforced by his later charters issued for the monastery where the Cherubim and Seraphim are given the primary place.[63] In addition, this focus on the Cherubim and Seraphim strongly suggests an awareness in Fulk's entourage (perhaps on the part of the count himself) of the writing of Denis the Areopagite, who discoursed on this topic. The source for the Angevins was probably the late ninth-century translation of Denis's Greek text into Latin by John the Scot.[64] That Fulk saw the Cherubim and Seraphim as among the "most powerful" in the celestial hierarchy is important in the present case because of the "military role" they played in the Bible as guards to the entrance of the Garden of Eden (Gen. 3:28) and as the supports and guardians of the Lord's throne (Ezek. 1).

Belli Locus was only one mile from the stronghold of Loches, which Geoffrey Greymantle had done much to develop both as a fortified center whose market dominated the middle reaches of the Indre River and as a religious center focused on the church of Saint Mary, which he had restored with papal support.[65] By choosing Belli Locus as the site for his new foundation rather than a field in some other jurisdiction where the *judicium Dei* was rendered in trial by combat, Fulk appears to have been following his father's lead in continuing the development of this rich and strategically crucial region as a center of Angevin power and influence in the southeastern Touraine on the frontier with Berry.

By early in the spring of 1006 Hildegarde was pregnant, and Fulk decided that she would stay at Loches until the child was born. Through the summer and early autumn of 1006 Fulk supervised the building of a tall and elaborate church at Belli Locus. As the church rose from its foundations, only a mile away the much anticipated heir swelled within the countess. On 14 October 1006 Hildegarde gave birth to a son who was named Geoffrey in honor of his paternal grandfather.[66] It is likely, following contemporary custom, that the child was baptized and formally named soon after birth, probably at Saint Mary at Loches, the only major church in the area and one to which Geoffrey Greymantle had been so generous.[67] Not long after, construction of the church at Belli Locus had advanced sufficiently that preparation for its consecration did not appear unseemly.[68]

The ferocious Angevin count whose natural anger had been calmed, at least for a time, by his pilgrimage to the Holy Land and by his marriage was in high spirits as these two new creations, one of flesh and blood and the other of stone and mortar, sprang to life, manifesting God's favor. Fulk's prayer, likely made more than once, that "Almighty God . . . would bestow sons on us . . . who would be able to inherit after us" had been answered.[69] His desire to find the *suffragium* needed "to destroy the armies of eternal fire" was all but complete in the new church at Belli Locus, which he dedicated to the "Holy Trinity and the holy Archangels and the Cherubim and Seraphim."[70]

A local account written down only somewhat after the event, but which we have no reason to doubt, indicates that Fulk had his baby son Geoffrey handed over to the wife of a blacksmith from Loches to be nursed.[71] At about the same time Fulk issued documents in which he handed over the lands at Belli Locus to the monks established there. He made clear that he strove to provide enough to sustain the community of holy men who would live at Belli Locus and to this end he gave all of the income from all of the taxes due from the land (*omnes coustumae terrae*) which normally would be collected by agents of the comital fisc. Fulk also granted the monks freedom from all of the land taxes that might be owed to the comital fisc from future comital gifts as well as from gifts that might be given by others or on the lands that the monks might buy in the future. Finally, Fulk gave the monks the comital license to hold the market that traditionally was held at the nearby comital villa on Sunday along with the taxes that traditionally went to the comital fisc from sales of all kinds at the market.[72]

Once the basic *acta* were executed to nurse the economic survival of the monastic community at Belli Locus, Fulk had a letter sent to Archbishop Hugh of Tours. In this letter the Angevin count briefly traced the history of his new foundation from the battle-stained reasons for his pilgrimage to the Holy Land, to his vow to build a church where monks would pray for his soul, to the role played by Countess Hildegarde in providing advice, and he concluded:

[I] built a very beautiful church a mile from the castrum of Loches, evidently in the pagus of Tours. And now finally that the work on the basilica is complete,

[I] ask [you], Hugh, archbishop of Tours, in whose diocese this church is located to come as soon as possible to consecrate it in any way that [you] might choose.[73]

Archbishop Hugh, a fidelis of Odo II, vehemently rejected Fulk's request and responded: "[I] cannot associate [myself] in the consecration to the Lord, the vow of a man who has seized more than a few of the estates and serfs of the mother church of [my] bishopric." It is likely that Fulk's usurpations, such as the seizure of the land at Montrichard which Gelduin of Saumur held from the archiepiscopal fisc of Tours and upon which the Angevin count built a stronghold, was in the forefront of Hugh's thinking. Thus the archbishop continued: "It seems more appropriate to [me] that first [you], Fulk, should restore what [you] have taken unjustly and then [you] might be able to give to the just God of justice those of [your] own things that [you] have vowed."[74]

Raoul Glaber, a later contemporary, who seems to be relying in part on information provided by those privy to this exchange and in part on copies of the correspondence, indicates that when Fulk received Hugh's response he was "exceptionally indignant" and that "his old ferocity returned." Fulk responded in turn, showering the uncooperative prelate with "vigorous threats." The Angevin count made it clear that he would seek papal support for his new foundation in order to protect it from the hostility of the archbishop.[75]

To this point in his career Fulk had pursued ecclesiastical policies that were typical of those great magnates like the dukes of Normandy and Aquitaine who operated in a context that scholars have justly characterized as a "lay theocracy."[76] Fulk Nerra, as we have seen, "disposed" of Bishop Renaud of Angers when he became a serious problem and replaced him with a candidate who was likely to be more supportive of comital policies regarding the use of episcopal resources. The Angevin count also exercised close control over the monasteries in the Angevin state by choosing "friendly" abbots. We may recall here how Abbot Guntarius of Saint-Aubin hurriedly took the pilgrimage road and the monastery was punished by the loss of various immunities. Basically, Fulk effectively exploited the resources of the churches and of the monasteries as the needs of the state demanded. This exploitation took place whether his plan to execute a *divisio* by which monastic facultates were recorded in the records of the comital fisc and half were relegated for government use was fully implemented or not. Yet with the exception of the *divisio*, Fulk was not an innovator. He merely followed family policies that sometimes can be traced to Fulk the Red, policies that Geoffrey Greymantle had developed to a fine art.[77]

Control of the archbishopric, however, escaped the Angevins. Whereas the duke of Normandy exercised direct control over the archbishop of Rouen and the duke of Aquitaine more often than not dominated the archbishop of Bordeaux, the Angevin counts had no role in the selection of the archbishop of Tours nor any power over him once he had been elected. Moreover, Fulk had little influence over the bishops, with the exception of those at Angers and le Mans, in regions where he had direct political control or sought to establish such control. In this context, therefore, Fulk's threat to seek papal support for his new foundation at Belli Locus was not unreasonable. Clearly Fulk realized that he had to bypass or undermine Archbishop Hugh's control over those ecclesiastical resources in the Touraine which the Angevins needed to control. But Fulk was not an innovator here, either. Geoffrey Greymantle had obtained support for his church of Saint Mary at Loches from Pope John XV.[78] Indeed, a series of popes during the later tenth and early eleventh centuries—John XIII, John XV, Gregory V, and John XVIII—had pursued a policy of strengthening the role of the papacy in the French kingdom at the expense of the ecclesiastical hierarchy.[79]

Raoul Glaber, who is likely to have had access both to Fulk's documents stored at Belli Locus and to people who witnessed the events under discussion, reported that before the Angevin count set out to see Pope John XVIII at Rome, he went about collecting a large quantity of gold and silver with which to influence a papal decision.[80] Raoul's well-documented antipapal bias, here highlighted by an implication of bribery, should not, however, lead us to discount this report. It was customary during this period and was to remain the norm for many years that the wheels of justice in Rome had to be liberally greased.[81] Fulk's vigorous tax system and his capital liquidity, which enabled him to hire mercenary troops for the Breton campaign in 992, certainly could produce what was required to obtain a favorable hearing at Rome.[82]

Before leaving for Rome Fulk looked once again toward his western frontier and more particularly to the spearhead pointed into Maine by the strongholds of Sablé and Craon. Sablé, held by Geoffrey, brother of the viscount of Maine, dominated the middle reaches of the Sarthe and controlled access from le Mans to Angers through the valley of the

Sarthe. Sablé was well supported in this strategic goal by a constellation of Angevin holdings to the south at Parcé, Precigné, Prignes, Noyau, Vaux, Thorigné, and Champigné. In contrast was the isolation of Craon, which had been held by the Suhard-Warinus family at least since early in the reign of Geoffrey Greymantle and which not only dominated the upper reaches of the Oudon but was Fulk's primary stronghold on the frontier with Rennes. To the south Pouancé, Segré, and Candé were largely undeveloped and the fifty-kilometer distance between Sablé and Craon left the valley of the Mayenne open to enemy penetration almost to the gates of Angers itself.[83]

Although this precarious strategic situation had existed for a long time, the Blésois-Norman war placed matters in a new light that at once presaged danger for the region and opportunity for Fulk. Odo II was firmly allied with the count of Maine, and Count Geoffrey-Berengar of Rennes seems to have been more inclined toward supporting his Norman brother-in-law than his Blésois *senior*. This complex of interests probably convinced Fulk that the frontier of Maine was likely to be an area of vigorous campaigning. Indeed, some sixty years later a very similar political configuration involving the duke William of Normandy, count of Rennes, and count of Maine brought the major powers into conflict in this same region.[84]

If Fulk were to do nothing in this threatening situation he could well expect that his castellans at Craon and Sablé as well as his lesser supporters in the region, lacking leadership and coordination, would be drawn into a conflict in which they had no natural role but as a result of which larger Angevin interests in the region would suffer.[85] Surely, Fulk knew that the count of Rennes and the count of Blois would not hesitate to take advantage of whatever opportunities came their way. If Fulk were to act vigorously, however, he could take advantage of the preoccupation of his adversaries to strengthen his spearhead into Maine and to reinforce his western frontier against Rennes. To this end Fulk had a castellum constructed at Bazouges on the right bank of the Mayenne twenty kilometers east of Craon and thirty kilometers west of Sablé, that is, within a day's ride of either stronghold.[86]

The castellum at Bazouges, which apparently was left under the command of a *villicus* of Fulk's named Guntarius and which later came to be called Château-Gontier, was strategically located to send troops to support Craon should that stronghold on the Breton frontier be attacked by Count Geoffrey-Berengar of Rennes and to support the garrison at Sablé if it were attacked by the count of Maine or his ally, Odo

II. Finally, from a defensive perspective the stronghold at Château-Gontier dominated the middle reaches of the Mayenne and stood directly astride the direct route to Angers from the north, that is, from Normandy. Troops stationed at both Sablé and Craon were well positioned to provide support for the garrison at Château-Gontier should it come under attack. From an offensive point of view, Fulk's bastions at Craon, Château-Gontier, and Sablé pointed the Angevins toward the count of Maine's stronghold of Mayenne only sixty kilometers to the north, the key to western Maine and the gateway to Normandy.[87]

A fact of substantial importance to our understanding of Fulk's ability to utilize various resources in pursuit of his policies is the ownership of the curtis of Bazouges, which belonged to the monastery of Saint-Aubin. Fulk held control of half of this curtis, probably in consonance with the *divisio* of monastic lands which Letaldus had so vigorously condemned in his *Miracles of Saint Martin* at the instigation of Abbot Robert and Bishop Renaud of Angers. Thus in 1007 Château-Gontier was built on monastic lands belonging to Saint-Aubin just as earlier Fulk had built Montbazon on lands belonging to Cormery.[88]

Fulk went to Rome before the end of 1007, before the Alpine passes were closed by winter snows, and gained an audience with Pope John XVIII at which he sought protection for his new foundation. The pope provided Fulk with a bull. The *arenga* lays down the principle that the pope has the obligation to support, strengthen, and protect the church and that this obligation is the case especially when the job is not being done in a satisfactory manner by the local authorities. In short, the *arenga* sets out what appears to be a somewhat obvious but less than specific criticism of the archbishop of Tours. The papal pronouncement follows this lightly veiled criticism of the archbishop with the identification of Count Fulk as "nobilissimus atque strenuissimus" and records that Fulk built the monastery from the ground up "in nomine et honore sanctae et individuae Trinitatis, Patris, et Filius, et Spiritus sancti, atque similiter in honore coelestium agminum super quae Deus assidet, hoc est Cherubim et Seraphim . . . pro suae animae redemptione." The terminology ostensibly follows that found in Fulk's foundation charter, but the image of "the heavenly troops upon whom [lit., over which] God sits" makes the crucial role of the Cherubim and Seraphim as military supporters of the seat of power even clearer than do Fulk's *acta*. The bull then indicates that Fulk has requested of the pope a *privilegium*, which the latter granted.[89]

This privilegium places the *monasterium* under the *tuitio* and *defensio* of the holy apostles Peter and Paul and their successors and it orders that the monastery be free of the *dominatio* of any king, magnate, archbishop, or bishop. The lands and other resources belonging to the monastery, whether given by Fulk or by the Angevin count in the future or by anyone else, are placed under papal protection. Finally, after listing a number of curses and penalties to frighten anyone who might dare to violate the rights of Belli Locus, John's privilegium is extended to indicate that the monastery may in no way be excommunicated by any archbishop or bishop; only the pope or his legates are to have such powers there. Pope John declared that if any rebellious archbishop or bishop should excommunicate that place it is freed by papal authority and those who imposed the excommunication are to be excommunicated in turn.[90]

While Pope John clearly provided the desired protection for Fulk's new monastic foundation, the pope issued no order to have the church consecrated. Apparently John was unwilling to overreach the substantial body of canons which strongly supported episcopal dominance in the diocese, and he may even have been deterred by the Roman law in Justinian's code which gave secular support to this position. Thus Pope John avoided the type of act characterized by "the bishops of the Gauls" as "sacriligious pretention" and the "fruit of blind cupidity"; according to a later contemporary, the prelates contended that such acts introduced "schism" into the Roman church.[91]

When Fulk returned to the west of France, papal bull in hand, he took steps to strengthen his foundation at Belli Locus; these actions hint at the development of a religio-political policy that would be far more aggressive than that pursued by his father. Thus a local tradition affirms that Fulk "consulted religious men concerning religion" and chose Odo, abbot of the monastery of Saint-Genou-de-l'Estrée in the environs of Buzançais, to be the first abbot of Belli Locus. Saint-Genou was firmly within the *mouvance* of Sulpicius and Adalhard, the lords of Buzançais, who were longtime Angevin allies, and the abbey lay within the archdiocese of Bourges.[92] Given Abbot Odo's connections, those religious men whom Fulk consulted probably included Herveus, treasurer of Saint-Martin of Tours and paternal uncle of the lords of Buzançais, and Archbishop Dagobert of Bourges, also a longtime supporter of the Angevins.[93]

Fulk's choice of a Berrichon abbot who maintained his position at Saint-Genou, which was under the jurisdiction of the archbishop of Bourges, while at the same time taking on the responsibility for heading

Belli Locus, which by Pope John's bull would owe obedience only to the papacy, suggests a maneuver to distance the Angevin count's new foundation from the potentially hostile efforts of Archbishop Hugh of Tours. Since Loches is less than ten kilometers from the Berry frontier, perhaps Fulk's advisors envisioned a redrawing of diocesan boundaries that would place Belli Locus within the friendly archbishopric ruled by Dagobert.[94] Such changes, while hardly commonplace, were certainly not impossible. Indeed, at this very time Bishop Hubert of Angers was in the process of adding part of the Mauges region to his bishopric. His effort was in support of Fulk's policy to dominate Saint-Florent-le-Vieil, which belonged to Saint-Florent de Saumur, whose abbot Robert had recently recognized the Angevin count as his *senior*.[95] In a more grandiose fashion the duke of Aquitaine only a few years earlier had transferred the bishopric of Limoges from the jurisdiction of the archbishop of Bourges to that of the archbishop of Bordeaux.[96]

That Herveus of Buzançais, who was Berrichon by origin, should support a policy diminishing the power and prestige of the archbishop of Tours is not inconsistent with his position as treasurer of Saint-Martin. As we have seen, the men of Saint-Martin strongly opposed the expansion of Blésois power to the castrum at Tours and traditionally worked to restrain all efforts to dominate them by the archbishop who controlled the nearby urbs.[97] In a similar vein Archbishop Dagobert of Bourges had good reason to oppose the Blésois and their archbishop at Tours. Odo II not only controlled the archbishopric of Tours but for much of the tenth century his family had provided the archbishops of Bourges. In fact, Dagobert's appointment in 987 by Hugh Capet was probably regarded by contemporaries as thwarting the efforts of the counts of Blois to make Bourges a family archbishopric.[98]

Fulk is reputed to have been very generous in providing Belli Locus with books, holy vestments, vessels for the altar, incense holders, candelabra, crosses, and phylacteries.[99] Some two centuries earlier Einhard had described Charlemagne's largess to the church and unwittingly established a quasiofficial list of the gifts to be offered by those seeking divine approval for their actions.[100] Fulk's largess conforms to Einhard's list; moreover, according to a tradition written down some two centuries after the events represented, Fulk went well beyond providing Belli Locus with the usual liturgical paraphernalia and "above all provided a piece of wood from the cross of the Lord that he miraculously acquired from the sepulchre of the Lord."[101]

In its present form this story seems to refer to events likely to have taken place during Fulk's second pilgrimage to the Holy Land, at which time he is credited with having stolen a piece of stone from the Holy Sepulchre.[102] Tradition, however, does attest to a relic at Belli Locus considered to be a piece of the true cross donated by Fulk Nerra. There is no reason to reject this tradition. In fact, during his visit to Rome in order to secure Pope John's privilegium, Fulk had both the opportunity and the means to obtain "a piece of the cross of the Lord" from the ubiquitous relic dealers who infested the city.[103] Fulk's largess, documented in the *acta* discussed thus far, as well as his religious sentiments, expressed both in letters and charters, reveal a consistent pattern of behavior which his generosity to Belli Locus supports.

The Norman-Blésois conflict combined with King Robert II's repudiation of Bertha and his marriage to Constance had provided Fulk with respite from the threat of attack by a major power. Fulk was therefore able to accomplish the construction at Belli Locus and make a journey to Rome. But when Duke Richard II soundly defeated the combined forces of Odo II and Count Hugh of Maine at the battle of Tillières and shortly thereafter introduced Scandinavian mercenaries into France, King Robert realized that war between Normandy and Blois had to be brought to an end.[104] Robert met with Richard at the Norman monastery of Fécamp at the end of May 1006 and probably met with him again at Senlis early in January 1007.[105] At the end of September 1007 the king met with Odo II and Archbishop Hugh of Tours.[106] These meetings, a sort of personal diplomacy orchestrated by the monarch, finally resulted in the peace of Coudres, which was in place before the end of 1007 and ended the war with a territorial settlement that saw Dreux go to Odo and the land on the Arve River go to Richard.[107]

Whatever King Robert's fundamental reasons for coming to a rapprochement with Odo II may have been—clearly, bringing an end to the war and seeing the Scandinavians leave France were worthwhile ends in themselves—the result of this peace would seriously jeopardize Fulk Nerra's prospects for continued aggrandizement of the Angevin state. Moreover, we may suspect that King Robert was interested in reestablishing his relationship with Odo II's mother Bertha. Queen Constance, Fulk Nerra's cousin, had done her duty for the Capetian house and produced several sons.[108] The king no longer needed her and could indulge his personal feelings for Bertha once again while at the same time not seriously injuring the royal position in the balance of power then prevailing in the west of France.[109]

Abbot Robert of Saint-Florent quickly saw that the new alignment of the powers provided an opportunity for him to escape Fulk's domination and perhaps to preserve the fisc of Saint-Florent from further depredation by the Angevin count. Thus Abbot Robert saw to the forgery of two documents. These *acta* emphasized that the monastery of Saint-Florent belonged to the counts of Blois who were by right the only legitimate lords of the house. These forgeries stipulated that the holdings of Saint-Florent in the Mauges region were exempt from episcopal taxation as well as from comital exactions. Furthermore, the bishop of Angers was forbidden to tax the lands of Saint-Florent in the pagus of Anjou except for synodal dues. Finally, Abbot Robert included a long list of properties that at one time, the forgery alleges, belonged to Saint-Florent. These lands, however, were at the time of the forgery mostly in Fulk Nerra's possession or in the possession of his supporters. The forgery proclaims that anyone other than Saint-Florent holding these lands was to be excommunicated.[110]

Abbot Robert's chances of having the forgeries accepted as genuine by Archbishop Hugh of Tours were good. Hugh was eager to limit the power of Fulk Nerra, who had seized control of archiepiscopal lands, and this opportunity could also be used to impose greater archiepiscopal authority on Hubert of Vendôme, the Angevin count's new bishop of Angers. In addition, Abbot Robert could rely on the support of Count Odo II of Blois, who could not have been pleased by Fulk's efforts to gain control of Saint-Florent. Finally, King Robert, who had made Robert of Saint-Florent the abbot of Saint-Mesmin-de-Micy in 996 and later abandoned him, demonstrated his new support by restoring control of Saint-Mesmin to him. With a hostile archbishop holding the see of Tours and a monarch prepared to support Saint-Florent, these forged documents threatened Fulk's possessions and the possessions he had bestowed on his fideles.[111]

Fulk's situation could be seen to deteriorate as King Robert, Odo II, and perhaps Duke Richard of Normandy turned their undivided attention toward the Angevin count under the pretext of defending the church from despoliation. Following the Council of Chelles on 17 May 1008, the Angevin position was markedly weakened as Queen Constance was set aside and Bertha, Odo II's mother, was reintroduced into the royal bed. Raoul Glaber reports that Fulk viewed the developing crisis as a strategy engineered by Hugh of Beauvais, a loyal supporter of the house of Blois who was marked for special honor at Chelles by the king whom he served as count of the palace.[112]

In response Fulk gathered a group of about a dozen of his trusted followers and instructed them to kill Hugh of Beauvais. The assassins apparently timed their attack on the count of the palace very poorly and they cut him down in the presence of the king while a royal hunting party was in progress. To make matters worse, the murderers were identified as Fulk's men, and when they fled to safety in Anjou, Fulk provided them with protection.[113] The murder precipitated a crisis that could well have led to war. According to Fulbert of Chartres, many people in the royal entourage demanded that the Angevin count be excommunicated and others accused him of treason. Both the monarch and the Angevin count, however, appear to have been willing to negotiate in order to avoid more serious consequences. Fulbert, who served as the king's representative, informed the Angevin count (represented by Abbot Hubert of Saint-Aubin) that a group of "secular judges" (*mundani iudices*) had determined that the murderers had committed a capital crime. The judges also pronounced Count Fulk guilty of treason according to Roman law because he had given protection to murderers.[114]

Abbot Hubert met with representatives of the royal party and conveyed Fulk's promise that he would prove his innocence, presumably by oath but perhaps by combat, if required, in order to satisfy King Robert. According to Fulbert, the king found Fulk's promise insufficient, but apparently Abbot Hubert was not instructed to go beyond conveying Fulk's offer. Fulbert recorded that he persuaded the king to postpone Fulk's excommunication if the Angevin count would agree to the following terms: (1) Fulk must stand trial, that is, he must fulfill the promise made through Abbot Hubert during the first round of negotiations to prove his innocence; (2) Fulk must bring the malefactors who murdered Hugh to trial; and (3) Fulk must repudiate the malefactors to show that he honors his king. If Fulk met these terms, according to Fulbert, King Robert promised not to exact punishment from the murderers in life and limb but would demand compensation only.[115]

King Robert's final demands as articulated by Bishop Fulbert, although they appear lenient, placed Fulk in a difficult position. If the Angevin count acquiesced, his credibility as a dominus who provided protection to his loyal fideles would be undermined. This would be a serious breach of the normally accepted obligations of a lord to his men.[116] Fulk's fideles provided the basic military support that enabled the Angevin count to defend his frontiers and expand his rule over border areas. Geoffrey Greymantle had made clear in word and deed to his sons Fulk and Maurice that the power of the Angevin counts rested on the loyal support of the milites. If, however, Fulk did not submit to the king, he would be excommunicated, perhaps charged with treason, and in all likelihood a coalition of Blésois and royal forces would be launched against the Angevin state.

The charge of treason against Fulk according to Roman law (*Codex Theodosianus*, IX, 14, 3) was vitally important to Fulk, not only because if successfully pursued it could result in the Angevin count's execution and the confiscation of his lands but because King Robert and his advisors, likely informed by Fulbert of Chartres, may be assumed to have seen an advantage in using Roman law to develop their case against the Angevin count. Moreover, we may infer that not only were there secular judges capable of applying the Roman law, as claimed by Fulbert, but that there was an audience capable of responding to its use. Fulk Nerra's representative, Abbot Hubert, must have been able to understand the legal situation, and even if the Angevin count was not prepared to grasp the significance of the application of the Roman law, we must assume that with instruction he would come to see the danger of the situation.[117]

Fulk did not find Roman law a mere curiosity. He can be shown to have affirmed the validity of the *lex antiqua* in a context relating to the *utilitas* of the *res publica*, as the Angevin state is described in a document from the cathedral of Saint Maurice.[118] In addition, the Angevin court used diplomatic instruments with a close connection to imperial tradition, especially the *mandatum* by which governmental authority was delegated. This pattern is fully consistent with Fulk's overall attraction to Roman ways of carrying on the business of government, particularly with regard to the organization of the military.

In what may be regarded as a surprise move, Fulk chose to go on a pilgrimage and again left his half-brother Maurice to rule in his place.[119] At first glance this seems risky strategy in light of the troubles that had beset the Angevin state during Fulk's first pilgrimage. Yet Fulk knew well that the situation early in 1009 differed markedly from that in 1003. Now Maurice was six years older and considerably more experienced than he had been in 1003. In addition, Anjou's western frontier had been greatly strengthened by the gains made in the Mauges region and by the construction of strongholds at Montrevault, Châteaupanne, and Passavant as well as by the elimination of the Renaud family. Furthermore, the death of Count Geoffrey-Berengar in 1008 while on a pilgrimage to Rome left Rennes without effective leadership.[120] Within Anjou itself Bishop Hubert, unlike his predecessor Bishop Renaud, was a loyal supporter of Fulk, and Abbot Hubert of Saint-Aubin apparently was considered a loyal supporter by the Angevin count.[121] Finally, Fulk's refusal to punish his men as King Robert had demanded surely raised the morale of the comital entourage. In fact, a much later and very confused account of this incident suggests that the assassins were richly rewarded.[122]

By contrast, the threat of excommunication should be seen as a substantial danger that Fulk recognized. Fulk had made clear on a number of occasions already that being "unprepared" to migrate from this world was a fate to be avoided at great cost. Although Bishop Hubert seems not to have supported his fellow prelates in their attack on Fulk nor permitted an interdict on Anjou to be pronounced in churches under his control, the problem had to be resolved sooner or later. By going first to Rome and then on a pilgrimage to the Holy Land, Fulk could undermine the threat of excommunication posed by the king's bishops. It would have been difficult to maintain the censure of a man who had been absolved by the pope and who would likely return from Jerusalem with a sack full of relics. Indeed, what saint would permit his or her relics to be transported by an unrepentant sinner? [123]

Fulk went to Jerusalem by way of Rome, where Pope Sergius IV had recently succeeded John XVIII, who died in June 1009. Among the traditions popularizing Fulk's pilgrimages was one that focused on his relations with Pope Sergius IV. According to this story, Sergius complained to Fulk that the Roman noble Crescentius was causing the papacy a great deal of trouble, and the pope asked the Angevin count to kill the malefactor. Fulk is portrayed as favoring Sergius's request but as being anxious about the impact this murder might have on his soul. Thus Fulk says to the pope: "I ask that you absolve me and my men from the sin of murder and from the crime of premeditation . . ." The pope replies: "I absolve you from sin and I will reward you with gifts as you are worthy." [124] As the story continues to unfold, Fulk's men killed Crescentius and returned to the pope, where crowds greeted the count and his followers with singing and the waving of banners. When Fulk again requested absolution for himself and his men, the pope declared that no expiation was necessary but that prayers should be said for those who had struck down God's enemy. Fulk received as a reward from the pope the relics of the holy martyrs Daria and Chrysanthus.

The Angevin count in his turn then rewarded those of his men who had carried out the assassination.[125]

Fulk Nerra's men clearly did not murder Crescentius.[126] Crescentius was killed by the supporters of Otto III in 998, but how can we explain the process by which this history became associated with the career of Fulk Nerra and the pontificate of Pope Sergius IV? In the historiographical traditions of the west of France the story survives in its earliest written form from the reign of the Angevin count's grandson. In explanation, first, we must note that Fulk's decision to go to Rome was likely conditioned partially by the friendly treatment he had received from Pope John XVIII only two years earlier. The Angevin count may even have understood that recent popes were pursuing a policy of strengthening the role of the papacy in the French kingdom at the expense of the ecclesiastical hierarchy.

Setting aside for the moment Sergius's "absolution" of Fulk and his men for murder, an examination of Pope Sergius's other decisions indicates that he adopted a policy favorable to Angevin interests broadly conceived. In 1010 the Capetian king Robert II and Odo II of Blois went to Rome with the aim of having Pope Sergius nullify the monarch's marriage to Fulk's cousin Constance. Robert hoped to gain acceptance for his previous marriage to Bertha. Sergius, however, sustained the Angevin position.[127] Shortly after defending Constance's rights, Sergius supported her mother Adelaide-Blanche of Arles in her efforts to maintain control of the monastery of Montmajour, which was threatened by a coalition of lesser nobles.[128] Finally, shortly before his death Sergius (like John XVIII) sustained Fulk's interests at Belli Locus against the prerogatives of Archbishop Hugh of Tours.[129] Obviously, Pope Sergius viewed Fulk Nerra as somewhat more than a penitent Frankish magnate seeking absolution. Like his father, Geoffrey Greymantle, Fulk was the head of a powerful family network, and he deserved serious political consideration.

The dominant theme of the Crescentius story, as told in the west of France, is Fulk's freedom from sin and guilt—religious and secular culpability—for having planned a murder and ordered its execution. One particular element of the Crescentius story has the ring of truth: "I ask that you absolve me and my men from the sin of murder and from the crime of premeditation," Fulk Nerra asked, and Pope Sergius answered: "I absolve you from sin . . ."[130] We then read: "The pope judged that Fulk needed no expiation but rather that prayers should be said for the man who had the enemy of God struck down."[131] This recalls the background provided to the murder of Hugh of Beauvais by Raoul Glaber, who writes that Hugh "intruded between the king and his wife and sowed seeds of discord. He made the queen odious to the king in the hope of securing his own advantage." Raoul continues: "Fulk, the Angevin count and a relation of the queen, sent twelve *fortissimi milites* who killed Hugh . . ."[132] Hugh had tried to destroy a marriage sacred in the eyes of God and upheld in solemn proceedings by Pope Sergius. Fulk and his twelve *milites*—the number requires no gloss now and needed none then—had indeed struck down God's enemy. Fulk went to Rome to obtain absolution for premeditated murder, not for the killing of Crescentius but for the death of Hugh of Beauvais. As the legend developed, the story of Fulk's absolution appears to have been merged with the more celebrated story of Crescentius's murder, and in the retelling Hugh of Beauvais' assassination was forgotten. Indeed, as we will see in chapter 5, Fulk's strategy appears to have been successful, for the murder of Hugh ceased to be an issue.

Fulk's rapprochement with King Robert II ended dramatically with the murder of Hugh of Beauvais, which brought to a halt an Angevin offensive that had flourished in the context of good relations with the monarch. During this offensive Fulk had been able to destroy the power of the Renaud family and to gain control of the Mauges region, where he built the strongholds of Montrevault and Chemillé. In the Vendômois Fulk had solidified the Angevin position by renewing good relations with his erstwhile brothers-in-law, Bishop Renaud of Paris and Abbot Theobald of Cormery, and by assuring the support of the viscomital house of Vendôme through the appointment of Hubert as bishop of Angers. Fulk had also struck farther east. Seizing lands that Gelduin of Saumur held from the archbishop of Tours, the Angevin count saw to the construction of a stronghold at Montrichard. At Semblançay and at Morand in the Touraine Fulk also built strongholds. At Saint-Florent Fulk made startling gains by maneuvering Abbot Robert into a position in which the cleric recognized the Angevin count as his *senior*. This submission allowed Fulk to use the resources of Saint-Florent's fisc to reward his supporters, and it gave the Angevins control of the stronghold of Châteaupanne. Along with Montrevault, Châteaupanne helped to strengthen the western frontier, which had been severely weakened by the defection of the Renaud family and the success of Count Geoffrey-Berengar at Nantes.

This whirlwind of activity by Fulk Nerra also included a fortunate marriage, the birth of a male heir, and the building of a monastery at Belli Locus near the castrum of Loches, a construction that would aid in the economic development of the region. Fulk was able to accomplish as much as he did during this short period of time in part because he enjoyed good relations with King Robert II, because Odo II of Blois was at war with the Normans, and because William of Poitou was either cowed by or under the influence of the Angevin family network in the south. The leaders of the major powers in the west are likely to have drawn the conclusion that their relations with one another were basic to the success of any plans they might have for limiting Fulk's future aggrandizement.

CHAPTER FIVE

The Second
Capetian-Blésois Axis

While Fulk was visiting Rome and the Holy Land to do what was necessary to undermine the advantages his adversaries enjoyed as a result of the murder of Hugh of Beauvais, King Robert II and Odo II of Blois were at work on several fronts to weaken the Angevins. Within the frontiers of the Angevin state, which Fulk's half-brother Maurice had the responsibility of protecting, the most serious threat to comital power arose with the defection of Landry of Dun, who abandoned his traditional loyalty and joined the supporters of Odo II.[1] Geoffrey Greymantle had given Landry a *domus munitissima* in the Châteauneuf district of Amboise many years earlier. Geoffrey had also given this fidelis from Berry many *casamenta* (estates) to support his followers.[2]

Landry's aim was to gain control of Amboise, but he was vigorously opposed by the brothers Archembaud and Sulpicius of Buzançais, who held the stronghold for the Angevin count and who supported his interests. There developed within the castrum of Amboise and its environs the kind of house-to-house urban warfare that the author of the *Gesta Ambaziensium dominorum* illuminated so vividly when a similar situation developed there about two generations later.[3] Briefly described, Sulpicius' and Archembaud's men based at the stronghold inside Amboise itself harassed Landry's men in Châteauneuf and made sallies against his *domus munitissima*. Landry's men attacked the count's supporters in a similar manner. This conflict within Amboise and its environs was inconclusive; the count's men were unable to drive out the enemy or to take the rebel stronghold, and Landry's followers were incapable of wresting control of the castrum of Amboise from the Angevins.[4]

Landry's inability to win a decisive victory at Amboise and to gain control of this important castrum for Count Odo II may have been a result of his decision to divide his forces. Part of Landry's force was occupied at Amboise while Landry himself personally led another element into the field. This contingent moved west through the environs of Tours and joined with a force led by Gelduin of Saumur to attack Anjou. The army led by Gelduin and Landry concentrated its efforts in la Vallée, the section along the Loire River between Saumur in the east and Ponts-de-Cé in the west. Thus they penetrated into the center of the Angevin heartland, virtually to the walls of Angers itself.[5]

After cooperating with Gelduin, Landry extended his operations to the south and harassed Fulk's fideles in the area of Loches.[6] It is likely there that he coordinated his efforts with Geoffrey the Young, the castellan of Saint-Aignan and a longtime supporter of Odo, who gained notice for his struggles during Fulk's absence with the Angevin count's fideles at Villentrois, Buzançais, and Graçay.[7] It is significant that the source that outlines Angevin opposition to Geoffrey—a source probably based on a contemporary report that no longer survives—omits mention of forces from la Haye supporting Fulk's interests. This omission permits the inference that Roscelinus of la Haye defected from Fulk's entourage during this period. An independent account indicates that Roscelinus cooperated with Plastulfus, another of Odo's important followers in the region, in opposing the Angevins.[8] In the course of these campaigns Fulk's newly built stronghold at Passavant was destroyed, and it is likely that both Montbazon and Langeais fell into Blésois hands.[9]

Despite these losses and defections, Angers itself was not attacked. The efforts by Landry and Gelduin, while more than local in nature, should not be seen as a full-scale invasion of the Angevin state but rather as raids carried out in search of booty and as probes mounted to test the will of Fulk's fideles to resist and maintain the interests of their dominus. Only three strongholds fell, although there were in excess of thirty in the hands of Fulk's castellans. So far as can be ascertained, the majority of Angevin magnates, as epitomized by Archembaud and Sulpicius of Buzançais at Amboise, remained loyal.[10]

The story of Landry's defection, juxtaposed to that of the loyal Archembaud and Sulpicius, is used by the authors of the *Gesta Consulum* to emphasize the importance of faithfulness to one's *senior* and the reciprocal nature of the connection between *superiores* and *inferiores*. The *superior* makes the *inferior* his *amicus*; as a result, the latter is elevated in character (*ingenium*), prosperity (*fortuna*), and rank (*dignitas*). The authors of the *Gesta* explain that those who serve in the manner required are rewarded not only in worldly goods but in reputation, while those who are disloyal suffer. We must note here that the values attributed to Maurice, Archembaud, and Sulpicius are drawn from classical texts. For example, the *Gesta Consulum,* in addition to being informed by the spirit of Cicero's *De officiis,* quotes his *De amicitia* (XX, 71–72) to emphasize that the man who grants "multa beneficia" deserves to be remembered even more so than the men who receive them.[11]

No less important than the nature of the relationship between *superior* and *inferior,* the giver and the receiver of beneficia, is the manner in which the authors of the *Gesta* point out (quoting an as yet unidentified Roman rhetorical text) that among his other accomplishments Maurice had acquired the skills of an orator ("oratoriis ornamentis") and was experienced in the judicial process ("peritus in causis").[12]

This tie between *forma fidelitatis* and classical rhetoric should not be considered twelfth-century romanticism. Rather, recall that a century earlier when Fulbert of Chartres, Fulk Nerra's contemporary, wrote on *forma fidelitatis,* he did so firmly in the spirit of Cicero's *De officiis* and utilized a rhetorical framework provided by the latter's *De inventione* (II, 157–159, 168) and *Ad herennium* (III, 4–5).[13] Is this early eleventh-century romanticism, or are these simply men of conviction seeing the world in light of their past?

In fact, Fulbert had more than an academic interest in the *forma fidelitatis* and this interest was directly in conflict with those of Fulk Nerra and his allies at Vendôme. In his role as bishop of Chartres Fulbert was overlord of the castrum of Vendôme. Many of the magnates of the Vendômois held beneficia indirectly from Fulbert through Bishop Renaud of Paris, who succeeded his father Bouchard as count of Vendôme. Moreover, Fulbert and (more to the point here) Odo II of Blois, who was also count of Chartres, imperiled Angevin interests when the bishop of Chartres demanded of Renaud:

Assurance concerning my life and limbs and the land that I have or shall acquire with your counsel, [assurance] concerning your *auxilium* against all men with the exception of [King] Robert, [assurance] concerning the rendering of the castrum of Vendôme for my use and for my fideles to use for which they will give you surety, [and assurance] from your *milites* who hold a beneficium from you from our *casamentum* that they will provide their military service (*commendatio*) to us with the exception of the *fidelitas* that they owe to you.[14]

If Fulbert succeeded in enforcing the rendability of the castrum of Vendôme and acquiring the military service of many of Renaud's fideles, then the entire northeastern sector of the defensive perimeter (*limes*) of the Angevin state which had been so laborously pieced together by Geoffrey Greymantle and Fulk Nerra during more than two decades would be at risk. In addition, Angevin communications in the northern Touraine and particularly Fulk's stronghold at Morand would be endangered. Whether Bishop Renaud fully understood the strategic importance of Fulbert's success for Odo II's operations against Fulk is not clear. But we do know that Fulbert was not able to persuade or to frighten Renaud, Fulk Nerra's erstwhile brother-in-law, into acceding to his demands.[15]

Fulbert, whose loyalty to Odo II was to be demonstrated throughout his career, pursued his efforts to secure a point d'appui in the Vendômois for his lord. In this case he corresponded with those of Renaud's fideles who held *casamenta* from the church of Saint Mary at Chartres as *dona* from the Vendômois count. Included in this group were Viscount Hubert of Vendôme, Gundacrus, Roger, Bouchard, Hugh the son of Hugh, Otredus, Hamelinus, Hugh the son of Herbrandus, and Guismandus's wife. Fulbert demanded that they all come to Chartres to do *servitium* for him under pain of excommunication, interdict on Vendôme and its environs, and the confiscation of their *casamenta*. Of these nine most were relatives or close associates of Bishop Hubert of Angers and they remained loyal to the Angevin connection. In the end Fulbert of Chartres was not able to press his claims to overlordship in Vendôme or the Vendômois successfully whether Fulk Nerra was in the region or away on a pilgrimage to the Holy Land.[16]

While the interests of the Capetian-Blésois axis were pressed during Fulk's absence by men such as Gelduin of Saumur, Landry of Dun, Fulbert of Chartres, and Geoffrey of Saint-Aignan, King Robert and Odo II were acting in a larger theater of political operations. Robert and Odo traveled to Rome in an effort to have Pope Sergius IV approve of the king's liaison with Bertha and to have the pontiff nullify the marriage to Constance. In October of 1010, following these unsuccessful negotiations in Rome, the king, "Queen" Bertha, and Odo II accepted an invitation from Duke William of Aquitaine to attend a great celebration to be held at the monastery of Saint-Jean-d'Angély in order to venerate what was widely believed to be the head of John the Baptist, which recently had been "rediscovered." At this gathering King Robert demonstrated his royal generosity and is reported to have given to Saint-John an immense bowl of solid gold weighing thirty pounds along with many other valuable gifts.[17]

Although the ostensible reason for this gathering was a religious celebration, the selection of great magnates invited by Duke William suggests that matters of political concern were not completely ignored. Shortly before this gathering took place, William had married Brisca, the sister of Duke Sancho of Gascony. This marriage followed hard upon the death of Adalmode, William's first wife and Fulk Nerra's cousin, and took place while the Angevin count was on a pilgrimage.[18] This marriage provided Duke William with an opportunity to diminish the influence of the Angevins which he had endured for more than a decade. The visit by King Robert, who was now once again estranged from Fulk, made possible an arrangement between the monarch and the duke which could help to undermine Angevin influence in Aquitaine while at the same time increasing royal influence as far south as the Pyrenees. In addition, viewed from King Robert's and Odo II's perspective (both men were William's cousins), with the duke of Aquitaine now as a potential ally against Fulk, the resuscitation of Odo I's plan to launch an attack on Anjou from the Poitou once again became a real possibility. The presence of Count Hugh of Maine, who had recently served alongside of Odo II in the Blésois conflict with the Normans, further raised the spectre of a multifront invasion of Anjou. An additional hint that the meeting at Saint-Jean-d'Angély was intended for the discussion of political matters inimical to Anjou is the absence of Count William of Angoulême, Fulk Nerra's brother-in-law, who customarily was a companion of Duke William during the period of Angevin influence from about the year 1000.[19] Also conspicuous by his absence was Joscelin of Parthenay, another of Fulk's fideles from the Poitou.[20]

We do not know why King Robert and Odo II did not take the opportunity afforded by Fulk's absence and by the undistinguished care of Count Maurice to launch a full-scale invasion of the Angevin state. Perhaps the death of Count Geoffrey-Berengar of Rennes in 1008, which eliminated a threat to Anjou's western frontier, discouraged the king and led him to Aquitaine in search of allies who could open a second front to complement an attack from the east. A coordinated attack that would result in a speedy victory was essential to the royal cause. Once Fulk had left for Rome and thence to the Holy Land, King Robert was in danger of losing the moral initiative in the effort to punish the Angevin count for Hugh of Beauvais' murder. An extended campaign, if necessary, would certainly have led to a debate about the propriety of pursuing a war against the lands and heirs of a man who was on pilgrimage and who, in addition, had been absolved by the pope. Recalling that Sergius IV had rebuffed King Robert's efforts to set aside his "Angevin" queen and had sustained Fulk Nerra and his aunt Adelaide-Blanche of Arles, Queen Constance's mother, in their separate struggles, we may even perhaps suspect that Sergius warned King Robert against invading Anjou.

Several other reasons for King Robert's hesitation can also be posited. For example, after news reached France of al Hakim II's vigorous persecution of Christians in Jerusalem and the burning of the church of the Holy Sepulchre, King Robert may well have come to believe that Fulk was dead, or at the very least, a prisoner of the Muslims. To invade the lands of a "martyred pilgrim" or perhaps a soon-to-be-martyred pilgrim and to deprive his legitimate heirs of their inheritance would hardly win widespread support in the French kingdom and would be even more unpopular in Rome. In addition, the king was no doubt aware that the magnates of the Angevin family network in control in Angoulême, Gévaudan, Forez, and Arles would not remain idle observers for long or simply watch as the Angevin state was dismembered by an invading army. Countess Hildegarde's royal relatives in Lotharingia were also to be considered a factor in the east. Surely King Robert remembered how effective this family network had been during the various military actions that took place from 994–999; any extended campaign would give Fulk's relatives and friends the opportunity to mobilize their forces and agree on a unified plan of opposition.

Instead of risking an invasion, King Robert and Odo II chose to probe the defenses of the Angevin state for weaknesses. In Landry of Dun they found an eager defector who tried to take Amboise for the Capetian-Blésois axis and who also harassed Fulk's supporters in the southeastern Touraine. Roscelinus of la Haye also defected in this region. At Amboise Fulk's forces, ably led by Archembaud and Sulpicius, dealt with the enemy adequately if not decisively. Lisoius of Bazougers, a young *miles* from the western region of the Anjou-Maine frontier, also seems to have acquired a reputation for bravery and military skill while defending Fulk's interests during this hectic period.[21] In general, it would appear that the majority of Fulk's fideles remained loyal and that the count's strongholds were by and large unscathed.

In short, the reestablishment of the Capetian-Blésois axis and Fulk's "holy exile" following the murder of Hugh of Beauvais had the effect of blocking the Angevin advance, which in the space of a few short years after the count's first pilgrimage had resulted in startling gains. These gains were solidly based and enabled Maurice to weather his brother's absence without great losses. It seems clear, however, that the Angevin position, despite the tergiversation of King Robert and Fulk's second lengthy absence from home, was stronger in 1011 than it had been in 1005.

In the winter of 1011 Fulk arrived at Rome, safe and sound, for a second meeting with Pope Sergius IV after a series of exploits in the Holy Land and on the journey there which later were embellished with epic grandeur.[22] This second visit to Rome may perhaps permit the inference that Pope Sergius himself had imposed the pilgrimage on Fulk as a penance for the murder of Hugh of Beauvais. In any case, two points are clear: (1) the murder of Hugh of Beauvais ceased to be an issue or even of interest after Fulk returned from his pilgrimage,[23] and (2) Pope Sergius agreed to have Fulk's church at Belli Locus consecrated by a papal legate.[24]

When Sergius and Fulk Nerra finished their business, the pope along with all of the clergy and people of Rome ("papa cum omni clero et populo Romano") escorted the Angevin count and his entourage one mile beyond the walls of the city ("extra muros urbis miliario uno").[25] This honor, which traditionally marked the departure of an important person from Rome as far back as the Republic, was the analogue of the *adventus,* which was of course a much more elaborate ceremony.[26]

In addition to orchestrating and leading this procession to the first milestone, Pope Sergius also is said to have given Fulk a collection of precious relics. These included parts of the saints Daria, Chrysanthus, and Lawrence. The first two, wife and husband, were believed martyred at Rome by stoning early in the first century and buried in a sand pit. St. Lawrence, however, in contrast to Daria and Chrysanthus, whose fame appears to have been rather local, was martyred according to tradition in 258; he had gained great fame because of the method of his execution, roasting on a gridiron, which caught the popular imagination.[27]

When Fulk finally reached his own territory, he was likely regarded as a hero favored by God. Not only had the Angevin count survived a shipwreck on the outward journey (through the efforts of Saint Nicholas, he and others believed),[28] but he had endured the persecution that al Hakim II had visited upon Christians in the Holy Land, especially in Jerusalem where, it was believed, the caliph had destroyed the Church of the Holy Sepulchre at this very time.[29] The exaggerated rumors of the caliph's cruelty doubtless served to make Fulk's actions that much more extraordinary in the minds of contemporaries.[30] Indeed, Fulk would have appeared to his people to have had the special help of the saints. He returned, according to tradition, with sack full of relics, some provided by Pope Sergius, and a piece of stone the Angevin count is said to have broken off the Lord's tomb.[31] Even allowing for the great exaggeration of Fulk's adventures during the century following his reign, we must marvel at his having completed a second successful pilgrimage to Jerusalem in the winter of 1011 while many of the most holy people in society had not ventured even once on this dangerous journey.[32] We are quite safe in concluding that Fulk Nerra was no ordinary man in the eyes of his contemporaries.

Following his triumphal departure from Rome, Fulk headed north across the Alps, but he did not return directly to his capital at Angers. Instead, he went to his castrum at Loches in the southeastern Touraine, the province of Archbishop Hugh of Tours, who as Fulk's major ecclesiastical adversary had refused to consecrate Belli Locus. At Loches Fulk saw to the orchestration of an *adventus* ceremony. This, however, was an arrival of a very special type, an *adventus* of relics, which had its origins as a government ceremony during the later Roman empire.[33] More than a century after Fulk's *adventus* John of Marmoutier, likely relying on his research into the oral traditions of the monks living at the monastery of Belli Locus, only forty kilometers south-southwest of Tours, records the following ceremony: "The *consul* [Fulk Nerra] transported the bodies of the abovementioned holy martyrs [Daria and Chrysanthus] to the castrum of Loches. There they were taken up [in procession] by all the clergy, people, abbot and monks of Belli Locus . . . and with appropriate reverence and honor they were buried."[34]

Although it is likely that Fulk learned of the problems at la Haye and Amboise shortly after crossing the frontier in the region of Buzançais, a long day's ride to Loches, he continued his northward journey to carry out the *adventus* at Belli Locus. It seems certain that through the *adventus* Fulk intended to spread the word far and wide that he had returned triumphant from his second pilgrimage to the Holy Land and that he had the support of Pope Sergius. The news that the pope would send a legate to consecrate the church was undoubtedly announced at this time as well.[35]

Before the beginning of March 1011 Fulk had returned to Angers after his harrowing but immensely successful second pilgrimage to the Holy Land. He appears not to have enjoyed the high spirits and exultation that followed his first voyage only a few years earlier. His normal ferocity seems not to have been pushed aside by good feelings. Rather than being euphoric, Fulk appears to have been angry, probably as a result of the defections and losses Maurice suffered during his absence. Indeed, a group of monks passing through Angers on 1 March 1011 stopped to attend mass, but while in the city they refrained from calling attention to a miracle performed during the rite through the intervention of Saint Rigomer, whose relics they carried. The monks reported to their abbot that they kept the joyous occurrence a secret because "they feared Count Fulk."[36]

Shortly after this episode, Fulk thoroughly terrorized Abbot Adhebertus of Saint-Florent (Abbot Robert's successor). Adhebertus admitted that he was so impressed by Fulk's "overwhelming ferocity" that he gave the count what he wanted. Indeed, at the *placitum* where the final agreement was made, Fulk was represented by his praepositus Berno and various other government officials (*servientes comitis*); the abbot did not hesitate to hand over to these mere functionaries half of a family of serfs the count claimed.[37] It may also be useful to remember here that Fulk had endeavored to register half of the *facultates* of the monasteries on the books of the comital fisc for governmental exploitation; this *divisio* may have been but the enforcement of this unpopular policy.[38]

With the beginning of the campaigning season of 1011 Fulk called out his levies and moved eastward to attend to the punishment of Landry.[39] The vigorous and above all speedy punishment of a disloyal fidelis like Landry was of paramount importance if Fulk was to provide a lesson for other potential defectors. Thus Fulk proceeded to Landry's stronghold at Châteauneuf and ordered the garrison to open the gates and turn the fortifications over to him. This action was taken in the traditional manner according to long-standing legal principle, dating at least to the later Roman empire, that the commander of a fortified place, whether a massive urbs or a rather modest castellum, might not deny a governmental order to turn over the fortifications to proper authority.[40]

Initially Landry's men balked at the count's command. When the count threatened a siege, the defenders quickly realized that their position was hopeless—their leader seems not to have been present—and sought to obtain terms of surrender for themselves from Fulk.[41] They obviously understood that if they held out or were captured when the stronghold fell, they risked serious punishment or even death. This was the thrust of the *lex deditionis* that governed military actions of this type during the late tenth and early eleventh centuries.[42] Following negotiations, the garrison of Landry's stronghold offered to surrender and provide Fulk with hostages if the count would promise to spare their lives. Fulk accepted and the stronghold was handed over to him. He then confiscated all of Landry's holdings and those of his men at Amboise and in its environs, for example, the many *casamenta* that Geoffrey Greymantle had given to Landry more than a quarter-century earlier so that he and his men would be able to defend the Châteauneuf district. Finally, Fulk razed Landry's stronghold, the *domus munitissima*, in Châteauneuf.[43] The lesson to defectors was as clear then as it is to the modern reader.

Landry's defection, the expulsion of his supporters, and the destruction of the *domus munitissima* seriously weakened the elaborate defensive arrangements that had been developed during the reign of Geoffrey Greymantle to keep Amboise secure. Amboise was of great value, not only because of its strategic location in military terms, for it controlled passage on the Loire between Blois and Tours, but because of its great economic importance for trade on the river and as a regional market for the rich agricultural land around it. Indeed, the growth of a merchant settlement outside the walls of the old Roman castrum of Amboise surely played a prominent role in Geoffrey Greymantle's decision to have the enclave protected both by a wall and an internal defensive bastion, that is, the *castrum novum* with the *domus munitissima* inside it.[44]

The security of Amboise was further undermined by the death about this time of Archembaud of Buzançais, perhaps as a result of the conflict with Landry. In any case, Sulpicius, Archembaud's brother, was left with sole responsibility for the defense of Amboise. Toward this end and with Fulk's license, Sulpicius used his own resources to strengthen the internal defenses at Amboise. He built a high stone tower where previously only a wooden stronghold had served. This addition to the defenses at Amboise was finally completed in 1013.[45] Fulk also made an effort to compensate for the loss of Landry's services and entered into negotiations with Lisoius of Bazougers, a military commander of noteworthy accomplishments from Maine, for the purpose of recruiting him to strengthen the defenses of Anjou's eastern frontier.[46]

Among the various other problems in the east which had arisen during his absence and which apparently consumed much of Fulk's attention following his return from the Holy Land was his need to retake the stronghold of Montbazon, which appears to have been lost by Maurice. This formidable stone tower, rising thirty meters above the hill on which it stood and girded by a curtain wall, held out successfully against the Angevin count.[47] Fulk apparently decided after some time that a lengthy siege was poor strategy and moved south to deal with Roscelinus of la Haye. The latter had supported Landry in a localized version of the operations carried out against Angevin interests; this phase of the conflict was called the "guerra Plastulfi." Fulk confiscated Roscelinus's holdings, and he does not appear at la Haye again.[48] Fulk's interests at la Haye were thereafter defended by his vicarius Hugh.[49]

Having restored a modicum of order in the Touraine by dealing ruthlessly with several defectors, Fulk turned his attention to Belli Locus and Loches. At the former, Fulk initially had made an effort to encourage economic development by giving the monks the right to all of the taxes (costumae) owed to the count from the villa he had given them. Fulk also provided the monks with the license to collect the taxes (mercatum) that formerly had gone to the comital fisc from the Sunday market traditionally held at the count's villa.[50]

During the five years following Fulk's foundation of Belli Locus there seems to have been substantial economic development. Thus, for example, we find the first mention of a burgus at the villa; this nucleus not only drew merchants but also attracted the settlement of serfs among others. In order to further this development Fulk now decreed that the entire tax traditionally paid to the comital fisc by the inhabitants of the burgus for the privilege of living there was to go to the monks and to the inhabitants of the burgus for their mutual use. In addition, Fulk gave the dominium of the burgus—that is, the erstwhile regalian rights that had devolved upon the count, such as the right to call up the levies for military services and other rights connected with the ban—to the inhabitants as a collectivity. Furthermore, Fulk established that all inhabitants of the burgus were free and that no one who lived in the burgus was to be "defamed by the taint of servitude." Fulk also exempted the inhabitants from many taxes: those normally owed by mills (molinagium) and ovens (furnaticum) as well as those on sales (*vendae*) and those due from the assarting of waste lands (*terragium*). The inhabitants of the burgus were also exempted from paying the tax on their vineyards (*vinagium*) wherever these might be located; Fulk also freed these vintners from the tax (*taberna*) on the retail sale of their wine. Finally, Fulk gave the inhabitants of the burgus the right to mint his coins in the same type as was minted in the nearby castrum of Loches.[51]

The case of the burgus at Belli Locus is an example of Fulk's effort to pursue economic development. This endeavor formed part of a more general Angevin comital policy of governmental intervention in the economy. For example, Fulk the Good, Fulk Nerra's grandfather, had provided substantial inducement in the form of remissions from taxes to attract new settlers from outside the Angevin pagus. He thus began a process of settling empty lands deserted as a result of the Viking invasions. He also pressed the assarting of waste lands.[52] His son Geoffrey Greymantle continued these efforts and also encouraged the development of burgi where merchants and artisans could gather under government protection and where markets and even fairs could be developed.[53]

The tax incentives offered by Fulk Nerra to the inhabitants of the burgus at Belli Locus require no labored explanation for readers familiar with medieval governmental efforts to stimulate economic productivity. Of more interest is Fulk's grant of freedom to all of the inhabitants of the burgus. This improvement in personal legal or social status was a powerful incentive, as Fulk's contemporaries in England, Flanders, and Catalonia also understood.[54] Since Belli Locus was on the border with Berry, where both the Capetians and the Blésois enjoyed a strong presence, Fulk's special incentives to lure productive people from the lands of his adversaries had political as well as economic significance.

Fulk's grant of the right to mint the count's coinage is an important index of the Belli Locus community's initial economic success. The need for readily available coins, and likely for large quantities, suggests that the market there was flourishing. If the *burgenses* at Belli Locus had been left to rely for their coinage on the mint controlled by their competitors at the castrum of Loches, less than a mile away, then the fluidity of their commercial transactions could have been adversely affected. This competitive situation was recognized not only by the merchants of Belli Locus, who we may assume desired the privilege, but also by Fulk Nerra who granted it.

The grant of the minting privilege, as set forth in Fulk's act, does not mean that the right had been withdrawn from Loches. Indeed, the wording of the text permits the inference that the identification with Loches was to be maintained. This is borne out by the archaeological evidence: all surviving specimens of "Loches coinage" from the eleventh century bear the legend *Lucas Castrum* or some orthographic variation such as *Locas Castrum*. They never mention Belli Locus. The inclusion in the design of a depiction of the Holy Sepulchre, however, signals the importance of Belli Locus. Thus we can conclude that a new coinage was not established, only a second mint.[55] There is no reason to believe that Fulk was supporting the economic development of Belli Locus in order to punish or to diminish the importance of Loches. During the next few years, Fulk acted favorably toward the inhabitants of that castrum. In short, it seems that Fulk came to understand that economic competition, like tax incentives and personal freedom, was good business, and what was good for business was good for government.

The Loches coinage served more than economic needs. A representation of the Holy Sepulchre on each coin undoubtedly was intended to distinguish Belli Locus wherever the coins were minted.[56] Belli Locus had been founded to commemorate God's role in Fulk's victory at Conquereuil and following his first pilgrimage to the Holy Land undertaken in part to expiate his sins for spilling Christian blood during this conflict. Fulk's second pilgrimage, if tradition is accurate, yielded a piece of stone believed to be from the Holy Sepulchre itself. Thus, it seems likely that this new Loches coinage was instituted in 1011 or shortly thereafter, that is, following Fulk's return from his second pilgrimage. Clearly, Fulk grasped the value of propagandizing his pilgrimages through a representation of the Holy Sepulchre on this coinage, much in the same way that on the coins minted in the city of Angers he was styled "Dei Gratia, Comes" in consonance with the family tradition of employing this usage on official documents as a symbol of their political independence from higher secular power.[57]

Fulk was interested not only in the development of the burgus at Belli Locus but also in the economic health of the monastery. The abbot of Belli Locus was made chief judicial official of the *vicaria* in which both the monastery and its burgus were located. This meant that those profits of justice that normally went to the count's officials (the vicarius or perhaps the praepositus, for Loches was administered for the count by a praepositus) would go toward the support of the monastery. Fulk also donated a nearby church and several estates in the region along with the woods pertaining to them, cultivated and uncultivated lands, and male and female dependents living on these lands. The monks also received the right to the services of comital dependents from nearby estates (whether male or female) who married a dependent of the monastery. Next, the monks obtained a free license to take wood for new buildings and for the repair of old buildings from the woodlands; they also could use wood from these woodlands to build houses and mills and for heating and for other work as needed. Finally, the monks were given free license to feed their pigs on the acorns that grew in the woods.[58]

All of the estates granted to Belli Locus appear to have been made immune from the tax on land. But this would seem to have benefited the monks only incidentally since they were not given the proceeds which normally accrued from this *consuetudo*.[59] The monks were permitted to collect for the monastery what formerly had been the government levies, but only on special occasions such as the election of the abbot rather than on an annual basis, as had been the case when the count's agents collected this *consuetudo*. The main benefit of this immunity, or perhaps more exactly partial immunity, went to those who normally paid the land tax, and thus it may be seen as an incentive to attract and to retain agricultural population in a frontier region that was in competition with landowners in Berry for relatively scarce human resources. Fulk himself also likely benefited by this policy insofar as all sales taxes (*vendae*) and other taxes (*costumae*), obviously excluding the said land tax, were to be paid to the count's official as before, according to what was normal practice in each locality (*locus*).[60]

At Loches Fulk not only worked to sustain the economic development of the region but prepared for the consecration of his new church at Belli Locus, which Pope Sergius had promised earlier in the year. This church was of monumental proportions: the so-called "arc triomphal" measured some fifty-four feet to its keystone and more than forty feet in width.[61] Its architectural function was to support the western part of the great lantern tower, "but it is hard to resist the idea that one reason for [its] size and splendour was to impress in this way, as in the imperial cities of earlier and later times."[62] Great men of the ancient and medieval worlds were generally great builders.

In addition to its monumental size, the church at Belli Locus was constructed of large stone blocks, one of the earliest medieval examples of the use of this size material. It was also well decorated;[63] the frieze depicting Fulk's "judicial victory" over Conan of Rennes at Conquereuil was probably already fixed in place by 1011. Apparently only a fragment of this frieze survives. It is approximately twenty feet in length and about three feet in height (figure 1). It depicts four mounted figures, each two registers in height; three figures face in the same direction as they do battle with a fourth, who opposes them. The continuity of this main scene is interrupted in the bottom register by two opposed figures in combat and in the upper register by a pair of quadrupeds tentatively identified by art historians as lions.[64] A more careful examination of the main scene of the four horsemen in double register makes clear that three of them are stumbling—this action is accentuated by the drooping horses' heads and feet splayed at various angles—while the fourth opposing figure stands straight, as evidenced by the upright position of the horse's head. Given the role of the battle of Conquereuil in the foundation of Belli Locus it is likely that this scene depicts the episode in which Fulk's men fell into the pits dug by Conan. As Richer, a contemporary, wrote of the Angevins: "They charged into the ditches and were sunk down into them."[65]

This episode was perhaps particularly worthy of depiction from the Angevin point of view because Fulk and his men overcame the traps dug by the Bretons. Moreover, these very traps dug by Conan's men led to the charge that the Breton count had violated the rules of the trial by combat, which had been prearranged with the Angevins. In short, this episode encapsulated the trial-by-combat aspect of the battle which connected Conquereuil to Belli Locus, where the *judicium Dei* was traditionally rendered.[66]

If the main thrust of the frieze was to depict the Angevin victory at Conquereuil or at the very least to highlight a crucial episode of the battle, what is to be made of the half-scale elements, the two opposing horsemen in the bottom register and the lionlike quadrupeds above them? It seems reasonable to suggest that these horsemen represented a traditional trial by combat which involved two contenders, principals or their champions, in a duel, or *Zweikampf* as one says more explicitly in German.[67] The appearance of two lions is not surprising on a monument commemorating a noble military victory won with God's help. Indeed, a complement of lions is quite appropriate given this animal's biblical reputation for strength (II Sam. 1.23) and courage (II Sam. 17.10). The scattering of lions throughout the Bayeux Tapestry strongly suggests that this animal was firmly associated with victory during the eleventh century.[68]

Returning to the main scene of the surviving fragment of the frieze,

Figure 1. *Frieze at church of Belli Locus (c. 20' × 3')*.

examination of the horsemen and their equipment provides two *exempla* that highlight late antique usage and may suggest copying from classical models. Where the shape of the riders' shields can be discerned on the frieze, they are rounded or oval. This type of shield is frequently found on Roman monuments of various types, but more important, these shields are markedly different from the kite-shaped shields commonly used by mounted fighting men in the eleventh century and even earlier. The kite-shaped shield, of course, is most clearly represented on the Bayeux Tapestry, which commemorated the victory of Fulk Nerra's younger contemporary, William the Conqueror, at the battle of Hastings.[69]

Our knowledge of the history of stirrups also suggests that a late antique model or perhaps even a "neo-Roman" *mentalité* lay behind the sculptures of the horsemen at Belli Locus. The horsemen ride in the classical manner, without stirrups. In addition, the horses display elaborate harnesses, devices used to help manage horses when the rider lacked stirrups.[70] One may recall the oft discussed tie between Trajan's column and the Bayeux Tapestry, among other possible imperial models for the commemoration of military victories. Many such ancient monuments were available to Fulk and his entourage as the Angevin count traveled to Rome, the Byzantine empire, and the Holy Land.[71] Fulk's affinity for things Roman, whether Vegetius's *De re militari* or Roman legal forms such as the *mandatum,* increases the likelihood that he was influenced by antique monuments when having his battle frieze designed.

This intriguing frieze, which originally may have been two or three times as long and which decorated the facade of the church just below the second-story windows, merits an even closer look at one of the three putative Angevin figures in the fragment (figure 2). Of the three figures, two carry pole weapons, but the third man carries a sword. Indeed, this sword deserves attention because its hilt is the very same rare upturned type carried by the statue of Fulk Nerra on his tomb at Belli Locus (see plate 3).[72] In light of the centrality of this horseman in the Angevin ranks, his unique position wielding a sword, and the design of the sword's hilt, I venture the hypothesis that this horseman represents Fulk Nerra at the battle of Conquereuil.

While Fulk Nerra was seeing to affairs at Belli Locus and awaiting the papal legate, perhaps even admiring his monumental new church and the battle frieze, a drama was unfolding in Rome. Archbishop Hugh of Tours, a loyal supporter of Odo II, journeyed to the Eternal

Figure 2. *Detail of frieze at church of Belli Locus.*

City in order to thwart the consecration of Fulk's church. It is likely that Hugh learned of Pope Sergius's promise to Fulk when the Angevin count carried out the *adventus* of the relics at Belli Locus on his return from Rome. As described in a papal bull preserved at Belli Locus for centuries, Archbishop Hugh was granted a hearing by the pope. In a formal proceeding before both lay and clerical judges, the archbishop's advocate argued on the basis of the canons and on the basis of a law of Justinian, probably *Novella* no. 131, ch. 8, that the sole right to consecrate in each diocese belongs to the bishop. The advocate for the pope's position, Bishop Peter of Piperno, who frequently acted as a papal legate in Gaul during the early eleventh century, stressed that Belli Locus had been founded by Fulk Nerra on his own property and stressed the rule of law which established the *consecratio* as a *res* adhering in the property rights and legally disposed of by the person holding the *dominium*. Peter summarized his case with the legal maxim "cujus est haereditas, ipsius est consecratio."[73]

The court found in favor of Fulk and the pope. Archbishop Hugh was required to recognize in a formal ceremony—by transferring the *virgula*—that he had lost the case. The bull Sergius issued says that Archbishop Hugh admitted that his case had "nullum verum aut rectum" and that he had "sinned and erred before the omnipotent Lord

and the holy Roman church . . . " After Hugh recognized his error
Pope Sergius ordered Bishop Peter of Piperno to go to Gaul and to
consecrate the church, which the bull confirms to be under papal
protection.[74]

A great crowd of local people and distant visitors, including several
bishops who, a later contemporary alleges, were forced to attend because of their fear of Fulk, gathered at Belli Locus early in May 1012
to celebrate the consecration over which Peter of Piperno presided. It
is important to emphasize that Peter consecrated the church in the
name of the Trinity and of the Cherubim and Seraphim and not in the
name of the Holy Sepulchre. Although Fulk had already begun to associate Belli Locus with the Holy Sepulchre, as for example with the
Loches coinage, the church was not rededicated until later in his reign,
probably after the rebuilding following the collapse of the roof.[75]

The consecration of Belli Locus took place with great pomp and display, but after the crowds departed, a great storm arose and blew down
the high roof and part of the west wall. Raoul Glaber, who likely ques-
tioned eyewitnesses to the catastrophe with technical knowledge of the
damage, wrote:

Just before the ninth hour of the same day, at a time when the heavens were
calm and fanned with gentle breezes, a hurricane struck from the south, filling
the church with turbulent air and pounding it long and hard. The tie-beams
having been dislodged, all the timber roof members together with all the tiles
along the length of the western arm of the church fell to the ground and came
to ruin.[76]

Raoul reported that *rustici* viewed such disasters as punishments or
as portents of future punishments and emphasized that the collapse of
the roof was understood by contemporaries as a sign that Fulk had dis-
pleased God and the saints. Raoul then concluded: "When many people
throughout the region learned what had happened, no one doubted
that the insolent boldness of his [Fulk's] presumption had rendered his
offering useless."[77]

A small group of bishops, probably headed by Archbishop Hugh of
Tours, perhaps taking heart from the calamity at Belli Locus, met in a
synod and condemned the papal action of sending Peter to consecrate
Belli Locus as a "sacrilegious pretention" and the "fruit of blind cupidity" which introduced "schism" into the Roman church. Pope Sergius
responded immediately with a blistering letter to the bishops reiterating
that Fulk's foundation was under papal protection and that Belli Locus
and its supporters were also protected from the archbishop, who him-

self would be excommunicated should he excommunicate anyone there. Sergius elaborated this last point to make clear that not only did papal protection extend to the place of Belli Locus itself but to the *servientes loci,* the *adjutores,* and the *amici.*[78]

The memory of the collapsed roof of the monumental church at Belli Locus, despite the fact that it was rebuilt and stood for generations, undoubtedly impressed the local populace, and it is even likely that some three decades or so later Raoul Glaber found *rustici* who attributed the dangerous winds to God's displeasure with Fulk. Whatever may have been the impact of the fallen roof on Fulk's reputation, his adversaries were unable to take advantage of the calamity. Thanks to Pope Sergius's vigorous efforts, the episcopal attempt to condemn Fulk's position failed.

When Fulk returned to Angers, the experience at Belli Locus seems to have had an effect on his program of church building. Work began to rebuild the church of Saint-Martin at Angers no later than the early spring of 1012.[79] The tenth-century efforts at reconstruction on the basis of the Carolingian plan called for an exceptionally high lantern tower similar to that at nearby Saumur. Under Fulk's patronage, however, the church of Saint-Martin was substantially redesigned with the tower a full story lower than originally planned. In addition, and perhaps even more important, the designers decided to alter the cruciform plan of the Carolingian structure in order to evoke a basilica at the expense of its appendages.[80] To destroy the arms would obviously have been very costly, but it is clear that at Saint-Martin's of Angers Fulk supported the Roman basilican tradition that found expression in the new style that has come to be called Romanesque.

In 1012 the cathedral school at Angers was also founded. Bishop Hubert contacted a learned scholar of Angevin origins named Bernard, who had been a student at the school of Chartres, and invited him to develop a school in connection with the cathedral of Saint Maurice. This Bernard apparently was given a three-year contract.[81] The sources do not tell us exactly what role Fulk Nerra played in the early development of the school, but there is circumstantial evidence for comital support from the start. Bishop Hubert, son of Viscount Hubert of Vendôme, was a very young man in 1012 and very loyal to Fulk, thus it is unlikely he would have undertaken a major project without the count's participation.[82] In addition, Bernard, a student of Fulbert of Chartres and thus closely connected with a loyal supporter of Odo II, would hardly have been chosen to head the school without the Angevin count's approval. The establishment of a cathedral school was potentially a costly enterprise, and Bishop Hubert, who was strongly committed to rebuilding the cathedral church of Saint Maurice (which had burned down in 1000), was in financial need for his projects. He obtained large donations from his father, the viscount of Vendôme, among others in order to carry out the reconstruction of the cathedral.[83] Fulk Nerra, however, was the obvious patron because he commanded the resources to support a cathedral school, and, as he later demonstrated, he had good use for its faculty as "chancery" clerks.[84] Finally, Angevin traditions surviving in their earliest written form only from the period after Fulk's death emphasize his praiseworthy efforts to combat ignorance; these comments may perhaps be taken to mean that Fulk played some role in the establishment of the cathedral school at Angers.[85]

The long-term political importance of church building and of higher education cannot be ignored, but in 1012 Fulk had pressing decisions to make. Joscelin of Parthenay, one of Fulk's supporters in the Poitou, died in 1012, and the right to dispose of his *honor* rested jointly with Fulk Nerra and Duke William of Aquitaine. The latter wanted to use this *honor* to gain the support of Hugh of Lusignan and to thwart his efforts to ally with Viscount Radulfus of Thouars. Fulk also had good reason to support a scheme that would keep the viscount of Thouars from strengthening his position. Ever since Fulk had deprived Viscount Aimery of Thouars of the countship of Nantes in 994, the viscomital family of Thouars had worked against Angevin interests. William and Fulk held a *placitum* at Poitiers where the Angevin count agreed to a *conventum* in which he promised to grant Hugh as a beneficium whatever was under Angevin control at Parthenay. In return, William promised to provide the Angevin count with valuable resources from the comital fisc in the Poitou. It was agreed between Fulk and William that Hugh would have Joscelin's *honor* and his widow as wife.[86]

Fulk's paramount interest was in the castrum of Parthenay, which protected his communications with the Saintonge and provided a base for military operations against Thouars, which was less than forty kilometers north. Thus Fulk made it clear to Hugh of Lusignan that any stronghold held from the Angevin count was to be at the disposal of the count or his agents on demand and without delay. Rendability was a basic requirement.[87]

We may add that Fulk also pursued his own policies to strengthen his position vis-à-vis the viscounts of Thouars. For example, Fulk developed a good working relationship with Abbot Gerard of Saint-Jouin-de-Marnes, whose monastery was in the *mouvance* of the viscounts of Thouars but only twenty kilometers northwest of Fulk's stronghold at Mirebeau, only thirty kilometers northwest of Parthenay, and only thirty kilometers west-southwest of the Angevin castrum at Loudun. Fulk granted Abbot Gerard a *licentia* to build a church at the Angevin stronghold of Vihiers, thirty kilometers from Thouars. Vihiers, however, was so prosperous that Gerard had two churches built there, and when these were completed Fulk granted to Saint-Jouin extensive privileges at the castrum. Among the most important of these were revenues from the annual fair (*feria*) and from the weekly market (*mercatum*).[88]

The pattern of development encouraged by Fulk in the Vihiers region on the Poitevin frontier was similar to that pursued in the neighborhood of Belli Locus and Loches on the Berry frontier. The strongholds of Loches and Vihiers served to protect communications between Angers and the count's eastern holdings, provided well-defended links along the *limes* that marked the southern border of the Angevin state, and served as offensive bases from which military power could be projected into enemy territory; in addition, they were also defensive bastions that gave protection to merchants and clergy. These were the two groups contemporaries regarded as essential to the growth of towns.[89]

Fulk's military organization at Vihiers at this time provides some useful insights into his close control of strongholds and thereby his avoidance of problems resulting from overambitious castellans. Geoffrey Greymantle had established his relative Albericus as dominus of Vihiers around 981. When he died about 1007, his son Albericus was not established at the castrum by the count. Rather, Fulk handed Vihiers over to Bouchard, a member of the Bouchard family, which was very important at Angers and in its environs. Bouchard was also given command of the stronghold of nearby Passavant; thus like Roger the Devil, who held Montrésor and Montrichard, Bouchard headed a small regional command. This regional command came to an end with the destruction of Passavant in 1010 and the death of Bouchard at about the same time. Following his policy, Fulk did not permit Bouchard's son Sigebrannus to replace his father as castellan; the position was given to the vicarius Gerald.[90]

Among those who served in the garrison at Vihiers under Gerald were Sigebrannus, Bouchard's son, and several of Fulk's fideles, such as Otgerius and Aimericus. Both of these men are seen in later documents to have held beneficia in the region, and the latter is very likely the Aimericus who succeeded Gerald as the commander (*oppidanus*) at Vihiers.[91] In addition to the garrison troops whom Fulk refers to as his *homines,* we can catch a glimpse of the administration at Vihiers. In addition to Gerald, who apparently served both as castellan and vicarius, there was a fidelis of Fulk's named Gausbertus who had responsibility for the main gate and thus received the cognomen "de Porto." As part of the remuneration for his service he received half of the income collected by the monks of Saint-Jouin from their church of Saint Hilaire at Vihiers. This may reflect the ongoing *divisio* of monastic *facultates* into halves which Fulk appears to have organized a decade or so earlier and about which the monks of Saint-Jouin had complained.[92]

Whatever schemes King Robert, William of Aquitaine, Odo II of Blois, and Hugh of Maine may have contemplated during their meeting at Saint-Jean-d'Angély about Fulk Nerra, nothing was done. Fulk was assured of continued Angevin influence in the Poitou by William's need to consult and compensate him for his support at Parthenay. At Nantes Count Budic recognized that he held the *comté* from Fulk and needed his help against Count Alan of Rennes, who had recently reached his majority. But Alan, without the aid of his overlord Odo II or his Norman relatives was unlikely to be much of a threat to Fulk's interests or to his supporters.[93]

Odo II, moreover, was having difficulties at his stronghold of Saumur in the middle Loire valley where Gelduin, the lord of the castrum and traditionally a loyal supporter of Blésois interests, disagreed with the count over the choice of a new abbot for the monastery of Saint-Florent. After considerable difficulty Odo, who wanted to use this office to strengthen his ties with the viscounts of Thouars, managed to install Gerald of Thouars as abbot over the strong opposition of Gelduin. In these circumstances Theobald I of Blaison, the son and successor of Cadilo, Geoffrey Greymantle's and Fulk Nerra's loyal supporter in la Vallée, seized the opportunity to take the offensive against Blésois interests in the region between Saumur and Saint-Rémy-la-Varenne from his nearby stronghold (*podium*) at Sazé.[94]

The count of Blois, Fulk's major adversary in the west of France, took no noteworthy initiatives against the Angevins. It is likely that Odo was distracted by King Robert II's actions. For the monarch once again set aside Bertha, Odo's mother, and took back as queen Constance, Fulk Nerra's cousin. Although Robert's tergiversation does not seem to have precipitated an open break with the count of Blois, it surely cooled relations between them considerably. The situation worsened as Odo and Robert vigorously disagreed over what should be done concerning Count Renaud of Sens. The latter, who had succeeded his father Frotmund in 1012, soon gained a reputation for heretical leanings and more particularly for actively supporting the Jews to the detriment of Christians.[95] As the situation developed, King Robert became preoccupied with the idea of depriving Renaud of his *honor*. Odo, by contrast, seems to have given his support to Renaud and may have been influenced in this by the Jewish community of Blois, which he surely regarded as an economic asset.[96] A useful index of the importance of this episode is provided by Bishop Fulbert of Chartres who was asked by his archbishop, Letaldus of Sens, to condemn Renaud and by King Robert to mobilize support for the royal position. Fulbert, however, temporized for at least a year, perhaps because Odo, as count of Chartres, was his dominus. The second Capetian-Blésois axis gradually disintegrated under these stresses so that when King Robert attacked Sens, Odo sided with Count Renaud. Fulbert belatedly supported his king, and the monarch also had the support of Fulk Nerra's cousin, Walter II the White, who was count of Valois, Amiens, and Pontoise.[97] The byproduct was freedom for Fulk Nerra once again to pursue the Angevin policy of aggrandizement in the west.

CHAPTER SIX

Struggle for Mastery in the West: Part 1

Fulk Nerra did not hesitate to take advantage of the dissension between his adversaries and turned his attention to Maine. By early in 1014 Fulk was at war with Count Hugh. In order to secure his northwestern frontier during this period of hostilities, Fulk arranged for the castellum at Château-Gontier on the Mayenne to be upgraded and made it a castrum by adding a formidable tower. He then installed as castellan Renaud, son of Ivo.[1] This new addition to Fulk's entourage was likely related to the lords of Bêlleme, whose *honores* lay less than sixty kilometers north-northeast of le Mans, virtually on the Norman frontier.

The defensive importance of Château-Gontier rested in part on its strategic location thirty kilometers to the east of Sablé and twenty kilometers west of Craon. Thus troops stationed at Château-Gontier could help defend the strongholds on either of its flanks, and the latter could reciprocate with regard to the castrum in the middle. From an offensive perspective these three strongholds formed a sound base from which to project Angevin military power into western Maine. Therefore, when Fulk opened negotiations with Lisoius, the latter's holdings at Bazougers and Sainte-Christine, strategically located only twenty-five kilometers north-northeast of Château-Gontier, potentially created a new configuration in the form of a spearhead pointed at the important stronghold of Mayenne thirty-five kilometers farther north and only twenty kilometers from the Norman frontier.[2]

From the spearhead Angevin forces struck to the north through the valley of the Mayenne. They bypassed the village of Laval, which apparently boasted no fortifications of importance, and attacked the stronghold of Mayenne. This castrum was in Fulk's hands well before the end of 1014. There he established as castellan one of his supporters, a certain Aimo.[3] This assignment provides an additional glimpse of Fulk's careful manipulation of his fideles to prevent any one of them from building up a strong local base. Lisoius was being considered for a post on Anjou's eastern frontier but he was not permitted to augment his holdings at Bazougers and Sainte-Christine by becoming castellan at Mayenne. Similarly, the installation of Aimo at Mayenne deprived Renaud of the opportunity to develop a "western march" from his base at Château-Gontier. Indeed, Fulk's new castellan Aimo seems to have been a longtime but otherwise undistinguished member of the count's military household who was rewarded for loyal service.[4]

Fulk's success at Mayenne appears to have been only a prelude to what was intended as a campaign to conquer Maine. Before the end of 1014 Count Hugh appears to have regarded his position as hopeless, for he could not stop Fulk's advances. Thus, as a later account indicates, Fulk "violently subjugated Hugh to him";[5] another chronicler reports succinctly, "Fulk acquired Maine."[6] Hugh was permitted to remain as count with Fulk as his overlord. Shortly thereafter, however, Hugh died, leaving his son Herbert as heir. The boy had not yet reached his majority, and Fulk had no difficulty in keeping him under Angevin control.[7]

Although Fulk's victory seems to have been accomplished easily, I emphasize that the Angevin count's success and indeed his rationale for subjugating Count Hugh were not the result of policy he had initiated. Fulk surely took advantage of a propitious situation to gain his ends, but in effect he was following a policy his father had developed almost a half-century earlier. Geoffrey Greymantle seems to have secured either from Hugh Capet or from King Lothair, perhaps from both men, some right, however vague, to the overlordship of Maine. But Geoffrey had been unable to secure recognition from the counts of Maine that they held their county from him as, for example, he had from Guerech, count of Nantes. His failure, however, did not mean that the Angevin counts had abandoned their longterm aims with regard to their northern neighbors.[8]

Fulk Nerra followed Geoffrey Greymantle's policy of strengthening the Angevin position in Maine against the time when the claim of overlordship could be made good. For example, Fulk made bishop of Angers Hubert of Vendôme, who was a relative of the viscount of le Mans, and later Fulk favored the viscount's son, Radulf, by supporting his marriage to the prelate's niece and granting him various *honores* in the strategic Mauges region.[9] Fulk also maintained a close relationship with the viscount's brother Geoffrey, who held the important stronghold at Sablé, by supporting the latter's *fideles*, men such as Herveus the Razor, whom Fulk established at Champigné-sur-Sarthe.[10]

From the reign of Geoffrey Greymantle the ties of the Angevin counts to the viscounts of le Mans brought the former into close contact with the lords of Bellême. Geoffrey had played the key role in getting Seginfredus of Bellême the bishopric of le Mans. Avesgaud, Seginfredus's successor, was the brother of William of Bellême, the son of Ivo of Bellême, and the brother-in-law of Haimo of Château-du-Loir, whose son Gervais would follow his maternal uncle to the bishopric of le Mans.[11] Haimo was also a *fidelis* of Fulk Nerra, who granted him the rich churches of Bousse and Arthezé which belonged to the monks of Saint-Aubin.[12] It is because of these close Angevin relations with the lords of Bellême that I proposed Renaud, whom Fulk established at Château-Gontier, was connected to the Bêlleme family. Ivo, the name borne by Renaud's father, was a *Leitname* of the Bellême family, and Hildeburgis, the wife of Haimo and sister of William, had a brother named Ivo. This latter Ivo would have been of the correct age cohort to have fathered Renaud. In addition, it should be emphasized that the name Ivo is not found in the *Namengüter* of the Angevin aristocracy during this period.[13]

In addition to maintaining ties with the viscomital family of le Mans, playing a vital role in choosing the bishop of le Mans, and cultivating a good working relationship with the house of Bellême, the Angevin counts also recruited men of military worth from Maine, especially from le Mans. We have already mentioned Fulk's negotiations with Lisoius and Herveus the Razor. Other examples such as Ellianus of le Mans, whom Fulk established as castellan of the castrum of Loudun on the southern frontier, and Joscelin of le Mans, who was granted the curtis of Saint-Saturnin in the environs of Angers, are worthy of our notice.[14]

At about the same time that Fulk was bringing Hugh and Herbert under his lordship, he moved to continue the process of establishing le Loir River as the northern frontier of the Angevin state. To this end he arranged for Hubert of Champigné-sur-Sarthe, the son of Aremberga who was a relation of the Angevin comital house, to marry the daughter of Isembardus of le Lude.[15] The castrum of le Lude, located on the right bank of le Loir, was one of the key fortifications on the river, only twenty kilometers west of Château-du-Loir, which was held by Fulk's fidelis Haimo, and twenty-five kilometers northeast of the Angevin count's own stronghold at Baugé, which he had entrusted to Joscelin of Rennes, a longtime supporter of Geoffrey Greymantle. Isembardus of le Lude appears to have been recruited from the Angevin-controlled region of Seiches-sur-Loir where his father, also named Isembardus, had the *honor* of Beauvais.[16]

It is in the context of securing the northern frontier that Fulk completed his negotiations successfully with Lisoius of Bazougers, who was given an extensive command on the eastern frontier of the Angevin state. Lisoius was the son of Hugh of Lavardin (his stronghold was on le Loir only fifteen kilometers downriver from Vendôme) by his second wife, Odelina. Lisoius's sister Avelina was the heir to the castrum of Lavardin, which she brought as her dowry to Sigebrannus of Mayenne, probably a younger son of Fulk's castellan Aimo of Mayenne. Lisoius's mother was the sister of Viscount Radulfus of le Mans and of Geoffrey of Sablé. Thus Lisoius was related also to Viscount Hubert of Vendôme and Bishop Hubert of Angers. When Lisoius was established at Amboise, he gave his stronghold at Bazougers to his brother Algerius and his inheritance at Sainte-Christine to his other brother Albericus.[17]

On the eastern frontier of the Angevin state where Lisoius was now posted, Landry of Dun's defection and the death of Archembaud of Buzançais surely had weakened the elaborate defensive arrangements that Geoffrey Greymantle had developed some three decades earlier. Lisoius's appointment not only strengthened Fulk's ties with the local aristocracy of le Loir valley but brought into Angevin service a man of outstanding military ability. In addition, Lisoius brought with him to Fulk's eastern frontier a personal armed following composed of relatives and friends who constituted a professional cadre of battle-hardened fighting men who could be expected to be more effective and especially more easily mobilized for offensive action than the levies that were raised through the normal process of proclaiming the ban or, as the Angevin terminology has it, "issuing a *submonitio*."[18]

Lisoius's extensive command in the east included both the castrum at Amboise and the castrum at Loches. Fulk delegated to Lisoius the power to command both *minores* and *majores,* as one chronicler records it, or, as another writes, to command *ignobiles* and *nobiles.* Many of the *majores* or *nobiles* may be assumed to have had personal armed followings of their own while the *minores* or *ignobles* included both those who were freemen and those who were dependents or unfree. This delegation of power by Fulk also likely included the full spectrum of comital rights usually exercised by the count's vicarii and praepositi in military matters. The major source of Lisoius's remuneration for this *servitium* was what was left over from the tax receipts after he met the expenses required to do his job.[19]

Fulk's creation of a special command for Lisoius embracing the central and southern sectors of the eastern frontier constituted a rather more elaborate version of the marcher-type organization he had developed earlier in his reign. We have seen how Renaud of Thorigné held a special command and great responsibilities on the western frontier in the Mauges region. On the southern frontier Roger the Old held both Loudun and Montrevault and Bouchard held both Vihiers and Passavant. In the east Roger the Devil held the strongholds of Montrichard and Montrésor. These frontier commands seem to have been established to provide a capacity for a rapid coordinated defense and perhaps also to enable individual commanders to pursue Angevin offensive aims within an overall scheme outlined by the count. Indeed, early in his service in the east, Lisoius appears to have ventured vigorously into Berry for the purpose of exploiting the resources of the monastery of Selles-Saint-Eusice.[20]

Fulk Nerra's successes in Maine seem to have caused King Robert II and Odo II of Blois some anxiety, for despite their growing differences they met at Tours where the monarch confirmed several acts made by supporters of the house of Blois.[21] Nonetheless, the king and the count of Blois were unable to agree on a common course of action with regard to Fulk. Robert was distracted by affairs in Burgundy which were further complicated by the king's problems at Sens. Robert had launched a surprise attack against Sens on 22 April 1015 and the heavily fortified urbs fell immediately, but Count Renaud of Sens managed to escape and found refuge with Odo II. Moreover, the king was unable to move effectively to follow up his capture of Sens because Renaud's brother Frotmund held the citadel against Robert.[22]

Odo II now rallied to Count Renaud's cause, or perhaps more accurately he set to work against the king. Apparently he spent some time with Bishop Fulbert of Chartres in order to convince the prelate to support the opposition to Robert.[23] Odo was unable to win over Fulbert, even though the bishop of Chartres was his fidelis, but he did obtain from Renaud the strategically located stronghold of Montereau, which dominated the lower reaches of the Yonne at its confluence with the Seine just thirty-five kilometers northwest of Sens. From a strategic perspective, Montereau was the key to the northern attack route into Burgundy for King Robert. We may perhaps speculate that Odo, who was well acquainted with the monarch's interest in Burgundy, chose to ally with Renaud as a means of gaining this valuable point d'appui in order to strike a bargain with the king.[24]

Fulk Nerra once again was well prepared to take advantage of the hostilities between King Robert and Odo and also to take advantage of the conflict between the count of Blois and Gelduin of Saumur over control of the abbey of Saint-Florent at Saumur.[25] Thus, late in the spring or perhaps early in the summer of 1015 Fulk advanced into the Touraine with the object of retaking the stronghold of Montbazon. This important fortification, only twelve kilometers south of Tours, had apparently been lost by the Angevins while Fulk was on his second pilgrimage to the Holy Land. Fulk had besieged Montbazon once before, probably after his victory over Landry of Dun at Amboise, but without success.[26] This time Fulk was determined to succeed and he made elaborate preparations. On a small hill only five hundred meters to the south of the castrum of Montbazon, Fulk ordered the construction of a siege camp at a place now called Bazonneau. This investment of time and resources proved effective and Montbazon fell to Fulk's forces before the end of 1015. The Angevin count established William of Mirebeau there to command the garrison stationed at the castrum.[27]

We should note that Fulk's efforts to recapture Montbazon enjoyed a modicum of moral and political support by King Robert's call to his fideles for aid against Odo. In fact, from the king's perspective Fulk's invasion of the Touraine might be seen as part of a larger effort aimed at the count of Blois and his allies. For example, Bishop Hubert of Angers led an army of considerable size into the Touraine "at the king's order" for the purpose of injuring the count of Blois. Hubert, however, ravaged the lands of the archbishop of Tours, one of Odo's supporters. Archbishop Hugh vigorously objected to this "outrage" and after an exchange of letters in which Bishop Fulbert sided with the Blésois, Bishop Hubert was excommunicated by his metropolitan, Archbishop Hugh.[28] While Fulk and Hubert were on the offensive in the Touraine, Odo made an effort to alienate Angevin supporters in Maine and Vendôme; this utterly failed.[29]

Odo's possession of the stronghold of Montereau near Sens, Fulk's success in recapturing Montbazon, and Count Renaud of Sens's continued resistance apparently convinced King Robert that a negotiated settlement was preferable to war. Robert made peace with Renaud, and before the end of 1015, perhaps even as early as 24 October of that year, Odo II and the king were once again at peace with each other.[30] The monarch, however, was still not interested in taking action against Fulk. The king's attention was riveted on Burgundy, where he spent the early part of 1016. Then in April of the same year Robert went to Rome.[31]

Fulk was not reluctant to take advantage of Robert's preoccupation with affairs in the south or his failure to provide support for Odo II in the Touraine. During the campaigning season of 1016 Fulk gathered a large army, including a substantial contingent led by young Count Herbert of Maine, and laid siege to the formidable urbs of Tours.[32] When Odo learned that Fulk's army had invested Tours, the count of Blois levied a very large force of his own with the intention of going on the offensive.[33] Fulk, who kept himself well informed of Odo's movements, decided that it was unwise to continue the siege of Tours and moved his forces upriver to Amboise.[34]

With the stronghold of Amboise at his back, Fulk was well positioned to engage Odo's forces on favorable terms. The Angevin position at Tours had been insecure because Odo's forces controlled both the urbs and the castrum and Fulk's men would have been caught between two enemy forces, even if the Angevins had withdrawn from their siege emplacements to face the Blésois in a unified manner. Had the Angevins remained scattered in their siege emplacements, they would have been even more vulnerable and could have been attacked and destroyed a few at a time.

When Fulk learned that Odo was moving south from Blois toward the Beuvron, probably with the intention of fording this small river in the area of les Montils, he realized that the Blésois were intent on attacking the Angevin stronghold of Montrichard and were not headed either for Amboise or Tours. Fulk responded by taking advantage of his interior line of communication and transportation and moved a picked force of both footmen and horsemen approximately twenty-one kilometers east to Pontlevoy (ca. seven kilometers northeast of Montrichard) astride Odo's route to Montrichard. Fulk then dispatched Count Herbert of Maine with a detachment of mounted troops to Bourré less than five kilometers to the south in order to establish a fortified camp and deploy as a reserve.[35]

While Fulk was preparing to block Odo at Pontlevoy, the count of Blois moved south slowly at the head of a large army of *milites* and *pedites*, probably encumbered with siege engines and other *impedimenta* for the projected attack on Montrichard. When Odo's army arrived at Pontlevoy on the afternoon of 6 July, Fulk's forces were drawn up before them ready for battle. A contemporary report recorded in a later source indicates that Odo was "astonished" when he saw the Angevins. Fulk took full advantage of the element of surprise and launched an attack along the Blésois front. Before the Angevins were able to scatter the surprised but tightly packed enemy, Fulk's horse went down and the count was badly shaken. It was probably at this time that Sigebrannus, the castellan of Chemillé who served as Fulk's standard bearer, was either seriously wounded or killed. At this point in the engagement the Angevins broke off the attack and retired from the field; traditionally, the lowering of the standard was the signal for retreat.[36]

The Angevins retired from the field and a messenger was sent to Count Herbert to bring up the reserve. The count of Maine launched a vigorous attack from the west on the Blésois left flank. Blinded by the early evening July sun, Odo's men did not perceive the full significance of Herbert's advance until it was too late. Their resistance crumbled in the face of a coordinated attack along the enemy front which sent Odo's *milites* fleeing for their lives. The allied forces slaughtered the slower-moving *pedites* and Fulk's army is said to have taken no prisoners. Odo managed to escape with a group of his *socii*, and the Angevins, after looting the enemy baggage train, returned to their base at Amboise.[37]

Examination of Fulk's planning for the operations at Pontlevoy makes it clear that he again employed Vegetian military maxims in a consistent manner. Among the points worthy of emphasis was the effort to protect his forces should they be defeated on the field of battle. Thus, if the Angevins were driven off the field at Pontlevoy they could retire to Fulk's stronghold at Montrichard only seven kilometers to the south-southwest or withdraw to the fortified camp at Bourré, which was closer. Fulk's establishment of the camp at Bourré also blocked the only road along which reinforcements could reach the Blésois from Odo's stronghold at Saint-Aignan fifteen kilometers to the east-southeast. By establishing a reserve, just as he did at Conquereuil in 992, Fulk was following a primary Vegetian maxim. Indeed, the launching of two surprise attacks, initially and in the second phase of the battle, follows Vegetian advice as does the deployment of troops to take advantage of the setting sun in order to shield movements from the enemy.[38]

Despite the losses that Fulk suffered at Pontlevoy, he wasted little time and hurriedly set in motion a major military operation to follow up his recent victory. His forces moved downriver from Amboise and deployed to the north and west of Tours on the right bank of the Loire. At this point only a kilometer from the walls of Tours in a place called Montboyau, Fulk gathered large numbers of laborers and built a formidable military encampment that was considerably larger than the works he had constructed at Bazonneau the previous year.[39]

Like Bazonneau, which had been built to serve as a base for an attack on Montbazon, Montboyau was to be used as a staging center for the conquest of Tours. Fulk established a garrison at Montboyau not only to defend the stronghold itself but also to harass the banlieu of Tours.[40] Montboyau, however, was not primarily a siege camp established for an immediate attack. For Fulk to take control of Tours, as he obviously had learned in 996–997, it was not sufficient simply to put his troops in the urbs and the castrum. He needed strategic control of the region, political support, and some form of legitimization. Clearly, as events in 997 proved, the fact that Fulk the Red, Fulk Nerra's great grandfather, had once been viscount of Tours was insufficient to legitimize his control of the city and its environs.

The significance of investing substantial resources in Montboyau was that it formed part of a system that could give the Angevins strategic control of the region around Tours. Indeed, Tours was virtually encircled. Montbazon was twelve kilometers south of the city, Semblançay fourteen kilometers to the north-northeast, Maillé on the Loire only ten kilometers from Tours, and Amboise about twenty kilometers upriver. Although these strongholds had not been built for the purpose of threatening Blésois control of Tours, in combination they provided protection for a besieging force and their garrisons were positioned to interdict reinforcements and supplies to the besieged.[41]

After bringing to a close the successful campaigning season of 1016, highlighted by the great victory at Pontlevoy, Fulk returned to Angers. There, perhaps for the second time, he made use of the Via Triumphalis that led to the city. Fulk le Réchin wrote of his grandfather: "He had two great battles in the field: one at Conquereuil against Conan the Breton consul . . . the other battle against Odo . . . at Pontlevoy . . . where by the grace of God he was victor."[42]

Fulk Nerra's demonstrated interest in ceremony, whether to cele-brate an *adventus* of relics or a great military victory, and his attention to the perceived Roman past led the Angevin count to adorn the setting of the Via Triumphalis in a particularly striking manner. In an act drawn up during the later 1030s but which concerned actions taken much earlier, Fulk observed: "Dedi illi ecclesiae, super ripam Brionel, vineas ac viridigarium . . . cum culturis quam extirpavi et complanivi." In short, Fulk makes clear that he personally did the arduous rustic labor of pulling up the tree stumps and leveling the land so as to make it ready for planting as a *cultura*.[43] Fulk's statement "extirpavi et com-planivi" should not be taken to mean "I ordered the land to be cleared and leveled" but rather "I myself cleared and leveled the land." Fulk should be taken at his word here; his son Geoffrey Martel did exactly that only a few years after the old count's death. Geoffrey confirmed Fulk's gifts to Saint-Nicholas and observed: "culturam . . . quam . . . pater meus proprio labore silva extirpata, complavit et exsartum fuit" (my father with his own labor, having cleared out the woods, leveled [the field] and made an assart).[44]

Indeed, Geoffrey Martel was at least as interested in making known his father's personal efforts in the matter of agricultural labor as Fulk himself had been. In an act given at about the same time as the one just discussed, Geoffrey described Fulk's work in the following manner: "terram . . . quam pater meus bubus propriis excolebat et dicebatur Cultura comitis."[45] Thus it can be seen that Fulk not only cleared the land but that he worked it with his own oxen. The field where Fulk did his clearing and plowing was called "the count's cultivation" so that his work was widely advertised by the place-name.

The *cultura comitis* straddled the Via Triumphalis. Fulk further de-veloped the setting by adding a barn for his oxen in the southeastern part of this cleared field. In the southern part of the same field Fulk called attention in one of his documents to the kennel where he kept his dogs.[46] Thus, in the cultura Fulk planted the symbols of rustic and noble activity, that is, the ox and the hunting dog, along the triumphal military way. This stagelike setting may catch the eye of the reader familiar with the Cincinnatus story. As told by Livy (III, 29, 4–6), the hero was summoned from the plow, soundly defeated the enemy, and was awarded a triumph. He entered Rome along a specially designated via triumphalis.

That Livy should have been the locus classicus for the Angevin adap-tion of the Cincinnatus story fits well with eleventh-century knowledge of that classical Roman work. By the later tenth century there seems to have been a renaissance of interest in Livy. The emperor Otto III obtained a copy of Livy some time between 996 and 1001. His successor, Henry II, had this manuscript deposited at Bamberg where it was copied and intended for heavy use. At about the same time efforts were made at Cluny to obtain copies of Livy's *Ab urbe condita,* but in the present context the history of this text at Chartres is of primary importance.[47]

Fulbert, who first dominated the curriculum as head of the cathedral school at Chartres and then as bishop, began using a copy of Livy by the early eleventh century. Among Fulbert's early students at the cathedral school was a young man named Bernard, who went from his native Anjou to study at Chartres. After he had completed his education, he was recruited by Bishop Hubert to head the new cathedral school that the prelate had founded at Angers with the probable support of Fulk Nerra. By no later than 1012 Bernard was firmly established at Angers and he was to remain at his post, with occasional trips to the Conques region for "historical" research on Sainte Foy, until about 1025. Bernard's research methods and particularly his skepticism about evidence marks his internalization of classical ideas concerning the recording of what was true in the past, that is, what really happened.[48]

Other students with an interest in history also were recruited from the cathedral school at Chartres for services in Anjou. Among the most prominent of these was Renaud, who rose to head the cathedral school at Angers by 1039. He is noted for having written several historical works, and, perhaps more important, he was relied upon because of his critical eye for authenticating documents at issue in court proceedings. His methods were not inferior to those used in the Roman world and indeed are employed by specialists in diplomatics to this day.[49] Renaud's contemporary Berengar of Tours, the noted heresiarch and critic, was given a prebend by Fulk Nerra and served on the count's staff.[50] Thus, we note with great interest that Renaud and Berengar together crafted the Latin text of the document in which Fulk Nerra referred to the land that he himself had cleared (the "Cultura comitis") and which describes the scene along the Via Triumphalis.[51]

Fulk Nerra's effort to convey a Cincinnatus-like image of himself with a tableau of rustic labor and military glory appears to have been grasped by historians at the Angevin court during the following century. Thus, for example, the authors of the *Gesta Consulum,* a history of the Angevin counts, refer to Fulk's ancestor as Torquatius, an obvious twisting of the name of Cincinnatus's *magister equitum,* Tarquitius (Livy, III, 27, 1–2), and they characterize the great success of the dynasty with a paraphrase of Livy: "It is not surprising for we often read that senators have lived on the land and emperors have been snatched from the plough."[52]

The authors of the *Gesta Consulum,* however, were not limited to Fulk Nerra's Cincinnatus tableau or descriptions of it in various documents for evidence that the Angevin counts in the late tenth and eleventh centuries had an interest in seeing themselves depicted in a Roman or neo-Roman manner. For example, Geoffrey Greymantle, Fulk's father, permitted himself to be described in legal documents by honorifics used by Roman consuls or thought to have been used by such important figures. Indeed, in light of Geoffrey Greymantle's use of a red cloak, the *trabea* customary for the Roman consul, he himself may well have insisted that scribes use the honorifics we encounter such as *illustrissimus, noblissimus,* and *magnificentissimus.*[53]

Fulk himself saw his *officium* characterized by the term *consulatus.* Indeed, as the following text seems to suggest, annals kept in Anjou used the years of Fulk's "consulship" for dating purposes: "Fulk the Jerusalemite succeeded to the rule of the *comté* and sustained the situation concerning both churches until the 28th year of his *consulatus* . . . at which time a partition was made . . . This partition was sustained until the 42nd year of the *consulatus* of the above-mentioned Fulk . . . "[54] Fulk likely used the term *consul* to describe himself, and his son Geoffrey Martel did so from early in his reign.[55]

The development of the complex of ideas which cast the Angevins in a Roman light was doubtless intended to play a role in legitimizing their usurpation of regalian rights. Among the most important of these rights was independent military command, which in Roman tradition was a consular or proconsular right. Indeed, unlike Geoffrey Greymantle who recognized that he was "count of the Angevins" by the grace of God and "senioris mei domni Hugonis largitione," Fulk confined his dependence to "gratia Dei" and did not recognize Capetian overlordship.[56]

Fulk's ability to maintain Angevin "independence" and his ability to strive to dominate the west rested in part on the economic and strategic base provided by his capital city of Angers, the Roman Juliomagus. As with so much else, however, Fulk was not an innovator but built upon the sound foundation his father and even his grandfather had established. Thus, for example, Fulk the Good (d. 960) had reversed the pattern of economic and demographic decline afflicting Anjou and more particularly Angers because of the Viking raids. Geoffrey Greymantle supported his father's initiatives by building mills, irrigations systems, and supporting the refounding of monasteries with burgs in their environs.[57]

An important index of Angevin economic and demographic success is Geoffrey Greymantle's increase of the perimeter of the city walls to protect the people who had settled in the *suburbia*.[58] When Juliomagus was first fortified around 275, the perimeter wall was barely 1,200 meters in circumference and enclosed nine hectares.[59] But from the late tenth century several expansions were carried out. The first by Geoffrey Greymantle and the second and third by Fulk Nerra, probably following the fires of 1000 and 1032, expanded the circumference to 1,900 meters and the area enclosed to twelve hectares.[60]

The population living within the walls combined with those dwelling in the burgs, located a bow shot or less beyond the defenses, likely numbered well in excess of six thousand. Indeed, in order to provide for the defense of a 1,900-meter perimeter, military doctrine of the period required that one man be assigned to defend each 1.37 meters of wall.[61] This indicates that the militia of *urbani* at Angers numbered about 1,600 able-bodied men between the ages of fifteen (the age of majority) and fifty-five.[62] The density of the population within the walls is difficult to calculate because it is not possible to ascertain how many people lived in the burgs and the latter must be subtracted from the total. For example, the area between the monastery of Saint-Aubin and the walls, about 125 meters, was fully built up with houses and shops.[63] Nevertheless, it would be surprising if the population density within the walls were less than 350 per hectare and it was likely much greater.[64]

This pattern of demographic growth beginning in the second half of the tenth century and not confined to Angers brought substantial wealth to the inhabitants of Fulk Nerra's capital through trade and manufacturing. Elements of the population became sufficiently wealthy to be called upon for military service beyond the obligation of local defense, which was incumbent on all eligible *urbani*. Thus, for example, within twenty-five years of Fulk's death well in excess of a thousand *cives* from Angers were available to serve in *expeditio*.[65] At the other extreme, poverty had not been eliminated, but the little charity that was required was provided in part by the count with the help of the church.[66]

Angers' dynamic growth was largely a result of its propitious location at the confluence of the Mayenne and Loire rivers. The Mayenne was the major artery for water transportation draining the rich agricultural lands of western Maine. The Angevins dominated the course of the river and its valley with a line of strongholds sited as far north as the castrum at Mayenne more than a hundred kilometers from Angers itself. On the Loire Angers stood between the port city of Nantes and Tours to the east. This stretch of the Loire, the major artery for commerce in western France, was under Angevin control, with the exception of Saumur, which would fall to Fulk in 1026.[67] I emphasize that Angers' location became an advantage because Fulk Nerra had developed a system of defense that protected his capital from enemy attack. In contrast, during much of the ninth century Angers had been easy prey to the Vikings because of its geography.[68]

In addition to the vast income from direct and indirect taxes on trade collected by the Angevin counts, Fulk Nerra appears to have played a dominent role in the production and sale of salt from "pans" in the environs of Nantes. Salt, one of the necessities of life, was shipped from Nantes along the Loire as far as the monastery of Saint-Benoit, east of Orléans, and perhaps farther. It also may have been one of the commodities traded at Nantes on oceangoing ships, that is, vessels with two or more masts as contrasted to river craft, which sailed into the Loire perhaps as far as Saint-Florent-le-Vieil about forty kilometers west of Angers as the crow flies.[69]

With the exception of the production and sale of salt, Fulk's government appears to have had little direct involvement in either manufacturing or commerce. Nonetheless, the count's officials kept a close eye on all aspects of business. For example, a *colliberta* named Christina and her son-in-law, a *collibertus* named Gauterius Nafragallus, who were dependents of the cathedral of Saint Maurice, owned a washing house (*domus lavandaria*) by the river outside the walls of Angers where they washed the bishop's clothing. After some time, it became clear that they were not able to make a living from this business, perhaps because they were limited to serving the bishop and his entourage. Thus, "compelled by the necessity of poverty," they sold the wash house, with the consent of the prelate, to Archardus *Barba Torta* and Bernardus, both freemen. The new owners retained the bishop's business.[70] This sale of a failing business to a pair of entrepreneurs unconnected to the episcopal establishment came to the attention of Fulk Nerra's officials at Angers, even though the wash house was located outside the walls of the urbs.

Michael, the *magister* in charge of Fulk's *ministri*, understood that the wash house had left the control of the bishop and concluded therefore that the exemption from taxes (*consuetudines*) previously granted to Saint Maurice for this property was no longer valid. Thus Fulk's agents, under Michael's leadership, went to the wash house and when they found no one there they broke in. Once inside they seized a chest, dumped its contents on the floor, and carried it back to Fulk's court ("curiam comitis").[71] Fulk's *ministri* clearly thought the new owners owed some taxes to the government. In lieu of payment, they seized the said chest. Apparently they were not set on looting the premises, for they left behind the rather valuable contents of the chest. In addition, they were aware of the previous tax exemption and concluded that it had lapsed upon the sale. The tax exemption, as Michael apparently understood the law, was not transferable with the property.

We may wonder how the situation at the wash house might have developed had Archardus and Bernardus been present with some of the prelate's retainers when Michael and his men arrived, especially if the new owners had known that Bishop Hubert argued that the tax exemption was transferable to the new owners.[72] Violence in such circumstances was not out of the question, as some of Fulk's men learned to their sorrow in a confrontation with the armed retainers of the abbot of Saint-Aubin. The details of this conflict, which took place within the walls of the town, are obscure, but five of the count's men were killed and the abbot had to pay a substantial compensation, which rankled the monks for many years thereafter.[73]

These cases highlight several aspects of the local government of Angers. The count's praepositus oversaw a bureaucracy that was sufficiently well staffed and well informed to take an active interest in a recently sold business of rather minor importance located outside the walls of the urbs. The *ministri* who served under the praepositus were led, at least on occasion, by junior officers like Michael who apparently were styled *magistri*. These officials obviously had access to records concerning land ownership, taxes owed or assessed, and exemptions granted. Some of these men surely were literate.[74]

The government of Angers should not be confused with the count's household staff, which often stayed at the *curia comitis* but was equally prepared to take the road with Fulk. This staff of *servientes comitis* saw to the functions of government and likely was more rather than less finely articulated, given the volume of business and breadth of concerns they handled. Some members of the government even had titles, such as *buticularius*. Dodo, who held this office toward the latter part of Fulk's reign, was of servile origin; this suggests that the Angevin count was not averse to rewarding merit regardless of social status. Theobald, Dodo's predecessor, was made a castellan after his service in the count's household. Fulk also had a chaplain and probably a chamberlain. The countess Hildegarde had at least a *cameraria*. She also employed a vicarius to head her *familia*. Those who performed the wide variety of other tasks required to keep the government running, like record keeping and writing up the *submonitiones* that called Fulk's subjects to serve in a *bellum publicum,* were often recruited, like Renaud and Berengar discussed above, from local religious establishments.[75]

Fulk Nerra's crowded and bustling capital city undoubtedly was a source of pride to the count as well as a vital source of income. The economic development of Angers, like Fulk's military victories, contributed to his image of success in the eyes of contemporaries. We have seen Fulk restore churches, encourage the building of burgs, and expand the city's defenses. He also sought to demonstrate that spiritual forces sustained his goals at Angers. Thus, for example, he donated relics to religious houses such as the chapel of Sainte-Geneviève near the comital palace.[76] Another helpful insight into Fulk's attitude in the matter of relics derives from a series of orders he issued concerning two caskets found by the monks of Saint-Aubin. When Fulk learned of the find, he went to the site at the monastery and first ordered that the caskets be opened in his presence. According to the report of the episode, an inscription—the transcription permits the inference that it was uncial and of high quality—which identified the bodies in one casket as belonging to the saints Lautho, Rumpharius, and Coronarius and those in the second casket as belonging to the saints Marculfus and Carrullus. After the relics had been identified, Fulk gave Saint-Aubin several items of worship and "decorations worthy of an entire monastery" and ordered that these be set up along with the saints' relics in a suitable place so as to provide an appropriate means for instructing those who visited the shrine to honor the saints in the proper manner.[77]

We cannot be sure of Fulk's personal religious feelings, but we can argue that his contemporaries would be impressed by such a display of spiritual wealth and perhaps, more important, by the favor shown by these saints to Saint-Aubin, to Angers, and to Fulk Nerra himself.[78] Parenthetically, it may also be noted that Fulk, as a result of his connections with Saint-Martin of Tours when he held the castrum in 996–997, was aware that well-publicized and powerful relics attracted large numbers of visitors who in turn increased the *fama* and the revenues of the locality.

After bringing the campaigning season of 1016 to a close and celebrating the triumph at Angers, Fulk still had to deal with King Robert. He chose not to take advantage of the strategic advantage the Angevins so obviously enjoyed at Tours. He did not lay siege to the city. Perhaps he did not consider his political situation sufficiently strong. Bishop Renaud of Paris, Fulk's former brother-in-law, had died very recently and thus there would be a new count of Vendôme. This situation presented an opportunity to secure an Angevin objective identified a generation earlier when Geoffrey Greymantle arranged for Fulk to marry Elizabeth of Vendôme, Renaud's sister.[79] Clearly Adele, the daughter of Elizabeth of Vendôme and Fulk Nerra, and her sons, none of whom had yet reached his majority, had some claim to the county as the only direct heirs of Count Bouchard the Venerable, Bishop Renaud's father. But the castrum of Vendôme itself and much of the surrounding territory was held, at least nominally, by the count of Vendôme from the bishop of Chartres. Although Bishop Renaud and the Vendômois aristocracy, which was closely allied to Fulk Nerra, had not submitted to Bishop Fulbert's claims, the death of Renaud would surely result in a reopening of the dispute. Bishop Fulbert thus was provided with an opportunity to renew his claims, and, because he was a fidelis of Odo II, these efforts were likely to be prejudicial to Fulk's interests. In these circumstances Fulk's failure to open a vigorous campaign to capture Tours suggests that he was waiting to see how the larger picture would develop.

Perhaps history had taught Fulk Nerra that the king would play a major role in decisions at Vendôme. Fulk needed only to recall Hugh Capet's disposal of the Gâtinais and Robert's settlement of affairs at Sens and Beauvais as well as the role the king played in Champagne. So, rather than attacking Tours in the summer of 1017, Fulk attended a massive royal conclave of lay and ecclesiastical princes held at Compiègne on 9 June to crown Robert II's son, young Hugh, and support his association in the kingship.[80] At this gathering not only did King Robert obtain recognition for his son as coruler and heir by the most important nobles of the *regnum Francorum* but many of the latter seem to have gained considerably as well. For example, in connection with the elevation of young Hugh, Odo II was promised the title "Count of the Palace" and had his rights to succession in Champagne recognized. William of Aquitaine's usurpation of control over the bishopric of Limoges appears to have been accepted.[81] Among the "deals" made at Compiègne, Bouchard, Adele's son and Bishop Renaud's nephew, was recognized as the legitimate heir to the *comté* of Vendôme. Fulk Nerra, young Bouchard's maternal grandfather, however, took active control of the region with the support of his daughter Adele and the magnates of the Vendômois headed by Viscount Hubert, the father of Bishop Hubert of Angers. It is also clear that young Bouchard's father, Bodo of Nevers, played no role in the succession.[82]

Whatever the diplomatic dynamics at the Compiègne summit meeting may have been, Fulk Nerra emerged as the dominant figure in the Vendômois following the death of Bishop Renaud of Paris. The acquisition of the stronghold of Vendôme, the plans for which had been laid more than thirty years earlier, was crucial to the development of defensible frontiers for the growing Angevin state. Vendôme was the anchor of the Angevin northern and eastern frontiers, one of which stretched south to Loches and the other westward along le Loir River.

When Fulk assumed control at Vendôme, arrangements had long been in force by which the count and important members of his entourage provided garrison troops for the defense of the castrum.[83] Some of these magnates were already Fulk's men before he assumed control of Vendôme, for example, Viscount Hubert and others, men such as Gundacrus, Otredus, Hilgaudus, Hugo, Fulcherius, and Hamilinus, soon submitted themselves to the new count.[84]

The strategic importance of Vendôme should not be underestimated, but Fulk also gained valuable economic resources when he took control of the region. For example, at about the same time that Fulk recognized the potential for the economic exploitation of the region of Loches–Belli Locus on the frontier with Berry, Bishop Renaud, acting in his capacity as count of Vendôme, carried out extensive assarting in the Gâtine (the wasteland) of the Vendômois and built a "new town" that he named Ville l'Evêque. There he built a church and established a market. With the resources that accrued from this establishment, Fulk secured the firm support of the Vendômois magnate Hamilinus.[85]

Another index of the economic viability of the Vendômois during the period was Fulk's decision that the economy could sustain "new" taxes without being depressed as a result. Thus Fulk mandated a toll called the *pedagium*, to be collected on all those who traveled within the region carrying goods to sell, and the *minagium*, a tax on salt. The complaints by local inhabitants that these were taxes that had never before been collected in the region are tendentious, at least with regard to the *pedagium*, which was in force during the Carolingian era. What is likely is that Fulk was not imposing a new tax but reimposing old ones that had ceased to be collected.[86] That Fulk's contemporaries, like

Frederick who became abbot of Saint-Florent in 1021, and presumably the count himself were aware that excessive taxation had a depressive effect on economic development is not at issue here.[87] The point to be emphasized is that Fulk moved quickly after gaining power in the Vendômois to integrate the region into the tax system that prevailed throughout the Angevin state and that provided much of the resource base to sustain government.[88]

Even after securing the Angevin succession at Vendôme, Fulk still did not move against Tours. Rather, he left the task of pursuing Angevin interests to Lisoius, who now commanded the eastern frontier in the Touraine. Lisoius was opposed on the local level by Odo II's *miles* Nevolus, who was the castellan of Chaumont, and by Burellus, who commanded the garrison at Blois.[89]

Although Fulk chose not to press home the Angevin military advantage at Tours, he did not remain idle. Closer to home, Fulk grasped the opportunity provided by the conflict between Gelduin and Odo at Saumur to exploit the monastery of Saint-Florent. When Abbot Adhebertus died in 1013, Gelduin sought to have his man Galo appointed as abbot, but Odo preferred to use the office as a means of strengthening his ties with Viscount Radulfus of Thouars and so appointed Gerald of Thouars. When Radulfus died about 1014, his successor Geoffrey showed himself to be considerably less hostile to Fulk. Thus Abbot Gerald of Saint-Florent, a loyal supporter of Viscount Geoffrey, found himself in a difficult position, at odds both with Gelduin and with Odo.[90]

In this awkward situation, Gerald had little choice but to deal with Fulk. Among the many concessions that he made to the Angevin count, several are worthy of note. For example, Gerald recognized the authority of the Angevin government at the villa of Saint-Georges-sur-Layon, which was an extremely wealthy economic unit. The villa was established as a vicaria or administrative unit of the government in which the count's officials administered justice, collected taxes, and mustered the population, both free and unfree, for various types of military service. The *servientes* of the count, who were assigned to the *officium* of the vicarius, collected the taxes on what was produced at the villa at a rate of ten percent (a *decima*) of the gross production. In addition, these *servientes* received a substantial part of their sustenance as part of the taxes they collected. In this regard the government's lowliest agents shared a similar source of income (if not a similar level) with the more highly placed, such as vicarii, praepositi, and castellans.[91]

While the losses suffered by Saint-Florent at Saint-Georges were not far from the monastery itself, Fulk's major efforts at utilizing the monks' resources appear to have been reserved for their holdings in the Mauges region where Saint-Florent-le-Vieil was located. Albericus, the son of the late Albericus of Vihiers and a relative of Fulk Nerra, was established in the Mauges region at the newly constructed stronghold of Montjean. Soon after, Gerald was forced to hand over to Alberic the church of Saint Aubin at Châteaupanne along with everything that pertained to it. (This stronghold at Châteaupanne had been conceded to Fulk's vassalus Drogo by Abbot Robert of Saint-Florent at the count's "request" a decade earlier.) Gerald also was persuaded of the necessity of giving the church of Notre-Dame at Menil, only six kilometers from Saint-Florent-le-Vieil, to a *miles* from Châteaupanne named Peter.[92]

Fulk's concentration on the Mauges region at this time was likely dictated by the problems of Count Budic of Nantes, who was engaged in a serious military conflict with Bishop Walter of Nantes and the latter's ally, Count Alan of Rennes. Budic had sought Fulk's aid and promised once again to recognize that he held the *comté* from the Angevin count. Budic also claimed extensive rights over the holdings of Saint-Florent in the Mauges region, but the dependence of the count of Nantes made it possible for Fulk to choose to ignore the claims made by this fidelis. The Angevin count provided *auxilium* to Budic during his war with Alan and on at least one occasion personally commanded troops within the walled city of Nantes itself. Alan's efforts, which at this time lacked support either from his Blésois overlord or Norman relatives, allowed Fulk to stabilize the situation at Nantes and thoroughly dominate the western frontier.[93]

In sum, this first phase of Fulk Nerra's struggle for mastery in the West saw him establish firm control of the valley of the Mayenne in western Maine and seize the stronghold of Mayenne, which lay within striking distance of the Norman frontier. Angevin relations with the Bellême family suggest the possibility of future aggression against Normandy. The situation in the Touraine following the battle of Pontlevoy was excellent. Odo II had been badly defeated and Tours, at least from the military perspective, was ripe for the taking. The Vendômois fell firmly under Angevin control and various fortified links on Fulk's northern frontier along le Loir rapidly were being forged. The western frontier and control of Nantes were for the moment firm. Thus by about 1020 the Angevin position in the west of Francia was well in the ascendance.

CHAPTER SEVEN

Struggle for Mastery in the West: Part 2

Following the series of successes that Fulk Nerra enjoyed in Maine, in the Touraine, and at Nantes in western Francia, the Angevin count turned his attention to the advancement of Angevin interests in Aquitaine at the expense of Duke William. Fulk's man Aimery I of Rancon held the stronghold of Gençay from the Angevin count and also possessed the stronghold of Mallevallis (the location of this fortification in the Poitou has not been identified). Aimery then took the stronghold of Civray from William's supporter Count Bernard of la Marche and Chizé from William himself. After the death of Aimery I, his son and successor, Aimery II, lost Civray to William and Gençay to Hugh of Lusignan. Hugh, however, was also Fulk Nerra's man and through a series of negotiations orchestrated by the Angevin count, Aimery was reestablished at Gençay.[1] We should recall that all strongholds held in the Poitou or in greater Aquitaine from Fulk were rendable to him on demand.[2]

The importance of the actions just described is not only that they illustrate that Fulk's fideles were prominent men in the Poitou who controlled various strongholds—although these realities were hardly unimportant—but also that these men kept the local situation throughout Duke William's lands in a state of continuous unrest. William was therefore in the unenviable position of having to engage in frequent diplomatic and military maneuvers, often of a dubious legal and ethical nature, in order to avert a large-scale civil war. These maneuvers, however, undermined William's credibility among the magnates, such as

Hugh of Lusignan, who perceived the duke's weak position and sought to take advantage of it. Moreover, William found it virtually impossible to act effectively without the support of Fulk Nerra and the latter's brother-in-law, William of Angoulême.[3]

Fulk had built upon the gains Geoffrey Greymantle had made in the south and by about 1020 he had secured control of much of the northern Poitou and the Mauges region. By the settlement of 999 William recognized Fulk as holding the castrum of Loudun and several other strongholds in the Poitou. These probably included Gençay, Parthenay, and Mirebeau.[4] Vihiers, on the border between the Poitou and Anjou, had been a longtime Angevin possession, and Faye-le-Vineuse may be considered in the Angevin sphere of influence when its lord Aimery appears in Fulk's entourage around 1020.[5]

By 1006 Fulk had gained control of numerous allods in the Mauges, a region traditionally disputed by the counts of Poitou and Nantes. These allods Fulk distributed to his *milites*. The Angevin position in the Mauges region was further strengthened by building or gaining control of strongholds at Montrevault, Montjean, Châteaupanne, and Chemillé. By dominating Count Budic of Nantes and coming to a rapprochement with Viscount Geoffrey of Thouars, Fulk was left with a free hand in the Mauges to exploit the resources of Saint-Florent-le-Vieil.[6]

In William's own pagus of the Poitou, Fulk Nerra's brother-in-law William of Angoulême controlled the viscounty of Melle and its formidable castrum. Like Fulk, William of Angoulême dominated extensive *honores* in Aquitaine, his being on the borders of the Poitou and in the Saintonge.[7] During the period from 1018 to about 1021 William of Aquitaine met at least four times with Fulk to obtain advice and support.[8] We should note, in addition, that without Fulk, or more often without the Angevin count's surrogate, William of Angoulême, Duke William of Aquitaine was virtually powerless to take effective military action.[9] Indeed, in contrast with Fulk, who for twenty years had been expanding Angevin power and influence on all fronts despite two lengthy pilgrimages and the opposition of a formidable array of adversaries, William of Aquitaine appears to have lost many of the prerogatives enjoyed by his father, William Iron Arm, and he was in serious danger of suffering even greater losses at the hands of his Angevin neighbor.[10]

While Angevin interests were being pursued on all fronts by Fulk's supporters, the count's personal attention turned to the final stages of building a monastery at Angers to be dedicated to Saint Nicholas. Several stories circulated to explain the delay of more than a decade between Fulk's obviously well-publicized vow to build the monastery and the flurry of activity that took place in the year or two before 1020 when the building was completed. Fulk also seems to have shown some reluctance to recruit monks, and this too appears to have attracted some attention.[11]

Two of these stories may be of some importance. In the first Fulk is described looking out the windows of the comital *aula* at Angers. From this vantage point, he often noticed a dove picking up small bits and pieces of mortar in its beak and carrying them to a rock where they were deposited in a hole that was gradually being filled up. The account continues and makes clear that by watching this dove Fulk's mind was drawn to the danger he had experienced at sea on his pilgrimage and the vow he had made to build a monastery in honor of Saint Nicholas.[12] The second account tells how Fulk rode his horse to be watered in the Mayenne River beneath the castellum of Saint Mary. At the watering site both horse and rider were struck with great fear, and Fulk is quoted as saying: "O enemy! I will send monks right now to that place [Saint-Nicholas]."[13]

Neither of these stories can be easily related to the particular circumstances surrounding Fulk's vow to build a monastery[14] or to the vast tradition associated with Saint Nicholas's activities.[15] In short, since these stories lack a source from which they may have been copied, they may in fact be true. Because of information recorded, provided the stories are not complete fabrications, only Fulk Nerra himself could have provided the relevant data about his thoughts. Some circumstantial evidence regarding topography suggests that the stories do reveal the count's perspective. The image of the count looking out of the windows of the *aula* above the Mayenne River is consistent with the castle's situation. Second, the *castellum Sanctae Mariae,* a free-standing tower of late Roman origins and its related fortifications about 150 meters west of the comital *aula* and the walls of Angers, was well located to guard the low point in the river where horses could easily be watered.[16]

How an energetic dove and a spooked horse were related in Fulk's mind to a near-disaster at sea and his vow to build a monastery might form the basis for some stimulating speculation, but rather than follow that path, I tend to agree with R. W. Southern, who described how Geoffrey Martel, Fulk's son, and his wife Agnes witnessed a meteor fall to earth and vowed to build an abbey dedicated to the Holy Trinity.

Southern concluded: "It was in the face of the miraculous that they became most human."[17] I only ask rhetorically, have humans really changed very much during the past millennium?

We cannot guess at the feelings that may have inspired Fulk to make a vow when he believed his mortal life in danger. Nevertheless, the building of a monastery based on such a vow would recall to everyone Fulk's heroic journey to the Holy Land, in fact, his second such *peregrinatio* at a time of persecution of pilgrims by the caliph al Hakim II. That Saint Nicholas saved Fulk during a storm that wrecked the ship and forced him ashore at Myra added yet one more holy protector to the array of those who looked after the Angevin count's welfare.[18]

Fulk's encounter with Saint Nicholas took place off the coast of Myra where the holy man was perhaps best known for saving travelers from the perils of the deep. By the year 1000, however, this former bishop of Myra was well known throughout Western Europe for a lengthy list of attributes. Among these were several on which Fulk might hope to capitalize. For example, Saint Nicholas was regarded as a patron of the military, and Fulk was first and foremost a soldier (*miles*). In addition, Nicholas was known as a patron of secular piety, and by restoring and building churches Fulk surely was trying to cultivate an image of himself as pious, perhaps with the aid of the memory of his grandfather, Fulk the Good, for whom he was named. Finally, Saint Nicholas was a patron of merchants, and, as we have seen, Fulk was working hard to develop trade and commerce throughout Anjou.[19]

The act of building and endowing a monastery could certainly do Fulk no harm in the eyes of influential churchmen like Fulbert of Chartres who in general seem not to have been favorably impressed by the Angevin count's treatment of the church. Still, the *fama* Fulk may have acquired among the *rustici* and the sophisticated (churchmen and laymen alike) by building and richly endowing Saint-Nicholas should not be ignored when it comes time to evaluate the methods by which a reputation was built and *auctoritas* established. Fulk himself in the foundation charter for Saint-Nicholas downplayed the role of the intellect in the attainment of salvation and stressed the importance of providing resources to places that were prepared for divine veneration. In this context of providing resources to Saint-Nicholas, he emphasized yet another of Saint Nicholas's attributes, care for the poor, which had been long established.[20]

Fulk's early charters for Saint-Nicholas also provide some indication of his efforts to establish a neo-Roman image. Thus the *proomium* of one act reads: "In earlier times some kings (*reges*) and princes (*principes*) cared to build churches in the name of Christ, and [now] I Fulk, count of the Angevins, despite being one of the last and least worthy of men, ordered a church to be built in the name of God and of Saint Nicholas . . . "[21] Here Fulk claims no great title such as *rex* or *princeps* within the institutional framework of the *regnum Francorum* but appears content only to see himself styled *comes*. Fulk, however, like his sometime adversaries, the Norman duke and the Aquitanian duke, was beginning to think of himself as *consul*.[22] We note in Livy (IX.46.6) that only an individual with consular rank or possession of the *imperium* (the power to command) "posse templum dedicare." Thus it was legitimate for a count/consul, not only a *rex* or *princeps,* to establish a religious foundation (*templum*).

Fulk chose to express several ideas in his charters for the foundation and support of Saint-Nicholas which more than intimated the legitimacy of some aspects of Angevin autonomy. In addition to the obligation of the ruler to look after the poor and found *templa,* Fulk discussed his *Via Triumphalis,* described his Cincinnatus-like rustic labor, legislated on military service, and identified one gift "as a royal allod" (that is, exempt from the *census*).[23] This complex of allusions was probably intentional and may perhaps have been associated in Fulk's mind with the connection of the cult of Saint Nicholas in the German empire with the imperial family through the efforts of the Empress Theophano and her entourage. In addition, Nicholas was strong in Lotharingia, the homeland of Fulk's wife, the countess Hildegarde, who was of royal blood. Nicholas was also a saint of late antiquity, a fact well known in the West, and firmly associated with imperial and neo-Roman matters in the contemporary world of Fulk Nerra.[24]

When Saint-Nicholas was completed, Fulk sought as the first abbot a monk from the monastery of Marmoutier, at this time the spiritual leader in the west of France. Abbot Evrard sent a very pious monk named Baldric who displayed a strong inclination for separation from the cares of the world. Baldric, indeed, abandoned his responsibilities and "secretly sought the desert," according to Fulk.[25] Baldric may have found his obligation as abbot to play a major role in the Angevin military organization too secular to tolerate.[26]

In a larger sense it is more important to note that Marmoutier, on the outskirts of Tours, was in the *mouvance* of the count of Blois. At the very moment that Fulk sought Evrard's support the abbot was taken up with the task given to him by Odo of repairing the damage done to Saint-Florent by Abbot Gerald (of Thouars) during his brief tenure there.[27] No source indicates why Fulk chose to establish a connection between Marmoutier and Saint-Nicholas and thereby risk the infiltration of potentially hostile Blésois influence into his new foundation and into the Angevin capital itself. We may speculate that Angevin religious enthusiasm had seriously degenerated since the days when Fulk's uncle Guy had reformed Saint-Aubin in the 960s. The Angevin count perhaps was seeking to kindle the spark of renewal with the Marmoutier flame. The potential political risks might therefore have been regarded as inconsequential shadows dimmed by the brilliance of reform. It certainly would be foolish to deny that a complex character like Fulk was capable of being spiritually motivated in an apolitical manner, at least for a brief period of time.

We would be equally shortsighted, however, to ignore any examination of the political ramifications of these actions simply because we are considering the foundation of a religious institution. Although Marmoutier was clearly in the sphere of influence of the house of Blois around 1020, this had not always been the case. Only a quarter-century earlier the Capetians had dominated Marmoutier.[28] Political realities were such during this period that the domination of religious foundations could pass quickly from one lay power to another. Fulk surely understood this when he set out to undermine Odo II's control of Saint-Florent by obtaining recognition as *senior* by Abbot Robert around 1006.

From a political point of view, domination of Marmoutier, along with domination of the canons of Saint-Martin and the archbishopric, was important to the control of Tours. The Angevins had frequently shown an interest in gaining favor with the monks of Marmoutier, and many of Fulk's newly acquired fideles in the Vendômois had traditionally been generous to this monastery as well. Indeed, within a short time of establishing a Marmoutier abbot at Saint-Nicholas, Fulk Nerra and the viscount Hubert of Vendôme, father of Bishop Hubert of Angers, made gifts to Marmoutier.[29] Whatever complex of reasons may have motivated Fulk to seek the Marmoutier connection, religious reform, personal *fama*, and political advantage should not be viewed as mutually exclusive.

Fulk's advances in Aquitaine and Maine and his increasing influence over the monastery of Saint-Florent as well as his initiatives in the west, where he tipped the balance in favor of Budic in the latter's conflict with Alan of Rennes, were not ignored by King Robert II and Odo

II, who drew closer together during the years immediately following the coronation of young Hugh in 1017. A high point in the good relations between the king and the count of Blois was reached, at least symbolically, when Robert awarded the title "Count of the Palace" to Odo. Robert also supported Odo's inheritance of major *honores* in Champagne.[30]

Cooperation between Robert and Odo historically had meant trouble for Fulk. Indeed, by 1020 Gerald of Thouars, who had permitted Fulk to have his way with the *facultates* of Saint-Florent, was forced by Odo to leave the monastery. The exiled abbot took the pilgrimage road to the Holy Land, and Odo replaced him on a temporary basis with Abbot Evrard of Marmoutier, who was brought in to undo the damage that Gerald had done. Gelduin of Saumur had been vigorously opposed to Gerald, and the ouster appears to have led to a restoration of good working relations between the lord of Saumur and Odo II.[31]

After this rapprochement between Gelduin and Odo, Gelduin launched a devastating raid into la Vallée downriver from Saumur which may be seen as part of a new Blésois plan to limit Fulk Nerra's advances. Gelduin's troops penetrated the Angevin heartland, and the monastery of Saint-Aubin, which only a few years earlier had acquired sole possession of substantial resources in this region, appears to have suffered greatly from this raid. In return for a promise to protect Saint-Aubin's holdings in la Vallée, Fulk obtained extensive rights from the monks in the forests of this region.[32]

Early in 1021 Fulk launched a punitive raid in force in the direction of Saumur. Gelduin apparently was unable to withstand Fulk's advance and sought a truce. According to a later but manifestly hostile source, "the tricky and greedy" Fulk, "fraudulently" interpreting Gelduin's use of the word *treva*, halted his forces four kilometers within the western border of the Angevin pagus at a place then called Clementiniacum (Trèves). There the Angevin count built another stronghold in apparent violation of the terms of the truce, or so our chronicle source favorable to Gelduin would have his readers believe.[33] While this story seems to have been shaped by a tradition defending the reputation of Gelduin, "a most noble man" and "an able fighter," against those who might charge that he had been bested by Fulk Nerra in an honorable manner, the fact remains that the Angevin count was able—by whatever means—to establish a stronghold at Trèves, which controlled access into the more westerly parts of la Vallée from Saumur.[34] The obvious defensive importance of Trèves in light of Gelduin's recent raid into la Vallée should not obscure the offensive potential of these new fortifications as a forward base for an Angevin attack on Saumur.

While Fulk was seeing to the construction of the stronghold at Trèves, Odo II sought to take advantage of the Angevin count's preoccupation in la Vallée and gathered a large army which included Count Galaran of Meulan. Odo launched an *expeditio* into the Touraine with Fulk's fortified encampment outside Tours at Montboyau as his objective. Montboyau was besieged, and Fulk responded by raising a relief column to aid his garrison at the stronghold. Odo, on learning of Fulk's approach and apparently not wishing to engage the Angevin army, withdrew. By early June 1021 the siege was raised.[35]

Fulk's successes in the Loire valley, first at Trèves and then at Montboyau, each gained through superior strategy and without the need to engage the enemy, are classic examples of the adroit implementation of Vegetian advice to avoid combat unless absolutely necessary. Fulk, Gelduin, and Odo were all reluctant to fight simply for the sake of glory or honor or even the thrill of combat. They behaved in a manner far different from the so-called "chivalric ethic" many modern scholars believe characteristic of this era.[36]

Fulk's aggressive strategy in meeting and then turning back Odo's initiatives was probably based in part on his understanding that the count of Blois had made heavy commitments in Champagne, the result of which was a cooling of relations with King Robert. Odo's efforts to dominate the episcopal succession at Meaux and his conflict with Archbishop Ebles of Reims were only two of many initiatives undertaken by the count of Blois which sent King Robert looking for support from King Henry II of Germany and Duke Richard of Normandy.[37] Finally, the monarch met personally with Fulk Nerra near Vihiers during the last week of March 1023.[38]

From the Angevin perspective, Odo's decision to concentrate his efforts, even temporarily, in Champagne and Lorraine was a boon. That Odo's actions alienated King Robert II made the situation even better for Fulk. With Odo busy in the east, Fulk had virtually a free hand to pursue his policy of territorial aggrandizement in the west. The king's need for supporters who by their actions or even by the threat of action would convince Odo that his preoccupation with matters in the east was inimical to Blésois interests in the west made Fulk Nerra a likely candidate to implement this royal policy. Yet King Robert II had to be careful that Fulk was not too successful. Robert had to appreciate that Fulk, with royal support and perhaps even without such encouragement, might capture Tours, dominate the Touraine, and perhaps even threaten Blois itself. It would be a hollow royal victory over Odo if the result were an Angevin power that was an even greater threat to Capetian interests than that posed by the house of Blois.

Whether Fulk or Robert saw the complexity of the developing political situation is not clear. For example, when Herveus, treasurer of Saint-Martin at Tours, died in 1022, King Robert had the opportunity to make an important appointment. The treasurer dominated the fisc of this rich institution, and the canons of Saint-Martin played a key role at the castrum, which stood only some eight hundred meters beyond the walls of Tours. Traditionally, the Capetians had used the position of treasurer to reward either a supporter of the house of Blois or a fidelis of the Angevin counts, depending on political circumstances at the time. Herveus, a member of the house of Buzançais and a supporter of the Angevins, appeared during his career to have transcended dynastic concerns and served Saint-Martin in a manner that might lead us to characterize him as an ecclesiastical statesman. When King Robert chose as treasurer Sulpicius of Buzançais, whose loyalty to Fulk was proverbial, Capetian policy obviously tilted toward the Angevins.[39]

Fulk responded quickly and in a positive manner to Sulpicius's appointment. The Angevin count moved to strengthen the latter's position as treasurer by promising to give up the *malae consuetudines* (new taxes) the Angevin counts had imposed upon various holdings of the church of Saint-Martin at Tours.[40] At this time Fulk also returned to ecclesiastical control other *facultates* held from Saint-Martin but under the *advocatio* of Marmoutier.[41] Surely, good relations with the canons of Saint-Martin and the monks of Marmoutier were essential to Fulk if he was to take control of Tours.

The third great ecclesiastical power at Tours was the archbishop, and the incumbent, Hugh, had from the beginning of his career been at odds with Fulk Nerra. Hugh's death in June of 1023 thus gave King Robert the opportunity to exercise influence in the Touraine while at the same time addressing the vital interests of both Fulk and Odo II. After deliberating for almost a half year, Robert chose Arnulf to succeed his maternal uncle Hugh of Châteaudun as archbishop. At first glance this may be seen as clear support of Odo II and a check to Fulk's initiative at Tours. The viscomital family of Châteaudun was traditionally under the influence of the count of Blois, who also held the *comté* of Châteaudun. We may recall that King Robert's acceptance of Hugh as archbishop in 1007 had occasioned a rapprochement between the monarch and Odo II. But Robert's choice of Arnulf was more subtle than it immediately appears. The new archbishop on his father's side was related to the house of Bellême. Among Arnulf's cousins were Bishop Avesgaud of le Mans and Haimo of Château-du-Loir who were closely tied to the viscomital house of le Mans; all were in the *mouvance* of Fulk Nerra.[42]

At this time Fulk's grandson Bouchard reached his majority, and the Angevin count formally handed over to him the *honor* of Vendôme. This was likely in fulfillment of the terms of succession agreed upon with the king in 1017; Fulk's prompt compliance very likely was intended to allay any fears Robert may have harbored about the Angevin count's maintenance of a personal rule at Vendôme. While Fulk surrendered formal control, however, he remained the real power in this important region. Thus following the death of Viscount Hubert of Vendôme, Fulk saw to the installation of Radulfus of le Mans as his successor. Radulfus, a member of the viscomital family of le Mans, was the husband of Viscount Hubert's granddaughter and the nephew by marriage of Bishop Hubert of Angers.[43]

The policy that Fulk pursued at Tours—military encirclement combined with the development of profitable working relationships with the important powers—was repeated at Saumur. Fulk seized the stronghold of Doué from Odo II. This stronghold, seventeen kilometers west-southwest of Saumur, had considerable strategic importance. While in Blésois hands, it blocked the Angevins from utilizing the direct route between their fortifications at Vihiers and Montsoreau and provided a base for attacks on the southern route between Angers and Loches which ran through Vihiers and Loudun. Furthermore, while Doué was in enemy possession, it provided a base for the harassment of the nearby villas of Saint-Georges-sur-Layon, Denezé, Meigné, and les Ulmes from which the Angevin counts collected taxes and levied troops.[44]

Once Fulk took possession of the stronghold at Doué—it had apparently surrendered without significant opposition—he set about integrating it into his strategic system. Fulk demanded substantial and burdensome services from the *villani* dwelling at Epinats, Saint-Denis, and Montfort. All of these villages belonged to the canons of Saint Maurice, the cathedral church of Angers, and none was located more than eight kilometers from Doué. Fulk required that these dependents of Saint Maurice provide hauling services (*carragium*) with oxen and donkeys, the *bidamnum* (repair work) on nearby fortifications at Vihiers, and service to build military installations on the frontier ("castello faciendo in marchia"). In addition, Fulk required the *villani* at these villages to respond to any order to perform military service against his enemies (*submonitio in praelio in adversario* [*comitis*]). These services, particularly the calling up of the host of *villani* (*submonitio pro praelio publico*), were probably placed under the control of the vicarius Fulk established at Doué.[45]

These military and military-related services—especially the duty to build military installations "in marchia," the *carragium*, which was essential for logistic support, and perhaps the levy to serve *pro praelio publico*—should remind us that the stronghold at Doué also had offensive as well as defensive value. Indeed, with Doué in Angevin hands, Meigné, les Ulmes, Epinats, le Coudrey-Macouard, Saint-Denis, and Distré can be seen to have been converted to a kind of frontier (*marchia*) enclave in depth that came to within five kilometers of the walls of Saumur and blocked the roads south and west from Odo's key stronghold in the region. Doué and its march helped to complete a semicircle of strongholds—Trèves fifteen kilometers downriver and Montsoreau ten kilometers upriver—ringing Saumur on the left bank of the Loire.

While Fulk worked to further his interests at Saumur through a strategy of encirclement, he also worked on the diplomatic front to strengthen his position with Saint-Florent and to undermine Odo II's control of that rich and important monastery. Fulk had done well previously in exploiting the fisc of Saint-Florent during the abbacies of Robert and Gerald. Indeed, Robert had even recognized Fulk as his *senior*. Gerald, however, had been exiled from Saint-Florent, in part because of his "misappropriation" of monastic resources to the Angevins, and Abbot Evrard of Marmoutier briefly had served as caretaker abbot to help reform the house and to restore morale. Abbot Frederick, Gerald's successor, was a man of servile origins and pious reputation from Marmoutier who was made abbot to continue the progress of reform started by Evrard.[46]

Fulk approached Frederick in a manner very different from that which he used in dealing with either Robert or Gerald. When Fulk met with King Robert in March 1023, shortly after Frederick became abbot, the Angevin count and his fideles supported a royal act giving important rights to Saint-Florent in the locality of Montilliers near the stronghold of Vihiers. Not long after this concession was made, Fulk supported and indeed even encouraged one of his *milites*, Sigebrannus of Passavant, to make a substantial gift to Saint-Florent.[47]

Before the end of 1024 King Robert's relations with the count of Blois had deteriorated to the point that the monarch not only summoned him to stand trial but, when Odo failed to appear, made public his decision to confiscate Odo's *honores*.[48] As a result King Robert was critically in need of Fulk's support, putting the Angevin count in a good position to pursue his own interests in the west in an exceptionally aggressive manner with little fear of being opposed. In early March of 1025 Fulk began the execution of a policy that had been in the planning stage for some time. The story is told by Adémar of Chabannes, a contemporary though hostile chronicler:

At this time the Angevin count, Fulk, not being able to overcome Count Herbert of Maine, son of Hugh, openly led him into a trap at the citadel in the urbs of Saintes by promising that he would give Saintes to him as a beneficium. Since Herbert came without any suspicion or thought that something evil might happen, he was captured through this underhanded trick and imprisoned in the citadel on the second day of the first week of Lent. On this very same day Fulk's wife tried to capture Herbert's wife through trickery before she could learn what had happened, but Herbert's wife guessed that there was danger and cautiously avoided capture.[49]

Fulk did not murder Herbert, and Adémar's claim that this was the Angevin's count's plan cannot have been based upon firsthand knowledge. Rather, Adémar is likely to have been repeating local gossip based on the general belief that Fulk was the kind of man who would commit murder if he thought it necessary. Fulk had executed his first wife and he had ordered the assassination of Hugh of Beauvais, who was in fact cut down in the king's presence by the Angevin count's men.

Fulk's plot to deprive Herbert of his *honor* had to have been the result of considerable planning, as illustrated even by the logistics of trying to coordinate the capture of both the count of Maine and his wife. If murder had been Fulk's aim, it is unlikely that he would have failed to carry out his part in the plan. Indeed, it would have taken at least two days under good conditions for Fulk to have learned that Countess Hildegarde had failed to capture Herbert's wife. Adémar's assertion that Fulk did not murder Herbert because he feared the retaliation of the count of Maine's supporters is not convincing. Indeed, the viscount of le Mans, the bishop of le Mans, and the men who held the important strongholds at Craon, Château-Gontier, Sablé, Mayenne, le Lude, Château-du-Loir, and Bellême supported Fulk. In addition, before his capture Herbert had been at war with Bishop Avesgaud of le Mans, who had excommunicated him.[50] Thus it is highly unlikely that Herbert's wife could have mounted any kind of campaign to intimidate Fulk.

If Fulk did not intend to murder Herbert of Maine, what was his plan to gain direct control of Maine? We know that Fulk had observed the course of action King Robert was pursuing against Odo II. When Robert decided that his fidelis Odo had acted against him, he ordered the count of Blois to stand trial; when Odo did not appear, the king declared Odo guilty and his *honores* forfeit.[51] Not surprisingly Odo refused to accept the king's judgment and asserted that: (1) his high birth was a sufficient condition to keep him from being deprived of his *honor*; (2) his beneficium was not part of his lord's fisc; (3) he held his beneficium by hereditary right and only additionally received it through the consent of his lord; and (4) he had earned the beneficium by military *servitium* both at home and abroad.[52] In his turn, King Robert by declaring Odo's *honores* to be forfeit, clearly took the position that the obligations established by the *forma fidelitatis* were such that despite high birth, despite the fact that the beneficium did not originate in the lord's fisc, despite certain previously recognized rights of inheritance, and despite the prior rendering of important military *servitium* both at home and abroad, an unworthy fidelis could be deprived of his *honores*.

The case made by King Robert against Count Odo provided many parallels that Fulk could use in a legal process against Herbert. As we have seen, Herbert and his father Hugh had both recognized that they held the *comté* of Maine from Fulk. Herbert, however, had gone to war against Bishop Avesgaud of le Mans, who was a fidelis of the Angevin count; he also had supported Count Alan of Rennes, a fidelis of Odo II, who was at war with Count Budic of Nantes, a fidelis of Fulk Nerra. Clearly, Herbert had violated that obligation outlined in the *forma fidelitatis* that he do nothing to injure his lord.[53]

Thus it seems likely that Fulk imprisoned Herbert not to murder him (as asserted by Adémar) but to hold him for trial as a fidelis unworthy to hold a beneficium from his lord. Like Odo, Herbert could argue that his high birth was sufficient to keep him from being deprived of his *honor*. Indeed, his family had been counts of Maine for more than a century.[54] Herbert could also maintain that the county of Maine was not and had never been a part of the Angevin comital fisc and that Fulk's claims to overlordship could only be traced to the reign of Geoffrey Greymantle but surely no earlier. Furthermore, Herbert could contend that he held Maine first by hereditary right and only additionally from Fulk as his *senior*. Finally, Herbert could point with pride to the valuable military *servitium* he had given Fulk at the battle of Pontlevoy. Of course if King Robert rejected this line of defense when offered by Odo, then surely Fulk was in a position to do the same with regard to Herbert.

There was, however, one basic difference in the two cases. Whereas Fulk had imprisoned Herbert, King Robert either was unwilling or more probably was unable to seize Odo. Yet if we try to rethink Fulk's plan that began with the capture of Count Herbert, it is hardly unreasonable to conclude that King Robert's process against Odo provided the Angevin count with a model for his own actions. I scarcely need emphasize that Robert would have little chance of succeeding against Odo without Fulk's help and that in return for this support the Angevin count is likely to have believed that he could rely on royal support for his attack on Herbert. Indeed, King Robert could hardly pursue his effort to dishonor Odo and not permit Fulk to pursue his effort to dishonor Herbert in a similar situation.

Our understanding of Fulk's treatment of Count Herbert is deepened if we examine Angevin relations with Count William of Poitou at this time. On 6 March 1025, the day before Fulk imprisoned Herbert in the Capitolium at Saintes, Count William of Poitou, who we should not forget was also duke of Aquitaine, held an important gathering of magnates at Poitiers. These men met to discuss what steps would be necessary to sustain the candidacy for the Italian throne of William the Fat, William of Aquitaine's son by Adalmode, Fulk Nerra's cousin.[55] At this meeting were Isembard, Roho, Arnaudus, and Jordanes, the bishops of Poitiers, Angoulême, Perigueux, and Limoges, respectively. In addition, Islo, who was bishop of Saintes and acting archbishop of Bordeaux, was present. His sister was married to Fulk Nerra's half-brother Maurice and his city was Herbert's prison. The most important laymen present were Fulk Nerra's brother-in-law, William of Angoulême, and the latter's son Hilduinus. Also at the gathering was Hugh of Lusignan, one of Fulk's many fideles in the region.[56] It would be naive to assume that the events taking place at Poitiers and those taking place at Saintes were a coincidence of which the principal actors, Fulk Nerra and William of Aquitaine, were mutually ignorant. It is far more likely that William had already agreed to support Fulk's plan to deprive Count Herbert of his *honor* in return for the Angevin count's support for William the Fat's pursuit of the Italian throne. Indeed, Fulk showed his willingness to support these efforts, and at William of Aquitaine's request he sought help for the project from King Robert. It was William's hope—relayed by Fulk to Robert—that the Capetian king would ally with Duke Frederick of upper Lorraine and others to keep them from coming to terms with the Salian king Conrad, which in turn would make it very difficult for the newly chosen German monarch to pursue the Italian throne for himself.[57] Fulk Nerra concluded his letter to King Robert outlining William's request for royal support: "I call upon you to indicate to me by your letter or through a messenger what is in your mind concerning this matter that he [William of Aquitaine] asks you about so that I can pass it on to him."[58]

Clearly the Angevin count was master of the west. The counties that bordered the growing Angevin heartland on the north and west were firmly under Fulk Nerra's control while those in the south and east were under his domination along the frontiers. As we have just seen, the counts of Maine had recognized Angevin overlordship; Herbert's efforts to follow an independent policy against Fulk's supporters made it possible for the Angevin count to begin the process of dishonoring Herbert, perhaps for the purpose of taking direct control of the *comté*. Within Maine the aristocracy was closely tied to the Angevin count, as was the case in the neighboring *comté* of Vendôme, where Fulk's youthful grandson held the title of count.

In the west the counts of Nantes recognized Fulk's overlordship, and during his career Fulk had demonstrated his ability to choose the man who held that office. Fulk commanded his own troops in the urbs of Nantes itself, and Count Budic was totally dependent on Angevin support for his survival. Just to the south and east, the Mauges region, bordering on Nantes, Anjou, and the Poitou, was in the process of being integrated into the Angevin state. The strongholds of Montjean, Châteaupanne, Montrevault, and Chemillé strengthened Fulk's position in the region.

To the south the northern third of the Poitivan pagus had for all intents and purposes been severed from William's *comté* and was firmly integrated into the Angevin state. The Angevin *limes* from Chemillé in the west through Vihiers, Doué, Montaglan, and Loudun protected Fulk's gains with a line of strongholds which not only provided a frontier but also an important part of Angevin communications between east and west. Although Fulk recognized William as his lord for a large number of beneficia throughout northern Aquitaine, especially in the Poitou, it was William who was really dependent on his fidelis in practical terms. Fulk's stronghold at Mirebeau posed a direct threat to Poitiers as a base for attacks against William's capital. Along with his brother-in-law William of Angoulême, Fulk controlled strongholds at Chéneché, Parthenay, Melle, Gençay, Civray, Ruffec, Chabanais, Rochechouart, Confolens, and Rancon. The ensemble gave the balance of power in the Poitou and its environs to the Angevin count and his supporters.

In the east much of the Touraine was under Angevin control. In the southwestern part of the Touraine the Angevins controlled the valley of the Claise and the middle Vienne with strongholds at Preuilly-sur-Claise, la Haye-Descartes, and Nouâtre. On the Indre the fortifications at Buzançais, Chatillion-sur-Indre, Loches, and Montbazon were in Angevin hands as was Montrésor on the Indroye. With the exception of a short stretch on the Cher controlled by Odo II's castrum at Saint-Aignan, Fulk's men held Graçay, Villentrois, and Montrichard in the southeastern Touraine. North of the Loire Fulk's strongholds at Maillé, Semblançay, Château-la-Vallière, Saint-Christophe, and Morand when combined with Montboyau, Amboise, Montrichard, and Montbazon surrounded Tours itself. In short, the Touraine was dominated by Angevin fortifications and, as we have seen, Fulk was working on the diplomatic front to strengthen his position both at the castrum and in the urbs by developing good relations with Marmoutier, Saint-Martin, and the new archbishop who was closely connected to families in the *mouvance* of the Angevin count.

Fulk's interests on the upper Indre at Châtillion-sur-Indre and Buzançais as well as at Graçay on the Cher brought the Angevins into Berry itself. The development of the Loches–Belli Locus economic initiative was intended to root Angevin control firmly in this frontier region. Farther afield in the southwest Fulk relied heavily on his brother-in-law William of Angoulême and on Bishop Islo to maintain the Angevin presence at Saintes. South of Parthenay, which was controlled by one of Fulk's fideles, the strongholds at Melle, Chizé, Tonnay, and Taillebourg provided a defended route to Saintes from the north.

On the more distant horizon were Fulk's interests in the north. With Maine firmly in Angevin hands, the stronghold of Mayenne some twenty kilometers from the Norman frontier provided a strategically located base for further operations against Duke Richard's lands and lordships. Farther to the east William of Bellême obtained the castrum of Alençon at Duke Richard's expense and extended his control over the Norman bishopric of Sées where Sigenfred was installed in the cathedral seat. The close ties of the Bellême with the viscounts of le

Mans and the Angevin counts, dating back to Geoffrey Greymantle's key role in making an earlier Sigenfred bishop of le Mans, suggests that Anjou was the great power behind William of Bellême's aggressive posture toward Duke Richard of Normandy.[59]

From Mayenne in the west to Alençon and Bellême, the Norman frontier was at risk, perhaps even under siege. Although the role of Fulk's relatives in the region of Amiens and Vexin at this time is problematic, they cannot be ruled out as being willing to benefit from the problems of the Norman duke. In this context Richard's reversal of the Norman policy that had entailed the close support of King Robert and peace initiatives may perhaps have been partially motivated by his perception that Fulk Nerra posed a substantial threat to his lands and lordships. Angevin offensive thrusts into Normandy during the next generation can be seen to have been built on the base established by Fulk.[60]

At home the contours of the Angevin state that Geoffrey Greymantle may well have imagined by the early 980s had rapidly developed. From Vendôme in the northeast along le Loir through Chartres-sur-le-Loir, Château-du-Loir, and le Lude then turning north to Sablé, Château-Gontier, and Craon, the northern frontier came to an end in the west. South from Craon to Champtocé and across the Loire to the valley of the Eavre marked the western frontier of the Mauges and the Angevin state. Fulk's southern *limes* ran from Montrevault, Chemillé, Vihiers, Montaglan, Loudun, Faye-la-Vineuse, la Haye-Descartes, Preuilly-sur-Claise, and Graçay. The eastern frontier followed the valley of the Cher north to Villentrois, Montrichard, Amboise, Morand, and Vendôme.[61]

Within this state that was defined by defensible frontiers and lacked respect for the traditional boundaries of the Carolingian pagi, a handful of enclaves survived under the control of Fulk's adversaries. On the lower reaches of the Vienne the strongholds of Île-Bouchard and Chinon were held by Odo II's castellans as were Saint-Aignan on the Cher and Château-Renault on the Brenne. These enclaves, however, were surrounded by Fulk's strongholds much in the same manner as Tours and Saumur were cut off. In short, the Angevin count seems to have been waiting with his customary patience, planning to pick off each one as the opportunity arose or could be created.

CHAPTER EIGHT

Master in the West

Fulk Nerra's position as master in the west, if such a characterization is not an exaggeration, depended in large part on his continued ability to dominate William of Aquitaine, Herbert of Maine, and Budic of Nantes while at the same time forcing Alan of Rennes and Odo II of Blois onto the defensive. Diplomatic developments during the late spring and summer of 1025, however, gradually made it clear that King Robert was not going to press his case against Odo as vigorously as earlier indications suggested. In fact, all along King Robert II may have merely been trying to persuade Odo to behave in order to restore the delicate balance of power that had existed prior to the Blésois count's aggressive movement in Champagne.

In fact, Robert took none of the more obvious steps that would have further isolated Odo and permitted the Capetian monarch to crush one of his most powerful adversaries. Instead, Robert once again drew closer to Odo and with a coalition of nobles from upper Lorraine led by Duke Frederick II of Lorraine opposed the new German monarch, Conrad. This temporary agreement surely delayed any plans Fulk may have had to put Herbert on trial. Then the situation clearly worsened for Fulk when young King Hugh died on 17 September 1025. King Robert broke off his efforts in Lorraine in order to make arrangements to have his second son, Henry, associated with him in the kingship. Robert would now need the support of both Odo and Fulk Nerra among others, such as the Norman duke Richard and William of Aquitaine. New plans would have to be formulated to meet new conditions.[1]

Two sources of opposition soon emerged to King Robert's desire to have Henry associated with him in the kingship. One group of magnates apparently let it be known that they preferred no associate at all while a second group, led by Queen Constance, Fulk's cousin, desired to have Henry's younger brother, Robert, associated in the kingship with his father. In this delicate situation William of Aquitaine informed Odo indirectly that he was not prepared to support King Robert's policy and oppose Queen Constance and Fulk. Odo, however, saw his opportunity to obtain some measure of royal support for a major campaign against Fulk in return for backing Henry. Ultimately, before the end of May 1026, William promised that he would give his full support to Odo's choice but he made it clear that he would not risk the wrath of Queen Constance and her supporters by attending the royal court in person. The death of Duke Richard II of Normandy and the much contested succession of Richard III at this time removed the Normans as a major force in the contest. The balance of the major powers was for the moment weighted against Fulk.[2]

In June of 1026, less than two weeks after King Robert's plans to associate Henry in the kingship had been approved by a gathering of important nobles, Odo II initiated a campaign against Fulk. Although it is not clear whether King Robert had made a formal military alliance with Odo against Fulk, there is no doubt that the monarch was far from being neutral, for he permitted the count of Blois to move a noteworthy military baggage train through royal territory. Odo advanced westward into the Touraine with the intention of attacking the stronghold at Montboyau, the key Angevin base for military operations against the city of Tours. In order to assure himself of an especially large force, Odo ordered Gelduin to muster the troops of Saumur, Chinon, and Île-Bouchard in the west.[3]

Montboyau had been built ten years earlier, initially as a siege encampment, and during the subsequent decade had been substantially improved. In 1026 the motte of earth upon which the original camp had been constructed was topped by a tall donjon (*domgio*), probably built of stone. Odo's forces laid siege to the stronghold, his engineers building a high wooden tower to overlook Fulk's fortifications. From such an engine, which required considerable skill to design and build so that it had the proper balance and strength, Odo's men could shoot their arrows and bolts down on the defenders. With a drawbridge appended to the engine's top the attackers could storm the parapet of Montboyau.[4]

When Fulk learned that Montboyau was under attack, he gathered a force hurriedly and moved toward Tours. When his army reached Brain-sur-Allonnes, a villa sixty-three kilometers east of Angers, Fulk received additional intelligence indicating that Odo had under his command a force that was too large for the Angevins to engage with their present numbers. He also learned, however, that Gelduin had virtually stripped Saumur of its defenders in order to provide a large force to support Odo II at Montboyau.[5] So instead Fulk marched to Saumur, where he found the walls of the castrum denuded of *defensores* and both the east and west gates poorly defended. Within a short time the castrum was in Fulk's hands, with the exception of the citadel (*arx*). Those who defended the latter quickly realized that their position was hopeless and understood that if captured while resisting they could expect to be executed. Therefore, after brief negotiations, the garrison capitulated "under the law of surrender" (*sub lege deditionis*) and their lives were spared.[6]

After securing control of the *arx*, Fulk garrisoned Saumur with his own *satellites* and apparently placed a fidelis named Fulchardus in command with the title of vicarius. Then Fulk sent Aimericus Pirus, the praepositus Gelduin had left in command at Saumur, along with some of his followers to the stronghold of Doué as prisoners. Finally, Fulk moved his army, which by this time is likely to have been reinforced considerably, into the Touraine with the aim of relieving the siege at Montboyau. He established his base at Montbazon, only about ten kilometers south of Tours.[7]

With Fulk's army in the field, Odo had to move his forces from their siege emplacements, sooner rather than later, either to engage the Angevins or to withdraw from the area. When the defenders at Montboyau executed a successful sally during which they managed to overturn and burn the great wooden siege tower (this is prima facie evidence that Montboyau was constructed of stone and did not fear fire) the Blésois engineers had constructed, Odo raised the siege. He reformed his army, which seems to have been composed in large part of *pedites* needed to do the basic work of besieging a stronghold, crossed the Loire, and advanced toward Fulk's army at Montbazon. When Fulk learned that the siege had been raised and that Odo's forces were seeking an engagement, the Angevin count ordered his army to break camp and began a slow withdrawal in the direction of Loches about thirty kilometers southeast.[8]

Fulk's intention was apparently to lure Odo into an unfavorable position in the southeastern part of the Touraine, which was dominated by supporters of the Angevin count, by maintaining sufficiently close contact with the Blésois to suggest that battle was imminent. This "feigned retreat," as one later chronicler characterizes Fulk's tactic, was executed because the Angevin count had no desire to fight a battle in the open field against Odo. In short, once the tactical victory of relieving the siege at Montboyau had been accomplished, nothing was to be gained by the Angevins in such an encounter. When Odo's forces had been lured well away from Montboyau into an area of even greater Angevin strength than the environs of Tours, Fulk secured the safety of his army within the stronghold of Loches.[9]

When Odo learned that the Angevins were not going to fight, he had the option of several courses of action; none of them, however, was very attractive. He could go home, end the campaigning season early, and admit failure. He could continue on to Loches, in the center of an area of Angevin domination, and lay siege to this formidable defensive complex which was defended not only by its normal garrison under Arraldus but was now reinforced by Fulk's recently arrived army. Moreover, Loches formed part of an overall eastern military command, including Amboise, which was commanded by Lisoius, who had a significant military contingent. If Odo found these two options unsatisfactory, he could retreat toward Tours and prepare a siege either of Montbazon or Montboyau. But if he did begin siege operations again, Fulk was likely to follow him, harass his line of march, and ultimately threaten in detail whatever siege emplacements Odo established, thus re-creating the status quo prior to the initial siege.

On the whole, Odo seems not to have assessed the ensemble of Angevin military strength in the Touraine with a great deal of accuracy. Fulk's strategy of building fortifications had by 1026 resulted in an articulated system of strongholds from which, for example, Angevin forces using Montbazon, Maillé, or even Semblançay as a base could be deployed to strike against an enemy force that laid siege to Montboyau. Similarly, Montrichard protected Amboise; both Montrésor and Amboise protected Montrichard; Loches and Montrichard protected Montrésor; and Châtillon-sur-Indre and Montrésor protected Loches. For Odo to have been successful militarily against this strategic system, a massive coordinated effort would have had to be undertaken requiring the construction of lines of circumvallation and contravallation to protect those mounting the siege of a particular stronghold and necessitating the use of reserves emplaced in fortified camps to interdict columns dispatched to harass the besiegers. Fulk had purposefully and opportunistically created a system of defense in depth over three decades during which he was consistently seen also to employ Vegetian or other late Roman military principles. Indeed, in this campaign as well he executed a surprise attack on Saumur, carried out an extended "feigned retreat," and avoided unnecessary combat when his tactical objective had been gained without a direct engagement with the enemy in the field.[10]

As the situation developed following Fulk's phased or "feigned" retreat to Loches, Odo did not choose to invest one or another of the many Angevin strongholds in the neighborhood nor did he elect to return to Blois. Rather, the political situation among his supporters demanded that to keep his army together—indeed, to maintain the loyalty of Gelduin—he needed to make an effort to retake Saumur. Although Odo is reported to have been unenthusiastic about launching an attack on Saumur at this time, he moved his forces westward and, unopposed by an Angevin field army, established a siege of the Saumur castrum. The Blésois engineers built another large and elaborate wooden siege tower so that Odo's men could shoot down on the defenders and storm the walls. But just as at Montboyau earlier in the year, the defenders made a successful sally, burned the tower, and inflicted substantial losses on the enemy. Odo's army had been in the field since late in the spring and was weary of a campaign that had seen nothing but one failure after another. In addition, the harvest time was drawing near and Odo's levies wanted to return home to bring in their crops. Thus, with autumn approaching and morale low, Odo raised the siege and retreated to his own lands, leaving both Saumur and the wealthy monastery of Saint-Florent in Fulk Nerra's hands.[11]

With the fall of Saumur the last remaining enemy stronghold in the Angevin pagus was in Fulk's hands and the road to Tours through the valley of the Loire was open. Fulk, however, was unable to follow up this opportunity. The shared interest of King Robert, Odo II, and William of Aquitaine in supporting the association of Prince Henry with his father in the kingship provided the basis for a tripartite agreement that resembled that of 996–997 and that greatly threatened the state of affairs which had made possible Angevin mastery in the west. In fact, sometime late in 1026 or early in 1027 William of Aquitaine and King Robert met at a gathering also attended by Bishop Fulbert of Chartres, who frequently represented Odo II.[12] William apparently had much greater independence to act against Angevin interests because Fulk's brother-in-law William of Angoulême had taken the pilgrimage road to the Holy Land on 1 October 1026.[13] In addition, about this time Viscount Geoffrey of Thouars began to create considerable trouble for the Angevins on the border between Poitou and the Mauges region.[14] Given this rapidly developing situation, whatever plans Fulk may have had for laying siege to Tours or bringing Count Herbert to trial were abandoned. In early March of 1027, after having held Herbert of Maine in prison for two years, Fulk sought to make the best of a deteriorating situation and agreed to set him free. In return for his freedom, Herbert once again recognized Fulk as his *senior* and swore that he held Maine from the Angevin count.[15] Herbert also provided Fulk with hostages; these men were then imprisoned in the stronghold of le Lude on the Loir.[16]

While Fulk was trying to ensure his continued dominance in Maine, Odo II and his supporters were preparing an offensive campaign against the Angevins. Following the coronation of Henry on 14 May 1027, attended by many important magnates, including Odo and William of Aquitaine but apparently not by Fulk, the count of Blois launched an attack on the Angevin stronghold of Amboise. Evidence for royal support for Odo's campaign is unambiguous: the newly crowned King Henry participated in the lengthy siege of Amboise at the side of the count of Blois. But Sulpicius of Buzançais, Fulk's castellan at Amboise who only a few years earlier had been made treasurer of Saint-Martin by King Robert, remained loyal to the Angevins and led a successful defense of the castrum.[17]

Odo's attack in the east, however, was not an isolated event. At this time, Count Alan of Rennes, who recognized Odo as his *senior* and was in the process of arranging to marry the latter's daughter Bertha, was diverted from the conflict in which he had been engaged with Count Budic of Nantes and renewed his alliance with Count Herbert of Maine.[18] Alan then launched an offensive deep into Fulk's territory and laid siege to the stronghold of le Lude about sixty kilometers east-northeast of Angers. The count of Rennes took le Lude and freed Count Herbert's hostages imprisoned there.[19]

Alan's offensive, it seems safe to conclude, was a raid in force aimed primarily at freeing the hostages; there is no report that he took further action. This raid, however, was probably coordinated with Odo's attack on Amboise, characterized by one chronicler as a "surprise attack," or perhaps more accurately as an attack that took Fulk by surprise. Perhaps also coordinated with these offensives was the effort by Viscount Geoffrey of Thouars to build a stronghold at Montfaucon only about seventeen kilometers south of the Mauges frontier.[20]

Fulk responded in a variety of ways to these enemy initiatives. In the Mauges Girorius, the castellan of Beaupréau, seems to have played a major role in halting Geoffrey. Although Girorius was killed, Montfaucon was taken by the Angevins. Count Budic of Nantes was encouraged to threaten Alan's lands in the west while Fulk moved his forces eastward toward Amboise.[21] The general turmoil at this time, however, is highlighted by Bishop Fulbert's repeated observation that warfare in the region between Chartres and Poitiers, that is, Fulk's lands, made it impossible for him to travel south.[22]

Following his heroic and successful leadership in the defense of Amboise, Sulpicius seems to have realized (we are unsure why) that his long tenure in Angevin military service was nearing its end. Fulk reportedly consulted with Arraldus, the castellan of Loches, who advised that a marriage should be arranged between Lisoius, who commanded the Angevin count's southeastern frontier, and Hersendis, Sulpicius's niece, so as to realign the family networks girding the military organization of the eastern frontier. Both Fulk and Sulpicius found Arraldus's counsel sound and at the count's request the marriage was arranged. Lisoius was granted the stone tower at Amboise along with all that pertained to it. He also received the estate at Verneuil-sur-Indre with all holdings pertaining to it, the Buzançais family *domus* at Loches, and another estate at Moré.[23] Sulpicius also arranged for a certain *vir nobilis* named Fulk from the region of Berry to marry Hersendis's younger sister, Hermensendis. With Count Fulk's support, Sulpicius granted to his new Berrichon nephew-in-law the stronghold of Villentrois. Similarly, Sulpicius arranged for his nephew Robert to obtain possession of Buzançais and Châtillon-sur-Indre; this too undoubtedly was done with Fulk Nerra's support. Not long after these matters were settled and before the end of 1027 Sulpicius was dead.[24] The crowding of all these and probably several other important dispositions into a relatively short period of time may permit the hypothesis (although no sources speak of it) that Sulpicius received a serious wound while defending Amboise earlier in the year and was not expected to recover. In other words, these acts together with several pious bequests may have constituted the greater part of Sulpicius's testament.

Fulk's reorganization of the eastern frontier following Sulpicius's death provides numerous insights into the direction of Angevin policy during the last years of the 1020s. Lisoius, after proving to be a loyal and effective military commander for a decade, was chosen by Fulk for a post that for all intents and purposes was Angevin governor of the eastern district between Amboise and Loches. In order to provide the support needed for this weighty task, Fulk delegated to Lisoius vicarial powers and what we may call procuratorial powers for the collection of fodder for the army in the region between the Cher and the Indre. Fulk also arranged for Lisoius to marry one of the heiresses of the Archembaud-Sulpicius clan of Buzançais, which for well over a century had been a mainstay of Angevin policy in the east. With this marriage Lisoius obtained substantial personal wealth as well as invaluable local family connections. These, along with his natural ability and governmental support, would provide a sound basis for his leadership in the region for the next quarter century.[25]

The house of Buzançais, however, was not pushed out of its traditional leadership role by Fulk's action. In the thinking of the time, lineages were reckoned in a political context cognatically, not agnatically. Thus the Sulpicius-Archembaud clan was represented at the highest level of Fulk's entourage by Hersendis and would later be represented by her offspring. With Arraldus's advice, Fulk seems to have decided (and Sulpicius agreed) that Lisoius was the best man to govern the eastern frontier. In short, he was regarded as a better man for the job than Robert, Sulpicius's nephew and Hersendis's brother, who in the settlement of 1027 was established at Buzançais and Châtillion-sur-Indre. There he had the responsibility for controlling the upper reaches of the Indre and defending the region against Berrichon incursions; he probably also had a warrant to extend his own and Angevin interests to the south and east.[26]

Although the advancement of Lisoius seems to have resulted from a consensus, we should note that the power and wealth of the Sulpicius-Archembaud clan was fragmented by Fulk's settlement, which resulted in the division of the lands and lordships that had been held by Sulpicius. Fulk Nerra thus established Fulk of Berry at the stronghold of Villentrois following his marriage to Hermensendis, Hersendis's younger sister. I emphasize here that Robert the nephew of Sulpicius appears to have had no absolute right to inherit all that his uncle had held. These lands and lordships that Robert the father of Sulpicius and Archembaud and the grandfather of the younger Robert had held and had passed on to his two sons were at base at the disposal of the count.[27] That Fulk Nerra could exercise this power highlights comital power and its supremacy over the aristocracy.

While providing Lisoius with the tools to represent the interests of the Angevin government in the region effectively, Fulk also moved to provide certain checks to his new governor's power. This is particularly evident at Amboise itself, which was Lisoius's headquarters. In the old Roman castrum of Amboise, Fulk permitted Lisoius to hold the new stone tower that had been built by Sulpicius. Fulk's officials, however, continued to function within the old castrum and collected the taxes owed there; noteworthy among these was the land tax (or *census*) which went to the comital fisc, not to Lisoius's operations.[28] The judicial authority in the castrum, that is, the control of the comital court there, apparently was delegated to Léon of Meung-sur-Loire. Also within the castrum Fulk strongly supported the church of Saint Florentin by providing prebends for the canons. If the choice of canons at Saint Florentin followed traditional lines, then Fulk was in effect endowing prebends for members of the local aristocracy who thus would look to the count for patronage rather than to Lisoius.[29]

In the Châteauneuf district of Amboise, which was outside the old Roman castrum, Lisoius played no role at all. Following the diminution of the Viking threat in the mid-tenth century, the area beside Amboise was likely settled by merchants seeking to take advantage of the town's location and the protection the Roman fortifications provided. Under Geoffrey Greymantle this district was walled and came to be called Châteauneuf (Novum Castrum). Within these walls Geoffrey Greymantle built a fortified *domus* where the count's officials undoubtedly lived and from which they collected the vast array of taxes levied on all aspects of economic activity, including those of merchants. Geoffrey also established Landry of Dun in the castrum, and Landry built his own castellum there. Landry was charged with the defense of Châteauneuf.[30]

Landry's defection, defeat, and the destruction of his castellum (see p. 127 above) did not deter Fulk Nerra from experimenting with the integration of various aspects of nonmilitary administration at Châteauneuf and the old castrum. Thus, in the reorganization of 1027 Fulk brought into his administration Léon of Meung-sur-Loire, who held an important stronghold some ten kilometers downriver from Orléans. Léon was given the task of administering justice in the castrum; in the nontechnical language of the chronicler "he had the *jus.*" Léon was established in the count's fortified *domus* in Châteauneuf, which suggests that he was to oversee the comital bureaucracy that collected taxes. He was also charged with defending the suburb. In addition,

Léon's responsibilities extended beyond the complex of jurisdictions at Amboise, for Fulk delegated to him the right to impose the *commendaticae* throughout the immense forest Silva Longa in the Blésois up to Romorantin. This assignment seems to have been a kind of warrant to establish Angevin military obligations (*commendaticae*) on the population of a region at least nominally under Blésois dominion as a step toward the integration of the land and its people into the Angevin state. By what right Fulk delegated this authority, other than by outright usurpation, is unclear.[31]

Fulk's reorganization of the eastern frontier seems to have improved his position in this region. Problems cropping up in other areas appear equally to have been controlled, although not without an occasional setback. For example, Fulk's men tried to capture Bertha of Blois, Odo II's daughter, while she was on her way west to marry Count Alan of Rennes, but they failed. Bertha, of course, would have been a valuable hostage in negotiations both with her future husband and her father, an ample substitute for those hostages Alan had freed at le Lude.[32] Even though Fulk was unable to stop the Blois-Rennes marriage alliance, he was able to motivate Budic of Nantes to renew his military operations against Alan.[33] The count of Rennes' interest in dominating Nantes at this time rapidly waned as the succession crisis in Normandy between his cousins Richard and Robert waxed. The establishment of Almond of Maine as abbot of the border monastery and stronghold of Mont Saint Michel and his subsequent close relations with Alan suggest the cooperation of Herbert "Wakedog," count of Maine, and the count of Rennes to establish a base for initiatives in Normandy.[34]

The preoccupation of Odo II's allies and potential allies left the count of Blois without the immediate support of a major power in his efforts to retake the stronghold of Saumur and reimpose his authority over the wealthy monastery of Saint-Florent. Following his failure to take Amboise with the help of young King Henry early in the campaigning season of 1027, Odo regrouped his forces and, joined only by his son Theobald, launched a major operation to take Saumur. With a large army Odo again besieged this stronghold, this time establishing his main camp at the small monastic enclave outside the walls of Saumur where the monks of Saint-Florent had begun to build a new monastery during the preceding year.[35]

Apparently before serious hostilities got under way Fulk led an army to relieve his garrison at Saumur. According to the "official" account kept by the monks of Saint-Florent, they intervened at this point and brought the two counts to the conference table. The interest of the monks and their abbot Frederick in avoiding bloodshed and further destruction makes this account plausible. For the moment battle was avoided. Fulk and Odo came to an agreement. This arrangement—treaty might even be a more accurate term—stipulated that Odo give formal recognition of Fulk's conquest of Saumur and relinguish the castrum with all pertaining to it to the Angevin count. In return, Fulk promised to destroy his stronghold at Montboyau in the environs of Tours.[36]

This "treaty" provides evidence of sound strategic and tactical thinking on both sides. Odo surely came to realize that even if he defeated Fulk's relief force in open battle beneath the walls of Saumur, his forces would be weakened and not in condition to mount a protracted siege of a strong fortification in hostile territory. Indeed, Odo's entire campaign against Saumur at this time had been ill conceived. By recognizing Angevin control of Saumur, Odo gave legal force to a situation he was powerless to change. In return he obtained the destruction of a dangerous fortification that threatened his position at Tours and that he had failed to take on two occasions.

For Fulk the agreement saved him from fighting a battle that could have been costly in lives and, if lost, potentially damaging to his position. Indeed, no good commander fights an unnecessary battle if combat can be avoided.[37] By obtaining an agreement in which Odo relinquished his right to Saumur, Fulk's conquest was legitimized and his control of the Saumurois, the stronghold of Saumur, and Saint-Florent acquired a juridical basis. By agreeing to destroy Montboyau, Fulk recognized that political realities in the Touraine made it unlikely that he would be able at that time to secure control over Tours, even with military superiority. The death of Sulpicius and his replacement as treasurer of Saint-Martin with Wanilo, one of Odo's supporters, not only seriously weakened the Angevin position at Tours but provided evidence—if any was needed after Henry's participation in the attack on Amboise—that King Robert II, who controlled the appointment of the treasurer, was cooperating fully at this time with the count of Blois in the Touraine.[38]

Once the treaty with Odo had eliminated the prospect of taking Tours (for the time being) and legitimized the conquest of Saumur, Fulk had the leisure to settle a new regime at the castrum and in the region. From Fulk's perspective, this settlement may have been viewed as the next or perhaps even the final step in a process that had been going on since his accession in 987. In what may be characterized as the first phase of Fulk's relations with Saint-Florent, the Angevin count had sought to exploit the monastery's wealth and to undermine the position of both the count of Blois and his fidelis Gelduin at Saumur. Fulk had made considerable progress in these efforts and had even maneuvered Abbot Robert (d. 1011) into recognizing him as his dominus. Militarily, Fulk had surrounded Saumur with strongholds and villages from which he could raise troops in order to harass his adversaries in the castrum.

The second phase embraced the period between Fulk's capture of Saumur, early in the summer of 1026, and the treaty with Odo late in the summer of 1027. Fulk had imprisoned the key figures of Gelduin's military and civil administration, detailed a garrison to defend the castrum, and temporarily placed affairs at Saumur in the hands of Fulchardus. Later in the summer, Odo had tried to retake the castrum, but the besiegers were greatly discomforted by Fulchardus's garrison troops and Odo withdrew.

The Saumur that Fulchardus defended against Odo was a far different place from the castrum Fulk had surprised earlier in the year. In the course of the conquest of Saumur the monastery of Saint-Florent had been burned, Fulk's men had stolen the relics of Saint Doucelin, and had tried to carry off the relics of Saint Florent. This attempt had failed, and Abbot Frederick thereafter effectively opposed Fulk's plan to translate the relics of Saint Florent to Angers, where the count wanted to relocate the monastery. Indeed, Frederick even refused to rebuild the monastery in the castrum itself. Thus after much discussion, Fulk promised Frederick to return to Saumur with Countess Hildegarde and to help the monks find a new place for their monastery outside the walls of the castrum. This relocation was accomplished after Odo's siege was raised late in the summer of 1026.[39]

Following the treaty between Fulk and Odo, the Angevin count initiated a third phase resulting in radical changes at both Saumur and Saint-Florent. Fulchardus's commission as vicarius was regularized and he was transferred from his previous position at Rochfort-sur-Loire to Saumur. This widely experienced government official, who seems to have been of Vendômois origins and was perhaps a relative of Bishop Hubert of Angers, had the task of carrying out Fulk's policies. These policies, however, were similar in all areas newly brought under Angevin control; broadly characterized they amounted to an effort to exploit fully the tax base and the military potential in the interests of the government.[40]

For almost three-quarters of a century the monks of Saint-Florent had worked diligently and with great success to obtain from the count of Blois and the lords of Saumur immunities from the broad spectrum of obligations owed to the government at all levels by its subjects.[41] Following the treaty between Fulk and Odo, the Angevin government acted to reimpose a vast array of obligations on Saint-Florent and its dependents and to ensure that those who dwelled in the region were burdened in a similar manner to those in other areas of the Angevin state. The well-documented arrangements at Saumur permit us to see the full panorama of the Angevin system at work and provide an opportunity to grasp the dimensions of the resources available to the Angevin government.[42]

The Angevin counts administered a complex system of taxation in which the government levied a wide variety of imposts directly and indirectly on immovables, movables, and persons. There were taxes on land (the *census*), which seems to have been focused on allodial property, although not exclusively so. Thus, for example, an allod was normally subject to the *census* owed to the count, but there were special allods that were by definition immune from the *census* and thus were treated as a royal allod ("ut regale alodium"). The point need hardly be made that this *census* cannot be considered a rent since an allod was real estate held in private ownership during this period in the west of France. Other examples of the *census* as a land tax can be noted on land and houses located within fortifications. Small pieces of land (*reicules*) subject to the *census* are also identifiable where this levy is described as one of the comital taxes (*consuetudines comitales*). This *census* was assessed yearly and is described as a *taxatio annualis*. The phrase *terra censuales* also on occasion can be shown to refer to lands subject to a land tax.[43]

Of more importance than the *census* were those taxes (generally called *consuetudines*) levied directly on the productivity of the land or other forms of production. At harvest time the count's agents went into the countryside and assessed the *consuetudo* on various crops: *avenagium* on the crop of oats, *fenagium* on the hay, and *frumentagium* on grain. The "crop" of animals was also taxed: the *friscingagium* was levied on suckling pigs, *multonagium* on yearling rams castrated for fattening before slaughter, the *bribigium* on new lambs, and the *vaccagium* on calves. In addition, the count's officials also collected direct taxes on the production of bread in ovens (*furnaticum*), on the production of wine (*vinagium*), and on the milling of flour (*molinagium*).[44]

Not only did the tax collectors go out into the countryside to collect these direct imposts but the taxpayers were responsible for paying the expenses of these government officials. We learn that when the count's *servientes* went to collect the *vinagium* at the villa of Saint-Georges-sur-Layon, which belonged to the monastery of Saint-Florent, each of the tax collectors received a daily ration of one denarius worth of bread, one denarius worth of meat, and a sextarius worth either of wine or of flavored wine (*mustus*). The total value of these payments considerably exceeded what was required for mere sustenance and clearly constituted an important part of the income these government officials received for their work.[45]

Unlike these *consuetudines*, which were usually levied at a rate of ten percent (a *decima*) of the total in the "field" and occasionally at a higher (even a much higher) percentage of the gross, there was a congeries of interrelated imposts more directly mandated to sustain the functioning of the state in war and peace. These obligations fell more broadly on society as a whole and were not as explicitly tied to productivity. Among the taxes in this latter group is the *fodrum*. This levy was originally intended to provide fodder for the animals used by the army and it was assessed as needed. The burdensome nature of this impost, which was limited only by what was available to fill the government's needs, is frequently attested because the count's officials appear to have found various creative ways to meet the requirements of the state. The burdensomeness of the *fodrum* may have been partially a result of requisitions of fodder and related supplies for the men not only when the Angevin army was *in hoste* or *in expeditione* but also *sine hoste*, at times when the military was not actually on campaign.[46]

Closely connected to the *fodrum*, which in peacetime would appear on occasion as "hospitium equorum," were levies of all types of foodstuffs for the army. The obligation to provide food for the army did not fall only on producers but also on *burgenses*. Because burgenses generally were not engaged in agriculture, they paid this tax in money rather than in kind. In peacetime, moreover, efforts appear to have been made to limit the tax to sustaining the count and the officials of his military household who traveled with him at all times. This *abergementum* encompassed not only the basics of food (including wine) and lodging for the men and appropriate supplies for the horses but even stipulated that such detailed requirements as blankets or bed-ding be provided for the itinerant comital household.[47]

For transport of supplies needed by the army in time of war and for the government in peacetime, the Angevin count imposed the *angaria* on all those who owned wagons, carts, oxen, and asses. Actually, the *angaria* included not only hauling service, which at times is called the *carragum*, but also a messenger service, called the *cavaugadum*, which was imposed on all those who owned horses. It is not exactly clear how this "post service" worked and what if any relation it may have had to the Carolingian system, which itself was based on the Roman *tractoria*. Parenthetically, we may note that fishermen who plied their trade in boats on the major rivers of Anjou were responsible for the *evectio*; this encompassed transport services for the count's household, including his military following, as well as more general hauling obligations and the carrying of messages.[48]

More thoroughly military in nature was the general obligation for all those under the jurisdiction of the Angevin government to perform the *bidamnum*. This was an annual service apparently owed by all land-holders, free and unfree alike, which generally entailed fifteen days of labor and was focused on the building or repair of fortifications within the Angevin state or on the frontiers. Those who found such service inconvenient or even demeaning were permitted to find substitutes; as one text from the estates of Saint-Florent puts it: "hoc bidamnum tale erat ut omnes qui in hac possession terram tenebant, aut ipsi aut laetati (sic) eorum . . . pergerent . . ."[49] These *laeti* obviously would then do two tours of service. Although lords were often eager to have their dependents avoid this burdensome public service, the counts rarely granted immunity. They did, however, permit commutation of this tax paid with labor for regular payments in money. Of more general scope than the *bidamnum* were *corvadae* that were imposed by a government official such as the vicarius or someone exercising vicarial power in his place on dependents of various lords in order to carry out public works.[50]

Another direct tax levied by the government was the obligation to perform military service, both for local defense and for operations beyond the frontiers; this obligation was universal in the Angevin state. Thus, for example, the count's *satellites,* that is, his *vassi* and *fideles,* were required not only to answer the *submonitio* (call to arms) themselves but were required to bring their *rustici,* their agricultural dependents, along with them. In addition, the *villani,* both those who were dependents of a lord, such as the *rustici* just mentioned, or the lowly *famuli* of a great *senior,* as well as those who were not dependents, were required to answer the comital *submonitio* "pro praelio publico" under the leadership of a government official such as the vicarius or under the command of their lord or his substitute in cases where the *senior* was an ecclesiastic. Even those who held very small plots of land, the *ruricolae,* owed military service, as did those who were inhabitants of the *burgi,* the *burgenses.* The townsmen, whose wealth more than likely was not in land and whose livelihood was probably earned through trade and commerce or as artisans, were explicitly warned that "nullam causu mercedis" will they be exempt from military service.[51]

Direct input to the comital government came also from licenses for the use of public lands and waters. Such revenues had been collected by the Carolingian kings in much the same manner and for the same reasons. The count held a broad spectrum of rights on all "wooded land" whether privately held by his subjects as *silva* or belonging to the comital fisc and called *foresta.* Thus, the count's subjects, such as the monks of Saint-Florent, were required to purchase licenses or obtain immunities in order to hunt, chop down oak trees for building, or carry out general land clearing for the purpose of developing arable, that is, assarting. Licenses, of course, were also required if anyone wished to hunt or chop down oaks in the forests of the comital fisc or to fish on the major rivers for commercial purposes.[52]

Not only did Fulk impose on the Saumurois the array of direct burdens just detailed, but he also imposed a no less daunting complex of indirect levies. These taxes fall into two groups. The first we can classify as tolls that were levied at the frontiers and internally on the circulation of merchandise. The term *theloneum* is often used in a general manner to describe this impost, but in a more specialized context *theloneum* appears to refer primarily to the toll paid by ships carrying merchandise up and down the Loire as well as on the lesser rivers of Anjou. Other specialized terminology can be discerned, such as the *pedaticum* imposed on all those (merchants and nonmerchants alike) who carried vendable or potentially vendable goods or the *rotaticum* or wheel tax, which identifies the vehicle carrying the goods for taxation along with a smaller tax for goods carried on pack horses. There are also references to the *pontaticum* paid for crossing a bridge. The bridges were also used as toll stations where the *theloneum* was collected from passing boats. The count's officials also exacted moorage charges and port charges, the *ripaticum* and *portaticum.*[53]

Levies on sales (*vendae* and *venditiones*) comprised a second group of indirect taxes that contributed significantly to the revenues collected by the government—and siphoned funds away from monasteries like Saint-Florent which had lost their immunities. All sales, retail and wholesale alike, wherever they were made and by whomever they were executed, freemen and dependents alike, were subject to sales taxes. These taxes were not limited to those "qui vivunt mercatore."[54] Of course, despite the army of minor officials who appear in the documents doing their duty, often with great zeal and officiousness, it would have been impossible to collect taxes on every transaction that took place. Yet before concluding that these officials operated solely in the markets and fairs where they normally did collect sales taxes, we should note that they went at least as far as collecting taxes on the retail sales of wine in taverns (*cauponae*), which suggests some rather detailed record-keeping mechanism.[55]

The profits of justice were yet another source of revenue collected by Fulk's officials. The system that prevailed in the Angevin state was a modified version of that which had functioned in the Carolingian empire. Under this system the counts had received one-third of all the fines paid in the local courts over which they or their subordinates presided. One-third of fines went to the king and one-third to the successful litigant. But with the collapse of royal control over local administration it is likely that the king's portion of the fines (or *freda*) went to the Angevin counts and thus the next lower range of functionary in the comital government was positioned to receive what earlier had been the count's portion. The importance of the income generated from these fines may be gauged in part by the government's policy of not permitting its subjects to obtain the profits of justice from the three major crimes—homicide, arson, and theft—and of only very rarely giving as gifts the income earned from lesser crimes. The vigorous efforts undertaken by some of the count's most influential subjects, including the monks of Saint-Florent, to obtain access to these profits, coupled with the production of forged documents to secure mere "crumbs" appear to be additional indices of the perceived value of this income.[56]

In addition to the more obvious strategic gains, the conquest of the Saumurois and the subjection of Saint-Florent clearly provided Fulk with substantial economic resources. Although only a few solid indices of wealth can be quantified, contemporaries conservatively estimated that the bridge across the Loire at Saumur earned from tolls a yearly average revenue after expenses of 2,000 solidi.[57] The value of this profit can be seen for military purposes in that the average price of a high quality war horse was forty solidi. Thus from the tolls provided by one bridge at Saumur, Fulk could purchase mounts of the best kind for fifty members of his military household.[58]

As we assess the strength of Fulk's government, the information provided as a result of the conquest of the Saumurois tells us that neither lay nor ecclesiastical landowners, regardless of their importance, intruded between their dependents and the agents of the government when it came to the assessment of taxes or public services. By contrast, in the Carolingian empire dependent cultivators were not directly liable to the state for military service.[59] Rather, about fifty percent of the so-called "rents" paid or performed by peasants were in fact "taxes" that went either directly or indirectly to sustain the Carolingian government's constant military operations through the mediation of the great lords.[60] It is important in gauging the direct authority exercised by the Angevin state to note that the government not only imposed the traditional fines on military levies of all classes who were delinquent in satisfying the *herribannum* (*submonitio*) but also fined the lord when a dependent was delinquent.[61]

Fulk's administrative reorganization of the Saumurois was only a part of the whole picture. The Angevin count carried out massive confiscations of lands and other resources belonging to the count of Blois and his supporters in the region. Gelduin of Saumur, whose family had been domini of the castrum for almost three-quarters of a century, appears to have lost everything. Lesser supporters of the Blésois regime, relatively undistinguished *milites* such as Renaud Cinifes, Berard, and Teucho, were also dispossessed; only a few of the most minor landholders in the region can be identified as having survived Fulk's policy of dispossessing his adversaries' men.[62]

Fulk used some of the confiscated resources to reward supporters who had served him loyally through the years. Thus we see *milites* such as Walter Titio and of course Fulcherius benefiting from the conquest. The overwhelming share of the gains made in the region, however, came under the jurisdiction of the comital fisc and was not parceled out by Fulk to his fideles as had been the case, for example, about 1005. At that time, the Renaud family allods came into Fulk's hands and the count distributed the lands to his *milites*. That Fulk did not feel it necessary to alienate, even on a limited basis, much of these newly acquired resources may be viewed as yet another index of his effective rule. His ability to retain for the comital fisc large amounts of income-producing land acquired through successful operations even further strengthened the government.

The treaty that Fulk made with Odo in the summer of 1027 ushered in a period of general peace in the west of Francia lasting through the campaigning season of 1028. Fulk took advantage of this respite to build a new stronghold at Montfaucon in order to strengthen his position in the Mauges region. Fulk imposed the *bidamnum* and compelled the local monks of Saint-Florent to participate in the building. In short, Fulk imposed the same types of *consuetudines* on the *homines* of Saint Florent-le-Vieil that he had previously imposed on the dependents of Saint-Florent at Saumur, the mother house. This appears to have been Fulk's first major effort to take advantage of his newly recognized control of Saint-Florent in order to assert his authority over Saint-Florent-le-Vieil and thereby to undermine whatever claims Count Budic of Nantes might have attempted to press in the Mauges region.[63]

From the strategic point of view the new stronghold at Montfaucon, located fifteen kilometers south-southeast of Beaupréau, was a departure from Fulk's previous focus on defending the valley of the Eavre. The new stronghold seems to have been intended in part to counter the viscount of Thouars, whose supporters apparently had raided the western reaches of the Mauges region in sufficient force or with sufficient regularity for the Angevin count to modify his strategy. While such a stronghold had little immediate offensive capacity, its garrison would be well positioned to deter or to cut off enemy raiders. Such a garrison can be especially effective in attacking an enemy whose homeward-bound forces are laden with booty.[64] Such a move is key to defense in depth strategy.

Closer to home, Fulk took the opportunity provided by the cessation of hostilities to deal with other pressing matters. Abbot Hubert of Saint-Aubin, who had loyally supported Fulk for more than a quarter-century, died in 1027, and a successor was needed. With the agreement of his fideles Fulk chose a monk of Saint-Aubin named Primaldus to lead this important monastic house at Angers. Perhaps in recognition of the lengthy and exceptionally loyal service that he had received from Abbot Hubert, Fulk gave the monks on the occasion of Primaldus's election all of the vicarial rights in their lands with the exception of those concerning theft, arson, and homicide. The economic value of the right to two-thirds of the judicial fines from minor crimes, the comital and vicarial portions, was undoubtedly substantial and likely was made possible by the immense gains the government treasury had reaped as a result of the conquest of the Saumurois.[65]

From the political point of view, Primaldus proved to be a good choice. With the abbot's help, Fulk reestablished a strong comital presence in the region of Montreuil-Bellay and Méron in the northern Poitou on the direct route from Thouars to Saumur. Through various means, not all of which were subsequently viewed in a positive light by the monks, Fulk was able to establish his men at Montreuil-Bellay, to impose on Saint-Aubin the right to subject their *homines* at Méron to the corvée in order to make hay for the count from fields belonging to the comital fisc at Montreuil-Bellay, and to place his vicarius at Méron. Finally, Fulk began construction of a stronghold at Montreuil-Bellay where he established one of his fideles, a certain Berlaius, to command the garrison.[66]

Fulk's interest in Méron had been shared by his predecessors Fulk the Red and Fulk the Good, who had seized this strategically located Poitevin villa from Saint-Aubin and had held it for several decades as part of a policy of encroachment into the Poitou. Geoffrey Greymantle, however, was closely allied with the viscounts of Thouars, whose stronghold was only eighteen kilometers south-southwest of Méron. Because of this alliance Geoffrey had apparently considered Angevin control of the villa expendable and had returned it to Saint-Aubin.[67] When hostilities with the viscount of Thouars threatened Fulk Nerra's encroachment on the south during the mid-1020s, the count responded first by building the stronghold of Montfaucon, then by reestablishing the Angevin position at Méron, and finally by building a new stronghold at Montreuil-Bellay. From Montfaucon in the west through la Tour-Landry, Vihiers, and Montreuil-Bellay, a line of strongholds served as a military frontier to defend against raids launched by the men of Thouars. At the same time these fortifications helped to establish Fulk's control of the northern third of the Poitou and provided a southern border for the greatly expanded Angevin heartland.[68]

Fulk garrisoned the new stronghold at Montreuil-Bellay with a troop of *caballarii* who served Fulk *in hostem* under their castellan Berlaius both outside the frontiers of the Angevin state and within its borders. Moreover, when these *caballarii* joined the comital host to serve outside of the count's territory, particularly against the men of Thouars, the *homines* of Méron, who were dependents of Saint-Aubin there, were required to leave their holdings and to travel to the stronghold of Montreuil-Bellay, where they were to serve under the command of Fulk's vicarius, to whom the *bannum* had been delegated so that he could provide for the defense of the area.[69]

The development of this southern frontier region appears to have encouraged Fulk to adopt the title *princeps*, at least in certain circumstances, so as to legitimize the wide variety of regalian rights he exercised in the diverse regions outside the Angevin pagus where he exercised the *bannum* or *imperium*.[70] The microcosm of this frontier region enabled Fulk (and those around him) to see that he was operating in the Poitevin pagus and commanding not only persons living on his own estates but those who normally would be under the jurisdiction of the Poitevin count or his officials. Exercising a plenitude of power, Fulk built fortifications and arranged for "civil" administration by appointing vicarii and for military administration by assigning men from his military household to serve as castellans. He issued the *submonitio* to raise troops, pronounced the *bannum*, and arranged a special *consuetudo* so that his subjects would be regulated for a *bellum publicum* against the people of Thouars.[71]

While Fulk's successes on the frontier may have stimulated his actions, it is clear that Fulk was already a *princeps* in fact if not in title, especially in relation to his contemporaries in the west, the dukes of Aquitaine and Normandy and the count of Rennes, who not only styled himself duke of Brittany but even king of Brittany. Fulk not only exercised a broad spectrum of regalian rights but had vanquished the powerful count of Blois and dominated the counts of Nantes, Maine, and Vendôme, controlled the bishopric of Angers, and had more than a little to say concerning who would be bishop of le Mans and perhaps a word or two as to who would be bishop of Saintes.[72]

The monks of Saint-Aubin, with their many possessions on the southern frontier, likely recognized Fulk's right as *princeps* to impose on them the *custodia* of his castra "in marginibus terrae suae" along with other *consuetudines* of a related military nature. An arrangement seems likely in the context of Primaldus's "election" and Fulk's concession of vicarial rights and revenues to Saint-Aubin: the monks agreed to fulfill the same kinds of military obligations in what was arguably Poitevin territory as they normally did within the Angevin state itself.[73]

Angevin movement southward, at Poitevin expense, was facilitated by Abbot Primaldus, who supported Fulk's efforts at Méron and at Montreuil-Bellay. But Fulk's appointment of Primaldus had ramifications well beyond the traditional comital interest in selecting a friendly and cooperative abbot. Although Primaldus was a monk, he had been a member of the entourage of Geoffrey of Sablé, the brother of the viscount of le Mans; both men were loyal supporters of Fulk Nerra. In addition, Bishop Hubert of Angers, who was related on his father's side to the viscounts of le Mans, had arranged for his niece Emma to marry Radulf, the man who in the normal course of events would become viscount of le Mans and whom Fulk had already made viscount of Vendôme. We are not then surprised to discover that Bishop Hubert's interests benefited substantially during Primaldus's tenure as abbot.[74] The viscomital house of le Mans had strong ties to Bishop Hubert and to the bishops of le Mans as well as to the house of Bellême; all were of vital importance to Fulk in his efforts to dominate Maine and threaten Normandy. Thus the appointment of Primaldus may be seen as one small part of Fulk's ongoing attempt to maintain his position as master in the west.

In March of 1028 the delicate balance of power that had enabled Fulk to extend Angevin control through the northern Poitou as well as in other parts of Aquitaine was threatened by the death of Fulk's brother-in-law William of Angoulême, who may have succumbed to poison. William's youthful sons Hilduin and Geoffrey could likely be counted on to continue their father's policy of close cooperation with the Angevins under the guidance of their mother, Hermengarde-Gerberga, Fulk Nerra's sister. Following the death of her first husband, Conan of Rennes, Hermengarde-Gerberga remained a vigorous supporter of Fulk's policies despite the fact that she had been made a widow by her brother.[75]

By 1027, however, King Robert appears to have developed a base of sorts in the south. This became evident when Duke William of Aquitaine either shared with the monarch or perhaps even lost to him control over appointing the archbishop of Bordeaux.[76] In this context, we take note when we find Fulk attending what appears to have been King Robert's Easter court at Paris; this appearance may well suggest that the Angevin count and the king were once again drawing closer together as their interests coincided.[77] Fulk's agenda for strengthening his position in Aquitaine following Count William's death may possibly have benefited from royal support, but the Angevin count had ambitions much closer to the center of Capetian power.

Fulk Nerra's family had a long-standing claim to the lordship of Château-Landon, which was the major town of the Gâtinais, that "wasteland" east of Orléans and mostly west of Château-Landon. As we have seen, when Fulk was unable to maintain his obligations to Hugh Capet in this region, the new monarch created a *comté* of the Gâtinais and placed Walter, Fulk Nerra's cousin, in control at Château-Landon. Now it came about that Geoffrey, Walter's heir, was in need of a wife and Fulk Nerra had a daughter, Hermengarde-Blanche, who was of marriageable age; a few years earlier Viscount Hugh of Châteaudun had tried unsuccessfully to carry her off.[78]

At Robert's court in Paris during Easter 1028 Bishop Odolricus of Orléans along with a host of his relatives were conspicuous, and they had a deep interest in the Gâtinais because of its proximity to their base of power. Also present was Lancelinus of Beaugency, a fidelis of Fulk's whose stronghold was only twenty-five kilometers downriver from Orléans.[79] Beaugency along with the stronghold of Meung-sur-Loire (whose lord Léon was also one of Fulk's fideles) provided essential defended links for the Angevin count's communications to the Orléanais and on to Château-Landon.

Fulk had inherited from his father a position of no little consequence in the Orléanais. This included close relations with the viscomital family (the Alberici) and local aristocratic families who influenced the fisc of the cathedral church of Sainte-Croix through the canons. During the intermittent and brief interludes of cooperation with King Robert, Fulk had kept alive Angevin interest in the region. Fulk had also managed a measure of cooperation with Theobald when he was bishop of Orléans. By about 1006 Fulk had obtained the support of Lancelinus of Beaugency. Another of Fulk's supporters in this area was Humbaldus Cortinus, who held the land of Portereau from the Angevin count.[80] Fulk furthered his position in 1027 when he gained the support of Léon of Meung-sur-Loire.

With a base of importance on the western frontiers of the Gâtinais and its environs, Fulk also seems to have sought the support (or at least he avoided the opposition) of the powerful monastery of Fleury to the resurgence of Angevin influence at Château-Landon. Fulk's control and brutal exploitation of the monastery of Saint-Peter of Ferriers had elicited a blistering attack from Abbo of Fleury late in the tenth century, but now Gauzelin, King Robert's half-brother, was abbot of Fleury.[81] It is likely that at the marriage of Fulk's daughter Hermengarde-Blanche to Geoffrey he and his mother Beatrix made a substantial gift to Fleury. At about the same time Fulk was even more generous and provided Gauzelin with an exemption from the toll on one of the monks' ships that traveled on the Loire, half of the revenues that the count normally received from the abbey of Notre-Dame de Nantes, and the revenue from the salt pans located nearby that monastery.[82] The marriage was carried out before the end of 1030, and as part of the deal, Fulk received the office of the *viceconsulatum* of Château-Landon.[83] In subsequent years Fulk appears far more frequently in the Orléanais than prior to the marriage.

During the twelve to eighteen months required to negotiate the marriage of Hermengarde-Blanche to Geoffrey and reestablish a significant Angevin presence in the Gâtinais, Fulk was far from idle. The highlight of 1028 was the round of ceremonies and festivities surrounding the consecration of the convent of the Ronceray at Angers in mid-July. Fulk had consented to cooperate with Countess Hildegarde, to whom he generally delegated the handling of largess to religious houses, in her long-desired goal of restoring the ruined church of Saint Mary at Ronceray and to build a convent there. Indeed, Fulk's gifts to the church and to the convent, even without considering those of his wife, were far in excess of what he had given to his earlier foundations of Belli Locus and Saint-Nicholas and certainly outstripped anything that he gave to already established houses such as Saint-Aubin and Saint-Serge or to the cathedral of Saint Maurice. Even his gifts to the church of Saint-Martin at Angers, which he and Hildegarde strongly supported, were small in comparison with what was provided to Ronceray.[84] The great gains Fulk made from the conquest of the Saumurois may have encouraged this unaccustomed liberality.

Fulk cooperated closely with his wife and son, Geoffrey Martel, in the founding of Ronceray, and we see the Angevin count on one of those rare occasions when he expressed a sense of good feeling and even "exhilaration."[85] Probably this is the moment chosen by the aging count, nearing his sixtieth year, to establish his son and successor, Geoffrey Martel, in a position of responsibility so that he could gain experience in the art of government. Thus in a spirit of practicality and generosity, Fulk gave Geoffrey, now in his early twenties, the castrum of Saumur.[86]

While Fulk was arranging affairs within the Angevin pagus, Odo II of Blois was exploring various opportunities to subvert Fulk's newly won position in the west. Thus in 1029 we find Odo at the castrum of Vendôme with an illustrious entourage that included Abbot Evrard of Marmoutier and Archbishop Arnulf of Tours. Odo's presence at Vendôme at this time and with these dignitaries may well have been a response to the weakening of his position in the region by King

Robert, who had maintained control of the bishopric of Chartres following Fulbert's death on 10 April 1028. Traditionally, the bishops of Chartres not only included the Vendômois in their diocese but laid some claim to overlordship of important holdings in the region, including the castrum of Vendôme itself. Fulk Nerra's interests at Vendôme, however, were conserved ably at this time by Bishop Hubert of Angers, a powerful lord in the region whose father had been viscount of Vendôme. Odo's initiative came to nothing.[87]

A second initiative against Fulk at about this time seems to have benefited Odo's interests somewhat more than the Blésois effort in the Vendômois. Since about 1013 Count Budic of Nantes had been at war with Count Alan of Rennes on an intermittent basis, with Fulk providing *auxilium* to Budic, who recognized the Angevin count as his *senior*. Alan was Odo's man and recognized that he held Rennes from the count of Blois. During the decade and a half following Budic's recognition of Fulk, the Angevin count repeatedly encroached on the rights and powers claimed by the count of Nantes. This was especially the case in the Mauges region, where Fulk built strongholds at Montrevault, Beaupréau, Chemillé, and Montfaucon. In addition, Bishop Hubert of Angers pursued a deliberate policy of integrating the religious institutions of the Mauges region into the diocese of Angers. Furthermore, Fulk exploited the resources of the monastery of Notre-Dame de Nantes for his own purposes and used the fisc of Saint-Florent-le-Vieil over which Budic claimed lordship.[88]

Before the summer of 1027 Fulk apparently had given nominal recognition to Budic's claims over the monks of Saint-Florent-le-Vieil, but when the Angevin count built the stronghold of Montfaucon (ca. 1027–1028) and required the *bidamnum* from the monks and their dependents for construction work, the count of Nantes probably realized that his claims were not being honored. By about 1030 Budic seems to have decided that having Fulk for his *senior* was more burdensome than beneficial. Thus, through the efforts of Bishop Junguenée of Dol, Count Alan's adviser, a secret agreement was concluded between Budic and the count of Rennes. Alan promised to grant various beneficia to Budic, who had become increasingly impoverished because of the lengthy war and Fulk's depredations. In return, Budic agreed that he would recognize Alan as his *senior*.[89]

Through some stratagem that has left no record in the sources, Budic managed to have Fulk remove his troops from Nantes. Shortly thereafter the pact between the count of Nantes and Alan of Rennes was made public and, at least for the time being, Fulk lost control of the important stronghold of Nantes. This loss, however, was not as serious as it might seem, for the inspiration for Alan's action was his preoccupation with affairs in Normandy. He no longer could maintain operations in the south against Nantes and in the north on the Norman frontier. In addition, even if Alan was successful in gaining a strong position in the western parts of the Norman duchy, it would have been difficult for him to mobilize a substantial Norman force for operations in Anjou. Finally, the spectre of an alliance of the kind that had materialized in 992 with Viking ships at Nantes preparing to move up the Loire in support of an army from Rennes was not in prospect. Since 1025 the traditionally close ties between Scandinavia and Normandy had been broken.[90]

Fulk evidently understood Budic's defection to present only a limited danger, at least in the short term, for he did not respond immediately with a punitive expedition. Rather, the Angevin count focused his attention on Aquitaine, where Count William of Poitiers, at sixty-one years of age, had retired to a monastery and left his eldest son, William the Fat, to rule in his place. On 31 January 1030 the elder William died, and William the Fat, whose mother had been Fulk Nerra's cousin Adalmode, took steps to secure his position. Agnes of Burgundy, William's third wife and William the Fat's stepmother, was banished from the court with her two young sons. The new count was probably correct in believing Agnes a danger to him. Her father had been count of Mâcon, and she was the aunt of Count Renaud of Nevers and the niece of the bishop of Langres.[91] These important magnates on the eastern frontiers of Aquitaine and Burgundy could well cause trouble for the new duke of Aquitaine in the name of looking after the interests of Anges's children.

Clearly, William's death in January 1030 presented numerous possibilities for Fulk and for others to aggrandize their positions in Aquitaine at the expense of William the Fat. This potentially fluid political situation was further destabilized by the revolt of the young Capetian king Henry and his brother Robert against their father Robert II. Although Queen Constance, Fulk's cousin, remained loyal to her husband, as did many of the important magnates of Burgundy, including Count Renaud of Nevers, the monarch's son-in-law, the rebels were surprisingly successful. King Henry operated in the north and deprived his father of Dreux while Robert, his brother, gained control of Beaune and Avallon in Burgundy.[92]

The war in Burgundy may well have kept Agnes's powerful relatives from intervening in her interest against William the Fat. Such intervention by "foreign powers" in the affairs of the duke of Aquitaine or more directly in the Poitou could have upset Fulk's plans as well. Indeed, for thirty years Fulk had systematically taken advantage of the elder William, whom paradoxically he had recognized as his *senior,* and robbed him of both land and power.[93] With the accession of William the Fat, the Angevins appear to have been in a strong position to continue this policy of gaining control of territory within the Poitou and establishing alliances throughout Aquitaine.

To this end Fulk set about constructing a formidable stronghold at Moncontour. This castrum, located just east of the Dive about midway between Loudun and Mirebeau, and Faye-la-Vineuse signaled Angevin efforts to dominate the region north of Poitiers between the Veude and the Dive. But Moncontour, which was a formidable stronghold with a stone tower standing at least 24 meters in height and having walls 2.80 meters thick, had the additional purpose of dominating the wealthy monastery of Saint-Jouin-de-Marnes, which stands less than a bow shot from its walls.[94]

Saint-Jouin itself was a worthy prize in the struggle for control of that part of the northern Poitou which traditionally had been in the control of the viscount of Thouars. The latter's long-standing interest in Saint-Jouin had been undermined by Fulk Nerra, who was systematically expanding his control of the region and was ensuring his domination with the construction of the stronghold of Moncontour. Indeed, by about 1030 Angevin fortifications at Moncontour, Loudun, Montreuil-Bellay, Maulévrier, Vihiers, and Parthenay—all within seventeen to forty kilometers of Thouars—surrounded the home base of the viscomital family and blocked its forces from the Mauges region to the north and from Poitiers to the east.

Fulk's forceful move into the Poitou was built on a strong base. In addition to the strongholds focused on Thouars, the Mauges region was in Angevin hands and protected with strongholds at Montrevault, Beaupréau, Montfaucon, la Tour-Landry, and Chemillé. To the east of the Mauges region, the viscounts of Thouars refused to recognize William the Fat's accession in Poitou; moreover the Angevin strongholds at Vihiers, Doué, Loudun, Mirebeau, and Faye-la-Vineuse placed the northern third of the Poitou in Fulk's hands. Add to these bases Fulk's rights over the strongholds of Parthenay and Gençay. Finally, Fulk's nephews, the sons of William of Angoulême, established at Melle and Chéneché, and the lords of Lusignan and Rancon, who recognized the Angevin count as their *senior*,[95] augmented the Angevin presence.

Documents issued by William the Fat make it clear that he was unable to secure recognition in northern Poitou. Indeed, William played no juridical role at the very important and rich church of Saint Hilaire, which had been one of his father's favorites, and the magnates of the north do not appear in his entourage. The canons of Saint Hilaire were so disheartened by the inability of William to protect their interests that they sought Fulk as their protector. In return for his promise to provide protection for them and to represent their interests, the canons gave Fulk various estates in the region of Loudun and Chinon.[96]

Fulk's position in 1031 as master of the west appears to have grown even more secure. The future may have looked even brighter than it had five years earlier when he took Saumur and held Count Herbert of Maine in prison. But before the Angevin count could take full advantage of the death of Duke William of Poitou or exploit Alan of Rennes' attraction to affairs in Normandy (which also distracted the Norman duke), King Robert II died.[97] The projection of young King Henry to the forefront was likely to create considerable destabilization from which a powerful magnate like the Angevin count could be expected to benefit. We must recall, however, that Fulk's plans and initiatives, although based in the long term on the work of his father and grandfather or even earlier ancestors, were developed in the short term in the context of King Robert's agenda. Henry could not simply be considered a weaker version of his father Robert, even if the young Capetian intended to continue his predecessor's rather consistent policies without alteration. On the basis of more than four decades of experience, Fulk no doubt surmised that regardless of Henry's intentions, the other great powers of the French kingdom such as Flanders, Blois-Champagne, and Normandy would likely reassess their own policies in light of Robert's death. Henry's accession would doubtless require Fulk to make adjustments in his plans.

CHAPTER NINE

The Angevin-Capetian Alliance

The fragile balance of power in France teetered on the verge of disintegration with the death of King Robert II. King Henry, who had been associated with his father in the kingship four years earlier, assumed sole power but was in a precarious position. His mother, Queen Constance, had earlier preferred her younger son Robert as king, and she was not one to shrink from taking vigorous action to accomplish her goals. At the outset, Constance had two natural allies to sustain her opposition to Henry. Fulk Nerra, her cousin, who may have given her some support in 1026–1027 when she first opposed Henry's succession, was the leading figure in the west of France. Fulk had little obvious reason to support King Henry since the latter had allied with Odo II to attack the Angevin stronghold of Amboise in the spring of 1027.[1]

Constance's other potential ally was her nephew William the Fat, duke of Aquitaine and count of Poitou. William's mother Adalmode and Constance were half-sisters, and their mother Adelaide, Fulk Nerra's aunt, had only recently died.[2] William, however, was in difficult straits at home, and Fulk Nerra was one of his major problems. Thus, if William and Fulk did not join to support Constance, the duke of Aquitaine could be of little or no help to his aunt. Whether Fulk would support his cousin Constance was therefore a major question for King Henry to ponder.

King Henry, however, acted quickly and decisively to stabilize a potentially volatile situation. He granted to his brother Robert the duchy of Burgundy and the title of duke. To his brother-in-law Baldwin V of Flanders he granted the abbey of Corbie.[3] Although Henry's brother Robert, now Duke Robert, was pacified for the moment, the king was not naive about Queen Constance's ability to subvert the settlement and lead her favorite son to revolt against his brother.

Queen Constance's position had some "constitutional" (for want of a better term) importance. The idea persisted that the kingship was elective. Since no legal process had been established to provide for the succession, scholars have argued that the queen likely believed that she had some right to play a role in determining who would be king. Moreover, from a practical perspective, Constance's future would likely be much less attractive with Henry on the throne since he well knew that she had opposed his association in 1027.[4]

King Henry had to find a way to deprive his mother of the support that she might hope to obtain from her cousin Fulk. William the Fat seems to have been of considerably less consequence at this time. Yet for Henry to ally with Fulk would mean almost certainly that Odo II of Blois would be alienated from the royal cause. Clearly, just as Henry's grandfather and his father had frequently had to choose between Blois and Anjou in order to maintain a favorable balance of power, the new monarch had to make this choice as well.[5]

As Henry pondered his options during the late summer of 1031, he could reflect on his brief and unsuccessful association with Odo II when their combined forces failed to take Fulk's stronghold at Amboise. In addition, Henry was well aware that no love was lost between Queen Constance and Odo, whose mother she had finally displaced on the throne, but only after much tribulation. In short, while Fulk Nerra was clearly a potential supporter of Constance, King Henry could plausibly conclude that Odo was not likely to give his support to the woman who had been the instrument of his own mother's humiliation and abandonment. Thus, whatever Henry's reasoning during the months following his succession on 20 July 1031, he bent his efforts toward depriving his mother of the Angevin alliance with Fulk.

A deal was struck between Fulk and Henry before the end of 1031. As a result Geoffrey Martel, Fulk's son and heir (by his second wife Hildegarde), was made overlord of Vendôme and held the title of count by year's end. Fulk's grandson Bouchard and his daughter Adele (by Fulk's first wife Elizabeth of Vendôme) then held the *comté* from Geoffrey. In constitutional terms, King Henry seems to have secured the Angevin alliance by transferring to Geoffrey Martel the overlordship of the castrum of Vendôme, which previously had been held by the bishop of Chartres, and also the countship of Vendôme, which was in the royal gift.[6] Thus the bishop of Chartres was removed from this aspect of Angevin affairs, and the potential for Odo II, who was also count of Chartres, to gain a foothold in the Vendômois through domination of the bishop was removed as well.

Not long after Fulk and Henry arranged for Geoffrey to obtain the county of Vendôme, the Angevins took up the pursuit of their interests in Aquitaine. On 1 January 1032 Geoffrey Martel, who was now count of Vendôme, married Countess Agnes, the stepmother of William the Fat. This marriage, which was manifestly contrary to canon law by reason of consanguinity,[7] could have had but one purpose and that was to press forward the long-held Angevin policy of dominating the Poitou and perhaps even Aquitaine. As a result of the marriage, the Angevins gained physical control of the two sons of Countess Agnes, who were potential heirs to the duchy of Aquitaine and to the Poitou.[8] If William the Fat refused to serve as a pliable tool for the advancement of Angevin policy in a manner similar to that of his recently deceased father, then Fulk and Geoffrey Martel could hardly be expected to withhold their support for the candidacy of Agnes's sons to their half-brother's *honores*. We might well hypothesize that in the long term the Angevins expected to eliminate William the Fat and his brother Odo of Gascony and give one of Agnes's minor sons the title. If Agnes produced a son by Geoffrey Martel as well—certainly it was not thought unlikely given the respective ages of Agnes and Geoffrey in 1032 that the newlywed couple would have a son[9]—then one day an Angevin might well rule not only Anjou, Aquitaine, Maine, Vendôme, Nantes, and the Gâtinais but probably the Touraine as well.

Surely this latter scenario depended upon acts of questionable legality that in some cases might have to be pursued by force. We must remember that Angevin overlordship of Nantes had been acquired in a similar manner: Fulk the Good, Fulk Nerra's grandfather, married the widow of the count of Nantes. He then did away with the deceased count's legitimate heirs and placed a man of his choosing in the office. Fulk's "right" to behave in this way seems to have stemmed in the first instance from his military might. Yet a "constitutional" relationship of sorts also seems to have been created through Fulk's marriage to the widow of the previous count, despite the fact that she had no prior claim to Nantes or its region from her paternal or maternal ancestors. The ability of Fulk the Good's son Geoffrey Greymantle and his grandson Fulk Nerra to maintain overlordship during the eight decades that bring us to our present place in the story seems to suggest that a modicum of "legitimacy" undergirded the acquisition of power through marriage to the widow of the erstwhile officeholder.[10]

In yet another strikingly similar context Geoffrey Greymantle took for his second wife Adele the widow of Count Lambert of Chalon. Geoffrey then ruled the region with the comital title and maneuvered Adele and Lambert's son Hugh into an ecclesiastical career. Geoffrey and Adele had a son of their own named Maurice, and he was placed in line to succeed as count of Chalon. Geoffrey, however, died prematurely, and in the settlement following his death Hugh and Maurice (still a minor) shared the comital title under the guardianship of their mother. In the long term Hugh drove Maurice out, and Geoffrey's plan failed.[11]

In 1031 Maurice was alive and well and a participant in Angevin affairs. If necessary, he surely could explain the thinking that the "hereditary" transfer of power through a widow was a plausible tactic for territorial aggrandizement, even if it had not succeeded in his own case.[12] It seems that during the late tenth and early eleventh centuries notions of legitimacy were less well developed than they were to become later in the Middle Ages; moreover, the level of political instability was sufficiently high that "far-fetched" schemes such as an Angevin effort to gain control of Aquitaine or at least of the Poitou through marriage to the widow of a recently deceased count fell squarely within the realm of the possible. We may recall that less than a decade before the events under discussion here, William the Fat had sought to become king of Italy,[13] and within a few years of Geoffrey's marriage to Agnes, Odo II of Blois took military action in an effort first to secure control of the kingdom of Burgundy and then of the kingdom of Italy for himself.[14] A generation later William of Normandy succeeded brilliantly in realizing a no less unlikely dream.[15]

As one apparent result of King Henry's quick actions in securing the support of Fulk Nerra, Baldwin of Flanders, and his brother Robert, no notable violence followed in the wake of the transition from the reign of King Robert to that of his son. This calm persisted through the winter of 1032, and during the Easter court held in April at Orléans Henry I met with the great lay and ecclesiastical magnates of his realm: Fulk Nerra, Robert of Burgundy, Robert of Normandy, Alan of Rennes, William the Fat, Baldwin of Flanders, Herbert of Maine, Odo II of Blois, Otto of Vermandois, Archbishop Aimo of Bourges,

Archbishop Letericus of Sens, Archbishop Arnulf of Tours, Bishop Odolricus of Orléans, Bishop Hildebertus of Paris, and Bishop Walter (?) of Meaux.[16]

Aside from the survival of one relatively routine grant to the monastery of Saint-Mesmin-de-Micy, we know very little of what transpired at this great Easter court. The appearance of harmony at this court, given the list of attestors to this act, seems to have masked substantial discontent. Odo II, who was not one to accept easily Angevin control at Vendôme, tried to press his interests in the region in 1029 following the death of Bishop Fulbert of Chartres. Henry, of course, supported Fulk and made Geoffrey Martel count of Vendôme. William the Fat, Odo's cousin, may certainly be thought to have sought royal support for his newly acquired and somewhat precarious position in Aquitaine and he surely wanted the condemnation of the patently illegal marriage of Agnes and Geoffrey Martel which further threatened his position. At this gathering, however, King Henry pointedly recognized William the Fat only as count of the Poitou and did not accord him the dignity of the title *dux Aquitanorum*. In addition, no evidence survives that would lead us to believe that the ecclesiastical magnates who were gathered at Orléans during Easter of 1032 offered a condemnation of the "incestuous" marriage that had been contracted between Geoffrey and Agnes. Count Alan of Rennes, who recognized Odo II as his *senior*, was married to the latter's daughter, and claimed lordship over Count Budic of Nantes was not accorded recognition with the title *dux Brittanorum* which he claimed. The situation at Nantes placed Alan in direct conflict with Fulk Nerra, Henry's ally, and the king recognized Alan only as count.[17] Finally, it may be observed that Queen Constance very probably did not play a role at this very important court.[18]

Odo II of Blois, William the Fat, Alan of Brittany, and Herbert of Maine formed a cadre among the greater magnates of the west which had good reason to oppose King Henry because the monarch had lent his support to the Angevins and in turn relied upon them. Queen Constance clearly was not satisfied with the course events had taken following her husband's death; she had wanted her son Robert to be king, and potentially she was the natural leader of those opposed to King Henry and his Angevin allies. Constance's "Angevin" blood gave her— as half-sister of the counts of Forez and Gévaudan, sister of the count of Arles, and aunt of William the Fat—a potentially strong following in Aquitaine with a possibility of undermining Fulk Nerra's position in the south. If her son Robert of Burgundy would play an active role, then Constance's position would be even stronger.[19] All that was necessary was a crisis that could be exploited to bring together the various elements who might benefit by deposing Henry and punishing Fulk Nerra.

On 26 June 1032 Archbishop Letericus of Sens died, and King Henry acted quickly to appoint as his successor Gelduin, who was of the family of the counts of Joigny near Sens. From a strategic point of view, Sens, which bordered on the county of Troyes in the east, was, along with the Gâtinais held by Fulk's son-in-law, a link between Odo II's holdings in Champagne and those in the Loire valley. In addition, the archbishop of Sens was in a position to exercise influence over the bishop of Chartres, who had a long-standing claim (now perhaps set aside by King Henry) to be overlord of Vendôme. Odo, as count of Chartres, could plausibly use the archbishop of Sens to help him pressure the bishop of Chartres to press Blésois interests in Vendôme.[20]

Earlier in his career Odo II had recognized the importance of Sens. He had tried to strengthen his position there during his conflict with King Robert in 1015. Thus, following King Henry's appointment of Gelduin as bishop, Odo acted decisively in opposition. When the canons of Sens cathedral rejected Gelduin and elected their treasurer Mainard as bishop, the count of Blois gave his support to Mainard, who was the father of Viscount Dagobert of Sens. Odo dispatched troops to Sens which were welcomed, and Count Renaud of Sens, who apparently supported King Henry, was driven out. Odo is said to have had the support of the canons, the viscount, and the *proceres* of Sens.[21]

By taking Sens under his control, Odo violated the treaty he had made with King Robert in 1015 and opened what was to be the first round in a revolt against King Henry. Once Odo had acted, Queen Constance was in a position to move as well. During the many years that she exercised influence at the royal court, Queen Constance had developed considerable personal power, especially among the second- and third-level magnates of Francia, the minor counts, viscounts, and lesser domini. A substantial group of these men made it known to the queen that they were willing to follow her against King Henry. Thus, the unlikely allies Constance and Odo came to an agreement to join forces against King Henry and his Angevin supporters. To seal their bargain, Constance recognized Odo's position at Sens. The canons of Sens cathedral remained loyal to the queen, apparently in return for her promise to accept the election of Mainard, and in her turn Constance granted half of the city of Sens to Odo. The other half of Sens as stipulated in an earlier treaty belonged to the archbishop.[22]

When Archbishop Gelduin tried to return to Sens after being consecrated in Paris, Odo II, Viscount Dagobert, and the rebels' archbishop, Mainard, refused to permit him to enter the city. The revolt was now out in the open, and King Henry could no longer ignore the maneuvering that saw a coalition led by Constance and Odo in possession of the strategically located city of Sens. Henry responded quickly. He gathered a large force and moved against Sens. At the same time he called for aid from his ally Fulk Nerra.[23]

Henry encamped at a villa near Sens while Fulk vigorously launched a force against the monastery of Saint-Pierre where he wrecked the abbey and burned the cloister. Fulk is reliably described as "first after the king in the *expeditio*"[24] and his enduring reputation as "elegantissimus bellicus rebus"[25] seems to permit the inference that the experienced Angevin count was the actual military decision maker rather than the young monarch. Fulk and Henry's operation was but a hastily organized counteroffensive. After testing the resolve of the enemy for three days with direct assaults on the walls of the city, the allies concluded that lengthy siege operations would be necessary if Sens was to be taken. In this era defense was far superior to offense from a technical point of view. Thus the allies withdrew leaving Sens in enemy hands.[26]

Through the end of 1032 and early 1033 King Henry's position continued to deteriorate. The Angevins, however, had their own problems. On the western frontier, Count Budic of Nantes, who had recognized Alan of Rennes as his *senior,* penetrated the Mauges region and tried to undermine the Angevin position there.[27] In addition, William the Fat seems to have thrown in his lot with his cousin Odo and his aunt Constance. Fulk had not recognized William as his *senior* for the many beneficia, including the Saintonge and the Loudunais, which he had held from the previous count of Poitou.[28] During the latter part of 1032 William the Fat held several courts at which he granted various concessions to the magnates of Aquitaine in order to rally support.[29] Reoccupation of the Saintonge, the most distant of Fulk's holdings from his home base, seems to have been William's primary objective.[30]

The rebel cause in Francia progressed so well that during the late autumn of 1032, following the successful defense of Sens, Odo II decided that he could employ his forces in a manner that was even more ambitious than the projected overthrow of King Henry and the radical realignment of the balance of power in the French kingdom. On 6 September 1032 King Rudolph of Burgundy died without direct heirs; he had designated the German emperor, Conrad II, as his successor. Odo, however, had been Rudolph's closest living relative, and the count of Blois saw the monarch's death as an opportunity to make himself king of Burgundy. Thus, while Constance's forces systematically reduced King Henry's position throughout the royal demesne and while William the Fat and Budic of Nantes occupied the king's Angevin allies, Odo invaded Burgundy with a large force. In the winter of 1033 he soundly defeated a German army sent by the emperor to defend his claim as Rudolph's successor.[31]

Despite the commitment of what seems to have been a substantial part of the rebel force to the Burgundian theater of operations—Odo took several well-fortified strongholds and cities and these in turn withstood Conrad's counterattack during the winter of 1033[32]—Queen Constance continued her successes against Henry. Major fortified cities such as Orléans, Senlis, and of course Sens either fell to the rebels or sided with the queen because their lords favored her cause. In addition, strongholds such as Melun, Poissy, le Puisset, Bethisy, Gournay-sur-Marne, Coucy, and Dammartin also either fell to Constance or saw their lords join the revolt. This list, of course, is incomplete since the surviving sources make no effort to provide comprehensive information.[33] For example, nothing specific is said of Paris, but this city too is likely to have been in Constance's hands, especially after the middle of April when King Henry was forced to flee from Francia with a small group of fideles to seek safety with Duke Robert in Normandy.[34]

Once in Normandy, King Henry worked to convince Duke Robert to support the royal cause. The duke, whose military forces appear to have been much less formidable than later Norman writers would have their readers believe, was not eager to enter the conflict. Alan of Rennes was causing considerable trouble on Robert's western frontier, and the lords of Bellême, who were allies of the Angevin count, continued to advance in the south contrary to Norman interests. Nonetheless, King Henry managed to prevail upon Robert, and in return for making the duke overlord of Dreux, Henry gained his support.[35] It is also likely at this time that Henry recognized the duke's illegitimate son William as the legitimate heir to Normandy. Indeed, this recognition seems to have been essential to Robert in light of the possibility of his death in battle defending Henry's throne.[36]

Duke Robert's support of King Henry was also made possible through the efforts of Fulk Nerra. The Angevin count's ally Robert of

Bellême turned his attention from his own interests in southern Normandy and joined with another of Fulk's fideles, Bishop Avesgaud of le Mans, to attack Count Herbert of Maine, who at this time was allied with Alan of Rennes. It is important to remember here that Alan's major support on the western borders of Normandy came from the abbot of Mont Saint Michel, who was from Maine and likely a fidelis of Count Herbert, the Breton count's ally.[37]

Thus Duke Robert attacked the rebel-held city of Orléans, where he had considerable success.[38] While Robert was at work in the west of France, Henry himself, under the guidance of Fulk Nerra, took the stronghold of Poissy and then gained control of le Puisset, where Queen Constance led the defense and was captured. About this time Melun also fell to the king's forces, and Henry imprisoned his mother there. With the capture of Constance, Henry and Fulk shattered the rebel coalition, putting Odo clearly on the defensive.[39] The chronicler Raoul Glaber, a later contemporary but no friend of the Angevin count, depicts Fulk as the architect of victory in the civil war and the man responsible for bringing about peace.[40]

Although the capture of Constance put victory within King Henry's grasp, the war was not yet over. Therefore, between 18 and 20 July 1033 Henry met with the emperor Conrad at Deville-sur-Meuse near Monthermé (south of Dinant) and made an alliance that was sealed by the betrothal of the emperor's daughter to the French monarch. Conrad, with Henry's permission, then launched a devastating campaign against Odo's holdings in Champagne. Odo counterattacked in Lorraine during late August of 1033.[41] At the same time Henry and Fulk defeated Odo's forces at Gournay and Clairoix. More rebel strongholds then fell and the allies sacked the environs of Sens.[42]

While Fulk was orchestrating Henry's victory over the rebels in the north, Geoffrey Martel was engaged against the forces of William the Fat in Aquitaine. Although the fullest account of Geoffrey's operations is provided by the rather late Gesta Consulum, which is somewhat confused both as to the duration of the campaign in 1033 and the place of the key battle fought against William, the general picture of what happened is basically accurate. For some four months (not four years, as the Gesta indicates) beginning in May 1033, that is, probably not long after the news that King Henry had been driven from Paris reached Poitiers, some of William's troops cut communications between Geoffrey Martel and Saintes in the south. Other units, perhaps commanded by the Poitevin count himself, struck the region around the Angevin stronghold of Mirebeau and then moved north and devastated the area around Loudun. From there some groups drove farther north into the Saumurois.[43]

Geoffrey, who clearly had been delegated by Fulk the full responsibility for dealing with William, responded on two fronts. Militarily, his forces drove south from Angers to William's capital where he "burned and destroyed whatever was around Poitiers on the near side of the river Clain and no less the suburb of the city beyond the river."[44] Diplomatically, Geoffrey negotiated an alliance with the frequently troublesome viscount of Thouars and managed to open communications with friendly factions in the Saintonge who promised support to the Angevins.[45]

William the Fat apparently came to believe that the war of attrition against Geoffrey was not in Poitevin interests as he saw the defection of important elements in the Saintonge and at Thouars. In addition, word of Queen Constance's capture and King Henry's alliance with Conrad in mid-July must surely have reached William by August. Only Odo II of Blois remained in the field with significant forces operating against the king and his Angevin allies. Odo's offensive into Lorraine late in August may well have stimulated William of Poitou to seek a major confrontation with Geoffrey. The Angevin forces at this time were still divided between Geoffrey, who was operating in the south, and Fulk in the north. But if William waited much longer and Henry's cause continued to prosper, large numbers of Angevin troops surely would be shifted very soon to the Aquitanian theater of operations, further disadvantaging the Poitevin count's position.[46]

By early September William, with a large force at his command levied from throughout Aquitaine, drove north to the Angevin frontier near the stronghold of Moncontour and the monastery of Saint-Jouin-de-Marnes. At Mont Couër not far from the monastery, Geoffrey Martel, apparently outnumbered, awaited William's attack.[47] In consonance with Vegetian tactics Geoffrey set his footsoldiers and archers in the vanguard to receive the enemy attack, and while these forces engaged he charged on the flank with his horsemen.[48] William's army was defeated and the count captured. Geoffrey followed up this victory by advancing to Saintes, which opened its gates to him.[49]

With the royal forces and their Angevin allies victorious on all fronts, Odo was forced to sue for peace. He surrendered Sens to King Henry and recognized the emperor Conrad as king of Burgundy.[50] As noted earlier, Raoul Glaber gave the Angevin count full credit for engineering both the victory and the peace. For the Angevins this victory meant new opportunities, and Fulk, Geoffrey, and the latter's wife Agnes met at Saint-Florent-le-Vieil either late in 1033 or early in 1034 to take collective measures to secure the Mauges region and the western frontier from the attacks of Count Budic of Nantes.[51] In a spirit of cooperation fully consistent with the century-old Angevin tradition of familial harmony, Fulk, Geoffrey and Agnes decided to build a defensive complex near Saint-Florent-le-Vieil. To help finance this project they confiscated from the monastery rights granted during the Carolingian era to collect tolls from ships passing on the river.[52]

This family meeting is doubly significant for it dispels the long-held myth that Geoffrey Martel's marriage to Agnes and his victory over William the Fat caused conflict with Fulk Nerra. But as we have seen Fulk had already handed Saumur over to Geoffrey, placing his son in a position to dominate the monastery of Saint-Florent. The abbot of Saint-Florent, moreover, also ruled over the priory at Saint-Florent-le-Vieil. Thus Fulk was laying the basis for his son to control Saint-Florent's two major centers of wealth. In addition, by providing Geoffrey with a major interest in a new stronghold at Saint-Florent-le-Vieil, the youthful count of Vendôme now had a substantial role to play in the problems of the southwestern frontier, that is, in Angevin efforts to rule the Mauges region and to dominate Nantes. These of course linked closely to the Poitou, where everything was up for grabs. Finally, we should recall that Fulk had established Fulchardus of Rochefort as the vicarius of Saumur, where he served directly under Geoffrey. Rochefort was a key stronghold in the Angevin defense system on the western frontier and stood only twenty-eight kilometers upriver from the newly constructed military complex at Saint-Florent-le-Vieil, where men from both Fulk's and Geoffrey's *clientela,* or military households, would be detailed to serve as garrison troopers.[53]

This obvious effort by Fulk to integrate Geoffrey into the administration of key areas of Angevin concern and to associate him with important members of the comital entourage is also attested in the Gâtine of the Poitou. The stronghold of Parthenay had been established either late in the tenth century or early in the eleventh century by the Angevins for the purpose of penetrating the western Poitou. A certain Joscelin, who most likely descended from a Touraine family in the *mouvance* of the Angevin count, was given control of this newly constructed fortification in the midst of the Gâtine. It is possible that Joscelin was brought south by Geoffrey Greymantle, who held estates and churches in northern Gâtine as well as in the area around Niort and Saint-Maixent to the south as early as about 970.[54] Geoffrey, who pursued a policy of moving supporters from one area to another, might well have been interested in following up his alliance with the viscounts of Thouars by establishing one of his own men directly to the south of Thouars. It is also possible, however, because of the youthfulness of Joscelin's oldest surviving children about whom we are informed, that Fulk Nerra established him in the Gâtine and oversaw the construction of the stronghold at Parthenay shortly after the settlement of about 999 with William of Aquitaine which brought Saintes and a substantial part of the Saintonge into Angevin hands.[55] Parthenay was constructed so that its garrison could control part of the main route from Angers to Saintes where it passed through the Gâtine.[56]

Fulk Nerra and later his son Geoffrey maintained close ties with William of Parthenay, Joscelin's son and successor. For example, even Countess Adele of Vendôme, Fulk's elder daughter and Geoffrey's half-sister, was called upon to lend her support to the alliance, and she granted William valuable holdings. William in turn supported the Angevin position in Aquitaine and with Angevin help built a stronghold at Germond twenty-five kilometers south-southwest of Parthenay, a day's journey for horsemen along the route to Saintes.[57]

The strategic importance of the strongholds at Parthenay and Germond to the maintenance of Angevin communications with the Saintonge deserves emphasis and points to the important efforts by Fulk and Geoffrey to secure control of Mauzé, Chizé, Tonnay-Boutonne, and Taillebourg along the route south from Parthenay. North of Parthenay, at intervals of no more than one day's travel, Fulk Nerra secured a line of strongholds which protected the Angevin lines of communication through Bressuire, Maulévrier, Passavant (or Vihiers), Chemillé, and Rochefort-sur-Loire to Angers.[58]

The entire 250-kilometer route between Angers and Saintes was protected by strongholds sited at no more than approximately thirty-kilometer intervals, that is, one day's ride for a horseman who intended to keep his horse in battle-ready condition throughout the journey and in good enough shape to cover the entire distance in about nine days. One day of rest was required for the mounts after five or six days on the road. This strategy, which conformed closely to Vegetian advice, meant that in the best case a mounted force from Angers could reach Saintes a little more than a week after mobilization. Knowledge of the capacity of the Angevin military in this situation may well have deterred William the Fat from laying siege to Saintes, thereby limiting the Aquitanian duke to the unsuccessful strategy he did pursue.[59]

As the year 1034 drew to a close, Fulk undoubtedly remained master in the west, and his son Geoffrey Martel had shown outstanding ability in pressing Angevin interests in Aquitaine. William the Fat was in prison, Odo II had been soundly defeated, and Herbert of Maine once again recognized Fulk as his *senior*. Although Count Budic was still nominally in revolt, his position was not threatening since his only possible ally, Alan of Rennes, was involved in Norman affairs. King Henry was in Fulk's debt. Only the city of Tours had eluded the Angevin grasp. When Duke Robert of Normandy, Fulk's recent ally in maintaining the royal cause against Odo II of Blois and Constance, decided to make a pilgrimage to the Holy Land, the Angevin potential for northward penetration surely brightened. Indeed, Fulk's Bellême allies were hard at work on the Normans' southern frontier.[60]

While diplomatic initiatives in the west of France could well be undertaken at this time to strengthen the Angevins throughout Poitou and indeed in much of Aquitaine, and the Norman frontiers could be effectively nibbled on by the Bellême, the climate was not propitious for major military operations. This was especially true in the Loire valley, where Fulk's major objective was the capture of the city of Tours. For at least two years, beginning during the last phase of the civil war and continuing for more than a year through all seasons, the region suffered exceptionally cold temperatures and excessive rainfall. Thus by early 1035 not only had consistent flooding made it impossible to carry out military operations in the Loire valley but at least two full years of failed crops had exhausted surpluses of grain. Famine, or at least the threat of famine, was widespread.[61] Moreover, from a military perspective, the large war horses of the Angevin army could not be properly fed. In short, the logistic underpinnings for a major Angevin offensive in the Loire valley or anywhere else for that matter had been thoroughly undermined by consistently poor weather.[62]

In this context of deteriorating natural, economic, and social conditions throughout much of France, Duke Robert of Normandy thoroughly surprised his contemporaries with the announcement that he would go on a pilgrimage to the Holy Land. Some scholars have long believed that the Norman duke was seeking to atone for the role that he is alleged to have played in the poisoning of his brother. The timing of Robert's decision from a political perspective—his illegitimate son and barely recognized heir was but eight years of age—has remained largely inexplicable. Yet if we try to rethink with Robert the cause of the scourge of bad weather and subsequent famine—was this a sign that he must expiate his guilt quickly and convincingly?— the duke's hurried and politically ill-timed *peregrinatio* becomes more comprehensible.[63]

Robert's example plus the effects of the weather and famine, which probably meant that the Angevins would not be able to mobilize for at least a year, may well have worked on Fulk's abiding "fear of Gehenna" to encourage the sixty-three-year-old Angevin count to follow in the Norman duke's footsteps. But by 1035 Fulk had suppressed such an urge for more than a quarter-century despite the spilling of Christian blood in vast quantities. Indeed, as long ago as 1016 Fulk had attracted attention throughout Western Europe with his dramatic and bloody victory at the battle of Pontlevoy.[64] Fulk, however, had had much to do after Pontlevoy and clearly he was not so obsessed with guilt that he would leave his responsibilities at home untended. Indeed, the timing of Fulk's first two pilgrimages shows that he only sought the Holy Land when matters were well under control or when the voyage itself was a stratagem to help bring a dangerous situation under control. Thus as Fulk came to ponder a third journey, he could see that matters at home were in hand. Geoffrey Martel, who was now well established at Saumur, had been count of Vendôme for almost five years and was in the process of consolidating Angevin control in the Poitou. He had also proved himself an able leader in war.

As Fulk considered a third visit to the Holy Land—a unique accomplishment among contemporaries—he could recall the dangers he had faced on previous trips and ruminate on the possibility, indeed the likelihood, that at almost sixty-four years of age he might not survive the journey. The rigors of the journey and the need to leave the Angevin state in the hands of Geoffrey Martel surely brought Fulk to think hard about his son and their relationship; the Angevin count averred early in his career that he never treated matters of importance with *levitas*.[65]

In many ways Geoffrey Martel's upbringing and training was, as Fulk knew, similar to his own. But there were also some very important differences. Both Fulk and Geoffrey Martel were their fathers' long-awaited heirs; Geoffrey Greymantle had been married at least fifteen years before his son's birth, and Geoffrey Martel was born some twenty years after Fulk's first marriage. Indeed, Fulk Nerra was so concerned during his second wife Hildegarde's pregnancy that she remained at

Loches throughout most of the nine-month period and he stayed at her side rather than pursuing his normal itinerant pattern of government. Fulk and Geoffrey both had elder sisters (although Geoffrey's was a half-sister), but both young women married and left home before developing a personal relationship with their infant brothers. Both, however, were to remain loyal and prove exceptionally helpful to their brothers during their careers. Fulk and Geoffrey also had younger siblings. Fulk's brother Geoffrey died at no more than two or three years of age, but the Angevin count was to enjoy during adulthood a lengthy and productive relationship with his half-brother Maurice. Geoffrey Martel, by contrast, seems not to have much appreciated his younger sister, Hermengarde-Blanche, who was born no later than 1013 and probably several years earlier and whose behavior appears to have been somewhat of an embarrassment.[66]

Beyond the central position in the family enjoyed by both Fulk and Geoffrey Martel as heirs and a similar pattern of sibling relationships, especially with an elder sister, the respective childhoods of father and son diverged sharply. Fulk's mother died when he was about four years old, his favorite uncle Guy left Anjou at about this time, his younger brother Geoffrey died shortly thereafter, then his father remarried and a half-brother was born. Fulk likely never saw his stepmother and had little contact with his half-brother until after their father's premature death. In short, Fulk suffered a continuous series of family losses in childhood of the type that engender feelings of abandonment, guilt, and insecurity. These in turn frequently manifest in the child and later in the adult feelings of anger and even rage. That Fulk was an angry man both he and his contemporaries attest. Whether Fulk's abiding ferocity was partially the result of his childhood experiences remains of course a matter of speculation.

Unlike Fulk, Geoffrey Martel grew up at the side of a mother who throughout her life was recognized both by her husband and by others as a woman of good sense, pious sentiment, and fair disposition. Indeed, Fulk often sought and followed his wife's advice and delegated to her substantial responsibilities. Thus, he is found to say shortly after their marriage: "Since [I] never undertake anything of this sort lightly, [I] began to ask very pious people . . . And among others at the suggestion of [my] wife, a woman of wise counsel, who gave [me] the idea that [I] fulfill the vow that [I] made in honor and memory of those cherubim and sublime seraphim . . . "[67] It seems to have been well known that Fulk, because he was so busy with military matters, delegated to Hildegarde the major role in sustaining religious foundations and in building new ones. Fulk seems to have made this clear in a charter for Saint-Martin at Angers,[68] and not long afterward, the Breton abbot Catwall wrote to Hildegarde with the flattering address, "Queen of the Angevins":

We give thanks because you have not scorned to visit our humble selves with frequent messengers and letters asking that we remember you in our prayers. Indeed, if you are sure that God will save you through our faith . . . we [who] are sinners remember you to God each day. For a long time it has not been unknown to us how very sincerely you show the cult of religion to God and show deference to the servants of God. Indeed, if the fame of these things were silent the shining character of these works would not remain silent.

Because we are rebuilding our monastery which is almost in ruins . . . we are sending to you this brother . . . who is selling the wine from our grape harvest. Because I am not unaware of the conflict between your lord and our prince of Brittany . . . we have committed our servant to your protection so that You may not neglect to assist him in whatever business . . . Particularly, we pray that he may go free from tolls in every place and port which is subject to your authority . . . [69]

Perhaps the highest praise for Hildegarde came from the nuns of Ronceray whose convent she had played the major role in founding. In a notice drawn up by the nuns sometime between 1040 and 1045 they wrote: "God-fearing and most pious of countesses, Lady Hildegarde, born of royal stock, who evidently as we believe and is manifested in things, God, the founder of all things, led from the Lotharingian territories to these western borders of the lands in order to restore those churches which were devastated in the past."[70]

That Geoffrey Martel's mother was a religious woman of distinguished lineage who exercised both influence and power in her own right seems clear. What this meant for the child whose care and education lay in her hands until the age of seven or eight is far less evident. An apparent bit of common wisdom concerning the relationship between Fulk and Hildegarde which found its way into the *Historia Sancti Florentii* may cast some light on Geoffrey's upbringing. The author of the *Historia* writes, albeit in a different context: "To this . . . the outstanding Countess Hildegarde, who was noted for her sanctity and piety, brought help . . . Although burdened by the heavy yoke of a husband, she mitigated his ferocity by wise deeds."[71]

If Hildegarde had any lasting influence on Geoffrey's habits, it was probably in encouraging him to be generous to the church. Indeed, when one compares Geoffrey's *acta* with those of his father, the son's grants show a far higher percentage of gifts and immunities to ecclesiastical beneficiaries. In terms of absolute wealth also, once allowance is made for the paucity of surviving grants by Fulk, Geoffrey can be shown to be much more generous to the church than was his father.[72] Although now it is suggested by psychologists that a tendency toward generosity is an inherited or genetically programmed characteristic, its development surely must be fostered in an encouraging environment. Clearly, Hildegarde provided such an environment for her son.[73]

At the end of Geoffrey's infancy at age seven, Countess Hildegarde's direct supervision of Geoffrey's education ended in a formal sense. The next stage, *pueritia*, from age seven to about fourteen, when the father's responsibility was paramount, focused on military training.[74] The surviving sources do not tell us whether Geoffrey learned to read or write, although he did make the sign of the cross with his own hand, an accomplishment in which he apparently took some pride, and he valued the use of the written word in matters of governmental concern.[75] Moreover, he seems to have gained some sense that things of importance could be learned from books,[76] and like Fulk he evidenced a command of Vegetian strategic and tactical principles.[77]

We may consider whether Fulk tried to "educate" Geoffrey during his *pueritia* in the same way that he himself had been trained. For example, there is evidence suggesting that Geoffrey traveled with Fulk's household government to places like Vihiers and Loudun where he attested documents and met his father's officials, members of the comital entourage, and other important persons. While still a boy, Geoffrey acted in an official capacity alongside such distinguished figures as Bishop Isembard of Poitiers, Abbot Gerald of Saint-Jouin-de-Marnes, and Guy the treasurer of the Angevin cathedral of Saint Maurice. Among Fulk's officials whom Geoffrey met were castellans such as Albericus of Montjean, Ellianus of le Mans, who commanded the stronghold of Loudun, Aimery of Faye-la-Vineuse, Harduinus of Maillé, and Renaud of Château-Gontier. There were also vicarii like Gerald of Vihiers.[78]

Meeting with these senior figures and acting officially with them no doubt gave young Geoffrey an increased sense of self-importance. Of even greater practical value were his contacts with garrison troops, especially those of aristocratic lineage, who were training as part of the count's military household and were likely to be men of importance when Geoffrey finally succeeded as ruler of the Angevin state. The younger men, like Sigebrannus who served at Vihiers, were much closer in age to Geoffrey. Sigebrannus's father Bouchard, a member of a powerful family at Angers which controlled the office of treasurer of Saint Maurice, had been castellan at both Vihiers and Passavant but died young. Ultimately, Sigebrannus would serve both Fulk and Geoffrey as castellan at Passavant.[79]

Other such young men were Geoffrey and Peter, the sons of Alberic of Montjean and the grandsons on their mother's side of Theobald the castellan at Trèves and Fulk's former *buticularius*. In their paternal lineage these boys were distant cousins of Geoffrey Martel.[80] Gerorius, who served in the garrison at Loudun, was the son of Joscelin, who was castellan at both Baugé and Beaupréau, and Theobald, whose father held Blaison and was the lay abbot of Saint-Lézin, were among the more important young men Geoffrey encountered.[81] Others of lesser pedigree were Walter Titio, who remained but a *miles* and is seen frequently at Geoffrey Martel's side after he reached his majority.[82] Also of interest here is Malrannus, a man whose family was of some standing in the Touraine and whose younger brother Geoffrey became a member of Geoffrey Martel's household soon after the latter reached his majority.[83]

Like other young heirs being trained in the art of government, Geoffrey Martel gathered around himself a personal entourage that formed a military household of sorts. In order to maintain this group of followers, however, Geoffrey was dependent on Fulk's largess. Like many fathers in this period, and presumably thereafter, Fulk remained to be convinced that his son was ready to be on his own and to exercise good judgment simply because he had reached the age where custom dictated that a young man was responsible.[84] In Fulk's earliest surviving grant to Geoffrey, the church at Mazé, the Angevin count particularly stipulated that Geoffrey hold the lordship himself and grant it to no one else.[85]

The church at Mazé was apparently a valuable property and a lucrative source of income; it previously had been held from Fulk by important men such as Viscount Hubert of Vendôme, Anastasius of la Haye, and the latter's brother Roscellinus. Very soon after Geoffrey Martel received the church, however, he granted the *fructus* to young Geoffrey, the brother of Malrannus. Fulk heard a distorted version of this act and believed that his son had granted the church in a manner that violated their agreement. Fulk then repossessed the entire church and all that pertained to it. When the son learned of his father's action, he appealed and explained that he had only granted the *fructus* but had maintained the lordship for himself. Fulk then restored the original grant to his son.[86]

This episode gives us a good glimpse of the father-son relationship. We see how Fulk supported Geoffrey while the youth "was on his own" how the latter took care of his own followers, but a certain amount of tension between father and son is also evident. Fulk's stipulation that Geoffrey maintain the lordship of Mazé suggests certain worries about his son's extravagance. Among young men in Geoffrey's position at this time, living beyond one's means was a frequent problem and was often a source of considerable hostility between father and son. We do not know whether Fulk harbored some fundamental lack of trust in the youth or was merely being prudent in light of experience. What is clear, however, is that Fulk was willing to act summarily to punish Geoffrey. Yet equally important is Fulk's quick reversal when he learned that he had acted on the basis of inaccurate information. I emphasize here that there is no basis for speculation that individuals would intentionally misinform Fulk in order to drive a wedge between father and son.

Fulk's trust in Geoffrey obviously grew strong through the 1020s. Geoffrey was given control of the castrum of Saumur when he was in his mid-twenties. Not long afterward Fulk pressed the policy of Angevin advancement into Aquitaine, which led to Geoffrey's marriage to Agnes and his leadership role in the war against William the Fat. Fulk can also be seen as the catalyst for King Henry's appointment of Geoffrey as count of Vendôme. The conference at Saint-Florent-le-Vieil following the victory over William the Fat and Odo II's capitulation during which Fulk involved Geoffrey in the affairs of the western frontier is but one more index of their close cooperation. Geoffrey showed that he had learned well the art of government when he and his wife Agnes founded the monastery dedicated to the Trinity at Vendôme in order to advertise his status as count.[87] The monastery of Belli Locus, which Fulk had founded and in the shadow of which Geoffrey was born, also had the Trinity as one of its dedicatees. Like a good Angevin, Geoffrey carefully followed the path his father had tread.

By early 1035 Fulk had made the decision to leave on his third pilgrimage to the Holy Land and to follow the road just recently trod by his grandnephew, Duke Robert of Normandy. Everything was in order. As William of Malmesbury, a contemporary of Fulk Nerra's grandson, indicates on the basis of sources that are no longer extant, the Angevin count "handed over his *principatus* to Geoffrey" along with the "insignia of the government."[88] Bishop Hubert of Angers, Fulk Nerra's loyal supporter, lent his weight to the new order as Geoffrey Martel took over the reins of government.[89]

When Fulk departed, the Angevin state was stronger than it had ever been in its history. The Capetian alliance had benefited the Angevins greatly. King Henry II owed his throne to Fulk, and Odo II of Blois had been defeated by a great alliance that included the German emperor. Normandy was in the hands of a boy who was barely eight years of age, and the duke of Aquitaine was Geoffrey Martel's prisoner. Geoffrey was count of the Angevins and of Vendôme and overlord of both Nantes (although Budic's loyalty was a problem) and Maine. His friends, allies, and resources were positioned to advance into Normandy, and the political situation in both the Poitou and Aquitaine was what he could make of it with Anges's sons as expendable pawns in a game for high stakes.

CHAPTER TEN

The Last Years

After placing the reins of the Angevin government in
Geoffrey Martel's capable hands, Fulk took the road to Jerusalem. His
journey probably took him first to Rome and then on to Constan-
tinople where the Angevin tradition recorded in the *Gesta Consulum* has
him meet Duke Robert of Normandy.[1] The account provided by the
Gesta is worth examining in some detail both because of the information it provides and several subjects it avoids. Thus, after telling of
Fulk's meeting with Robert in the Byzantine capital, the author of the
Gesta continues:

Richard, duke of the Normans, by his wife Judith, the daughter of Count
Conan of Brittany, had two sons, Richard and Robert. Richard, the first born,
was killed by his brother Robert with poison. The latter, in order to satisfy
God for having perpetrated this crime, undertook this journey barefoot in the
seventh year of his ducal rule. That man Robert, before becoming duke, had
by a concubine [a son] William [who became] an honorable man and acquired
England.[2]

Although this text took its present form after the Angevin-Norman alliance had been sealed by the marriage of Geoffrey Plantagenet and
Matilda, the granddaughter of William the Conquerer, the *Gesta* presents the Normans of Fulk Nerra's era in a guardedly negative manner
consistent with Angevin-Norman relations prior to the death of Duke
Robert in 1035. It is taken as fact that Robert murdered his brother
by poison; thus the reader is to infer that he acquired the ducal title in
an illegitimate manner. Indeed, the charge that Robert had poisoned

Richard was well publicized before the former's death.[3] Moreover, the theme of illegitimacy is carried over to William, the son of a concubine, who was "honorable" not because of his lineage but because of his accomplishments.

These themes are carried forward in the discussion of Duke Robert's maternal lineage. The *Gesta* makes clear earlier in the treatment of Fulk Nerra that the Angevin count had thoroughly bested Conan of Rennes, Robert's grandfather. Indeed, Fulk is well known to have decisively defeated Conan at the battle of Conquereuil in 992. This important and highly publicized fact is omitted from the *Gesta*. Also not mentioned is the fact that Fulk's sister, Hermengarde-Gerberga, was Conan's wife and Duke Robert's maternal grandmother. In short, anything that could reflect negatively on Fulk is omitted, such as his responsibility for the defeat and death of his brother-in-law Conan or his family ties to a poisoner.[4]

The account in the *Gesta* continues: "Fulk having met up with Robert joined with him . . . Both of these men . . . at the order of the emperor were escorted through the land of the Saracens. During the journey Robert died in Bythinia. Fulk under guidance was led to Jerusalem."[5]

The theme that juxtaposes Angevin worthiness (Fulk went on the pilgrimage because "he feared God") to Norman evil (Robert went to expiate fratricide) is replayed in this section of the *Gesta* as the Angevin count reaches the Holy Land and Jerusalem but the Norman duke dies along the way.[6] What is truly startling, however, is the omission from the account in the *Gesta* of the report found in Anglo-Norman tradition that Robert died of poison. Well within the lifetime of those who accompanied the Norman duke on his final journey, the author of the *Miracula S. Wulframni* observed: ". . . we are told he died from poison at Nicaea."[7] Before the present version of the *Gesta* was redacted, William of Malmesbury noted that Robert "died of poison administered to him by a servant (*minister*) named Radulf Mowin."[8]

The murder of a murderer, the poisoning of a poisoner, and a plague on those bloody Normans from the era of Fulk Nerra surely would have been both good literary drama and served the theme of this part of the *Gesta*. Unless, of course, something more important was to be gained or perhaps avoided by suppressing the story of Duke Robert's murder. Radulf Mowin (or Monin) may have been the man to drop the draught, but clearly he was not nor was he likely to have been the greatest gainer from the Norman duke's premature death. Indeed, for two

decades following Robert's murder, those who benefited most from the
anarchy in Normandy were the Angevin counts. Geoffrey Martel's efforts against young Duke William may have failed, but not for want
of trying. In short, Robert's murder made possible Angevin aggression
against Normandy.[9]

Could Fulk Nerra have been the man behind the poisoning? The
possibility cannot be ignored. As we have already seen, Fulk did not
shrink from murder, and the long-term destabilization of the Norman
duchy through the death of a single individual surely could not have
been an unattractive prospect. The repercussions after Fulk was identified as the man behind the *milites* who murdered Hugh of Beauvais
in the presence of King Robert were overcome only with difficulty.
Anticipation of such a prospect might well have deterred a lesser man
in the future. Fulk, however, would have been more than likely to have
learned from his previous error and seen to it that Duke Robert died
in a manner that would be less easily traceable.

While Fulk was pursuing his spiritual health in the Holy Land, a
series of events occurred which had the potential for bringing about
drastic political changes in the west of Francia. Not only did Duke
Robert die but before mid-October 1035 Count Herbert "Wake Dog"
of Maine and Bishop Avesgaud of le Mans were also in their graves.
Duke Robert of Normandy's son was a minor; so too was Count Herbert's heir. Thus a fluid political situation existed and contemporaries
did not doubt that new forces had the potential to emerge.[10] King
Henry I had recognized the right of Robert's illegitimate son William
to succeed as duke of Normandy. But Count Alan of Rennes, William's
cousin, emerged along with Archbishop Robert of Rouen as the future
conqueror's protectors. When violence erupted following William's
succession, Bishop Hugh of Bayeux held a court where Count Odo II
of Blois appears to have had considerable influence along with Archbishop Robert.[11]

The situation in Maine perhaps was even more complicated than in
Normandy. Fulk Nerra had been successful in forcing the counts of
Maine to recognize him as their *senior* and in acquiring direct control
over large parts of the *comté* along le Loir River and in the west as far
north as the castrum of Mayenne. In order to maintain this dominant
position effectively, however, the Angevin count had to manipulate
a coalition of forces headed by the viscomital family of le Mans and
the lords of Bellême. Between them these houses also controlled the
bishopric of le Mans, subject to the royal right of appointment and

Angevin influence, and the very important stronghold of Château-du-Loir. But through what appears to have been the clever exploitation of differences between Haimo, lord of Château-du-Loir, and his son Gervasius, Odo II of Blois was able to acquire the latter as his fidelis. This relationship had great potential for undermining the Angevin position in Maine. Bishop Avesgaud of le Mans was the youth's maternal uncle, and thus Gervasius was likely to succeed to the bishopric, following the well-defined tradition of the region and presupposing a pro forma royal confirmation that had been forthcoming since the reign of King Lothair IV thanks to the Angevin connection. King Henry permitted custom to follow its course and in December 1035 Gervasius was made bishop of le Mans.[12]

Although Geoffrey Martel was firmly in command of matters in Anjou, Vendôme, and the Poitou during Fulk's absence, his problems in the north and west were not inconsiderable. King Henry took seriously his responsibility for securing William's position in Normandy and this of course meant that Angevin interests in that direction would have to be blunted. Thus Henry's support for Gervasius's appointment at le Mans not only confirmed a long-standing Manceaux tradition but one that assured the see to a member of the Bellême family. The Bellêmes had been Fulk Nerra's most powerful allies in Angevin efforts to encroach on the southern frontiers of Normandy. King Henry's policy now drew the Bellêmes closer to royal interests while at the same time driving a wedge between the Angevin count, who opposed having a fidelis of Odo II on the episcopal throne of le Mans, and his erstwhile northern allies.

King Henry also came to a rapprochement of sorts with Odo II, and the count of Blois reestablished a position of influence at the Capetian court. This accord is evidenced not only by Henry's appointment of Odo's fidelis Gervasius as bishop of le Mans but also by the cooperation of the king and the Blésois count in the Touraine.[13] It seems that King Henry had concluded that the time had come to counterbalance the immense growth of Angevin power in the preceding decade.[14]

In addition to the revival of Odo, whose return to action in the west could not be regarded by Geoffrey Martel as a good sign, Alan of Rennes now also became a threat. When Duke Robert of Normandy had allied with King Henry and the Angevins against Odo II, Alan apparently had remained neutral.[15] But when Duke Robert died and Odo II and King Henry reached an accord, Alan was in a good position to pursue his long-standing vendetta against the Angevins. He no longer had to choose between his father-in-law Odo II, from whom he held Rennes, and his king.

Geoffrey Martel, despite substantial responsibilities during the previous five years, had relatively little experience in taking independent action and even less in the formulation of long-range policy. Geoffrey's reaction to the death of Avesgaud was to oppose the appointment of Gervasius, whom the Angevin count saw as Odo of Blois' surrogate in le Mans. But Geoffrey could not call on the traditional ally of the Angevin count in le Mans, the viscount, to thwart Gervasius's assumption of power because the latter two men were cousins. We must also remember that it was through this coalition of the viscomital house and the house of Bellême, which were closely related and which also dominated the episcopal office of le Mans, that the Angevin counts had in large part assured their dominance over the counts of Maine.

Geoffrey Martel was short on experience but not lacking in self-confidence. Indeed, he tended toward arrogance,[16] but now he faced a difficult situation calling for careful planning and subtlety. He wanted to stop Gervasius from assuming power in le Mans, but success would alienate the new prelate's viscomital relatives on whom the Angevin count depended. At the same time, Geoffrey wanted to assure that his dominance over the new count of Maine would be recognized. Geoffrey saw it as vital for him to gain physical control of Count Herbert's heir, Hugh, a young boy under the immediate control of his great-uncle and closest relative, Herbert Bacho. Thus, the boy heir became the key to Angevin policy. Geoffrey established Herbert Bacho as the guardian of the young count and in return Angevin dominance of the count of Maine was recognized. In addition, Herbert Bacho, acting for Geoffrey, took control of le Mans and barred Gervasius from the city. Gervasius went to war.[17]

Close examination of Geoffrey Martel's policy and hindsight allow us to see that his approach was somewhat poorly conceived. By opposing Gervasius Geoffrey endangered the long-standing alliance with the house of Bellême, which was crucial for Angevin advancement into Normandy as well as for dominance in Maine. Moreover, Gervasius had also succeeded his father as lord of Château-du-Loir, a key stronghold in the defense of the northeastern frontier of the much expanded Angevin state. The stronghold of Malicorne on the Sarthe only one day's ride (twenty kilometers) east of Sablé was commanded for the Angevin counts by Waldinus I, who had been a fidelis of Haimo of Château-du-Loir and who now recognized Gervasius as his lord.[18] Geoffrey's policy also endangered the Angevin alliance with the viscounts of le Mans, whose consistent family interest lay in opposing the count of Maine and keeping him out of le Mans. Finally, Bishop Hubert of Angers was closely tied to the viscomital family of le Mans and had great influence in both the Vendômois and in the Mauges region.

When Fulk returned from his pilgrimage, it appears that he was greatly angered by the manner in which the situation in Maine had developed in his absence. Form a variety of sources, some written and others oral, William of Malmesbury, a contemporary of Fulk's grandson, provides a conflated and telescoped account of the points at issue. Geoffrey is reported to have been harsh in his treatment of the inhabitants of the Angevin state (*principatus*) and to have acted in an arrogant manner toward Fulk when the latter returned and demanded an explanation. Indeed, William relates that Fulk was so annoyed he ordered Geoffrey to give up control of the administration and to surrender "the insignia of government." [19]

While it is likely that Geoffrey Martel had acted both harshly and arrogantly, as William of Malmesbury reports, these behavioral characteristics would hardly have caught Fulk Nerra by surprise. The old count surely was well aware of his son's shortcomings, if indeed he saw them as shortcomings. What undoubtedly rankled was the possibility that Geoffrey's policy in Maine might undermine the Angevin effort to dominate the region, an effort that had been under way for almost a century. Fulk certainly did not want to alienate either the viscounts of le Mans or the house of Bellême and surely he desired to maintain dominance over the count of Maine and stop Odo II's fidelis Gervasius from exercising power as bishop of le Mans. But while Geoffrey acted vigorously to ally with Herbert Bacho, increase the power of the count of Maine in le Mans to the detriment of the viscount, and close the city to Gervasius, which in effect was an act of hostility toward the house of Bellême, Fulk counseled patience. Fulk apparently grasped the essential point that Gervasius was only a threat insofar as he had Odo II's direct support. An acute political observer like Fulk, who had witnessed Odo II's broad-gauged interest in such distant regions as Normandy, Aquitaine, the Rhineland, and the Alps, likely suspected that the count of Blois, who never sustained a policy with single-minded ruthlessness, would soon lose interest in a backwater like le Mans and seek new horizons to conquer.

Geoffrey Martel had played into Odo's hands by using Herbert Bacho against Gervasius. Fulk demanded a reversal of his son's policy.

Geoffrey, however, having committed himself against the bishop of le Mans, refused to alter course. As a result, Fulk, whose violent temper was legendary even during his own lifetime, was greatly angered by this intransigence, and great dissension developed between them. It seems that there was no outright military conflict between the two men, despite William of Malmesbury's report that Geoffrey wanted to take up arms against his father. Rather, Fulk appears to have decided to inhibit his son's ability to wage a vigorous contest against the bishop of le Mans. Thus, the only two documents contemporary with these events state that Geoffrey was "occupied" by the anger of his father and because of this "dissension" with his father was unable to prosecute the war against Gervasius effectively.[20]

Geoffrey's major problem in carrying on the war with Gervasius seems to have been a lack of funds. According to William of Malmesbury, Fulk deprived Geoffrey of control of the administration and thus cut off access to the tax revenues and troop levies normally under comital control. Fulk did not deprive Geoffrey of his lordship of the castrum of Saumur. This lordship, however, did not entitle Geoffrey to the normal comital taxes (or *consuetudines*) so he levied special and putatively illegitimate taxes on the holdings of the monastery of Saint-Florent at Saumur. Geoffrey gave as his excuse for this high-handed action his poverty.[21] Because of this shortage of funds, Geoffrey also found it necessary to offer to free William the Fat—an act clearly contrary to Angevin interests in the Poitou and in Aquitaine—in return for a substantial ransom. Once the money ws raised, Geoffrey set William free; this took place before the end of 1036.[22] But even the ransom was not enough to sustain a costly war, for Gervasius was able to purchase the support of some of Geoffrey's *homines* by offering them a better deal.[23]

By the autumn of 1037 Geoffrey could no longer sustain his opposition to Gervasius financially or even physically, for he had recently suffered a broken hip, which apparently immobilized him completely. By mid-November, almost two years after his consecration, Gervasius entered le Mans; Geoffrey had agreed to make peace and to pay compensation.[24] Geoffrey was compelled to hand over to the bishop *casamenta* that previously he had granted to his own fideles in order to pay the settlement.[25] That Gervasius settled for his bishopric, from which Geoffrey was no longer able to block him, and for compensation, which, though difficult for the Angevin to pay, was hardly monumental compared to the ransom paid by William the Fat, requires some explanation. For Geoffrey Martel's much weakened position would normally be seen by an adversary as an invitation to press home the advantage.

It is important to note that Fulk Nerra sided, at least diplomatically, with Gervasius; this explains the description in the Angevin chronicles of the war as "more than a civil war" since Geoffrey was opposed by a relative as well as by those not related to him.[26] Once Geoffrey agreed to make peace with Gervasius, however, Fulk no longer had any reason for supporting the bishop of le Mans. No less vital to Gervasius's position was Odo II's policy. The bishop was really little more than the Blésois count's surrogate for pursuing Odo's policy of trying to undermine Angevin control in Maine, and indeed Gervasius was to play that role again later in his career but with the Norman duke William making the decisions.[27]

Gervasius must have recognized his isolation by late in the spring of 1037, almost a half-year before he came to terms with Geoffrey, because of Odo's ambitions in the empire. By that time a conflict between the emperor Conrad II and Archbishop Aribert of Milan had reached the point of reciprocal deposition. Aribert then offered the crown of Italy to Odo II. To win this prize, Odo was to attack Conrad's supporters in Lorraine and perhaps later in Burgundy with the aim of forcing the emperor to abandon Italy. Odo, whose penchant for becoming involved in grandiose schemes appears to have been chronic, gathered a large army and went on the offensive against Conrad. By early autumn he had captured Bar-sur-Aube and garrisoned the stronghold with his supporters. His next objective was Aix-la-Chapelle, but he was delayed when Duke Goscelinus of Lorraine gathered an army to support Conrad and moved against Bar-sur-Aube. Odo retraced his line of march and on 15 November 1037 the armies met. In the battle that followed Odo was killed and his forces were soundly defeated.[28] Thus, Odo's decision to pursue the Italian crown left Gervasius isolated, and although Geoffrey Martel was immobilized with a broken hip, Fulk Nerra at the age of sixty-seven was still very active. Gervasius would have little chance of success in pursuing a policy hostile to Angevin interests against the old count in the absence of Odo II.

Geoffrey's capitulation to Gervasius also seems to have been the signal for his surrender to Fulk. Although William of Malmesbury telescoped Fulk and Geoffrey's estrangement from perhaps as long as eighteen months to "a few days," the chronicler is correct in observing that through "wise counsel he [Fulk] broke the revolt of his son." William then described the ceremony of reconciliation in which Geoffrey, "after carrying his saddle on his back for a few miles, threw himself down along with his load at his father's feet. Fulk, fired up again with his old spirit, prodded and poked the prostrate Geoffrey with his foot and exclaimed: 'You are finally conquered, you are conquered.' He repeated this several times."[29]

How William of Malmesbury learned of this victory ceremony or even if he understood it to be a victory ceremony partially in the Roman imperial tradition cannot be ascertained. Several points, however, are clear. The ceremony was in part Germanic, or, more accurately, Carolingian, and in part Roman. With regard to the former, we see the "exercise of the arbitrary power to pardon" of the victor who has the power of life and death over the vanquished. In the capitularies of the ninth century this was called *harmiscara*. The Norman dukes Richard II and Robert I, Fulk Nerra's contemporaries, are well known to have received their conquered adversaries seeking pardon in a ceremony that saw the supplicant carrying a saddle on his back.[30]

The Roman aspect of Fulk's victory ceremony is the *calcatio colli,* or, as it is often called in English, "the trampling of the defeated." The ritual appears to have first been used in the Roman Empire as part of a ceremony celebrating victory over a usurper during the early fifth century, and the Visigoths can be shown to have adopted it no later than the second half of the seventh century. In the Byzantine empire the *calcatio colli* was in continuous use and widely known during the tenth and eleventh centuries.[31] Several acts were fundamental to the imperial victory ceremony over a usurper. First the usurper was stripped of the insignia of office that he wrongfully held. Then the right arm was cut off and he was required to perform the *proskynesis,* or prostration at the foot of the victor. At this point the victor could perform a wide variety of acts symbolizing his victory. These ranged from a simple placing of his booted foot (*calceus*) on the neck (*collum*) of the vanquished to the most extreme act of walking all over the prostrated body.[32] Then the usurper was generally subjected to one or more severe punishments. These ranged from having other extremities cut off to blinding and at the extreme to decapitation. When a usurper was merely mutilated, he was usually further humiliated by being paraded backward on a donkey before the army or perhaps in the circus. When beheading was carried out, the head was placed on a pike and displayed for various audiences.[33]

William of Malmesbury's account of Fulk's victory ceremony captures the essentials of the initial phases of the Roman triumph over a usurper. He makes specific mention of the necessity of surrendering the insignia of office, and the surrender of these by Geoffrey Martel to Fulk is surely implied by what follows in William's account. The *proskynesis* is described by the statement that Geoffrey "threw himself down . . . at his father's feet." Finally, the *calcatio colli* is described. Here the act is depicted as a poking and prodding of the vanquished by the victor. The Angevin count clearly had no intention of executing or even mutilating his only son and heir. This merger of a Roman victory ceremony with a Carolingian pardoning rite in a manner consistent with the historical facts of Fulk Nerra's conflict with Geoffrey and the subsequent working out of their differences strongly suggests that William of Malmesbury was recording an historical event.

Although medieval chroniclers were preoccupied with the conflict between Fulk Nerra and his son, the sources show the old count pursuing his traditional policies with vigor during the period of estrangement from Geoffrey. One example at Angers itself concerns Fulk's dealings with the monastery of Saint-Aubin. The policy of both Geoffrey Greymantle and Fulk Nerra had been to keep this wealthy and influential house under close comital control. Thus when Abbot Hubert, who had served Fulk loyally for more than a quarter-century, died in 1027 the Angevin count rewarded the monks of Saint-Aubin by granting to them vicarial rights with the attendant income in taxes and fines in all of their lands, only keeping for himself control over the adjudication of major crimes: theft, homicide and arson.[34] Thereafter, however, under the leadership of Abbot Primaldus, the monks of Saint-Aubin seem to have become less cooperative than they had been under Abbot Hubert. On one occasion relations deteriorated so much that a group from the abbot's military *clientela* inflicted at Angers a bloody defeat on members of Fulk's military household and five members of the latter were killed. Fulk demanded compensation from Primaldus, who "unwillingly" surrendered at least one major landholding to a fidelis of the count, Stephen Stultus, in lifetime tenure.[35]

Fulk continued his religious policies in his effort to popularize the holy places in the Angevin state by calling attention to the relics sheltered there. He usually received church support for this policy, which not only advertised saintly approval of the comital regime—it was popularly believed that saints did not permit their relics to abide with unworthy patrons—but also brought visitors with money to spend. The abbot of Saint-Aubin apparently was not eager to support Fulk's policy (unlike, for example, the monks at Belli Locus), for when two caskets of obvious antiquity were found at the monastery, the count had to order Primaldus to open them. The find was a rich one: the caskets contained many items of worship, decorations, and a document that identified the bones as those of the saints Lautho, Rumparius, Coronarius, Marculfus, and Carrullus. Again Primaldus appears to have been unwilling to act, for Fulk ordered the abbot to have them displayed "in order to instruct them [the people] in the honor of their saints."[36]

Primaldus died about the time that Fulk returned from the Holy Land and for almost four months after the abbot's death the monks of Saint-Aubin were without a leader. The monks greatly lamented their lack of a "rector," suggesting that Fulk may perhaps have been disciplining the monastery for its failure to provide the kind of support traditionally required by the comital government and which Primaldus, after a promising start, had not been eager to provide. When Fulk finally gave his assent to the election of an abbot in December 1036 or shortly before, "a brother . . . named Walter who was humble, sober, chaste, and endowed with other virtues" was named by the count to succeed Primaldus.[37]

Unlike Primaldus, Walter was a political nonentity who in the course of a tenure lasting almost two decades appears only in three extant comital acts and seems to have accomplished nothing to benefit either the spiritual or the material resources of Saint-Aubin.[38] Quite to the contrary, he presided over substantial losses. Fulk denied to Saint-Aubin a renewal of the vicarial rights over "low justice" in their lands and thus deprived the monastery of substantial income and influence.[39] Finally, Fulk vigorously enforced the obligations of Saint-Aubin to play an active and costly role in providing garrisons (*custodia*) for the count's strongholds on the frontiers (*in marginibus*). Although the monks of Saint-Aubin regarded these obligations to the government (*consuetudines*) as a "danger to their souls," "humble" Abbot Walter dutifully served as *custos,* first of the strongholds of "Prince" Fulk and then of those of "Prince" Geoffrey (*castra principum*).[40] In short, after the trouble caused by Primaldus, Fulk saw to it that the right kind of man, from the government's perspective, was chosen as abbot of Saint-Aubin in December of 1036.

In addition to reasserting vigorous control over Saint-Aubin while at the same time keeping Geoffrey Martel "occupied," Fulk maintained a strong Angevin position in the Poitou vis-à-vis William the Fat, whom Geoffrey had recently released from captivity. Among those who likely supported Fulk's policies in the Poitou were William of Parthenay and members of the viscomital house of Thouars. How thoroughly the Angevins had undermined the position of the count of Poitou is not clear and in addition the situation was evolving. Thus it would be anachronistic to assume that the overwhelming support provided to the Angevins following the death of William the Fat and his brother was firmly in place by 1036–1037.[41] Nevertheless, it is worth emphasizing that communications between Angers and Saintes had been secured by a series of strongholds south of Vihiers, Passavant, and Maulévrier which proceeded from Bressuire to Parthenay, Germond (?), Mauzé, Chizé, Tonnay-Boutonne, and Taillebourg. North of Poitiers the area was defended in depth by Angevin fortifications at Loudun, Moncontour, Faye-la-Vineuse and Mirebeau.[42] Eastward from Mauzé a line of strongholds constituting a fortified communications route stretched to Lusignan, Gençay, and Rancon where Fulk Nerra's fideles were in command.[43]

With matters under control in Aquitaine, the establishment of peace in Maine, and the removal of the source of friction between father and son, Fulk was prepared to take advantage of Odo II's death (Odo's lands were divided among his sons Theobald III and Stephen) and Count Alan of Rennes' involvement in Normandy[44] in order to advance Angevin interests in the Touraine once again. The treaty of 1027 with Odo II had required Fulk to destroy his stronghold at Montboyau, which was the key Angevin base for a direct attack on Tours. Despite this loss Fulk had continued to work toward the domination of the region. Among diverse methods we encounter his effort to cultivate the support of the monks of Marmoutier, whose moral position as leaders in church reform and economic success made them influential in the region. Thus the Angevin count gave his support to gifts in favor of Marmoutier and maintained the cause of the monks against Archbishop Arnulf of Tours, who not incidentally was in the *mouvance* of the count of Blois.[45] Fulk also cultivated a relationship with Wanilo, treasurer of Saint-Martin at Tours, who had been a member of Odo II's entourage. Wanilo can be seen at Fulk's side favoring the Touraine monastery of Cormery, which was under Angevin control. In addition, Fulk supported the building in the Touraine of an abbey at Notre-Dame de Noyers, which was close to the stronghold of his supporter Guenno of Nouâtre.[46]

In addition to these efforts to win over key elements in the ecclesiastical establishment of the Touraine, Fulk took other more aggressive steps. Before the end of 1037 Fulk had seen to the construction of a stronghold at Sainte-Maure, only twelve kilometers east of Île-Bouchard.[47] This base, which was well positioned to provide support for a siege of Île-Bouchard, Fulk placed under the command of a certain Joscelin, who appears to have been a member of the count's military household like so many other Angevin castellans.[48]

The strongholds at Île-Bouchard and at Chinon were Odo II's only remaining bases west of Tours and south of the Loire. Fulk had made clear his designs on Chinon as early as 1033 when he made an arrangement with the canons of Saint-Hilaire, outside Poitiers, to "protect" their tithes at Beaumont-Veron, which was an easily fortifiable position only five kilometers north-northwest of Chinon itself.[49]

Soon after Fulk learned that Odo II of Blois had been killed in battle at Bar-sur-Aube, he gathered a substantial force and launched an offensive into the Touraine. The primary objective of this winter campaign was the recapture of the stronghold at Langeais, which had changed hands several times since Fulk had completed its construction in 994. That Langeais was a formidable stronghold is shown not only by the two lengthy sieges it withstood between 994 and 996 but also by its surviving remains.[50] In about 1032 or perhaps a year or two later Fulk had placed Hamelinus, the son of the Vendômois magnate Walter, as castellan there. It is likely, however, that Blésois forces working in concert with Gervasius took Langeais during Fulk's absence and Geoffrey's war with the bishop of le Mans.[51] It is in this light that the report of Fulk's building of lines of circumvallation in order to prosecute a siege is fully understandable.[52] Indeed, such efforts were required by military theorists, such as Vegetius, for the protection of one's men for the same reasons that a fortified camp was established after each day's march.[53] By the end of spring 1038 at the latest the garrison at Langeais surrendered. The defenders likely concluded that Theobald, the new count of Blois, would not relieve the stronghold. They had to surrender before Fulk suffered losses in trying to take the castrum by storm, for a well-timed surrender could avoid the harsher consequences of the *lex deditionis*. Once Langeais was retaken, Fulk reestablished Hamelinus as castellan.[54]

Following the fall of Langeais, Fulk pressed his offensive in the Touraine. His next objective was the stronghold of Chinon on the right bank of the Vienne about twenty-two kilometers southwest of Langeais. When the Angevin army appeared before Chinon after crossing both the Loire and the Cher, the garrison responsible for defending the stronghold for the count of Blois sought terms from Fulk.[55] The defenders undoubtedly knew that Langeais had fallen to the Angevins and it is also likely that they lacked any real hope that Count Theobald would come to their rescue. Indeed, supporters of the Blésois count had seen an increase in Angevin success throughout the region without significant response from their new leader. Thus after some discussion, the defenders of Chinon surrendered without resistance. Fulk promptly established a fidelis named Alberic from his military household as castellan.[56]

While Fulk was in the Touraine, Angevin interests in Aquitaine were being pressed by William of Parthenay, who with some of his own men and with a contingent of Angevins had built a stronghold at Germond twenty-six kilometers south of Parthenay on the road from Angers to Saintes. William had been placed in command of this stronghold, and it may be suggested that he was given responsibility for protecting Angevin communications with Saintes or at least responsibility for the northern part of the route.[57] As we have seen in the case of Roger of Loudun, Roger of Montrésor, and especially Lisoius of Amboise, Fulk often established commanders over geographical areas or logistic assets that included several strongholds.

When William the Fat died on 15 September 1038 the political situation in the Poitou once again became potentially unstable. William the Fat, following his release from prison, had shown no inclination to oppose the Angevins as they strengthened their position with new strongholds and supporters and through a new alliance with the viscount of Thouars.[58] Odo of Gascony, William's younger half-brother, who had appeared only briefly in the Poitou following the latter's release from captivity, sought to use his base in Gascony as a means for securing his succession to the countship. The Angevins, however, opposed Odo and lent their support to Agnes's minor son, William Aigret, who was also Geoffrey Martel's stepson.[59]

Odo opened hostilities against the Angevin-supported candidate with an attack on the stronghold of Germond. There Odo was vigorously opposed by William of Parthenay. After laying siege to Germond for perhaps as long as two months during the winter of 1039, Odo finally withdrew to the south.[60] Apparently frustrated by his lack of success at Germond and still looking for a victory in order to give some plausibility to his claim to succeed as count of the Poitou, Odo hurled his forces against the stronghold at Mauzé in an effort to take the fortifications by storm. William the Bastard, who commanded the defense at Mauzé and obviously had refused to recognize Odo's claim, held his ground in support of the Angevin candidate. In what was to be his final effort to take Mauzé on 10 March 1039, Odo received a mortal wound and died soon after.[61]

With the initiatives in the Touraine and Aquitaine going well, the Angevins turned their attentions to the western frontier. Count Budic of Nantes had died in 1038 leaving his young son Mathias as his heir. Bishop Walter of Nantes, Count Alan of Rennes' man, continued to act in the interest of his *senior*, who was occupied with affairs in Normandy. In furtherance of his own and his lord's interests, Walter saw to it that his own son, Budic, succeeded him as bishop of Nantes. Bishop Budic followed his father's policy and maintained Alan's dominant position at Nantes. Young Mathias, however, resented the domination of Bishop Budic just as Count Budic had resented the domination earlier in his career of Bishop Walter. Mathias thus sought Fulk's aid and promised to renew recognition of Angevin control of Nantes.[62]

This discord in Nantes clearly was in Fulk Nerra's interest, but the situation was extremely complex. Bishop Budic, before purchasing the see of Nantes, as a student in Châteauneuf had been associated with the canons of Saint-Martin at Tours. In addition, the choice of the man who would be bishop of Nantes rested in part with Archbishop Arnulf of Tours, who was from Châteaudun (Theobald of Blois, Odo II's successor, was count of Châteaudun), and in part with King Henry I.[63] Thus, in political perspective, Budic's acquisition of the bishopric of Nantes appears to indicate King Henry's support for Odo of Blois' and Alan of Rennes' policies with regard to Anjou's western frontier.

The key figure in the threat to Anjou's western frontier was Count Alan III of Rennes. His position was greatly strengthened by his marriage to Bertha, daughter of Odo II and sister of Theobald, who had succeeded as count of Blois. In addition, Alan was the grandson of Duke Richard II of Normandy. Another of the latter's grandsons, William, the illegitimate son of Robert I, claimed the Norman ducal title but was a mere child.

Alan III, following the death of his great-uncle, Archbishop Robert of Rouen in 1037, appears to have become young William's most powerful defender. Alan's primary adversary at this time was the Bellême family, who had already worked closely with Fulk Nerra during the reign of Robert the Devil to penetrate deeply into Normandy. Ivo, bishop of Sées, and his brother William Talavas, lord of Bellême, sought to press farther north with the help of Roger I of Montgomery, who was viscount of the Hiémois. Roger's mother-in-law Sa[g]infri[d]a appears to have been a member of the Bellême clan.[64] Indeed, the Bellême-Montgomery alliance remained strong through the 1040s as Roger II of Montgomery married Mabel, the daughter of William Talavas, no later than 1050 and perhaps as early as 1048.[65]

Nonetheless, a decade earlier Alan III, acting ostensibly in defense of Duke William's interests, laid siege to Roger I's main stronghold at Montgomery just north of the Sées frontier. There in 1039 or perhaps in 1040, the count of Rennes is reported to have died of poison. The siege was broken and yet another strong hand to guide the Norman polity was withdrawn through surreptitious means, as had been the case with the poisoning of Robert the Devil in 1035.[66]

In the very near term Roger I and his Bellême allies were the immediate beneficiaries of Alan's death and it is on them therefore that initial suspicion for the poisoning must fall.[67] In the wider view, however, the major beneficiaries of Alan's death were Fulk Nerra and Geoffrey Martel. With Alan's death the entire structure of opposition to Angevin interests on the western frontier crumbled. Then, with Angevin support, Alan's brother Éon seized power at Rennes. He banished his sister-in-law Bertha of Blois and his nephew Conan. This action cleanly severed ties between Rennes and Count Theobald III of Blois, whose position as the overlord of the Breton count was undermined.[68] The Angevin position at Nantes was restored. Thus Bishop Budic was isolated and Count Mathias served as a dutiful supporter of the Angevins. In Normandy the political situation continued to deteriorate in favor of various factions of magnates and the diocese of Sées saw an increase in the number of Angevin supporters.[69]

If the Angevin counts had the most to gain by Alan's sudden death, then they must be considered prime suspects in arranging for the poisoning. That no contemporary or even later report rumored their responsibility is hardly reason to quell our suspicions. Such was the value system of the time that an individual in a position of power could be discredited for having a noble adversary poisoned—and a relative in the bargain. Fulk was Alan's great uncle. Moreover, poisoning would certainly have been kept secret, for it was too easy a way to eliminate important leaders to allow it to become popular.

Our suspicions should be heightened because in 1035 Fulk Nerra not only had much to gain by Robert the Devil's death but he was there when the duke died. To have poisoned one grandnephew perhaps would have made a second murder easier. In this context we should give serious thought to Fulk's fourth and final pilgrimage to the Holy Land. Fulk Nerra was almost seventy years old and it was rumored he had inflicted on himself horrendous and humiliating punishment while in Jerusalem. According to William of Malmesbury's report:

... the old man, having seen to his secular concerns, now thinking to provide for his soul, went to Jerusalem. There, by two servants (*servi*) whom he had compelled by oath (*sacramentum*) so that they would do as he ordered, he was dragged naked in public, with the Turks looking on, to the sepulchre of the Lord. One of the servants had twisted a rope around Fulk's neck and the other hit him on the bare back with a stick. While this was happening, Fulk cried out: "O Lord receive wretched Fulk, Your oathbreaker, Your fugitive [from justice]. O Lord Jesus Christ look after my repentent soul."[70]

Obviously, too much should not be made of Fulk as a perjurer and a "fugitive" in a specific criminal sense, but we can note the Angevin count's putative self-indictment as a sinner. And we cannot ignore the pathos of the account of Fulk's last pilgrimage, which is so thoroughly different from reports of his second journey to the Holy Land during the persecutions of the caliph al Hakim II. On his second voyage Fulk is depicted as a powerful trickster who fools the Saracens, visits the Holy Sepulchre, and even comes away with a fragment of it as a relic.[71] Fulk himself reported on his return from this journey that he was "exultant" and that his "ferocity was replaced by a certain sweetness."[72]

That two such very different traditions are recorded may lead us to wonder whether Fulk was more "guilty" in 1040 than he had been some three decades earlier for the murder of Hugh of Beauvais. Did Fulk have his grandnephews Duke Robert and Count Alan murdered? We will never know, and that surely is what one should expect of properly conducted covert operations. Fulk undoubtedly learned that an open assassination, such as that of Hugh of Beauvais, brought considerable trouble, as did the mere allegation that he planned to murder Count Herbert of Maine and his wife after capturing them by trickery. Yet it must be emphasized that political assassination was a weapon in Fulk's arsenal, and thus he must remain a suspect in the deaths of both Robert and Alan.

The documentary record provides little firm evidence of Fulk's preparation for his fourth pilgrimage to the Holy Land, which he began late in 1039 and during which he is thought to have had imposed on himself the severe punishments described by William of Malmesbury. Nonetheless, a flurry of *acta* made along with Countess Hildegarde in favor of their new convent at Ronceray likely were executed toward the end of the 1030s.[73] Indeed, the *notitiae* on which these gifts were inscribed had not yet been put in a systematic form when the nuns asked Geoffrey Martel to confirm them. Geoffrey indicated that he would be pleased "to confirm all the donations which my father of good memory, the *illustrissimus comes* recently dead to worldly things, had made . . ." Geoffrey, however, also ordered that all of the *acta* be gathered up and copied into a pancarte that he calls a *summa*.[74]

Such *summae,* whether they included all previous acquisitions or merely those from a single benefactor, were obviously regarded as important by the Angevin counts, for Fulk had drawn up a pancarte of sorts sometime between 1032 and his third pilgrimage to the Holy Land in 1035. After his return from this pilgrimage but before leaving a fourth time, Fulk apparently had some aspects of this document redrawn and commented: "I strengthened it with my own hand before leaving for Jerusalem the last time."[75]

During the later 1030s as Fulk was nearing seventy years of age, this concern for the religious houses that he had founded hardly seems unreasonable. Thus, we should not be surprised that he also paid considerable attention to Belli Locus, where he decided his mortal remains would find their final resting place. Despite damage done during the Middle Ages and later restorations, Fulk's tomb at Belli Locus was still open for public inspection in the seventeenth century and probably was only finally destroyed during the French Revolution.[76]

Thanks to the work of an artist working for Roger Gaignières in the late seventeenth century a drawing of Fulk Nerra's tomb has survived (fig. 3).[77] The tomb is obviously in the form of a building with a peaked roof and an archway entrance; the count, resting on his bed with a sheathed sword in his right hand, appears to block or guard the entrance in a calm manner. The structure as a whole recalls the west front of a Romanesque church of the eleventh century many examples of which still exist in Anjou and its environs. The closest match to the tomb building is the church of Saint-Maur at Glanfeuil only twenty-five kilometers east of Fulk's capital at Angers. Other examples can be found at Saint-Pierre-en-Vaux, Savennières, Esvière, Lasse, and Bourgueil.[78]

Like the tomb building itself, the decoration is thoroughly consistent with Angevin style in the first half of the eleventh century. For example, the fluted design of the arch is a virtual copy of one from the north wall of the cathedral of Saint Maurice at Angers (completed before 1025).[79] The columns and their capitals and bases resemble those common in Anjou and its environs during the eleventh century and are

Figure 3. *Tomb of Fulk Nerra with* gisant.
(Courtesy Oxford, Bodleian Library, Ms. Gough Drawings—Gaignières 14, fol. 171a)

of the same basic style as the column decorations from the church at Belli Locus, which was completed under Fulk Nerra's patronage before 1012.[80]

Like his contemporary Abbot Isarn of Saint-Victor at Marseille (d. 1049), Fulk chose to have his tomb adorned with a *gisant* in the antique manner. Indeed, Fulk may have been an innovator in this matter in the west of Francia, as he was in so much else from building stone towers to commissioning a battle relief sculpture. Fulk's recumbent statue on his tomb raises some problems that likely result from restorations, but on the whole the count's clothing, shoes, hairstyle, and clean-shaven face are consistent with late tenth- and eleventh-century practices. Perhaps most important in this context is the design of the guard on Fulk's sword. This rare upturned style is the same as that on the sword of the leader of the equestrian figures on the "battle relief" (see plate 2) that decorated the church at Belli Locus and likely commemorated Fulk's victory at Conquereuil.[81]

While Fulk's interest in the Roman past and his innovative nature may have played a role in the adorning of his tomb with a *gisant,* a somewhat different though not unrelated set of values may have inspired the design of the tomb complex as a whole. Fulk's tomb house resembled in form the traditional west front of Angevin churches built during the eleventh century. Moreover, the structure bore more than a passing similarity to the house placed over the grave of Charlemagne. Thus, for example, an eleventh-century chronicle that purports to convey an eye-witness account of the opening of Charlemagne's tomb in the year 1000 describes it as being covered by a house (*tugurium*). Einhard, who lived at Charlemagne's court, reported concerning the emperor's interment: "He was buried the same day that he died, and a gilded arch was erected above his tomb with his image and an inscription . . ."[82]

Similarity, of course, is not identity. Yet if the art historians are correct, exact copying was not necessary during the Early Middle Ages for observers to make explicit connections. As Richard Krautheimer has observed: "The architect of a medieval copy did not intend to imitate the prototype as it looked in reality; he intended to reproduce it *typice* and *figuaraliter,* as a memento of a venerated site . . ."[83]

By the time of Fulk Nerra's death, Carolingian propagandists and their descendants had been laboring on the symbolic level for more than two centuries to identify Charlemagne with Constantine the Great in the popular consciousness. This was but part of an even more elaborate effort to identify both Constantine and Charlemagne with Christ. The Ottonian emperors and especially Otto III, Fulk's contemporary whose pope took the name Sylvester II (Sylvester I was Constantine's pope and baptizer), supported these efforts and labored to integrate themselves into the pattern.[84] Indeed, one did not have to be an emperor in order to have one's supporters orchestrate such a symbolic lineage. Thus, for example, Fulk's neighbor William the Great (d. 1030), count of Poitou and duke of Aquitaine, was associated with Charlemagne in the effort by his panegyrist Adémar of Chabannes (d. 1034).[85] Ultimately, Christ, Constantine and Charlemagne were markers that identified those who would exercise power as having Christian and Roman legitimacy for their positions and their actions.[86]

The church of the Holy Sepulchre in Jerusalem and the tomb of Jesus were two of the many elements used in the process of association and identification. It is important to note that Jesus' tomb house came to be called an edicule and that that term came to be associated with all such *tuguria*. Many of the edicules were built in churches in Western Europe before the first Crusade to imitate the Holy Sepulchre or to associate the deceased within the *tugurium* with Christ, as was the case in Charlemagne's burial.[87] The symbolic importance of the edicule surely permits us to suggest that Fulk Nerra's tomb house was intended to associate him with Roman and Christian figures of the greatest power and prestige.

During the eleventh century and earlier many sources, such as an illumination done for the German emperor Henry II in 1017, make clear the importance of seeing the edicule and the church of the Holy Sepulchre as an integrated whole.[88] Thus it is noteworthy that neither Fulk's church at Belli Locus nor the count's tomb physically resembled the church of the Holy Sepulchre.[89] Only the arch of Jesus' tomb as seen in Henry II's sacramentary and the columns as mentioned in Eusebius's description of the edicule suggest similarity in the mind of a modern observer.[90] Nevertheless, we must remember Krautheimer's clarification that the architect of a medieval copy did not intend to imitate the prototype.[91]

Among the important characteristics that facilitated the identification of a church with its putative prototype during the eleventh century were the dedication and relics.[92] It is therefore worth recalling that Fulk made three pilgrimages to the Holy Land and returned safely from each by 1036. These journeys associated the Angevin count in the popular mind with the church of the Holy Sepulchre and Jesus' tomb.[93] Indeed, Fulk's decision to build the church and monastery at Belli Locus followed his return from the first of these pilgrimages. Within less than a decade of Fulk's death, the chronicler Raoul Glaber paraphrased from one of the Angevin count's letters: "He went to the sepulchre of the Savior in Jerusalem. As a result of this pilgrimage he was in high spirits . . . and conceived in his mind the idea of constructing a church . . . so that monks would be joined together there and pray day and night for the salvation of his soul."[94]

Among the dedicatees of Fulk's church at Belli Locus was the *Dominici Sepulcrum*. This dedication was likely added to the list of dedicatees after the roof was rebuilt and the church was reconsecrated following the wind storm of May 1012.[95] Probably at the time of the reconsecration Fulk made a point of emphasizing his donation of relics from Jerusalem to Belli Locus. The author of the *Historia Sancti Florentii*, writing considerably after the event, rather conflated the chronology when he wrote: "The things he had carried off from the Holy Sepulchre and from the Roman see he established in the place [i.e., Belli Locus] as relics . . ."[96]

The story of these relics, no doubt as Fulk wanted it told, finally came to be written down in the *Gesta Consulum*: "He [Fulk] prayed with a flow of many tears. Soon he sensed that a Divine command (*imperium*) turned soft the hardness of the stone, and the count, kissing the tomb, tore off a big piece with his teeth and hid it. . . . He took it away with him."[97]

Fulk's efforts to associate his church at Belli Locus and his tomb with the Holy Sepulchre and all that this meant to the intellectual as well as the popular *mentalité* was carried on at several levels at once. Fulk's tomb house might appeal to the more sophisticated, but his re-dedication of the church to the Holy Sepulchre and his gifts of relics required little learning or imagination to appreciate. In an even more obvious effort to bring the message to the populace, Fulk had constructed within the precincts of the monastery, as distinct from the church, a pyramid-shaped monument recalling more realistically than *typice* or *figuaraliter* the Holy Sepulchre itself[98] (figure 4). Clearly, even while preparing for death, Fulk worked diligently to strengthen the position of his dynasty.

When all was in order at home—both the smooth transition of power to Geoffrey Martel and the latter's kind observations on his father in several documents suggest that Fulk and his son parted on good terms—the Angevin count left on what was to be his fourth and final pilgrimage to the Holy Land in late 1039.[99] The accounts of his self-imposed physical punishments at the Holy Sepulchre will always remain problematic. Yet both Fulk and his entourage returned to the West, and the latter were eyewitnesses fully able to tell the story. In addition, a short time after Fulk's death, Countess Hildegarde went on pilgrimage to the Holy Land and her people also returned. They too could have relayed information about Fulk's exploits or corroborated stories told by members of his entourage.[100]

On returning to Europe from the Holy Land late in the spring of 1040, Fulk proceeded north and east to Lorraine. This was the homeland of his wife, Countess Hildegarde, and Fulk likely made this detour from the normal route to Angers either to meet her or members of her family. Fulk reached the city of Metz on 21 June, took ill, and was dead before sunset. A local doctor (*medicus*) was entrusted with the task of opening Fulk's cadaver and removing his intestines. These were buried in a church cemetery at Metz and a stone was placed above

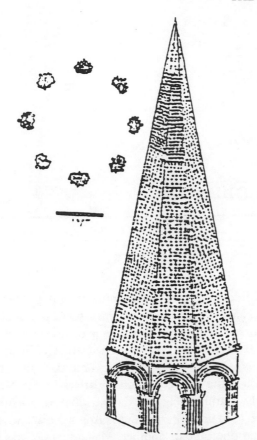

Figure 4. *Le pyramide at Belli Locus.*

this partial grave. The inscription on this stone—"The sepulchre of Count Fulk of the Angevins"—could still be read a century later.[101]

Fulk's unburied remains were preserved with fragrant spices and carried in an honorable manner—presumably with the ceremonial dignity worthy of a man considered in some quarters second only to the king—about six hundred kilometers, a minimum of three weeks' travel with a horse-drawn vehicle, from Metz to the castrum at Loches in the Touraine. From Loches the body was again moved. This time the journey was less than two kilometers to the monastery of Belli Locus. There the monks buried Fulk with great honor in the elegant tomb located in the chapterhouse (*capitulum*).[102]

CHAPTER ELEVEN

Summing Up

In the Middle Ages, as in the Roman world, politics was a family matter. Fulk Nerra came to power as his father's heir with the support of a family network that had been built up throughout the course of the tenth century and that was positioned strategically in various parts of the *regnum Francorum*. Although some ties failed from time to time to produce the desired results, relatives in the Valois, Amiens, the Vexin, the Gâtinais, Nevers, the Vendômois, Vienne, le Puy, Gévaudan, Forez, la Marche, Périgord, the Angoumois, and Arles appeared to aid Fulk at one time or another. Major support was provided by Fulk's uncle Guy, his half-brother Maurice, his cousin Walter, his father-in-law Bouchard, his cousin-in-law Aldebert, and his brother-in-law William Taillefer of Anguolême.

This family network supported Fulk largely in his "foreign policy," that is, in his expansion beyond the castra-defined *limes* of the Angevin state. The family had an important analogue in the Angevin aristocracy. These local magnates, many of whom held military commands as castellans, overwhelmingly saw their dynastic interests as inextricably connected to the continued success of the Fulconians. These fideles of the count acted in a manner that facilitated Fulk Nerra's policies, many of which had been set in motion by Geoffrey Greymantle and even by Fulk the Good; thus they supported his initiatives both at home and abroad. Defections were rare.

In about 985, Geoffrey Greymantle advised his sons publicly that the real strength of the Angevin count rested on the *generositas* of the *milites,* and Fulk appears to have listened carefully.[1] This insight, which carried more than a faint echo of Septimius Severus's advice to his sons as to the important role played by the army in the successful exercise of the *imperium,* was diligently cultivated by Fulk, who won the loyalty of his *milites.* Nevertheless, he rigorously enforced the *forma fidelitatis,* that is, the *sacramentum* taken to the dominus whether *imperator Romanorum* or *comes Andegavorum,* by the *milites.* Indeed, the oath was the base on which both imperial and Angevin service was constructed.

The legacy in material wealth and human capital that Geoffrey Greymantle and his predecessors had developed as part of long-term policies provided Fulk with opportunities a leader with the right abilities and some good luck (*fortuna*) could use as the basis for greater successes. Thus those familiar with Fulk Nerra's lengthy career would probably not quibble at a comparison with William the Conqueror, whom John Le Patourel described as "ambitious, ruthless, possessed of a ferocious energy and of great organizing ability, and perhaps very lucky at certain critical moments in his career."[2] We might also add that Fulk was parsimonious and patient.[3] Indeed, I anticipate no serious disagreement if I follow Richard Southern in suggesting that Fulk possessed "a kind of inspired opportunism" and perhaps even "an instinctive feeling for strategic advantage."[4] Unfortunately, an argument for Fulk's success based on the abovementioned descriptions is a circular one insofar as these descriptions have been deduced from the pattern of behavior they are intended to explain.[5]

Nonetheless, at least some of these qualities—several of which were recognized by Fulk's contemporaries, very probably through the same deductive process used by modern scholars—may perhaps be seen as prerequisites for political success during the first half of the eleventh century.[6] Indeed, historians working at the Angevin court in the twelfth century who had access to far more information about Fulk Nerra than what survives today saw his virtues as comparable to those of Julius Caesar.[7] In making such comparisons these writers were doing what William of Poitiers had done for Fulk's younger contemporary, Duke William, when he compared him to Julius Caesar, following the Norman conquest of England in 1066.[8]

Viewed by the scholars at the Angevin court, Sallust's Julius Caesar (*Catilina,* 54), appropriately edited, caught the essence not only of the Fulk Nerra they wanted their audience to appreciate but the Fulk Nerra they found in their sources.[9] Through the Angevin count's *acta* as well as various contemporary chronicles and in consonance with Sallust's

Caesar, Fulk "was held to be great (*magnus*) for his kindnesses, bountifulness, clemency, compassion, charity, relief of the poor, and pardons for the defeated."[10] Fulk's "panegyrists," following Sallust, continue: "Those in misery found a refuge in him"—here Fulk's acceptance of political fugitives from his adversaries' camp mirrors Caesar's behavior[11]— "intent on the business of his friends he often neglected his own."[12] Like Caesar, however, Fulk helped his friends, such as King Henry, and almost invariably helped himself at the same time.

The historians at the Angevin court, once again following Sallust's text, observe that Fulk had fixed in his soul the virtues of hard work and vigilance and that "he did not deny the appropriate gift to any worthy man." Indeed, the *milites* who shared Fulk's labor and vigilance required support, or as Septimius Severus advised his sons with perhaps some exaggeration: "Be harmonious, enrich the soldiers and despise the rest" (Dio., 76.12.2). The authors of the *Gesta* concluded, following Sallust, that Fulk "earnestly desired a *magnum imperium* [and] a new war where his *virtus* could shine forth." In this final observation, Sallust had included "exercitus" before "novum bellum" but the historians at the Angevin court omitted the word because they knew that Fulk already had an army.

Conspicuous by their absence from the twelfth-century appreciations of Fulk's persona are two very personal characteristics: his immense or ferocious temper and his abiding fear of hell. These traits are well attested in the Angevin count's own documents as well as in those of his contemporaries. We cannot doubt that the writers at the Angevin court were aware of these aspects of Fulk's personality, and their concern for his bad temper is manifest in the way they edited Sallust's description of Caesar. Just as they omitted "exercitus" from the list of Fulk's *desiderata* because it would obviously have struck a false note, they excised "facilitas" (easygoing, or even-tempered) from the description of his personality, even though Sallust had made a point of ascribing this characteristic to Caesar.

Fulk Nerra, unlike a Roman aristocrat, was not embarrassed to have deeply emotional aspects of his personality publicly bruited about; rather he took advantage of them.[13] Fulk's temper reached almost legendary proportions during his own lifetime. Thus, for example, Abbot Adhebertus and the monks of Saint-Florent testified that they agreed to the Angevin count's demands because "of his overwhelming ferocity."[14] The tradition at Saint-Florent recorded in its *History* also em phasized Fulk's ferocity and cunning; the author compared both Fulk and his son to wild beasts.[15]

Fulk's reputation for ferocity no doubt played a significant role in cowing potentially uncooperative clerics. But this reputation for ferocity combined with his widely recognized *strenuitas* resulted in his being considered *elegantissimus bellicus rebus*.[16] Fulk's adroitness in military activities is noted to have encouraged enemy garrisons to surrender *sub lege deditionis,* before actual fighting was begun, so that the wrath of the victor might be circumscribed by legal limitation. Thus, the historians at the Angevin court could observe in good faith that Fulk, like Caesar, came to be known for pardoning those he conquered.

Fulk also felt it desirable to publish his deep fear of Gehenna and his anxiety that "the last moment of life may come to an end in a very sudden manner."[17] Indeed, Fulk ascribed to a presentation of the latter idea in a style that was much beholden to Seneca.[18] Fulk dealt with his deep feeling in an unusual manner: his four pilgrimages to the Holy Land. Yet the Angevin count clearly did not have the type of "religious" personality exhibited by rulers like Louis the Pious, whose excesses made him a hostage to the bishops, nor did he have the "irresponsible" personality of Robert of Normandy, who left a child as heir to his unsettled duchy.

Fulk's first pilgrimage to atone for the great slaughter of Christians at the battle of Conquereuil in 992 was undertaken in 1003, more than a decade after his "sins" had been committed. Fulk left for the Holy Land only after the political situation in Anjou had been stabilized and the succession of an adult male, his half-brother Maurice, had been arranged. Fulk's second pilgrimage in fact commenced shortly after the murder of Hugh of Beauvais in 1009, but this journey was not primarily an act of atonement but a stroke of naked *Realpolitik* designed to avoid the consequences of the murder he had ordered. In the same vein as his first pilgrimage, the journey in 1035 had the primary aim of atoning for a massive slaughter of Christians, this time at Pontlevoy. This battle, however, was fought in 1016, almost two decades earlier. Fulk's final pilgrimage, as he was nearing three score and ten, may have been one of atonement for orchestrating the murder of Robert of Normandy and/or that of Alan of Rennes. It is also likely that this last journey was Fulk's way of gracefully retiring and leaving the reins of the Angevin government in the capable hands of Geoffrey Martel.

Family support and the appropriate personality traits go a long way toward explaining Fulk Nerra's success. But among the more important aspects of Fulk's personality had to be the ability to create and pursue productive policies. This talent we might characterize as a combination of judgment, intelligence, and insight based on a sound or realistic evaluation not only of resources but also of the strengths and weaknesses of adversaries. Here a brief comparison of Fulk with his contemporary and archrival Odo II of Blois can be instructive. Odo began his career with substantially greater material resources and a much more powerful family network than Fulk. Perhaps encouraged by this comparatively strong base, at his most audacious Odo attempted to gain control of the kingdoms of Burgundy and Italy. These efforts led on both occasions to war with the German emperor. In these campaigns as well as in his less ambitious schemes Odo routinely overestimated his own strengths and underestimated the capacity of his adversaries. Odo's pattern of behavior was characterized by the grand gesture and the overextension of his resources. The result was setback after setback and the ultimate victory of his rivals on virtually every front.

Fulk, by contrast, generally acted conservatively or modestly and with a clear sense of his position. The observation by Fulk le Réchin that his grandfather's *probitas* was both "great " and "admirable" catches the tone of Fulk Nerra's pattern of behavior if not of his personality very well.[19] Fulk Nerra built upon the efforts of Geoffrey Greymantle, who in the last few years of his reign began the process of organizing a territorial polity from the congeries of lands and lordships under Angevin jurisdiction in the west of the *regnum Francorum*. Fulk constructed stone stronghold after stone stronghold in order to create defended interior lines of communication and transportation between his widely scattered holdings in Anjou, the Touraine, the Vendômois, Maine, and the Poitou. These fortifications, established at approximately thirty-kilometer intervals in accord with the teachings of Roman military science, came to define a compact *principatus* that was further strengthened through additional fortifications in order to create a virtually impenetrable defense in depth for the Angevin state.

When Fulk discovered early in his reign that his interest in Château-Landon and the Orléanais stretched his resources too thin, he pulled back and left the exploitation of the Gâtinais to his cousin Walter. In a similar appreciation of his resources and the problems that could well have been created by overextension, Fulk pressed his interests in the Saintonge only after arranging the marriage of his sister to Count William of Angoulême, the marriage of his half-brother to a daughter of the viscomital family of Mussidan, which dominated many of the major church offices in the region, and securing a defended line of communication from Anjou south.

Fulk tended to build carefully, slowly, and incrementally, avoiding sudden policy shifts and grand gestures. Indeed, Fulk's encirclement of Tours was carried out so gradually and with such a defensive as well as an offensive purpose to the building of each permanent stronghold that the task was accomplished with a minimum of warning to his adversaries. These very same techniques were also used in the Saumurois, along the approaches to Poitiers, and even in the Angevin advance toward Normandy, which Geoffrey Martel would later pursue much more aggressively.

The development of the Angevin state under Fulk Nerra was made possible in large part because his father and grandfather had carefully rebuilt the fiscal system and tax base that had been undermined by the Viking invasions. The frequent complaints, particularly by literate clerics, concerning *malae consuetudines* and *novae exactiones* are reminders that the Angevin counts were reimposing long-dormant levies on land, production, sales, and people throughout the Angevin state both by means of direct and indirect taxation. The assarting and resettlement begun by Fulk the Good set in motion an economic revival that Geoffrey Greymantle and Fulk Nerra sustained and stimulated in a variety of ways, such as providing stimuli for the development of markets and privileges to attract merchants to newly built burgs.

Fulk and his contemporaries knew as well as the Romans that taxation was the business of government. They learned the lesson early in life as the background to the Nativity: "There went out a decree from Caesar Augustus that all the world should be registered [on the tax lists]" (Luke 2.1). As Fulk brought new lands under his control, he imposed the same broad schedule of both direct and indirect taxes which existed in areas already integrated into the Angevin state. In order to assure maximum income from these *consuetudines,* Fulk undertook various administrative efforts which to some extent have left a parchment trail that recalls Augustus's decree "ut describeretur universus orbis" (Luke 2.1).

Fulk Nerra labored to ensure that what was owed to Caesar was rendered to him. As a result, government revenues from taxes of all kinds as well as income for the comital fisc far outstripped the returns the Angevin magnates received from their estates. One important development from this immense imbalance in wealth and income was that magnates were attracted to government service as castellans, praepositi, and vicarii. Thus, as government officials they obtained a share of the tax revenues from fines, tolls, and tithes as payment for their services. Since magnates were not permitted in their capacity as private persons to mediate between their dependents and the state either in the collection of taxes or in the Angevin military organization, those members of the aristocracy who were *servientes comitis* did obtain a share of publicly generated revenues from the offices they held.

Fulk appears to have well understood that the magnates who served in the government had a family interest in augmenting their wealth and power. Fulk also understood that over time such a trend would be detrimental to the interests of the state, which was the creature for comital dynastic success. In order to maintain a creative tension between his interest and that of his *servientes,* keeping the latter in their place relative to the government, Fulk pursued a variety of policies that were made possible largely through the expansion and economic development of the resource base of the Angevin state.

Fulk acted toward his fideles in a consistent and predictable manner. Those who were loyal and able he rewarded. Those who failed these basic tests, which were administered to the potential heirs and successors of his proven officials during service in the count's military household, Fulk did not favor. While incompetence might be treated comparatively gently on occasion, disloyalty was ruthlessly crushed.

Fulk's rules for control of the Angevin aristocracy were rather simple and straightforward. The loyal and able sons of castellans would likely be made castellans in their turn, but they were generally not permitted to succeed to their fathers' offices. It was rare for a son to obtain in direct succession even one of the strongholds his father had commanded. This was especially the case if the castellan held a regional command that included several strongholds. Generally, the new castellan was placed in a region rather distant from his family's center of wealth and influence. When one family seemed to gain substantial influence in a region, Fulk made it a practice to introduce officials from the outside. The praepositi and vicarii were usually not chosen from the same families as the castellans for a particular district. Fulk carefully orchestrated the preferment of his fideles in an effort to keep them from developing bases of power that could threaten the effectiveness of comital administration.

In light of attitudes prevalent in the early eleventh century and even more particularly in view of the popular appreciation of Fulk Nerra, I have found it useful to emphasize the neo-Roman facade that adorned the Angevin state.[20] Although I have discussed artistic and architectural matters only where they specifically related to Fulk's political activities, specialists describe Angevin expression in the arts during this era as Romanesque.[21] It is clear that Fulk's battle relief at the church at Belli Locus and his tomb at the same church owed much to antique influence. Indeed, like Fulk's massive use of Romanesque stone fortification, his battle relief and tomb sculpture appear to have been innovations in the west of the *regnum Francorum*. The Romanesque artistic facade of Angevin society had its analogues in a variety of ceremonials, for instance, Fulk's triumph following the campaign of 992, his *adventus* of relics at Belli Locus, and his victory celebration in 1036 which included the *calcatio colli*. These rites were complemented on the ground by Fulk's apparent cultivation of the Cincinnatus image in his stagelike setting of the "Cultura comitis" for the *Via Triumphalis*. The use of terms such as *illustrissimus, princeps, consul,* and *consulatus* in various documents kept this neo-Roman image before Fulk's literate public and his posterity.

Fulk's neo-*romanitas* was not merely patina but structural as well. This antique support is perhaps best seen in the Angevin military where the influence of Vegetius's *De re militari* is manifest. Fulk's military organization, strategy, and tactics need not be reviewed here in detail to recall how, from the siting of strongholds to the use of a tactical reserve prepositioned with the sun at its back, Roman military science was not neglected. We may also observe that in fighting the *bellum publicum* and in developing the Angevin tax system concepts such as the "*utilitas* of the *res publica*" appear to have had some influence. The *lex antiqua* (or the *leges Romanorum*) seems to have manifested itself in both law and administration as indicated, for example, by Fulk's use of the *mandatum*.

Fulk Nerra himself, though an innovator, often initiated something new by reintroducing something old. A good example is the use of stone fortifications on a massive scale to create a system of defense in depth. It should also be made clear that Fulk had great respect for and doggedly pursued policies that had been initiated by his predecessors. He was a man of little or no *levitas,* the greatest of Roman personal and social sins. *Gravitas* dominated his personality, and he averred that he always took important matters seriously. His feelings of exultation were so rare that he thought them worthy of note when they occurred.

We catch a brief glimpse of Fulk's neo-*romanitas* when he ascribed to the view that his daughter was raised "inter paternos Lares nobiliter et pudice per matris diligentiam . . ."[22] It would be difficult to invent a more thoroughly neo-Roman indicator of Fulk's *mentalité* than this reference to his home as the "paternal Lares." The description of his daughter's upbringing as being done "pudice," with modesty, is thoroughly consistent with the Roman values surrounding the Lares. Indeed, it is little wonder that with information of this sort available for Fulk the authors at the Angevin court compared him with Julius Caesar.

Some of Fulk's neo-Roman investment, such as in military matters, obviously had practical value. But what of the rest: sculpture, ceremony, titles? Here, of course, one can only speculate because Fulk never revealed why he celebrated a triumph or carried out a *calcatio colli*. It might be suggested that all this was merely play acting, *homo ludens,* for no purpose other than pure entertainment. Such a conclusion, however, would contradict a very basic tenet of Fulk's personality: he rejected *levitas*.

Fulk Nerra seems to have understood that images of himself and of his government were important in influencing the behavior of those around him. Fulk's great ferocity cowed adversaries, his successful pilgrimages evidenced God's support for his efforts, his collection of relics manifested the positive manner in which the saints regarded him, his massive fortifications deterred invasion, and his consistent policy toward his fideles earned their loyalty.

Fulk's neo-Roman image may be seen as another means of influencing contemporaries. As a consul with a legitimate right to the *imperium,* Fulk could raise armies, build fortifications, levy taxes, mint coins, and build monumental churches. Indeed, he could rule autonomously without his legitimacy being challenged by the newly crowned Capetian kings. All of the surviving diplomatic instruments and narrative sources give us no reason to believe that Fulk recognized that he held the Angevin pagus from the Capetian kings who had replaced the Carolingians in 987.[23] Indeed, Fulk's views on Capetian legitimacy seem to have been summed up in Vendômois annals:

[*anno*] DCCCCLVI Hugh died. [He was] duke and abbot of Saint-Martin's, the son of Robert [I] the pseudo-king, father of the other Hugh [Capet] who was also made pseudo-king, at the same time as his son Robert [II], whom we saw ruling most unskillfully [*inertissime*]. The latter's son Henry [I], the present kinglet [*regulus*], has not deviated from his father's worthlessness.[24]

Indeed, at this time Fulk was not alone in treading a road to state building that had a neo-Roman patina. William the Great's panegyrist Adémar of Chabannes, who worked to have his principal thought of as Augustus and father of the Roman senate, also attacked Capetian legitimacy. Dudo of Saint-Quentin cast his principals, the dukes of Normandy, as consuls and patterned his history of their dynasty after the *Aeneid*, the father of state-building epics in the Roman tradition. With Normandy to the north and Aquitaine to the south, Fulk Nerra led the western reaches of the *regnum Francorum* in working to establish a neo-Roman basis for the independence of the Angevin state.

Genealogies

Genealogy 1
The Angevin Comital Patrilineage

TORTULFUS,[1] d. after 843
TERTULLUS,[1] d. after 877
INGELGARIUS, d. ca. 886?
FULK I THE RED, d. 942
FULK II THE GOOD, d. 960
GEOFFREY GREYMANTLE, d. 987
FULK III NERRA, d. 1040
GEOFFREY MARTEL, d. 1060
GEOFFREY THE BEARDED, deposed 1068
FULK IV LE RÉCHIN, d. 1109
GEOFFREY MARTEL II,[2] d. 1106
FULK V, resigned 1129
GEOFFREY LE BEL (Plantagenet), d. 1151
HENRY (II, king of the English), d. 1189

---

[1] did not hold the comital title
[2] son of Fulk V, coruler, died before his father

Genealogy 2
Angevin Patrilineal Marriages

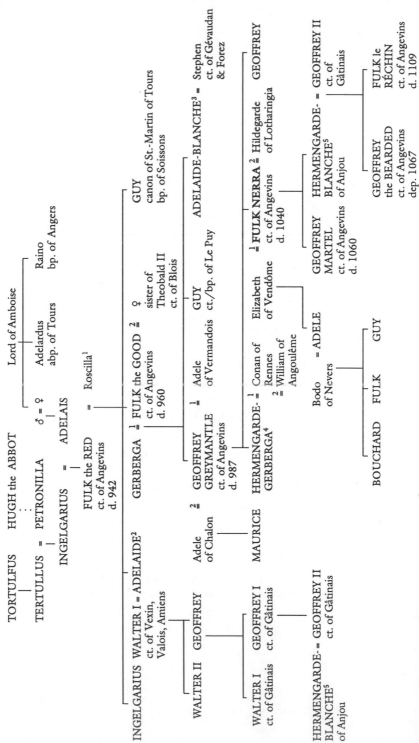

[1] See gen 3   [2] See gen. 4   [3] See gen. 5   [4] See gen. 6   [5] See gen. 4 and same person, this genealogy

Genealogy 3
Roscilla

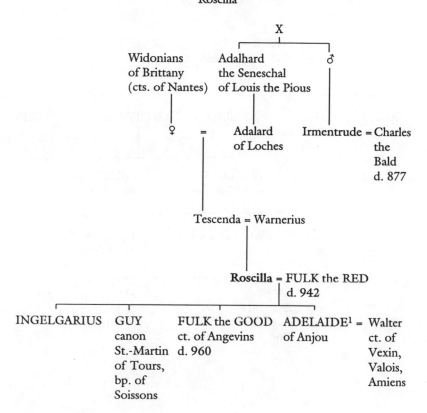

Genealogy 4
Adelaide of Anjou

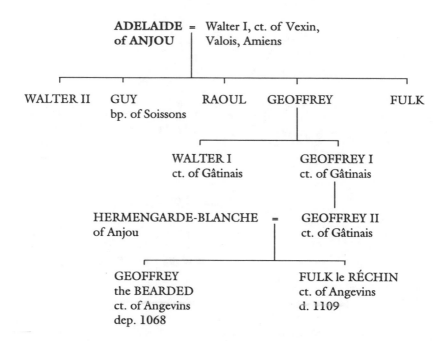

Genealogy 5
Adelaide-Blanche of Anjou

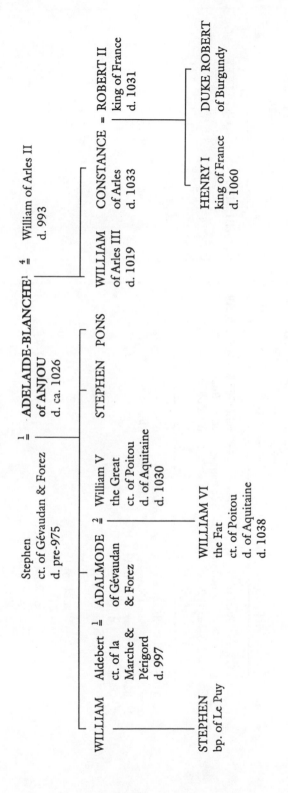

¹ Also married (2) Raymond of Gothia?
 (3) Carol. king Louis V
 (5) Otto-William of Burgundy?

Genealogy 6
Hermengarde-Gerberga of Anjou

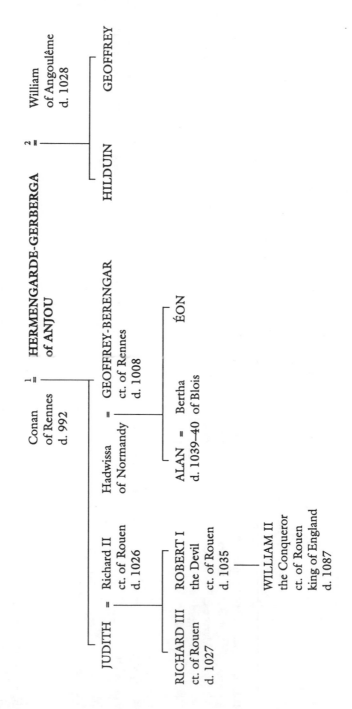

Genealogy 7
Counts of Blois-Champagne

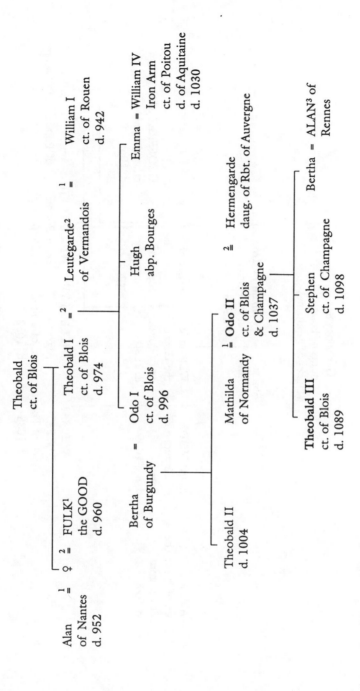

[1] See gen. 2   [2] See gen. 13   [3] See gen. 6

Genealogy 8
Counts of Poitou
(Dukes of Aquitaine)

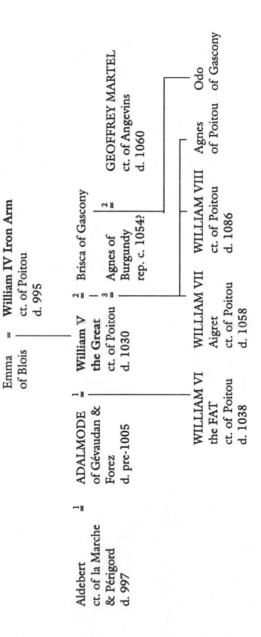

Genealogy 9
Counts of Nantes

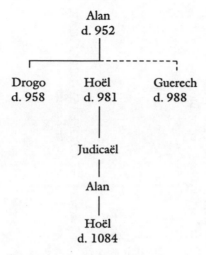

Genealogy 10
The Normans – Counts of Rouen (Dukes of Normandy)

Rollo
ct. of Rouen
d. 933

William I =¹ Leutegarde = Theobald I
ct. of Rouen   of Vermandois   ct. of Blois
d. 942

Breton concubine =²

Richard I
ct. of Rouen
d. 996

= Emma
sister of
Hugh Capet

Mathilda = Odo II   Hadwissa = GEOFFREY-BERENGAR
ct. of Blois   ct. of Rennes
& Champagne   d. 1008
d. 1037

JUDITH
of Rennes

ROBERT I
the Devil
ct. of Rouen
d. 1035

WILLIAM II
the Conqueror
ct. of Rouen
king of England
d. 1087

Richard II =
ct. of Rouen
d. 1026

RICHARD III
ct. of Rouen
d. 1027

Genealogy 11
The Carolingians

Charlemagne

Louis the Pious

Charles the Bald

Louis II

Louis III

Carloman

Charles the Simple

Louis IV

Lothair

Louis V

(Charles of Lotharingia)

Genealogy 12
The Capetians

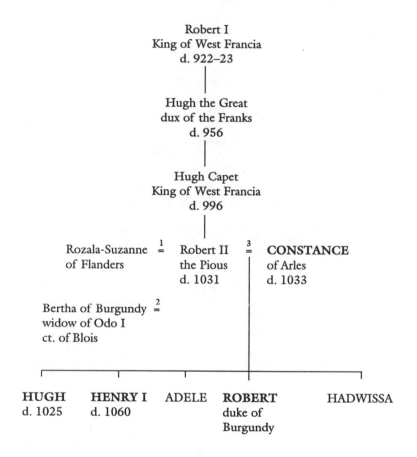

Robert I
King of West Francia
d. 922–23

|

Hugh the Great
dux of the Franks
d. 956

|

Hugh Capet
King of West Francia
d. 996

|

Rozala-Suzanne $\overset{1}{=}$ Robert II $\overset{3}{=}$ **CONSTANCE**
of Flanders   the Pious   of Arles
                     d. 1031   d. 1033

Bertha of Burgundy $\overset{2}{=}$
widow of Odo I
ct. of Blois

HUGH   **HENRY I**   ADELE   **ROBERT**   HADWISSA
d. 1025   d. 1060   duke of
                                        Burgundy

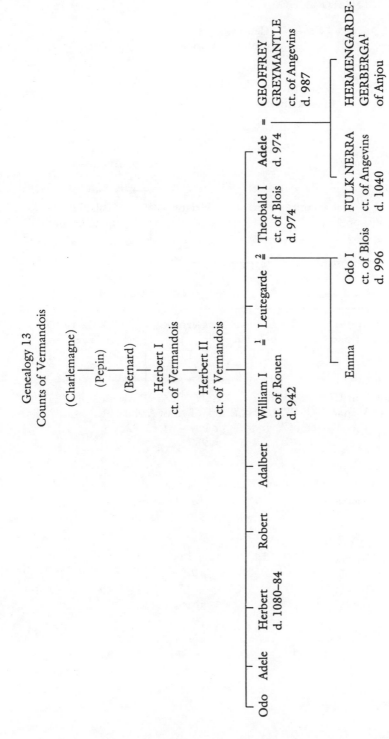

Genealogy 13
Counts of Vermandois

(Charlemagne)

(Pepin)

(Bernard)

Herbert I
ct. of Vermandois

Herbert II
ct. of Vermandois

Odo Adele Herbert   Robert Adalbert William I   ¹ Leutegarde ² Theobald I   Adele   =   GEOFFREY
          d. 1080–84   ct. of Rouen =   =   ct. of Blois d. 974   GREYMANTLE
                                             d. 942   d. 974   ct. of Angevins
                                                                                                      d. 987

                                                        Emma   Odo I   FULK NERRA   HERMENGARDE-
                                                                     ct. of Blois ct. of Angevins   GERBERGA¹
                                                                     d. 996   d. 1040   of Anjou

¹ See gen. 6

Genealogy 14
Viscounts of Vienne

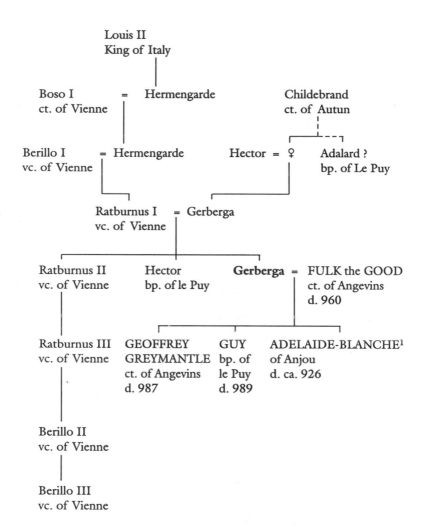

Genealogy 15
Abbots of Saint-Aubin

Guntarius, resigns in 987

Renaud, 988–996(?)

Girard, 996–1001

Hubert, 1001–1027

Primaldus, 1027–1036(?)

Walter, 1036–1056(?)

Abbots of Saint-Florent de Saumur

Amalbert, 956–985

Robert of Blois, 985–1011

Adhebert of Chinon, 1011–1013

Gerald of Thouars, 1013–1020

Frederick of Tours, 1021–1055

Fulk Nerra: Brief Chronology of Major Events

970	Birth of Fulk Nerra
971	Fulk's sister marries Count Conan of Rennes
973–974	Fulk's brother Geoffrey is born
974	Fulk's mother, Adele of Vermandois, dies
975	Fulk's paternal uncle Guy becomes bishop of le Puy
976	Fulk's brother Geoffrey dies
978	Geoffrey Greymantle marries Adele of Chalon
980–981	Maurice, Fulk's half-brother, is born
986	Fulk associated in the comital title
986	Fulk marries Elizabeth of Vendôme
987, 21 July	Geoffrey Greymantle dies
987	Fulk becomes sole count of the Angevins
988–989	Fulk leads raids into the regions of Blois and Châteaudun
992, 27 June	Fulk wins victory at Conquereuil; Count Conan of Rennes killed
992	Fulk gains full control of Nantes
992	Fulk's allies win battle of Orsay
992–994	Fulk constructs stronghold at Langeais
994	Fulk withstands a siege at Langeais by Odo I of Blois

995–996	Fulk withstands a second siege of Langeais; Odo I dies
996	Fulk captures Tours and Châteauneuf (violates cloister of Saint-Martin) with ally Aldebert of la Marche and Périgord
997	Fulk captures the stronghold of Montsoreau
997, Pre-25 July	Fulk's forces driven from Tours and Châteauneuf
999–1000	Treaty with William of Aquitaine by which Fulk gets Loudunais and Saintonge
1000	Fulk executes Elizabeth of Vendôme for adultery(?)
1000	The city of Angers suffers a serious fire
1000	Fulk builds the stronghold of Montrevault
1001–1002	Fulk undertakes the execution of a *divisio* of church resources
1003	Fulk advances into Berry
1003	Maurice, Fulk's half-brother, associated in the comital title on a temporary basis
1003, autumn	Fulk leaves on a pilgrimage to Jerusalem
1003–1004, winter	King Robert marries Fulk's cousin Constance
1004–1005, winter	Fulk returns home from pilgrimage
1005	Bishop Renaud of Angers leaves on a pilgrimage and dies
1005	Fulk resumes diplomatic relations with Bishop Renaud of Paris, his erstwhile brother-in-law, and with King Robert II
1005	Fulk marries Hildegarde, a woman of royal blood from Lotharingia
1005–1006	Fulk builds the stronghold of Montrichard
1005–1006	Fulk builds the stronghold of Montbazon
1005–1006	Fulk builds the stronghold of Mirebeau
1005–1007	Fulk builds the monastery of Belli Locus
1006	Fulk takes over vast allodial lands in the Mauges region
1006	Fulk appoints Hubert of Vendôme as bishop of Angers, consecrated on 13 June
1006, 14 October	Fulk's son Geoffrey Martel is born
1006–1007	Fulk is recognized as *dominus* of the monastery of Saint-Florent de Saumur

1007	Fulk builds a stronghold at Château-Gontier
1007	Fulk goes to Rome
1007	Peace of Coudres
1008, summer	King Robert II puts aside Queen Constance
1008	Fulk has Hugh of Beauvais, King Robert's advisor, murdered
1008	Geoffrey Berengar, count of Rennes, dies
1009, summer	Fulk goes to Rome, then on pilgrimage to Jerusalem
1009–1011	Count Maurice left in charge and Angevin interests suffer
1011, winter	Fulk returns to Anjou via Rome
1011, spring	Fulk goes on offensive to recover losses suffered by Maurice
1012	Cathedral school founded at Angers
1013	Hermengarde-Blanche, Fulk's second daughter, born (latest date)
1014	Fulk takes the stronghold of Mayenne
1015	Fulk campaigns to retake the stronghold of Montbazon
1016, 6 July	Fulk wins a major battle at Pontlevoy against Odo II of Blois
1017	Fulk exercises de facto control of the Vendômois
1017	Fulk builds a stronghold at Montboyau
1018	Fulk's forces raid in the Touraine
1018–1020	Monastery of Saint-Nicholas at Angers built
1018–1021	Fulk extends Angevin control into the northern Poitou
1020	Fulk builds a stronghold at Trèves in the middle Loire valley
1023, March	Fulk meets with King Robert
1025–1027	Count Herbert of Maine captured and imprisoned by Fulk
1026	Fulk captures the stronghold of Saumur
1027, summer	Blésois-royal attack on Amboise fails
1027	Fulk retakes Montbazon
1027	Odo II of Blois cedes Saumur to Fulk

1027–1028	Fulk builds stronghold at Montfaucon
1028	Fulk and Hildegarde build the convent of Ronceray
1030	William the Great of Aquitaine dies
1030	Fulk gives Geoffrey Martel the stronghold of Saumur (latest date possible)
1031	King Robert II dies and is succeeded by his son Henry I
1032	Geoffrey Martel marries Agnes, widow of William the Great of Aquitaine
1032–1033	Civil war over royal succession; Fulk leads King Henry's armies to victory
1033	Geoffrey Martel wins the Aquitanian phase of the war with a victory over William the Fat at Mont Couër
1033	Queen Constance dies
1034	Fulk and Geoffrey Martel build a group of strongholds near Saint-Florent-le-Vieil
1033–1035	Flooding, loss of crops, famine
1036	Fulk goes on third pilgrimage, handing government over to Geoffrey Martel
1036–1037	Geoffrey Martel at war with Bishop Gervais of Le Mans
1037	Fulk returns, Geoffrey surrenders government, and the latter loses war to Gervais
1037	Odo II of Blois killed in battle
1037–1038	Fulk retakes Langeais and captures Chinon
1039	Fulk makes fourth pilgrimage to Holy Land
1040, 21 June	Fulk dies at Metz and is buried at Belli Locus

Notes

Preface

1. Concerning the Carolingian Empire and its dissolution see the readily available survey by Rosamund McKitterick, *The Frankish Kingdoms under the Carolingians, 751–987* (London, 1983); also Jean Dunbabin, *France in the Making: 843–1180* (Oxford, 1985), 1–123, who provides a very useful guide to the period from 843 to 987.

2. For the general theme of continuity see Karl Ferdinand Werner, *Les origines (avant l'an mil): Histoire de France,* ed. Jean Favier, vol. 1 (Paris, 1984); and note that Richard Sullivan, "The Carolingian Age: Reflections on Its Place in the History of the Middle Ages," *Speculum* 64 (1989): 267–306, after an extensive review of several major areas of research, stresses that recent scholarship tends to emphasize continuity from the late antique world to the late tenth century. See in this context the brilliant treatment of continuity which focuses on public finances in relation to the dynamic of the composition and decomposition of the larger political entities, that is, the Christian Empire, the Romano-German kingdoms, and the Carolingian Empire: Jean Durliat, *Les finances publiques de Dioclétien aux Carolingiens (284–889)* (Sigmaringen, 1990); and my review of this work in *Francia* 19, no. 1 (1992): forthcoming. Recall the acute observation by J. M. Wallace-Hadrill, *The Barbarian West, 400–1000* (1st ed., 1952; 3d rev. ed., 1967), 163: "Historical interests and imaginative background do not radically change in Western Europe during the period [400–1000] covered in this essay. That is why it has unity."

3. See the helpful survey provided by Dunbabin, *France in the Making,* 124–245, with the relevant bibliography, 442–446. Regarding family relations, the dominant work in this area has been carried forward by Karl Ferdinand Werner, "Untersuchungen zur Frühzeit des französischen Fürstentums

281

(9.–10. Jahrhundert)," *Die Welt als Geschichte* 18 (1958): 256–289; 19 (1959): 146–193; 20 (1960): 87–119, and "Bedeutende Adelsfamilien im Reich Karls des Grossen: Ein personengeschichtlicher Beitrag zum Verhältnis von Königtum und Adel im frühen Mittelalter," in *Karl der Grosse, Lebenswerk und Nachleben: 1 Persönlichkeit und Geschichte,* ed. Helmut Beumann (Düsseldorf, 1965), 83–142, translated as "Important Noble Families in the Kingdom of Charlemagne: A Prosopographical Study of the Relationship between King and Nobility in the Early Middle Ages," in *The Medieval Nobility,* ed. and trans. Timothy Reuter (Amsterdam, 1978), 137–202, which, however, does not include Werner's appendices (pp. 137–142) from the original. This cognatic kinship structure demonstrates basic continuity with the early medieval period as presented by Alexander Murray, *Germanic Kinship Structure: Studies in Law and Society in Antiquity and the Early Middle Ages* (Toronto, 1983); see my review of Murray's book in *Speculum* 60 (1985): 1003–1004 as well as Bernard S. Bachrach, "Some Observations on *The Medieval Nobility,* in *Medieval Prosopography* 1, no. 2 (1980): 15–33.

From time to time various efforts, largely unsuccessful on the whole, have been made to overturn Werner's basic view concerning the connections of the West Frankish aristocracy to the Carolingians and the fundamental cognatic structure of their lineages. See, for example, the literature cited by Constance Bouchard, "The Origins of the French Nobility: A Reassessment," *The American Historical Review* 86 (1981): 501–532, and Constance Bouchard, "Family Structure and Family Consciousness among the Aristocracy in the Ninth and Eleventh Century," *Francia* 14 (1986): 639–658; these articles have tended to confuse the situation.

4. The basic works for the details of political history are still Ferdinand Lot, *Etudes sur le règne de Hugues Capet et la fin du Xᵉ siècle* (Paris, 1913), and Christian Pfister, *Etudes sur le règne de Robert le pieux (996–1031)* (Paris, 1885). The monograph was never written on the reign of Henry I, but a cluster of articles by Jan Dhondt (see bibliography) are very helpful. Elizabeth Hallam, *Capetian France: 987–1328* (London, 1980), 64–110, provides an accessible summary and a useful bibliography (334ff.). See also Dunbabin, *The Making of France,* 162–169, who also provides a sound tour of the horizon.

5. For Normandy the basic works are David Bates, *Normandy before 1066* (London, 1982), and John Le Patourel, *The Norman Empire* (Oxford, 1976). Eleanor Searle, *Predatory Kinship and the Creation of Norman Power, 840–1066* (Berkeley, Los Angeles, London, 1988), is exceptionally important; see my review in *Albion* 21 (1989): 609–611.

6. For a detailed account one must still turn to Alfred Richard, *Histoire des comtes de Poitou, 778–1204* (Paris, 1903), 2 vols. Dunbabin, *France in the Making,* 173–179, provides a useful introduction; see p. 421 for additional bibliography.

7. Karl Ferdinand Werner's long-awaited study of Blois–Chartres may well appear soon since his retirement as director of the German Historical Institute in Paris several years ago has provided the time for writing. Until this work appears we must cobble together the history of this important dynasty for the bulk of the period under consideration here from articles in rather obscure jour-

nals and the important monographs by André Chédeville, *Chartres et ses campagnes, XIe–XIIIe siècles* (Paris, 1973), and Michel Bur, *La formation du comté de Champagne v. 950–v. 1150* (Nancy, 1977). For a brief introduction see Dunbabin, *France in the Making,* 190–196.

8. The two fundamental works for the period under consideration here remain Olivier Guillot, *Le comte d'Anjou et son entourage au XIe siècle* (Paris, 1972), 2 vols., and Louis Halphen, *Le comté d'Anjou au XIe siècle* (Paris, 1906). Dunbabin, *France in the Making,* 184–190, provides an introduction. Concerning Juliomagus see Carlrichard Brühl, *Palatium und Civitas: Studien zur Profantopographie spätantiker Civitates vom 3. bis zum 13. Jahrhundert,* vol. 1: *Gallien* (Vienna, 1975), 152–160.

9. For the view that England was conquered in 1154 see the compelling argument by John Le Patourel, "The Norman Conquest, 1066, 1106, 1154?" *Proceedings of the Battle Conference on Anglo-Norman Studies,* ed. R. Allen Brown (Ipswich, 1978), 1:103–120, 216–220. Regarding the Angevin aspect of the conquest, however, see John Le Patourel, "The Plantagenet Dominions," *History* 50 (1965): 289–308, and Bernard S. Bachrach, "The Idea of the Angevin Empire," *Albion* 10 (1978): 293–299. With regard to the importance of the various *regna* see Karl Ferdinand Werner, "Königtum und Fürstentum des französischen 12. Jahrhunderts," in *Probleme des 12. Jahrhunderts* (Sigmaringen, 1968), 177–225, and the translation "Kingdom and Principality in Twelfth-century France," in *The Medieval Nobility,* ed. and trans. Timothy Reuter, 243–290.

10. Regarding the centrality of Fulk Nerra see A. de Salies, *Histoire de Foulques Nerra* (Angers, 1874); Kate Norgate, *England under the Angevin Kings* (London, 1887), 1:97–200; Halphen, *Le comté d'Anjou,* 1–111; Guillot, *Le Comte d'Anjou,* 1:15–55; and Richard Southern, *The Making of the Middle Ages* (New Haven, 1953), 81–89.

11. In the not so distant past some medievalists became particularly exercised about the use of the term *state* to describe the great many polities that functioned in pre-Crusade Europe and indeed even about such polities later in the Middle Ages. Despite an occasional problem, however, this dispute is rather moribund. For some background see, for example, Sidney Z. Ehler, "On Applying the Modern Term 'State' to the Middle Ages," in *Medieval Studies Presented to Aubrey Gwynn S. J.,* ed. J. A. Watt et al. (Dublin, 1961), 492–501. For an able demonstration of the sterility of many such controversies that have bedeviled medieval historiography see Susan Reynolds, *Kingdoms and Communities in Western Europe: 900–1300* (Oxford, 1984), esp. 323–326, regarding the state. With regard to the notion of an Angevin empire see: Le Patourel, "The Plantagenet Dominions," 289–308; Bachrach, "The Idea of the Angevin Empire," 293–299; and for a brief overview Dunbabin, *The Making of France,* 346–350 (426 for additional bibliography).

12. See Bernard S. Bachrach, "The Angevin Strategy of Castle Building in the Reign of Fulk Nerra, 987–1040," *The American Historical Review* 88 (1983): 533–560, where the outlines of this strategy are discussed.

13. See Bernard S. Bachrach, "The Practical Use of Vegetius' *De re militari* during the Early Middle Ages," *The Historian* 47 (1985): 239–255, where the

methodology is developed with a focus on the behavior of Fulk Nerra so that historians can ascertain whether a particular military commander was using Vegetian ideas as contrasted to the possibility that: (1) the source or sources that provided the information had access to Vegetian ideas and then credited the principal with such knowledge, and (2) the commander himself simply used an appropriate tactical or strategic idea that also happened to have been a standard of Vegetian or late Roman military science but did so on his own initiative without knowledge of historical precedents (a case of reinventing the wheel).

14. Bernard S. Bachrach, "Neo-Roman vs. Feudal: The Heuristic Value of a Construct for the Reign of Fulk Nerra, Count of the Angevins (987–1040)," *Cithara* 30 (1990): 3–30, provides a preliminary treatment of this view.

15. Werner, "Untersuchungen," 264–286.

16. See Bernard S. Bachrach, "Geoffrey Greymantle, Count of the Angevins, 960–987: A Study in French Politics," *Studies in Medieval and Renaissance History* 17 (1985): 1–67 (two maps), for the reign of Fulk Nerra's father and some attention to his grandfather. See also Bernard S. Bachrach, "The Angevin Economy, 960–1060: Ancient or Feudal?" *Studies in Medieval and Renaissance History,* n.s., 10 (1988): 3–55, for the economic background.

17. Bernard S. Bachrach, "Some Observations on the Origins of the Angevin Dynasty," *Medieval Prosopography* 10, no. 2 (1989): 1–23, for some of the early history of the establishment of marriage alliances.

18. Not only have the major secular figures been neglected but this is also true for the large number of bishops who, as Fanning observes, "were among the most powerful figures of the post-Carolingian period." For a model treatment of a rather ordinary bishop see Steven Fanning, *A Bishop and His World before the Gregorian Reform: Hubert of Angers, 1006–1047* (Philadelphia, 1988); see p. 92 for the quotation.

19. This is not the appropriate place to disentangle the various trends pursued by a plethora of scholars more or less connected to the *Annales* school during the postwar era in their various phases as they have affected the writing of French medieval history. Nor is there space to draw fine distinctions in order to delineate the nuances, for example, that differentiate the efforts of Duby, Le Goff, Fossier, and their respective admirers from one another. The point to be made here is that as a group these scholars have diminished the role traditionally given to political history and more particularly the centrality of the individual as decision maker on the stage of history. See, for example, Georges Duby, "Les sociétiés médiévales: Une approche d'ensemble," *Annales: Economie, société, civilisation* (January-February 1971), vol. 26. This inaugural lecture, given when Duby became professor at the Collège de France, is cited here for convenience in George Duby, "Medieval Society," in *The Chivalrous Society,* trans. Cynthia Postan (Berkeley, Los Angeles, London, 1977), 1–14, where he writes (p. 3), "Social history is, in fact, all history." See also *La nouvelle histoire,* ed. Jacques Le Goff et al. (Paris, 1978), and Robert Fossier, *Enfance de l'Europe: Aspects économiques et sociaux* (Paris, 1982), 2 vols. Jean-Pierre Poly and Éric Bournazel, *La mutation féodale, X^e–XIe siècles* (Paris, 1980), provide what now passes for political history in the milieu adumbrated above. Cf. Charles T. Wood, Review article: "The Return to Medieval Politics," *The*

American Historical Review 94 (1989): 391–404, who draws attention to some interesting trends in the writing of political history.

20. Cf. the emphasis on these areas of history by Fossier and to a lesser extent by Le Goff (see note 19 above).

21. Elizabeth A. R. Brown, "The Tyranny of a Construct: Feudalism and Historians of Medieval Europe," *The American Historical Review* 79 (1974): 1063–1088, is still useful; but see in particular Bachrach, "Neo-Roman vs. Feudal," 3–30.

22. Fredric Cheyette, "Some Notations on Mr. Hollister's Irony," *Journal of British Studies* 5 (1965): 1–14, provides a lucid discussion of the inherent circularity in the creation of constructs.

23. Edward Peters, *Europe: The World of the Middle Ages* (Englewood Cliffs, N.J., 1977), 1–7, provides a straightforward introduction for the beginner.

24. For the English background see J. G. A. Pocock, *The Ancient Constitution and the Feudal Law: English Historical Thought in the Seventeenth Century* (Cambridge, 1957), and Brown, "Tyranny of a Construct," 1064. While everyone is aware of the notion "la chose avant le mot," it should be clear that neither the "feudal system" nor "feudalism" is a "thing," however much some would like to reify such constructs.

25. Brian Stock, *The Implications of Literacy: Written Language and Models of Interpretation in the Eleventh and Twelfth Centuries* (Princeton, 1983), 517–521, provides some useful observations and bibliography that may serve as a convenient introduction to the topic of "modernity" in the eleventh century. See also Stock's quotation (p. 270) from Heriger of Lobbes (d. 1007), characterizing his contemporaries as writers of the "modern age." Stock's general views on this matter, however, might have been altered a bit had he encountered Rhabanus Maurus's dedication, ca. 856, of his *Epitome* of Vegetius's *De re militari* (*De procinctu Romanae militae,* ed. E. Dümmler in *Zeitschrift für deutsches Alterthum* 15 [1872]: 450) to King Lothair where he makes clear to his royal patron that he has included only those matters that are of interest "tempore moderno" and has omitted everything else.

26. Bachrach, "Neo-Roman vs. Feudal," 3–30.

27. J. Chydenius, *Medieval Institutions and the Old Testament* (Helsinki, 1965), and J. M. Wallace-Hadrill, "The *Via Regia* of the Carolingian Age," in *Trends in Medieval Political Thought,* ed. Beryl Smalley (Oxford, 1965), 22–41; reprinted in J. M. Wallace-Hadrill, *Early Medieval History* (Oxford, 1975), 181–200; see my review of the latter in *The Historian* 38 (1976): 729–730.

28. Wallace-Hadrill, *Early Medieval History,* 181–190. It may be of some importance that King Robert II, Fulk Nerra's contemporary, saw an effort made to merge the imperial and the biblical or at least the religious. See Dunbabin, *The Making of France,* 133–135, for an introduction to this aspect of Capetian kingship. For more detail on the entire subject see Andrew Lewis, *Royal Succession in Capetian France: Studies on Familial Order and the State* (Cambridge, Mass., 1981).

29. Stephen G. Nichols, *Romanesque Signs: Early Medieval Narrative and Iconography* (New Haven, Conn., 1983), 66–94; see also Bernard S. Bachrach,

"'Potius rex quam esse dux putabatur': Some Observations concerning Adémar of Chabannes' Panegyric on Duke William the Great," in *The Haskins Society Journal: Studies in Medieval History,* ed. Robert B. Patterson (London, 1989), 1:11–21, where it is shown that Adémar wanted to have his principal, Duke William, compared with Charlemagne, Constantine, and Christ as well.

30. Sir Ronald Syme, *The Roman Revolution* (Oxford, 1951), 12, of the revised second impression; this work originally appeared in 1939 but due to the distractions of World War II, its greatness was only fully appreciated somewhat belatedly.

31. Richard Southern, *The Making of the Middle Ages* (New Haven, Conn., 1953), 86. Southern justifies his notion of the emergence of feudal government in the following terms (p. 81): "Perhaps more simply than anywhere else in Europe, the shaping of a new political order may be seen in the valley of the river Loire. There was here so clean a sweep of ancient institutions, title deeds, and boundaries that the emergence of new forms of loyalty and authority was facilitated." This view of conditions in the Loire valley west of Orléans is simply incorrect at a basic factual level. See, for example, Jean-François Lemarignier, "La dislocation du 'pagus' et le problème des 'consuetudines' (X^e–XIe siècles)," *Mélanges d'histoire du moyen âge dédiés à Louis Halphen* (Paris, 1951), 401–410, and "Structures monastiques et structures politiques dans la France de la fin du Xe et des débuts du XIe siècle," *Settimane di Studio de Centro Italiano di Studi sull'alto Medioevo* 4 (1957): 357–400, revised by the author and reprinted as "Political and Monastic Structures in France at the End of the Tenth and Beginning of the Eleventh Century," in *Lordship and Community in Medieval Europe,* ed. and trans. Fredric Cheyette, 106–108, who makes clear that the Angevin *pagus* did not dissolve; Jacques Boussard, "L'origine des familles seigneuriales dans la région de la Loire moyenne," *Cahiers de civilisation médiévale* 5 (1962): 303–322, who demonstrates continuity among the aristocracy; and Guillot, *Le comte d'Anjou,* 1:2, who shows that Geoffrey Greymantle, Fulk Nerra's father, was "un personnage encore carolingien" in terms of his government.

If we were to try to search out a region that fit Southern's description of "so clean a sweep," it would not be the valley of the Loire west of Orléans but the Mâconnais as presented by Georges Duby, *La société aux XIe et XIIe siècles la région mâconnaise* (Paris, 1953, and reprinted with different pagination in 1971).

32. Southern, *The Making of the Middle Ages,* p. 81, n. 1, regarding his awareness and indeed, reliance on these twelfth-century sources, and p. 82, for the quotation on "romantic prejudice." Regarding Southern's use of these complicated texts see Bachrach, "Neo-Roman vs. Feudal," 3, 22, n. 18.

33. It is important in this context that when Fulbert of Chartres composed his famous letter (*Epist.,* no. 51) to Duke William of Aquitaine regarding *forma fidelitatis,* which is commonly considered the *locus classicus* for the "feudal" obligation between a *dominus* and his *fidelis,* he drew directly on two classical books on rhetoric, the *Ad herennium,* which at one time was attributed to Cicero, and the latter's *De inventione.* See on this point the detailed analysis by Claude Carozzi in the introduction (pp. lxiv–lxviii) of his edition and translation of Adalbéron de Laon, *Poème au roi Robert* (Paris, 1979). Concerning the

consensus that attributes a key role to Fulbert's letter in the development of "feudalism" see, for example, F. L. Ganshof, *Feudalism*, trans. Philip Grierson (3d English ed., New York, 1964), 83–84. For a treatment of the more practical nature of relations in the west of France in terms of the *forma fidelitatis* see Bernard S. Bachrach, "Enforcement of the *Forma Fidelitatis*: The Techniques Used by Fulk Nerra, Count of the Angevins (987–1040)," *Speculum* 59 (1984): 796–819.

34. In addition to Cheyette, "Some Notations on Mr. Hollister's Irony," 1–14, see Bernard S. Bachrach, "Was There Feudalism in Byzantine Egypt?" *Journal of the American Research Center in Egypt* 6 (1967): 163–166.

35. See, above, nn. 24 and 31.

36. A core of helpful work dealing with methodological questions is available. See, for example, Donald A. Bullough, "Early Medieval Social Groupings: The Terminology of Kinship," *Past and Present* 45 (1981): 3–18; Murray, *Germanic Kinship Structure*; David Herlihy, "Family," *The American Historical Review* 96 (1991): 1–16; and Stephen D. White, *Custom, Kinship, and Gifts to Saints: The 'Laudatio Parentum' in Western France, 1050–1150* (Chapel Hill, N.C., 1988), esp. 127, where he suggests that attention be paid to the family as "the 'practical' kin groups that actually engaged in particular social activities" and correctly observes that "they could assume different forms, depending upon the nature of the activity in which they were engaged." White's interest here is in those "families" he studied in light of the *laudatio parentum* and within the context of gifts to saints; this context is very different from the political family network detailed with regard to Fulk Nerra in the present work. Fulk's family network or political family looks in some respects rather like a large cognatic group. Cf. Marc Bloch, *Feudal Society*, trans. L. A. Manyon (Chicago, 1961), 138–139.

It has often struck me as somewhat paradoxical that social scientists, especially those anthropologists and sociologists whose works have found favor with medieval historians, tend to ignore real science, i.e., biology and genetics, when developing their "theories" concerning the family. For some further observations along scientific lines see Jerome Kroll and Bernard S. Bachrach, "Medieval Dynastic Decisions: Evolutionary Biology and Historical Explanation," *Journal of Interdisciplinary History* 21 (1990): 1–28.

37. A valuable effort to develop a sense of the political family of the Norman ruling house and its allies is provided by Searle, *Predatory Kinship and the Creation of Norman Power*. For a somewhat different approach to the Angevins see Bernard S. Bachrach, "Henry II and the Angevin Tradition of Familly Hostility," *Albion* 16 (1984): 111–130.

38. Syme, *The Roman Revolution*, 12. It is very important to emphasize that in law the Roman family was agnatic in structure. But as the material Syme masterfully marshals for the Republic throughout *The Roman Revolution* makes clear, in politics the Roman aristocratic family was cognatic. Southern, *The Making of the Middle Ages*, 88, points out that "a careful marriage" often played a key role in the process of taking over new territory. Of course, this is a central point for Werner, "Untersuchungen," 264–286, concerning the Angevin comital family.

39. *The Roman Revolution*, 157. For Fulk, however, like the Roman *nobiles*, the political *familia* (p. 13) extended beyond blood and marriage ties. As Syme put it: "The dynast required allies and supporters, not from his own class only. . . . Above all, it was necessary to conciliate the second order of society, the Roman knights." For a preliminary study on the way Fulk Nerra developed his relations with his fideles, "the second order of society," in Syme's terms, see Bachrach, "Enforcement of the *Forma Fidelitatis*," 796–819, and Herlihy, "Family," 1–7, for background.

Chapter 1: Family Background and Childhood

1. Werner, "Untersuchungen," 264–286; with the revisions and additions by Bachrach, "Some Observations on the Origins of the Angevin Dynasty," 1–24.

2. The best edition of the *Gesta Consulum* remains *Chronica de gestis consulum Andegavorum*, in *Chroniques des comtes d'Anjou et des seigneurs d'Amboise*, ed. Louis Halphen and René Poupardin (Paris, 1913), 25–73, and the intro., vii–lvi.

3. For a detailed examination of the genealogical material along with a review of the previous literature see Bachrach, "Origins of the Angevin Dynasty," 1–24.

4. *Gesta Consulum*, 26–29, with the discussion by Bachrach, "Origins of the Angevin Dynasty," 2–7. Cf. Werner, "Untersuchungen," 271, n. 71; and Bouchard, "Origins of the French Nobility," 514–515.

5. *Gesta Consulum*, 26–27; *Cartulaire de Saint-Aubin d'Angers*, no. 285, regarding Limelle; and Bachrach, "Origins of the Angevin Dynasty," 3–7, regarding the methodological question at issue.

6. *Gesta Consulum*, 26–27; and Bachrach, "Origins of the Angevin Dynasty," 3–7.

7. *Gesta Consulum*, 29; and Bachrach, "Origins of the Angevin Dynasty," 19–20, for a discussion of the text's accuracy at this juncture.

8. *Gesta Consulum*, 27–28; Werner, "Untersuchungen," 277–278; and Bachrach, "Origins of the Angevin Dynasty," 16–18.

9. Bachrach, "Origins of the Angevin Dynasty," 14–15.

10. *Gesta Consulum*, 29–30; Emile Bourgeois, *Hugues l'Abbé, margrave de Neustrie et archichapelain de France à le fin du IXe siècle* (Caen, 1885), remains basic; see the discussion by Bachrach, "Origins of the Angevin Dynasty," 10–11.

11. Werner, "Untersuchungen," 269–270.

12. *Gesta Consulum*, 30; and Werner, "Untersuchungen," 272–273.

13. John of Salerno, *Vita S. Odonis*, book 1, chs. 11, 18, 21 (*PL* 133).

14. Charles Lelong, "L'enceinte du Castrum Sancti Martini (Tours)," *Comité des travaux historiques et scientifiques: Section d'archéologie* (Paris, 1971), 43.

15. *Gesta Consulum*, 30, with the methodological observations by Bach-

rach, "Origins of the Angevin Dynasty," 10–12. Cf. Werner, "Untersuchungen," 265–271.

16. *Gesta Consulum*, 33.

17. Werner, "Untersuchungen," 270, 274–275, 279. Cf. Bouchard, "Origins of the French Nobility," 527, n. 78, who does not appear to have understood Werner's compelling and complex argument regarding Roscilla's lineage and thus does "not find it necessary" to accept the conclusion he has drawn from the substantial body of evidence provided. In drawing this conclusion Bouchard gives exceptional weight to an observation by Gerd Tellenbach, "Zu Erforschung des hochmittelalterlichen Adels" (9.–12. Jahrhundert), in *XXIe Congrès internationale des sciences historiques* (Vienna, 1965), 1:326, that not all men named Wido can be proven to have been related. Werner, of course, does not take the position that all men with the same name are related; he made this very clear from a methodological perspective in "Noble Families," 152–153.

18. Werner, "Untersuchungen," 265–271.

19. Werner, "Untersuchungen," 269–270, 274–275. Cf. above, ch. 1, n. 17.

20. *Gesta Consulum*, 33, and the discussion by Werner, "Untersuchungen," 270.

21. Werner, "Untersuchungen," 265–267, 283–284, for the documentary evidence.

22. John of Salerno, *Vita S. Odonis*, book 1, chs. 11, 18, 21 (*PL* 133).

23. Halphen, *Le comté d'Anjou*, 4.

24. Werner, "Untersuchungen," 267–268.

25. Werner, "Untersuchungen," 265–267 and 283–284, for the documentary evidence.

26. Ibid.

27. Walther Vogel, "Die Normannen und das fränkische Reich bis zur Gründung der Normandie (799–911)," *Heidelberger Abhandlungen zur mittleren und neueren Geschichte* 14 (1906): 92, 137, 139, 145, 197, 218, 234, 238–244, 250.

28. Bachrach, "Geoffrey Greymantle," 4, 9–10.

29. Bates, *Normandy before 1066*, 12; Cf. Searle, *Predatory Kinship*, 54–55, and my review of Searle, 609–611.

30. Philip Grierson, "L'origine des comtes d'Amiens, Valois, et Vexin," *Le moyen âge* 49 (1939): 96–97, with genealogy.

31. Flodoard, *Annales*, 78, 99, 113, 116–120, 154; *Cartul. de Saint-Aubin*, nos. 2, 38, with the discussion by Guillot, *Le comte d'Anjou*, 1:3–4; and the overall view of Grierson, "L'origine des comtes," 96–97.

32. Regarding the marriage see Bates, *Normandy before 1066*, 12; and Searle, *Predatory Kinship*, 54–55.

33. Bernard S. Bachrach, "Some Observations on the Origins of Countess Gerberga of the Angevins: An Essay in the Application of the Tellenbach-Werner Prosopographical Method," *Medieval Prosopography* 7, no. 2 (1986): 1–23.

34. Concerning the role of the matrilineage in the appointment of bishops

associated with the Angevin family network, see, for example, Bachrach, "Geoffrey Greymantle," 25–26; Steven Fanning, "Les origines familiales de Vulgrin, abbé de Saint-Serge d'Angers (1046–1056) et évêque du Mans (1056–1065), petit-fils du vicomte Fulcrade de Vendôme," *La Province du Maine* 82 (1980): 246–252; Grierson, "L'origine des comtes," 96–97; and the general discussion by Bachrach, "Origins of Countess Gerberga," 8–9. Obviously, the Angevins were not the only nobles of the Frankish kingdom to follow this pattern.

35. See *Chron. S. Petri Aniciensis*, 152, with the discussion by Bernard S. Bachrach, "The Northern Origins of the Peace Movement at Le Puy in 975," *Historical Reflections/Reflexions Historiques* 14 (1987): 408–413, regarding its value for Guy's activities.

36. Ferdinand Lot, *Les derniers Carolingiens: Lothaire, Louis V, Charles de Lorraine: 954–991* (Paris, 1891), 126–129, 367–368, and the perspective introduced by Bachrach, "The Idea of the Angevin Empire," 296.

37. See the discussion by Werner, "Untersuchungen," 266–269; and Guillot, *Le comte d'Anjou*, 1:8–10. The most complete source for these matters is *Chron. de Nantes*, chs. 37, 38, 42. The redating of this text to the twelfth century or later is questionable in light of the manner of its transmission and survival. What is important is ascertaining the sources the author had available. Cf. Guy Devailly, "L'Eglise médiévale," in Guy-Marie Oury, ed., *Histoire religieuse de la Bretagne* (Paris, 1980), 47. F. Leseur, *Thibaud le Tricheur, comte de Blois, de Tours, et de Chartres* (Blois, 1963), is simply not up to modern scholarly standards.

38. Lot, *Les derniers Carolingiens*, 13, 34; Jacques Boussard, "L'origine des comtés de Tours, Blois, et Chartres," *Actes du 103ᵉ congrès national des Sociétés savantes: 1977* (Paris, 1979), 85–112.

39. See the discussion by Bachrach, "Geoffrey Greymantle," 9–10.

40. Bates, *Normandy before 1066*, 10, 13; and Searle, *Predatory Kinship*, 54–55.

41. Guy-Marie Oury, "La reconstruction monastique dans l'Ouest: L'abbé Gauzbert de Saint-Julien de Tours (v. 990–1007)," *Revue Mabillon* 54 (1964): 70; and René de Lamothe-Dreuzy, "Saint-Florent-le-Vieil des origines à 1500," *Bulletin de l'Académie des sciences et belles-lettres d'Angers*, ser. 9, 2 (1968): 73.

42. For a good example of close relations between Fulk the Good, Theobald, and various important Bretons see Bib. Nat., Coll. Dom Housseau, vol. 2, pt. 1, no. 181.

43. *Chron. de Nantes*, chs. 37, 38. Scholars vigorously disagree concerning the death of Drogo. For example, some like Merlet in his edition of *Chron. de Nantes*, 10, n. 1, consider the murder to be a legend. But Lot, *Derniers Carolingiens*, 347, and Halphen, *Le comté d'Anjou*, 5, lean toward accepting the account of the murder of Drogo. Guillot, *Le comte d'Anjou*, 1:10, n. 5, accepts it. See Bachrach, "Geoffrey Greymantle," 47, n. 35, for various historical parallels.

44. Southern, *The Making of the Middle Ages*, p. 83, discusses Fulk's sobriquet. See, however, Jacques Boussard, "La charte de fondation de Notre-Dame de Loches," *Actes du colloque médiéval de Loches (1973)*, in *Mémoires de la Société archéologique de Touraine* 9 (1975): 8, where he publishes an act in which Geoffrey Greymantle recalls his father's "bitter and fearful deeds."

45. Bur, *Comté de Champagne,* 513, and Bachrach, "Geoffrey Greymantle," 47, n. 36, for the date.

46. *Cartul. de Saint-Aubin,* no. 3.

47. Lot, *Derniers Carolingiens,* 34, 346–357, and the discussion by Bachrach, "Geoffrey Greymantle," 10.

48. Lot, *Derniers Carolingiens,* 81, 127, 367; Marius Balmalle, "Les comtes de Gévaudan et de Brioude," *Almanach de Brioude* (Brioude, 1964), 251–252; Bernard S. Bachrach, "A Study in Feudal Politics: Relations between Fulk Nerra and William the Great, 995–1030," *Viator* 7 (1976): 113; Bachrach, "Northern Origins," 412, which discusses in detail the evidence from the *Chron. S. Petri Aniciensis,* 152, which makes it unambiguously clear that Adelaide had married Stephen. Christian Lauranson-Rosaz, *L'Auvergne et ses marges (Velay, Gévaudan) du VIIIe au XIe siècle* (Le Puy-en-Velay, 1987), 88–90, 93, sees Adelaide first marrying Stephen and then Raymond of Gothia within a chronological framework that is consistent with the argument presented here. Cf. Bouchard, "Origins of the French Nobility," 42, who insists on repeating the long discredited view that Adelaide never married Stephen but married Raymond of Gothia as her first husband.

49. See the material developed by Bachrach, "Origins of Countess Gerberga," 1–23.

50. Werner, "Untersuchungen," 270, develops this naming pattern or custom in detail.

51. Concerning Guy of Anjou see Guy-Marie Oury, "La frère de Geoffrey Grisegonelle: Guy II d'Anjou, moine et évêque du Puy (+ av. 998)," *Actes du colloque médiévale de Loches (1973),* in *Mémoires de la Société archéologique de Touraine* 9 (1975): 61–68, and "La situation juridique des monastères de Cormery et de Villeloin sous l'abbatiat de Guy d'Anjou (v. 964–975)," *Bulletin de la Société archéologique de Touraine* 9 (1975): 551–563; Bachrach, "Northern Origins," 405–421.

52. Bachrach, "Northern Origins," 409–419; and Lauranson-Rosaz, *L'Auvergne,* 87–95, who apparently was not aware of Bachrach, "The Idea of the Angevin Empire," 295–296, and "Geoffrey Greymantle," 20–25.

53. Bachrach, "Geoffrey Greymantle," 3–67, remains the basic work on this important figure; for details on Adele's background see Bur, *Comté de Champagne,* 89, 116, 417, 513.

54. Regarding the size and longevity of Adele's family see Bur, *Comté de Champagne,* 513.

55. See the useful observations on fertility and longevity by Frank Barlow, *William Rufus* (Berkeley, Los Angeles, London, 1983), 8.

56. The genealogical problems in Gerberga's family are worked out by Bachrach, "Origins of Countess Gerberga," 1–23; Hermengarde-Gerberga's double name is established in Bachrach, "Henry II and the Angevin Tradition," 117, n. 35.

57. For the date of Fulk Nerra's birth see the arguments developed by Bernard S. Bachrach, "Fulk Nerra and His Accession as Count of Anjou," in *Saints, Scholars, and Heroes: Studies in Medieval Culture in Honor of Charles W. Jones,* ed. W. Stevens and M. King (Collegeville, Minn., 1979), 2, 331–342.

58. *Archives d'Anjou,* ed. Marchegay, 2:60.

59. Listed below are the few surviving documents in which Geoffrey Greymantle played a juridical role during the first decade of his reign: Robert Latouche, *Histoire du comté du Maine pendant le Xe et le XIe siècles* (Paris, 1910), *p.j.* 1; *Cartul. de Saint-Aubin,* nos. 2, 18, 21, 38, 224; *Gallia Christ.,* vol. 14, cols. 60–62; *Cartul. de Saint-Maurice,* nos. 18, 21; and "Fragments de chartes . . . Saint-Julien de Tours," ed. Grandmaison, no. 21.

60. Bachrach, "Geoffrey Greymantle," 3–67.

61. For the basic work on Guy see ch. 1, n. 51, above. Guy did, however, become a monk in the early 960s (*Cartul. de Saint-Aubin,* no. 38), which illustrates his inclination for the spiritual life.

62. It is, of course, possible that Adele was frequently pregnant during this period and could even have given birth to several children, who died very young, but no record of such events has survived.

63. The chronology for the births of Fulk and his younger brother Geoffrey is discussed in detail by Bachrach, "Fulk Nerra and His Accession," 334–335.

64. For a discussion of the date of young Geoffrey's birth see Bernard S. Bachrach, "The Family of Viscount Fulcoius of Angers: Some Methodological Observations at the Nexus of Prosopography and Diplomatics," *Medieval Prosopography* 4, no. 1 (1983): 3–4. Cf. the discussion by Guillot, *Le comte d'Anjou,* 2:22, and Halphen, *Le comté d'Anjou,* 244.

65. The estimation of Adele's age is based on data provided by Bur, *Comté de Champagne,* 513.

66. Werner, "Untersuchungen," 277, regarding naming patterns and their relation to office holding.

67. See above, ch. 1, n. 61.

68. Georges Duby, *Medieval Marriage: Two Models from Twelfth-century France,* trans. Elborg Forster (Baltimore, 1978), 25–81, provides some interesting insights on divorce. The title of the work, however, is misleading since much of the key data is developed from tenth- and eleventh-century cases. The well-known effort of King Lothair II to divorce his wife because she produced no heir is treated by Suzanne Wemple, *Women in Frankish Society: Marriage and the Cloister, 500–900* (Philadelphia, 1981), 84–87.

69. Arthur le Moyne de La Borderie, *Histoire de Bretagne* (Rennes-Paris, 1898), 2:423; *Cartul. de Saint-Aubin,* no. 906; and the discussion by Bachrach, "Geoffrey Greymantle," 11.

70. See below, ch. 2, n. 123.

71. Jean-Louis Flandrin, *Families in Former Times: Kinship, Household, and Sexuality,* trans. R. Southern (Cambridge, 1978), 198–203, who argues on the basis of demographic evidence that breastfeeding is a useful means of contraception. According to a story recounted in *Historia Sancti Florentii,* 260, Fulk Nerra's son Geoffrey Martel was nursed by a blacksmith's wife.

72. *Cartul. de Saint-Aubin,* no. 3, and Halphen, *Le comté d'Anjou,* 244, who establishes the date.

73. *Cartul. de Saint-Aubin,* no. 3, actually embodies two acts. The first concerns a fragment of Adele's testament bequeathing various holdings to the monastery of Saint-Aubin. This initial act was confirmed by Geoffrey Greyman-

tle and his two sons, Fulk Nerra and Geoffrey, and dealt with aspects of Adele's *dotalitium*. Cf. Guillot, *Le comte d'Anjou*, 2:21–22.

74. See below regarding the conflict of Hermengarde-Gerberga's husband, Conan, with Geoffrey Greymantle, her father.

75. C. Easton, *Les hivers dans l'Europe occidentale* (Leiden, 1928), 44–45. A general weather pattern extends from the northern Rhine region west and south into the Loire valley and across the Channel to much of southern England.

76. *Cartul. de Saint-Aubin*, no. 3, pt. 2; Cf. Halphen, *Le comté d'Anjou*, 244; and Guillot, *Le comte d'Anjou*, 2:20–23.

77. Yvonne Mailfert, "Fondation du monastère bénédictin de Saint-Nicholas d'Angers, *Bibliothèque d'Ecole de Chartes* 92 (1931): *p.j.* 4.

78. C. Tennant et al., "Parental Death in Childhood and Risk of Adult Depressive Disorders: A Review," *Psychological Medicine* 10 (1980): 289–299.

79. Mary McLaughlin, "Survivors and Surrogates: Children and Parents from the Ninth to the Thirteenth Century," *The History of Childhood*, ed. Lloyd de Mause (New York, 1974), 105, 108, 127–128, 168 (nn. 158, 162).

80. Lot, *Derniers Carolingiens*, 81–82, and *Chron. S. Petri Aniciensis*, 152–153, where Bishop Guy is characterized as an advisor to King Lothair. The king is reputed to have made clear to Guy that he expected him to be a most faithful administrator (*fidelissimus procurator*) for him as well as for his flock. Guy is identified "cui erat frater germanus noblissimus comes Gaufridus, cognomento Grisagonella." For a discussion of these events and the viability of the source see Bachrach, "Northern Origins," 408–410.

81. Bachrach, "The Family of Viscount Fulcoius," 3–4, for the establishment of the date of young Geoffrey's death.

82. For Fulk at Orléans with Geoffrey in 975 see *Hist. Fr.*, 9:733, as dated by Guillot, *Le comte d'Anjou*, 2:21; Fulk at Angers with his father in September 976 see *Cartul. de Saint-Aubin*, no. 34, it is discussed by Bachrach, "Enforcement of the *Forma Fidelitatis*," 802, n. 27; Fulk with Geoffrey at Besse in Anjou during January 978 and at Tours between 978 and 980 as seen in "Fragments de Chartes . . . Saint-Julien de Tours," nos. 23, 27, respectively, along with Bachrach, "Fulk Nerra and His Accession," 339, n. 19, for the identification of Fulk's participation in the latter act. See also for Fulk's role in the restoration of Saint-Serge, Bachrach, "The Family of Viscount Fulcoius," 4, and Boussard, "La charte de fondation de Notre-Dame de Loches," 7–9, for Fulk's participation in the restoration of Notre-Dame de Loches.

83. Bachrach, "Geoffrey Greymantle," 20.

84. McLaughlin, "Survivors and Surrogates," 103–105; Wemple, *Women in Frankish Society*, 59–60, 103; Jerome Kroll and Bernard S. Bachrach, "Child Care and Child Abuse in Early Medieval Europe," *Journal of the American Academy of Child Psychiatry* 25 (1986): 562–568; and Herlihy, "Family," 1–8.

85. R. H. C. Davis, "William of Poitiers and His History of William the Conqueror," in *The Writing of History in the Middle Ages: Essays Presented to Richard William Southern*, ed. R. H. C. Davis and J. M. Wallace-Hadrill (Oxford, 1981), 84.

86. Barlow, *William Rufus*, 19.

87. Tennant et al., "Parental Death in Childhood," 289–299.

88. "Fragments de Chartes . . . Saint-Julien de Tours," nos. 23, 27; *Cartul. de Saint-Aubin,* no. 3; and the discussion of these sources noted above in ch. 1, n. 82.

89. See above, ch. 1, n. 82, for various examples.

90. *Chartes de Cluny,* nos. 1474, 1701, 2484; *Cartul. du prieuré de Saint-Marcel-lès-Chalon,* no. 6. See also Boussard, "La charte de fondation de Notre-Dame de Loches," 1–10; Lot, *Derniers Carolingiens,* 328–329; and Bachrach, "Geoffrey Greymantle," 20–21.

91. Saint Maurice was one of the patron saints of the cathedral church of Angers and he also was the patron saint of the cathedral of Brioude. The latter region was in close contact with the Gévaudan, Forez, and Le Puy where the Angevins already were well positioned. In addition, young Maurice was not given a name traditionally associated with the man who would succeed as count of the Angevins.

92. *Chartes de Cluny,* no. 1537 (30 November 980); Hugh is not yet a cleric. In *Cartulaire du prieuré de Saint-Marcel-lès-Chalon,* no. 6, in which Hugh appears with Count Geoffrey, the youth is already designated as a cleric. The chronology concerning Geoffrey's activities is provided by Boussard, "La charte de fondation de Notre-Dame de Loches," 8. In dating Hugh's removal from the succession and his apparent replacement by an Angevin it is important to remember that King Lothair had demonstrated both in 957 and in 978–979, when Geoffrey Greymantle married Adele and ruled the county, that the king had a role to play in legitimizing the succession. Thus, it seems clear that some type of royal authority would have been exercised to support Geoffrey's plan to have Maurice recognized as heir in place of Hugh. For the chronology regarding the succession see Bachrach, "Geoffrey Greymantle," 59, n. 98, with the literature cited there.

93. Fulk's relations with Maurice are traced in Bernard S. Bachrach, "King Henry II and Angevin Claims to the Saintonge," *Medieval Prosopography* 6, no. 1 (1985): 23–45.

94. For Fulk's absence from Geoffrey Greymantle's entourage while the latter was in the east see *Chartes de Cluny,* nos. 1417, 1701, 2484; and *Cartul. du prieuré de Saint-Marcel-lès-Chalon,* no. 6.

95. Boussard, "La charte de fondation de Notre-Dame de Loches," 7–9.

96. *Chron. de Nantes,* ch. 45; La Borderie, *Histoire de Bretagne,* 2:423; with the discussion by Bachrach, "Geoffrey Greymantle," 11.

97. Boussard, "Origine des comtés," 98–104; Lamothe-Dreuzy, "Saint-Florent-le-Vieil," 69–77; and the general discussion by Bachrach, "Geoffrey Greymantle," 29–31.

98. *Chron. de Nantes,* ch. 40; Halphen, *Le comté,* 6; Bachrach, "Geoffrey Greymantle," 12–13.

99. Richard, *Comtes de Poitou,* 1:102, n. 3; Lot, *Derniers Carolingiens,* 347; Oury, "La reconstruction monastique," 69–124, outlining the family cooperation; and Bachrach, "Geoffrey Greymantle," 12–13.

100. See the discussion by Halphen, *Le comté d'Anjou,* 6.

101. Lot, *Derniers Carolingiens,* 81, 127, 367; Balmalle, "Les comtes de

Gévaudan et Brioude," 251–252; Bachrach, "The Idea of the Angevin Empire," 296–297; and cf. Lauranson-Rosaz, *L'Auvergne,* 87–95.

102. Bachrach, "Geoffrey Greymantle," 28–33.

103. Lot, *Hugues Capet,* 229; *V. Domini Burcardi,* intro. p. xii; Guillot, *Le comte d'Anjou,* 1:21–22.

104. *Livre des serfs de Marmoutier,* no. 1; Halphen, *Le comté d'Anjou,* 62; and concerning the association Bachrach, "Fulk Nerra and His Accession," 331–342.

105. *Cartul. de Saint-Aubin,* no. 2, with the discussion by Bachrach, "Geoffrey Greymantle," 48, n. 39. The details of Bouchard's relations with Hugh Capet and Geoffrey Greymantle's relations with both men see Bachrach, "Geoffrey Greymantle," 27–28.

106. Boussard, "La charte de fondation de Notre-Dame de Loches," 7–9, publishes this act in which Geoffrey Greymantle sets out his estimation of the importance of his *milites.* For a discussion of this text and of the meaning of *generositas* in this context see Bachrach, "Geoffrey Greymantle," 38–39.

107. Concerning continuity between Geoffrey's fideles and those of his son see "Fragments de Chartes . . . Saint-Julien de Tours," no. 27; *Livre des serfs de Marmoutier,* no. 1; *Archives d'Anjou,* ed. Marchegay, 60; *Cartul. de Saint-Maurice,* nos. 22, 27; Bib. Nat., ms. lat. 17127, 157–159; and for an analysis of the names see Bachrach, "Fulk Nerra and His Accession," 340–342.

108. Historians' use of a diplomatic instrument, especially the *prooemium* or *arenga,* for the purpose of identifying one or another particular personal concern of the dominant participant, especially emotional sentiment and intellectual preference, raises several methodological questions requiring attention. In many places in Western Europe throughout the greater part of the Middle Ages diplomatic instruments were highly formulaic in structure and content. Often these formulae endured for decades if not generations and were a sort of template available in the writing office of the institution generating the document. Thus, in general, no particular connection can be assumed regarding the specific feelings or beliefs of the dominant participant in a particular act and the sentiments or beliefs set forth in formulaic parts of the *acta.* There are, however, at least two specific situations in which this generalization cannot be sustained even in the most formulaic milieu. First, we can assume that the overall thrust of the sentiments expressed in the formulae are not sharply in conflict with the dominant figure's views or, perhaps more accurately, not markedly hostile to the manner in which such a person wanted his views to be seen by those who read or heard the document. Second, when a particular formula is significantly altered, it surely is not methodologically unsound for the historian to draw the inference that those men in a decision-making capacity either had reevaluated the nature of their sentiments or that they wished their audience to believe that a noteworthy change had taken place in their thinking regarding the matter provided in the formula.

The *acta* of the Angevin counts, unlike much of the stylized documentation generated in medieval Europe, as well as many of the noncomital *acta* produced in the Angevin state during the period under consideration here and in some cases for several generations thereafter, should be considered idiosyncratic. This is especially the case for Angevin *acta* in comparison with the norms discussed above. Geoffrey Greymantle and Fulk Nerra did not employ repetitive formulae to express personal sentiments in their *acta* and this was so whether the scribes who wrote the documents were attached to the comital court or employed by the beneficiaries.

In addition to the absence of repetitive formulaic structures, the idiosyncratic nature of the Angevin comital *acta* is evidenced by "sentiments" expressed in stylistically unique locutions fundamentally consistent with the particular content of the diplomatic instrument in which they are found. This is not to say that the ideas or sentiments put forth in these *acta* are themselves unique. I do not argue here that Fulk Nerra and those around him were original thinkers or for that matter that they experienced unique sentiments. But from what the reader has seen of Geoffrey Greymantle's behavior thus far and from what will be seen of Fulk's behavior, it is unthinkable that scribes could attribute even marginally displeasing personal views to either count. In this context, decades after Fulk's reign some and perhaps even many of the ideas and sentiments he is found to express in his *acta* were incorporated into formulaic language and employed in diplomatic instruments in the Angevin state. Chronology here is exceptionally important, however, and anyone who might wish to argue that Geoffrey's and Fulk's sentiments are merely diplomatic commonplaces must document these putative formulae as repetitive in prior Angevin *acta*.

A useful introduction to the basic ideas and literature regarding the formulaic aspects of medieval diplomatic instruments is Leonard E. Boyle, "Diplomatics," in *Medieval Studies: An Introduction,* ed. James M. Powell (Syracuse, 1976), 69–101. There has been no general study of the diplomatic aspects of the comital *acta* of Geoffrey Greymantle and Fulk Nerra. But Guillot, *Le comte d'Anjou,* 2:1–65, provides a substantial corpus of information and much learned discussion regarding many of the *acta* under consideration here. The overarching and influential generalizations by Fredric Cheyette, "The Invention of the State," *Essays in Medieval Civilization: The Walter Prescott Webb Memorial Lectures,* ed. B. K. Lackner and K. R. Phillip (Austin, 1979), 153, that the terms used by scribes "may have corresponded only distantly to actual relations" and his skepticism regarding the relation between diplomatic *acta* and "accepted patterns of social life" (p. 156) are given far too much weight in relation to the research base that he provides. See, for example, White, *Custom, Kinship, and Gifts,* 3, 41–42, 253.

There is no good reason to believe that men like Geoffrey Greymantle and Fulk Nerra were any less aware of the world around them or understood their situations less well than the major decision makers in the Roman world, the Early Middle Ages, or the twelfth century. See, for example, Walter Goffart, *The Narrators of Barbarian History (A.D. 550–800): Jordanes, Gregory of Tours, Bede, and Paul the Deacon* (Princeton, 1988), who presses this theme in regard to the so-called barbarian historians; see my review article in *Francia,* 17, no. 1 (1990): 250–256.

A second question may be raised regarding the use of these documents in the manner discussed above, and this question arises from the fact that many of these documents are not originals but rather copies made during the subsequent seven or so centuries (see Guillot, *Le comte d'Anjou,* vol. 2, nos. 1–77). Thus, it is possible that from time to time one or another copyist altered the text before him, either intentionally or unintentionally, and therefore the surviving document does not reflect the terminology originally used. Nonetheless, it is unsound from a methodological perspective to assert that a document is corrupt at any particular point simply because it survives only in a copy. The burden of proof that a copy of a document is corrupt at a particular point rests with the person who asserts that there is a corruption.

Two additional methodological points require clarification. First, if one particular aspect of a copy can be shown to be corrupt, such demonstration does not prove that the copy as a whole is corrupt, nor does it prove that any other particular part of the document is corrupt. Second, one cannot legitimately argue that, for example, a particular part of a copy is anachronistic simply because it can be shown that at a date subsequent to the issue of the original, one or another particular terminology became common. The person who would argue in such a case for an anachronism in the copy as proof of corruption is in the difficult, though not impossible, position of demonstrating a negative, that is, that such a usage was unknown during the period in which the original was generated.

109. Guillot, *Le comte d'Anjou,* 2:12–20, discusses this matter from a diplomatic point of view. The conclusion is inescapable that those who agreed to witness or to support an act had to know what was said in it. Of course, it would be imprudent to assume that everyone involved understood Latin; therefore it is necessary to conclude that much was done orally in the vernacular. For a good example of Angevin court practice with regard to assuring that the content of *acta* were widely known, but using Latin, see *Cartul. du Ronceray,* no. 6. See also W. Mary Hackett, "Aspects de la langue vulgaire du Poitou d'après un document latin du onzième siècle," *Mélanges offerts à Rita Lejune* (Gembloux, 1969), 1:13–32; for the background, Rosamund McKitterick, *The Carolingians and the Written Word* (Cambridge, 1989), 1–22, with my review of the latter in *Journal of Interdisciplinary History* 21 (1990): 321–323.

110. *Cartul. de Cormery,* no. 47; "Fragments de chartes . . . Saint-Julien de Tours," no. 26; Boussard, "La charte de fondation de Notre-Dame de Loches," 8; *Cartul. de Saint-Aubin,* nos. 2, 21, 22, 222, 281, and 821 for the quotation. Note in light of n. 108, all of these sentiments are not expressed in every act, and the content of the act is in consonance with the sentiment expressed. As observed at n. 59, Geoffrey does not mention his wife, and this is another example of his idiosyncracy.

111. *Cartul. de Saint-Aubin,* nos. 2, 21, 22.

112. Bachrach, "The Angevin Economy," 11–12, with the literature cited there.

113. When the monks of Saint-Aubin drew up their cartulary toward the end of the eleventh century, they incorporated the election charters issued by Geoffrey Greymantle and Fulk Nerra but defaced them in an effort to obliterate evidence for comital control. See the discussion by Guillot, *Le comte d'Anjou,* 1:149–151, regarding the background.

114. *Cartul. de Saint-Maurice*, no. 25; Richard Hogan, "The *Rainaldi* of Angers: 'New Men' of Descendants of Carolingian *Nobiles?*" *Medieval Proso-pography* 2, no. 1 (1981): 32–62, for the background; and Bachrach, "Geoffrey Greymantle," 10–11.

115. Boussard, "La charte de fondation de Notre-Dame de Loches," 7–9.

116. Ibid., 8–9; and the discussion by Bachrach, "Geoffrey Greymantle," 38–39. For the background see Joseph Lynch, *Simoniacal Entry into Religious Life from 1000 to 1260: A Social Economic and Legal Study* (Columbus, Ohio, 1976).

117. *Cartul. de Saint-Aubin*, no. 21. In this act, as with most texts that detail Viking destruction, there is a tendency to exaggerate. Here this tendency is compounded because Geoffrey takes credit for the postinvasion pacification and rebuilding of fortifications which he carried out and which the king, dukes, and princes had not been able to hold. Thus, Geoffrey legitimizes his independent military action while at the same time making clear that the erstwhile authorities had lost their legitimacy by failing to fulfill their duty to provide for the common defense.

118. Boussard, "La charte de fondation de Notre-Dame de Loches," 7–9, with regard to fortifications; Bachrach, "The Angevin Economy," 29–31, regarding economic development.

119. *Cartul. de Saint-Aubin*, no. 21.

120. The association of Fulk in the comital title is established in Bachrach, "Fulk Nerra and His Accession," 331–342.

121. The idea of the importance of books as an aid to successful government is well developed by Alexander Murray, *Reason and Society in the Middle Ages* (rev. ed., Oxford, 1985); see p. 124 for the quotation. See also Bachrach, "The Practical Use of Vegetius' *De re militari*," 239–255, where this idea is pursued in relation to Fulk Nerra.

122. Notker, *Gesta Karoli*, book 1, ch. 3.

123. "Piété de Foulque le Bon," in *Chroniques des comtes d'Anjou et des seigneurs d'Amboise*, ed. Louis Halphen and René Poupardin (Paris, 1913), 140; for a lively discussion see V. H. Galbraith, "The Literacy of the English Medieval Kings," *Proceedings of the British Academy* 21 (1935): 201–238; Southern, *The Making of the Middle Ages*, 83.

124. Michael Clanchy, *From Memory to Written Record: England, 1066–1377* (Cambridge, 1977), 177–181.

125. "Piété de Foulque le Bon," 140, with the discussion by Southern, *The Making of the Middle Ages*, 83.

126. *Historia Gaufredi ducis Normannorum et comitis Andegavorum*, in *Chroniques des comtes d'Anjou et des seigneurs d'Amboise*, ed. Louis Halphen and René Poupardin (Paris, 1913), 218. See the observations by Murray, *Reason and Society*, 129, and the discussion by Bachrach, "The Practical Use of Vegetius' *De re militari*," 242–245.

127. *Cartul. du Ronceray*, no. 64.

128. Fulk le Réchin, *Fragmentum historiae Andegavensis*, in *Chroniques des comtes d'Anjou et des seigneurs d'Amboise*, ed. Louis Halphen and René Poupar-

din (Paris, 1913), 232–238; the discussion by Louis Halphen, "Etude sur l'authenticité du fragment de chronique attribué à Foulque le Réchin," *Bibliothèque de la faculté des lettres de Paris* 13 (1901): 7–48.

129. Flodoard, *Annales,* 78, 99, 113, 118–120, 188, 211, 217.

130. *Chron. S. Petri Aniciensis,* 152; and *Cartul. de Saint-Aubin,* no. 23, with the discussion by Bachrach, "Northern Origins," 406.

131. Boussard, "La charte de fondation de Notre-Dame de Loches," 8, with the methodological discussion in ch. 1, nn. 108, 109, above.

132. "Documents inédits . . . Sainte-Croix de Poitiers," ed. Monsabert, no. 1.

133. Boussard, "La charte de fondation de Notre-Dame de Loches," 9.

134. Adémar of Chabannes, *Chron.,* book 3, ch. 55, with the discussion by Bachrach, "Potius Rex," 11–21.

135. Helgaud de Fleury, *Vie de Robert le Pieux,* 61, and the discussion by Joel T. Rosenthal, "The Education of the Early Capetians," *Traditio* 25 (1969): 370–371.

136. Pierre Riché, *Ecoles et enseignement dans le haut moyen âge de la fin du Ve siècle au milieu du XIe siècle* (Paris, 1979), 128–131, 287–313.

137. See the discussion by Barlow, *William Rufus,* 14–15.

138. *Gesta Consulum,* 47.

139. Tennant et al., "Parental Death in Childhood," 289–299, for a review of the relevant literature.

140. Isidorus, *Etymologiae,* book 11, ch. 2.

141. Rhabanus Maurus, *De procinctu Romanae militae,* 252–254; for a discussion of the continued currency of the proverb see Rosenthal, "The Education of the Early Capetians," 373.

142. Barlow, *William Rufus,* 22–23.

143. Regarding the general use of hit-and-run tactics see Bachrach, "The Practical Use of Vegetius' *De re militari,*" 247. As specialists in military history generally recognize, the use of hit-and-run tactics is less noteworthy from the point of view of complexity than is the use of a prepositioned reserve. For Fulk's use of the reserve in 992 see Richer, *Hist.,* book 4, ch. 85, i.e., the "posterior exercitus" as compared with the "prior exercitus."

144. Regarding the foundation of the cathedral school at Angers and Fulk's use of various *magistri* see Fanning, *A Bishop and His World,* 69–72, and Bachrach, "The Practical Use of Vegetius' *De re militari,*" 252–253.

145. See, for example, Mailfert, "Fondation du monastère . . . Saint-Nicholas d'Angers," *p.j.* 4.

146. Fulk le Réchin, *Fragmentum historiae Andegavensis,* 233.

147. Murray, *Reason and Society,* 125–127, examines the vernacular culture and makes clear that although the earliest surviving manuscript of *The Song of Roland* dates to the beginning of the twelfth century, the naming phenomenon discussed here goes back almost a century earlier.

148. For a discussion of the methodological complexities involved in discussing personality and persona see Bachrach, "The Enforcement of *Forma Fidelitatis,*" 814–818, with the literature cited there.

149. Fulbert of Chartres, *Epist.*, nos. 13, 72, 104, 109; Bernard S. Bachrach, "Pope Sergius IV and the Foundation of the Monastery at Beaulieu-lès-Loches," *Revue Bénédictine* 95 (1985): 245–247.

150. Bachrach, "Pope Sergius IV," 245–247.

151. See the list of Fulk's *acta* in Guillot, *Le comte d'Anjou*, 2:21–66.

152. Einhard, *Vita Karoli*, ch. 25.

153. Barlow, *William Rufus*, 15–16.

154. See ch. 1, n. 109 above, esp. *Cartul. du Ronceray*, no. 6.

155. See the discussion of this maxim by Bachrach, "The Practical Use of Vegetius' *De re militari*," 252.

156. See below, ch. 4, p. 92.

157. See, for example, Georges Duby, "Youth in Aristocractic Society: Northwestern France in the Twelfth Century," *The Chivalrous Society*, trans. C. Postan (Berkeley, Los Angeles, London, 1980), 112–122.

158. For a preliminary discussion of this matter see Bachrach, "The Enforcement of *Forma Fidelitatis*," 817–818.

159. Concerning the association of depression with a black mood see Stanley W. Jackson, *Melancholia and Depression from Hippocratic Times to Modern Times* (New Haven, Conn., 1986), 7–11, 42–43, 46–77. In addition, Tennant et al., "Parental Death in Childhood," 289–299, indicates that there is some noteworthy association between early family losses and a risk for depressive illness.

160. This matter of sobriquets is discussed by Halphen, *Le comté d'Anjou*, 209–212.

161. *Archives d'Anjou*, 1:60; Bachrach, "Pope Sergius IV," 245, with the methodological discussion in ch. 1, n. 108, above, concerning the use of the former.

162. *Cartul. de Saint-Maurice*, no. 27.

163. *Cartul. du Ronceray*, no. 4.

164. Bernard S. Bachrach, "The Pilgrimages of Fulk Nerra, Count of the Angevins, 987–1040," in *Religion, Culture, and Society in the Early Middle Ages* (Kalamazoo, Mich., 1987), 205–217, where each pilgrimage is examined and dated.

165. Bachrach, "Pope Sergius IV," 245, for the reconstruction of the text of the letter.

166. This is examined in a preliminary manner in Bachrach, "The Enforcement of *Forma Fidelitatis*," 816–818. But it is not clear whether Fulk's natural inclinations melded with a long-term imperial notion of the ferocity of the ruler. See, for example, *In laudem Iustini Augusti minoris, libri IV*, ed. and trans. with commentary by Avril Cameron (London, 1976), book 4, l. 5ff. and 250.

167. See the discussion by Bachrach, "The Practical Use of Vegetius' *De re militari*," 251–252.

168. Bachrach, "Pope Sergius IV," 245.

169. See the discussion by Bachrach, "Geoffrey Greymantle," 38–39.

170. See the letter published by Bachrach, "Pope Sergius IV," 245–246.

171. Bib. Nat., Coll. Dom Housseau, vol. 2, pt. 1, no. 407.

172. See, for example, Ferdinand Lot, "Geoffroi Grisegonelle dans l'épo-

pée," and "Traditions sur Geoffroi Grisegonelle et sur Helgaud de Montreuil," *Romania* 19 (1890): 377–393 and 46 (1920): 376–381; for additional literature see Bachrach, "Geoffrey Greymantle," 40, n. 1.

Chapter 2: The Struggle for Survival

1. When I first decided to title this chapter "The Struggle for Survival," I was aware that David Douglas, *William the Conqueror* (Berkeley and Los Angeles, 1964), ch. 3, had labeled the period of William the Conqueror's life from 1047 to 1060 "The War for Survival." When I found that John Baldwin, *The Government of Philip Augustus: Foundations of French Royal Power in the Middle Ages* (Berkeley, Los Angeles, London, 1986), entitled chapter 1 "The Struggle for Survival," I began to wonder if there was some basic relationship between a difficult early reign and great success thereafter. In this context, of course, the reign of Louis XIV comes readily to mind.

2. *Gesta Consulum,* 47, and the discussion by Bernard S. Bachrach, "Robert of Blois, Abbot of Saint-Florent de Saumur and Saint-Mesmim-de-Micy (985–1011)," *Revue Bénédictine* 88 (1978): 126, n. 1.

3. For Odo see the still useful older works by Josef Landsberger, *Graf Odo I. von der Champagne (Odo II. v. Blois, Tours u. Chartres), 995–1039* (Berlin, 1878), 1–16, and Léonce Lex, "Eudes, comte de Blois, de Tours, de Chartres, de Troyes, et de Meaux (995–1036) et Thibaud, son frère (995–1004)," *Mémoires de la Société des sciences et lettres du Loir-et-Cher* (1891), 192–283, who provide considerable background material throughout. See also the more recent work by Bur, *Comté de Champagne,* 114–116, 121–123, 167–168, and *passim.*

4. Bachrach, "Geoffrey Greymantle," 18–20.

5. Halphen, *Le comté d'Anjou,* 6–7.

6. Bates, *Normandy before 1066,* 25.

7. Lot, *Derniers Carolingiens,* 210–215, 226 (n. 3), 270–271.

8. Richard, *Comtes de Poitou,* 1:143, 149.

9. Bachrach, "Study in Feudal Politics," 112–113.

10. Oury, "Le frère de Geoffroy Grisegonelle," 68.

11. *Chron. de Nantes,* ch. 43, p. 114 (n. 3), 126.

12. Bachrach, "Abbot Robert," 126.

13. *Hist. S. Florentii,* 275.

14. Bib. Nat., n. a. lat. 1930 = *Livre noir,* fol. 116r; along with the discussion of the text by Bachrach, "Abbot Robert," 126.

15. Archives de Maine-et-Loire, H. 2191, and the discussion by Bachrach, "Abbot Robert," 128.

16. *Cartul. de Saint-Aubin,* no. 23, and Bachrach, "The Angevin Economy," 5–13, regarding taxation. Cf. Guillot, *Le comte d'Anjou,* 1:444–455.

17. Abbo of Fleury, *Epist.,* no. 1, where the abbot speaks of Fulk's exploitation of the resources of Ferrières, which the Angevin count granted as beneficia to his vassali. Fulk and Abbo were in fact personally acquainted and in this

letter Abbo makes clear that the Angevin count had given him a *mandatum* to act for him with Pope Gregory V. Concerning the use of the *mandatum* by the Angevin counts in the sense that was intended by Roman law see Olivier Guillot, "La droit romain classique et la lexicographie de termes du latin médiéval impliquant délégation de pouvoir," *La lexicographie du latin médiéval et ses rapports avec les recherches actuelles sur la civilisation du moyen-âge: Paris 1978* (Paris, 1981), 153–166, with the additions provided by Bachrach, "Neo-Roman vs. Feudal," 26, n. 60.

18. Regarding Bishop Renaud see Bib. Nat. n. a. lat. 1930, *Livre noir*, fols. 23v–24v; Archives de Maine-et-Loire, H. 2191, as discussed by Bachrach, "Robert of Blois," 128 (nn. 1, 2) and 130 (n. 1).

19. Bachrach, "Study in Feudal Politics," 12–15.

20. Lot, *Derniers Carolingiens*, 328–329.

21. Horst Zettel, *Das Bild der Normannen und der Normanneneinfälle in westfränkischen, ostfränkischen und angelsächischen Quellen des 8. bis. 11 Jahrhunderts* (Munich, 1977), 230.

22. The ability to obtain titles and resources through the female line should not be underestimated. In chapter 1, for example, we have seen how Fulk the Good and Geoffrey Greymantle gained control of Nantes and Chalon, respectively, through their wives.

23. Bachrach, "The Idea of the Angevin Empire," 293–298.

24. *Chartes de Cluny*, no. 1728; and the discussion by Bachrach, "Henry II and the Angevin Tradition," 116–117.

25. Concerning the situation see Bachrach, "Henry II and the Angevin Tradition," 117, n. 33, and Lauranson-Rosaz, *L'Auvergne*, 87–98, 412–432; cf. Constance Bouchard, *Sword, Miter, and Cloister: Nobility and the Church in Burgundy, 980–1198* (Ithaca, N.Y., 1987), 309, n. 22, who tries to account for Maurice's use of the comital title and conjures up the unsupported notion that *comes* was "the ordinary title for a dead count's son," whether he was intended to inherit the *comté* or not. In addition, she is incorrect in asserting that Maurice is styled *comes* in only one act from Chalon.

26. Bachrach, "Geoffrey Greymantle," 23–25.

27. Bachrach, "Study in Feudal Politics," 14–15.

28. Oury, "Le frère de Geoffrey Grisegonelle," 65–66.

29. Bachrach, "Northern Origins," 405–429, for a discussion of the development of "Angevin" military capability in the region.

30. Bib. Nat., n. a. lat. 1930, *Livre noir*, fols. 23v–24v, with the discussion by Bachrach, "Abbot Robert," 130, n. 1.

31. Bib. Nat., n. a. lat. 1930, *Livre noir*, fols. 28r, 28v, and 116r, with the discussion by Bachrach, "Abbot Robert," 129–130.

32. Jacques Boussard, "Le trésorier de Saint-Martin de Tours," *Revue d'histoire de l'Eglise de France* 47 (1961): 61–68; and Bachrach, "Abbot Robert," 129, n. 2, for a detailed discussion with additional bibliography.

33. *Cartul. de Saint-Aubin*, no. 18; O. Desmaizières, *Essai d'inventaire des camps* (Le Mans, 1911), 26–27; Halphen, *Le comté d'Anjou*, 99, n. 1; and *Chron. de Nantes*, ch. 41, with the discussion by Bachrach, "Abbot Robert," 127.

34. *Cartul. de Saint-Aubin,* no. 23, with the discussion of the evidence by Bachrach, "Henry II and the Angevin Tradition," 117, n. 34.

35. *Cartul. de Saint-Aubin,* no. 23; and for the reservation of major crimes nos. 2, 22, 24, 26.

36. Bachrach, "Angevin Economy," 11–12.

37. *Cartul. de Saint-Aubin,* no. 23; cf. Guillot, *Le comte d'Anjou,* 1:444–455.

38. The *acta* are listed and discussed by Bachrach, "Fulk Nerra and His Accession," 341; and Bib. Nat., ms. lat. 5441, 1:391, for the earliest of this group of texts.

39. Bachrach, "The Enforcement of *Forma Fidelitatis,*" 799–802, for these men.

40. For the association, see Bachrach, "Fulk Nerra and His Accession," 331–342.

41. Bachrach, "The Angevin Strategy of Castle Building," 543–544.

42. Bib. Nat., n. a. lat. 1930, *Livre noir,* fols. 26v, 28r–v; and for the latter Halphen, *Le comté d'Anjou, p.j.* 2.

43. See the discussion by Bachrach, "The Angevin Economy," 8–10.

44. Bib. Nat., n. a. lat. 1930, *Livre noir,* fol. 116r; and the discussion by Bachrach, "Abbot Robert," 126–127.

45. *Cartul. de Saint-Aubin,* no. 85, with the discussion of the document by Bernard S. Bachrach, "Fulk Nerra's Exploitation of the *facultates monarchorum,* ca. 1000," in *Law, Custom, and the Social Fabric in Medieval Europe: Essays in Honor of Bryce Lyon,* ed. Bernard S. Bachrach and David M. Nicholas (Kalamazoo, Mich., 1990), 38–39.

46. Bachrach, "The Angevin Strategy of Castle Building," 543–544.

47. *Cartul. de Saint-Aubin,* no. 85.

48. Ibid.

49. Ibid.

50. Ibid.

51. Bachrach, "Fulk Nerra's Exploitation," 29–49, where the argument is made that the evidence provided by Letaltus in *Mirac. S. Martini,* ch. 7, applies to Fulk's government.

52. All of the available information regarding the Bouchard family is to be found in Bachrach, "Geoffrey Greymantle," 43–44, n. 18.

53. Bib. Nat., n. a. lat. 1930, *Livre noir,* fols. 116r–v; *Gesta Consulum,* 48; with the discussion of the texts by Bachrach, "Robert of Blois," 138–140.

54. Bachrach, "The Angevin Economy," 8–10.

55. Bernard S. Bachrach, "Angevin Campaign Forces in the Reign of Fulk Nerra, Count of the Angevins (987–1040)," *Francia* 16, no. 1 (1989): 67–84.

56. Richer, *Hist.,* book 4, ch. 79, with the discussion by Bachrach, "Angevin Campaign Forces," 73–75.

57. This text is discussed by Bachrach, "The Practical Use of Vegetius' *De re militari,*" 252–254.

58. Concerning the activities of Odo's men see *Gesta Ambaz. dominorum,* 79–80; Fulk le Réchin, *Fragmentum historiae Andegavensis,* 234, n. 1; and the discussion by Halphen, "Etude," 27–28.

59. Bachrach, "Geoffrey Greymantle," 32.

60. Bachrach, "The Angevin Economy," 11–12.

61. *Chron. de Nantes,* ch. 44; Lot, *Derniers Carolingiens,* 164–165.

62. Lot, *Hugues Capet,* 159, 188–189.

63. Concerning the family relations see Grierson, "L'origine des comtes," 96–97; Werner, "Untersuchungen," 270; Abbo of Fleury, *Epist.,* no. 1; and the discussion by Bachrach, "The Angevin Strategy of Castle Building," 540.

64. *Cartul. de Saint-Aubin,* no. 85; the establishment of the chronology of this act depends on seeing it in relation to the subsequent grant made by Fulk to Alberic of Vihiers, concerning which see Bachrach, "Enforcement of *Forma Fidelatitis,*" 805, n. 47.

65. Abbo of Fleury, *Epist.,* no. 1, and the discussion by Bachrach, "The Angevin Strategy of Castle Building," 550, n. 20.

66. Because of their international currency, I have decided to use two basic German prosopographical terms: *Leitname* and *Namengut.* The former may be defined as the most common name or one of two very common names used by an aristocratic family over many generations, e.g., Geoffrey and Fulk among the Angevin counts. *Namengut* refers to the stock of names used by both ancestral branches of a family. It is from this group of names that parents customarily selected the names for their children.

67. Lot, *Hugues Capet,* 189–190.

68. *Act. Pont.,* 353–355, with the discussion of this text by Bachrach, "Geoffrey Greymantle," 25–27; Bachrach, "The Angevin Strategy of Castle Building," 553, n. 68.

69. Lot, *Derniers Carolingiens,* 201–277, esp. 271–272; Robert Coolidge, "Adalbero, Bishop of Laon," *Studies in Medieval and Renaissance History* 2 (1965): 32–53.

70. Richer, *Hist.,* book 4, ch. 79 (cf. editor's footnote, p. 277, n. 3); *Chron. de Nantes,* ch. 44; and cf. Raoul Glaber, *Hist.,* book 2, ch. 3, where Conan is said to have styled himself "king." See Lot, *Hugues Capet,* 164–165.

71. Richer, *Hist.,* book 4, ch. 79; see Bur, *Comté de Champagne,* 116–117, concerning possible lands in dispute.

72. Lot, *Hugues Capet,* 160–161, 160 (n. 3).

73. *Gesta Consulum,* 47; and Halphen, *Le comté d'Anjou,* 18–19.

74. Lot, *Hugues Capet,* 174–175.

75. Richer, *Hist.,* book 4, ch. 82 (cf. editor's footnote, pp. 282–283, n. 1). But Conan's closeness to the Normans during this last year of his life is amply demonstrated by the arrangement for his burial in the monastery at Mont Saint Michel. See Bates, *Normandy before 1066,* 70, and Le Patourel, *The Norman Empire,* 15, who correctly places the marriage of Geoffrey-Berengar, count of Rennes, to Hawisse, daughter of Duke Robert I, about 996. Cf. Searle, *Predatory Kinship,* 139–140.

76. *Chron. de Nantes,* ch. 44; Richer, *Hist.,* book 4, chs. 81–82; Lot, *Hugues Capet,* 166, n. 5; and Halphen, *Le comté d'Anjou,* 20.

77. Bachrach, "Early Medieval Fortifications," 544.

78. Richer, *Hist.,* book 4, chs. 81–82; *Chron. de Nantes,* ch. 44; and Ber-

nard S. Bachrach, "Early Medieval Fortifications in the 'West' of France: A Revised Technical Vocabulary," *Technology and Culture* 16 (1975): 554.

79. Urban military organization is discussed by Bachrach, "Angevin Campaign Forces," 78–81.

80. Bernard S. Bachrach and Rutherford Aris, "Military Technology and Garrison Organization: Some Observations on Anglo-Saxon Military Thinking in Light of the Burghal Hidage," *Technology and Culture* 31 (1990): 1–17.

81. Richer, *Hist.*, book 4, chs. 81–82; *Chron. de Nantes*, ch. 44; and Halphen, *Le comté d'Anjou*, 20, n. 1.

82. Richer, *Hist.*, book 4, chs. 81–82.

83. The history of the rules or laws governing surrender and the related matter of the treatment of prisoners of war has not been examined for pre-Crusade Europe. Thus, I have gathered several examples from Fulk's reign. Of importance here is *Gesta Consulum*, 47–48, and *Hist. S. Florentii*, 277, for the use of the term *lex deditionis*; see the discussion by Bachrach, "The Angevin Strategy of Castle Building," 139. A useful treatment of this topic for the later Middle Ages is Maurice Keen, *The Laws of War in the Late Middle Ages* (London, 1965), 128, who discusses the *lex deditionis* briefly. More generally see, for example, Philippe Contamine, *War in the Middle Ages*, trans. Michael Jones (Oxford, 1984), 33, 35, 42, 57, 73, 151–152, 256–257, 265, 274, 276, who provides a few references regarding prisoners; most of these are from the period following the first Crusade.

84. Concerning these campaigns see Lot, *Hugues Capet*, 160–161, and Halphen, *Le comté d'Anjou*, 18–19.

85. Bachrach and Aris, "Military Technology and Garrison Organization, 1–17, examine the relationship of fortifications, technology, and military demography.

86. For examples of technology available at this time in the west of France see *Annales Vindocinenses*, 60; and *Annales . . . Rainaldi*, 86.

87. See, ch. 2, n. 85, above.

88. *Chron. de Nantes*, ch. 44; Richer, *Hist.*, book 44, chs. 81–82.

89. Richer, *Hist.*, book 4, chs. 81–82.

90. The chronology is discussed in detail by Halphen, *Le comté d'Anjou*, 20–21.

91. *Chron. de Nantes*, ch. 44; Richer, *Hist.*, book 4, chs. 81–82.

92. Richer, *Hist.*, book 4, ch. 82.

93. Bachrach, "Geoffrey Greymantle," 19, 25–26.

94. *Chron. de Nantes*, ch. 44; Richer, *Hist.*, book 4, ch. 82.

95. The sources have conveniently been assembled by Halphen, *Le comté d'Anjou*, 21–25.

96. A useful background sketch to "trial by battle" is provided by Robert Bartlett, *Trial by Fire and Water: The Medieval Judicial Ordeal* (Oxford, 1986), 103–126. Nonetheless, the entire subject of a prearranged battle for entire armies needs more research. See, for example, Gregory of Tours, *Hist.*, book 4, ch. 16, and book 5, ch. 17. In addition, the casting of a battle in terms of God's judgment is relevant here, as, for example, William of Poitiers, *Histoire de Guil-*

laume le Conquérant, who tells the story of the Norman victory in this vein beginning at book 2, ch. 12.

97. *Chron. de Nantes,* ch. 44; Richer, *Hist.,* book 4, ch. 84; Raoul Glaber, *Hist.,* book 2, ch. 3, para. 4.

98. Richer, *Hist.,* book 4, ch. 84.

99. *Hist.,* book 2, ch. 3, para. 4.

100. *Chron. de Nantes,* ch. 44.

101. Ibid.

102. See J. F. Niermeyer, *Mediae Latinitatis lexicon minus* (Leiden, 1959), fasc. 7, pp. 599–600, re: *levare.*

103. Nicole Belmont, "Levana, or, How to Raise Up Children," *Family and Society: Selections from the Annales: Economies, Sociétés, Civilisations,* ed. Robert Forster and Orest Ranum, trans. Elborg Forster and Patricia M. Ranum (Baltimore, 1976), 1–2.

104. The idea, also inherited from the Romans, that the "family," what we may think of as the "patronage family," for want of a better term, extended considerably beyond those related by blood or marriage. See the useful observations by Herlihy, "Family," 2–5; and, below, p. 54, the discussion of the wergild of a fidelis being claimed by his dominus.

105. *Chron. de Nantes,* ch. 44.

106. See J. F. Verbruggen, *The Art of Warfare in Western Europe during the Middle Ages,* trans. Sumner Willard and S. C. M. Southern (Amsterdam, 1977), 86–89, regarding the honor and the vital tactical role played by the standard bearer. It is also made clear in *Chron. de Nantes,* ch. 44, that Fulk was fighting to avenge the murders of various members of Judicaël's family; see ch. 2, n. 100, above, and also note that the standard bore the insignia of both the count of the Angevins and the count of Nantes.

107. *Chron. de Nantes,* ch. 44.

108. Richer, *Hist.,* book 4, ch. 85.

109. Richer, *Hist.,* book 4, ch. 84. Concerning this controversial tactic, the feigned retreat, see Bernard S. Bachrach, "The Feigned Retreat at Hastings," *Mediaeval Studies* 33 (1971): 344–347, and Verbruggen, *The Art of War,* 89–90.

110. Raoul Glaber, *Hist.,* book 2, ch. 3, para. 4. It is arguable that Viscount Aimo was the man responsible for launching the precipitous charge of the *prior exercitus* because the advance of the standard was the normal signal for the movement forward of the unit. Concerning such signals see Verbruggen, *The Art of War,* 81–89.

111. Richer, *Hist.,* book 4, chs. 85–86; Raoul Glaber, *Hist.,* book 2, ch. 3, para. 4; *Chron. de Nantes,* ch. 44; Fulk le Réchin, *Fragmentum historiae Andegavensis,* 234, with the discussion by Lot, *Hugues Capet,* 167–169, and Halphen, *Le comté d'Anjou,* 21–25.

112. Halphen, *Le comté d'Anjou,* 23–24; Bachrach, "Angevin Campaign Forces," 74–78.

113. Raoul Glaber, *Hist.,* book 2, ch. 3, para. 4; Richer, *Hist.,* book 4, ch. 86.

114. Raoul Glaber, *Hist.,* book 2, ch. 3, para. 4. Note the "Conventum,"

ed. Martindale, p. 543, provides evidence for the mutilating of the right hand of *milites* who were deemed guilty of treasonous acts.

115. Michael McCormick, *Eternal Victory: Triumphal Rulership in Late Antiquity, Byzantium, and the Early Medieval West* (Cambridge, 1986), 57–58, 160–166, 313–314, for the relevant ceremonies.

116. See Bernard S. Bachrach, "Gildas, Vortigern, and Constitutionality in Sub-Roman Britain," *Nottingham Medieval Studies* 32 (1988): 126–140, for a discussion of tyrants and the general literature on the subject.

117. Raoul Glaber, *Hist.*, book 2, ch. 3, para. 4, and the discussion by Bachrach, "Neo-Roman vs. Feudal," 24–25.

118. Concerning Raoul's sources and the quality of his research see the discussion by Bachrach, "Pope Sergius IV," 241–247; cf. Raoul Glaber, *Hist.*, pp. 60–64, for the editor's observations on this matter. With regard to Belli Locus as the original name for Fulk Nerra's abbey see Bernard S. Bachrach, "The Combat Sculptures at Fulk Nerra's 'Battle Abbey' (c. 1005–1012)," in *The Haskins Society Journal: Studies in Medieval History*, ed. Robert B. Patterson (London, 1991), 3:63–79.

119. The Via Triumphalis under discussion here was the final few miles, at the least, of the old Roman road from Nantes to Angers. Although we do not know at what place this road was renamed, the renaming had taken place by the time the road reached Pruniers (commune of Bouchemaine). The topography is discussed by Célestin Port, *Dictionnaire historique, géographique, et biographique de Maine-et-Loire* (Angers, 1874), 1:786. This is the road along which Fulk's army had to return in the summer of 992; thus there can be no serious doubt that it was renamed at this time in order to celebrate the Angevin victory. There is absolutely no reason to believe that some Roman emperor had celebrated a triumph along this road in the environs of Angers and that an ancient name had remained. Indeed, no evidence has been found to indicate that any Roman augustus even stayed at Angers much less won a great victory in the area. There are no great Merovingian or Carolingian victories recorded at Angers or in the region. Although Angers from time to time changed hands as a result of military action, nothing noteworthy occurred along the western approach to the city before Fulk's victory in 992 at Conquereuil and his recapture of Nantes. For this background material see Brühl, *Palatium und Civitas*, 1:152–160.

120. Richer, *Hist.*, book 4, ch. 86, and the discussion by Halphen, *Le comté d'Anjou*, 24–25.

121. Richer, *Hist.*, book 4, ch. 91, and the discussion by Guillot, *Le comte d'Anjou*, 2:25–26.

122. The failure of the alliance developed by Geoffrey Greymantle by which he attempted to link the interests of the Angevin counts to those of the counts of Rennes through the marriage of Hermengarde-Gerberga to Conan is the most glaring in the history of the Angevin family network. For a discussion of the political dynamics that helped to undermine this alliance in the period prior to Fulk Nerra's accession, see Halphen, *Le comté d'Anjou*, 6, and, in considerably greater detail, Bachrach, "Geoffrey Greymantle," 11–15.

123. René Merlet, "Les origines du monastère de Saint-Magloire de Paris,"

Bibliothèque d'Ecole de Chartes 56 (1885): 248, 270, n. 1; Lot, *Hugues Capet,* 199.

124. Fulk le Réchin, *Fragmentum historiae Andegavensis,* 234.

125. See Halphen, *Le comté d'Anjou,* 24, n. 2, and Lot, *Hugues Capet,* 169, n. 1, who is correct when he observes, "Cette lutte frappa l'imagination des contemporains . . ."

126. Richer, *Hist.,* book 4, ch. 84.

127. Regarding the importance of the vulgar Roman law in this region at this time see Fulbert, *Epist.,* no. 13, and the discussion by J.–F. Lemarignier, "Apropos de deux textes sur l'histoire du droit romain au moyen âge (1008 et 1308)," *Bibliothèque d'Ecole de Chartes* 101 (1940): 157–168, with the further discussion by Bachrach, "Neo-Roman vs. Feudal," 13–14.

128. *Cartul. de Saint-Aubin,* nos. 20, 23, 34, 131, 180, 196, 197, 932, with the discussion by Bachrach, "Neo-Roman vs. Feudal," 4.

129. Bachrach, "Neo-Roman vs. Feudal," 29–30.

130. Eleanor Searle, "Fact and Pattern in Heroic History: Dudo of Saint-Quentin," *Viator* 15 (1984): 61–67.

131. Adémar of Chabannes, *Chron.,* book 3, chs. 41, 54, and the extended discussion of this text by Bachrach, "Potius Rex," 11–21.

132. For the background on Fulbert see L. MacKinney, *Bishop Fulbert and Education at the School of Chartres* (Notre Dame, Ind., 1957); and more specifically regarding Livy the literature cited by Bachrach, "Neo-Roman vs. Feudal," 23, nn. 29–31.

133. *Chron. S. Petri Aniciensis,* 152, with the discussion of this text by Bachrach, "Northern Origins," 405–409.

134. Bachrach, "Neo-Roman vs. Feudal," 10–12.

135. Concerning the background on mercenaries see Jacques Boussard, "Services féodaux, milices, et mercenaires dans les armées, en France, aux Xe et XIe siècles," *Settimane di Studio del Centro Italiano di Studi sull'alto Medioevo* 15 (1968): 131–168; for the economic background in Anjou see Bachrach, "The Angevin Economy," 3–55.

136. Lot, *Hugues Capet,* 161–162; Bachrach, "The Angevin Strategy of Castle Building," 540, n. 20. The only date that fits all of the sources is the campaigning season of 992.

137. For a detailed discussion of the text on which this identification of Renaud rests see Bachrach, "Geoffrey Greymantle," 45, n. 21.

138. Oury, "La reconstruction monastique dans l'Ouest," 77–84.

139. Bib. Nat., ms. lat. 17127, p. 156; cf. Guillot, *Le comte d'Anjou,* 1:42.

140. Bachrach, "Angevin Economy," 28–29.

141. Bernard S. Bachrach, "Animals and Warfare in Early Medieval Europe," *Settimane di Studio del Centro Italiano di Studi sull'alto Medioevo* 31 (Spoleto, 1985), 1:716–722.

142. *Hist. S. Florentii,* 274, with the discussion by Bernard S. Bachrach, "Fortifications and Military Tactics: Fulk Nerra's Strongholds circa 1000," *Technology and Culture* 20 (1979): 535, n. 13.

143. *Hist. S. Florentii,* 274, for the quotation.

144. Richer, *Hist.,* book 4, ch. 90; Vegetius, *De re militari,* book 1, ch. 25.

145. Richer, *Hist.*, book 4, ch. 90, and the discussion by Bachrach, "Fortifications and Military Tactics," 534–541.

146. Bachrach, "Early Medieval Fortifications," 531–565.

147. Bernard S. Bachrach, "The Cost of Castle Building: The Case of the Tower at Langeais, 992–994," in *The Medieval Castle: Romance and Reality,* ed. K. Reyerson and F. Powe (Dubuque, Iowa, 1984): 46–62 (four plates); cf. R. Allen Brown, *English Castles,* 3d ed. (London, 1976), 24. It is likely that Fulk's architects used the Roman foot in laying out the dimensions for Langeais. See on this point Bernard S. Bachrach, "The Tomb of Fulk Nerra, Count of the Angevins (987–1040)," *Cithara* 29 (1989): 7–8.

148. For the background data see André Chatelain, *Donjons romans des pays d'Ouest* (Paris, 1973), and Bachrach, "Fortifications and Military Tactics," 534–541.

149. Boussard, "L'origine des comtés de Tours, Blois, et Chartres," 99.

150. Bachrach, "The Cost of Castle Building," 47–48. With regard to the ditch, however, see Bachrach, "Fortifications and Military Tactics," 534; but cf. Marcel Deyres, "Les Châteaux de Foulque Nerra," *Bulletin Monumental* 132 (1974): 16, who argues that the main ditch was of little importance because it was not very wide. Today, the ditch still measures more than two meters in width, and there is reason to believe that it was both wider and deeper when Fulk had it dug; through erosion it has probably been filled in somewhat. The problem, however, concerns the basis for comparison; for example, Vegetius, *De re militari,* book 1, ch. 24; book 3, ch. 8, makes clear that a ditch of less than two meters in width and one meter deep is nevertheless a significant obstacle. We must also remember that the earth extracted from the ditch was used to help in the construction of a wall at least 1.5 meters high; the wall may have been topped with a palisade. See J.–F. Finó, *Forteresses de la France médiévale: Construction, attaque, défense* (3d ed., Paris, 1977), 415, regarding general practice in this period.

151. Bachrach, "Fortifications and Military Tactics," 535–536, for the establishment of the chronology.

152. Bachrach, "The Cost of Castle Building," 52–54.

153. Roger Grand, "Une curieuse appelation de certaines corvées au moyen âge: Le 'bain,' biain,' ou bien,'" *Mélanges dédiés à la mémoire de Félix Grat* (Paris, 1946), 1:289–300; Guillot, *Le comte d'Anjou,* 1:382–384; and the discussion by Bachrach, "The Angevin Economy," 8–9.

154. Bachrach, "The Cost of Castle Building," 52–53.

155. Bachrach, "The Angevin Economy," 7–10.

156. Ibid., 27, for lists of officials.

157. *Hist. S. Florentii,* 278, for evidence of the use of both lists of workers and a payroll check-off system at a construction site.

158. For comparative purposes with regard to William the Conqueror's operations see Bernard S. Bachrach, "Some Observations on the Military Administration of the Norman Conquest," *Anglo-Norman Studies,* ed. R. Allen Brown (Woodbridge, 1986), 8:1–25.

159. Lot, *Hugues Capet,* 170–174; Coolidge, "Adalbero, Bishop of Laon," 55–56. Regarding the chronology, see Lot, *Hugues Capet,* 172, n. 1; and cf.

Mathilde Uhlirz, *Jahrbücher des deutschen Reiches unter Otto II. und Otto III.* (Berlin, 1954), 184–185, who does not appear to appreciate the fullness of Otto II's itinerary.

160. Richer, *Hist.*, book 4, ch. 90.

161. Cf. Richard, *Histoire des comtes de Poitou*, 1:136–137, who brings together the evidence but misreads what transpired.

162. Bachrach, "Robert of Blois," 130.

163. Bib. Nat. n. a. lat. 1930, *Livre noir*, fol. 21r; "Chartes poitevines de Saint-Florent," ed. Marchegay, nos. 34, 35; Guillot, *Le comte d'Anjou*, 2:26; and Bachrach, "Robert of Blois," 130. Richard, *Histoire des comtes de Poitou*, 1:136–137, provides additional evidence regarding the cooperation of Viscount Aimery and William.

164. Pierre de Maillezais, *Relatio*, fol. 249r.

165. Cf. F. Lot, *Hugues Capet*, 183, n. 1.

166. *Chron. de Nantes*, ch. 45, and esp. p. 134, n. 1.

167. See above, ch. 2, n. 123.

168. Richer, *Hist.*, book 4, ch. 90; Lot, *Hugues Capet*, 174, n. 4.

169. "Fragments de chartes . . . Saint-Julien de Tours," no. 34; "Notices sur les chartes originales relatives à la Touraine," ed. Delaville le Roulx, no. 13.

170. Richer, *Hist.*, book 4, ch. 90; Norgate, *England under the Angevin Kings*, 1:150, provides some useful insights concerning the character of Odo I.

171. Syrus, *Mirac. S. Maioli*, 262–263; Richer, *Hist.*, book 4, ch. 91, with the discussion by Lot, *Hugues Capet*, 183–184.

172. *Cartul. de Saint-Aubin*, no. 20.

173. Richer, *Hist.*, book 4, chs. 92–93.

174. Ibid., ch. 91, seems to reverse the roles of Fulk and Odo in order to strengthen the chronicler's attack on Fulk. Among the more useful comments on this text see Lot, *Hugues Capet*, 176, and F. L. Ganshof, "Depuis quand a-t-on pu, en France, être vassal de plusieurs seigneurs," *Mélanges Paul Fournier* (Paris, 1929), 261–270.

175. Note that the taking of the wergild provides a sense of "family" relationship between the dominus and his fidelis.

176. In the context of family, it is worth noting here the development of a three-generational sequence.

177. Richer, *Hist.*, book 4, chs. 92–93, as understood by Lot, *Hugues Capet*, 176–178. However, cf. Halphen, *Le comté d'Anjou*, 26, n. 2.

178. *Chron. de Nantes*, ch. 45, and p. 134, n. 1; Richer, *Hist.*, book 4, ch. 91.

179. Bib. Nat. n. a. lat. 1930, *Livre noir*, fols. 23v–24v, and the discussion by Bachrach, "Robert of Blois," 129–130.

180. Madeleine Dillay, "La régime de l'église privée du XIe au XIIIe siècle dans l'Anjou, la Maine, la Touraine," *Revue historique de droit français et étranger*, 4th ser., 5 (1925): 253–294; William Ziezulewicz, "'Restored' Churches in the Fisc of St.-Florent de Saumur (1021–1118)," *Revue Bénédictine* 96 (1986): 106–117, for background on the problem in regard to the region under consideration here.

181. Lamothe-Dreuzy, "Saint-Florent-le-Vieil," 69–77.

182. Hogan, "The *Rainaldi* of Angers," 35–62.

183. Pierre de Maillezais, *Relatio,* fol. 249r–v.

184. *Cartul. de Saint-Cyprian,* no. 103.

185. *Cartul. de Saint-Aubin,* no. 85. Some explication of this very important text is to be found in the articles by Bachrach: "Robert of Blois," 138–140; "The Angevin Strategy of Castle Building," 543–544; and "The Enforcement of *Forma Fidelitatis,*" 805, n. 47. The genealogical information found in *Chronique de Parcé,* p. 2, is suspect.

186. Bachrach, "Robert of Blois," 138–140.

187. Richer, *Hist.,* book 4, ch. 93. See, above, ch. 2, n. 177, regarding chronology.

188. Pierre de Maillezais, *Relatio,* fols. 247v, 248r, 249v, 250v. Bachrach, "Study in Feudal Politics," 114–115, n. 13, for a discussion of the situation in detail.

189. *Mirac. S. Benedicti,* book 3, ch. 7; Adémar de Chabannes, *Chron.,* book 3, ch. 24; Pierre de Maillezais, *Relatio,* fols. 249r–v, with the discussion by Bernard S. Bachrach, "Toward a Reappraisal of William the Great, Duke of Aquitaine (995–1030)," *Journal of Medieval History* 4 (1979): 11–21.

190. Richer, *Hist.,* book 4, ch. 94; and Archives de l'Indre-et-Loire, H 24, piece 51; with the discussion by Lot, *Hugues Capet,* 177–178 (n. 2), 179–180, 423–426; Bur, *Comté de Champagne,* 144, 173, 183; Halphen, *Le comté d'Anjou,* 29, n. 1; and cf. Guillot, *Le comte d'Anjou,* 1:25.

191. Adémar de Chabannes, *Chron.,* book 3, ch. 34; *Brevis Hist. S. Juliani,* 228, with Lot, *Hugues Capet,* 351 ff., and Halphen, *Le comté d'Anjou,* 29–30.

192. Bachrach, "Study in Feudal Politics," 114–115, and Bachrach, "Robert of Blois," 137, n. 2.

Chapter 3: The First Capetian-Blésois Axis

1. Adémar of Chabannes, *Chron.,* book 3, ch. 34, with the embellishments by Pierre de Maillezais, *Relatio,* fol. 249v.

2. Lot, *Hugues Capet,* 108–109, 119 (n. 3), 183–185, 298–303; cf. Pfister, *Robert le pieux,* 50.

3. Boussard, "Le trésorier de Saint-Martin," 76.

4. Halphen, *Le comté d'Anjou,* 348–349, for a critical edition of this text. The date is established by Guillot, *Le comte d'Anjou,* 2:27. Cf. Patrick Geary, "L'humiliation des saints," *Annales* 34 (1979): 32, reprinted with the author's corrections concerning the identity of the Angevin count and the date as "Humiliation of Saints," *Saints and Their Cults: Studies in Religious Sociology, Folklore, and History,* ed. Stephen Wilson (Cambridge, 1983), 130–131, n. 11.

5. Halphen, *Le comté d'Anjou,* 348–349.

6. Bachrach, "Geoffrey Greymantle," 37–38.

7. Cf. Geary, "L'humiliation des saints," and ch. 3, n. 4, above.

8. *Vita S. Odonis,* book 1, ch. 21.

9. Boussard, "Charte de fondation de Notre-Dame de Loches," 7–8, for the text, with the discussion by Bachrach, "Geoffrey Greymantle," 37–38.

10. Werner, "Untersuchungen," 176–177; Bachrach, "Geoffrey Greymantle," 58, n. 89; and Lot, *Hugues Capet,* 183.

11. *Vetera analecta,* ed. Mabillion, 99.

12. Gerbert, *Epist.,* nos. 207, 209, and the discussion by Jacques Boussard, "Les évêques en Neustrie avant la réforme grégorienne (950–1050 environ)," *Journal des Savants* (1970): 161–196; and Boussard, "L'origine des familles seigneuriales," 117.

13. Petrus "Bechin," *Chronicon, anno* 992, though late is accurate and dates events from the capture of Charles of Lorraine. Cf. Lot. *Hugues Capet,* 359–360.

14. Bachrach, "William the Great," 13.

15. See above, ch. 3, n. 2.

16. Adémar of Chabannes, *Chron.,* book 3, chs. 34, 45, and the discussion by Bachrach, "William the Great," 13.

17. Grierson, "L'origine des comtes," 95–101.

18. Abbo of Fleury, *Epist.,* no. 1, which describes a process that had begun earlier.

19. "Chartes de Saint-Julien de Tours," ed. Denis, no. 5, and the discussion by Bachrach, "Fortifications and Military Tactics," 242–243, 549. Cf. Marcel Dyres, "Le château de Montbazon au XIe siècle," *Cahiers de civilisation médiévale* 12 (1969): 147–159.

20. Fulk le Réchin, *Fragmentum historiae Andegavensis,* 234, and *Gesta Consulum,* 52. See the discussion by Bachrach, "Fortifications and Military Tactics," 542–543.

21. Bachrach, "William the Great," 13.

22. Pierre de Maillezais, *Relatio,* fol. 249r–v.

23. Ibid., with the discussions by Bachrach, "Study in Feudal Politics," 114–122, and "William the Great," 11–12.

24. Richard, *Histoire des comtes de Poitou,* 1:108.

25. See Bachrach, "Geoffrey Greymantle," 18–20, regarding the policy pursued by Fulk's father.

26. Bachrach, "The Angevin Strategy of Castle Building," 549–550.

27. Pierre de Maillezais, *Relatio,* fol. 249r–v.

28. Bachrach, "William the Great," 12–13.

29. Pierre de Maillezais, *Relatio,* fol. 255v, provides this view; see also Lot, *Hugues Capet,* 396.

30. Bachrach, "Study in Feudal Politics," 115–116.

31. Ibid.

32. Adémar de Chabannes, *Chron.,* book 3, ch. 41. Bachrach, "Potius Rex," 11–21, regarding Adémar's parti pris, and Bachrach, "Early Medieval Fortifications," 555–556, 568–569, n. 136.

33. Bachrach, "Study in Feudal Politics," 115–116.

34. Bachrach, "The Angevin Tradition," 117–118.

35. Bachrach, "William the Great," 16.

36. Bachrach, "Geoffrey Greymantle," 17–25.

37. Bib. Nat., Coll. Dom Housseau, vol. 2, pt. 1, no. 326, with the discussion by Bachrach, "The Enforcement of *Forma Fidelitatis*," 809–810, n. 67. For a general discussion of taxes see Bachrach, "The Angevin Economy," 5–13. The translation of *malae consuetudines* as "new taxes" requires some explanation insofar as the phrase seems literally to mean "bad taxes," as characterized by the person upon whom they were imposed. A "bad tax" in this perspective, within the Angevin state during this period, could either be a "new tax" or an "old tax" that was being reimposed by the count or his agents. The term *consuetudo* in the present context is often translated as "custom" and that is not incorrect, provided the proper association is made with the modern English context of "customs duties." The latter, of course, is redundant. The generalizations attempted by Dunbabin, *France in the Making*, 148–150, are on the right track but of necessity do not precisely mirror the Angevin situation under consideration here.

38. Bib. Nat., ms. lat. 17127, 157–159; and Bib. Nat., Coll. Dom Housseau, vol. 1, no. 282.

39. Bib. Nat., Coll. Dom Housseau, vol. 2, pt. 1, no. 326.

40. *Vita Burcardi*, intro., vi ff.

41. Lot, *Hugues Capet*, 126–129.

42. William M. Newman, *Catalogue des actes de Robert II, roi de France* (Paris, 1937), nos. 9, 10, 13, 16.

43. *Chartes de Cluny*, no. 2485; Bachrach, "Robert of Blois," 132–133.

44. Guillot, *Le comte d'Anjou*, 1:21–22, n. 107; Bachrach, "The Accession of Fulk Nerra as Count," 335–336; *Archives d'Anjou*, ed. Marchegay, 2:60.

45. Halphen, *Le comté d'Anjou*, 348–349; Abbo, *Epist.*, no. 1; Bachrach, "Robert of Blois," 126–127; Richer, *Hist.*, book 4, ch. 79; *Cartul. de Saint-Maurice*, nos. 22, 27.

46. Lot, *Hugues Capet*, 127–129.

47. See the *acta* cited above in ch. 3, n. 42.

48. *Cartul. de la Trinité de Vendôme*, nos. 6, 95. Cf. Guillot, *Le comte d'Anjou*, 2, <14>, who is correct in observing that the latter act, in its present form, is not authentic. But the information concerning the marriage is correct. A date of ca. 1000–1001 is fundamentally consistent with Adele's age.

49. Lot, *Hugues Capet*, 234, 414–422; Coolidge, "Adalbero, Bishop of Laon," 60; Halphen, *Le comté d'Anjou*, 63 (n. 2), 272–273.

50. Ernest Petit, *Histoire des ducs de Bourgogne* (Paris, 1885), 1:67–71.

51. Ibid.

52. *Chartes de Cluny*, no. 1794.

53. Ibid., no. 2484.

54. Pfister, *Robert le pieux*, 189; *Gesta pont. Autissiod.*, 48; and René Poupardin, *Le royaume de Bourgogne (888–1038): Étude sur les origines du royaume d'Arles* (Paris, 1907), 417.

55. Abbo of Fleury, *Epist.*, no. 1.

56. Fulbert, *Epist.*, no. 86, represents the king's view on the confiscation of *honores*.

57. Mansi, vol. 19, col. 226.

58. Devailly, *Le Berry,* 142; Oury, "Guy II d'Anjou," 67–68; Bachrach, "Northern Origins," 405–421.

59. Alfred Gandilhon, *Catalogue des actes des archevêques de Bourges antérieurs à l'an 1200* (Paris-Bourges, 1927), no. 27; Lot, *Hugues Capet,* 44, 76; Devailly, *Le Berry,* 138, n. 7.

60. Aimo, *Vita Abbonis,* ch. 10, (*PL* 139).

61. Bachrach, "Fortifications and Military Tactics," 541–543.

62. L. Raynal, *Histoire du Berry* (Bourges, 1844), 1:350 (n. 2), 424 (n. 1), with the discussion by Guillot, *Le comte d'Anjou,* 2:29.

63. Devailly, *Le Berry,* 133.

64. Pfister, *Robert le pieux,* 276–277.

65. *Chron. Masciacense, anno.* 999. Note the error by Pfister, *Robert le pieux,* 162, 277, as corrected by Devailly, *Le Berry,* 157–158. See also Newman, *Robert II,* no. 17.

66. Newman, *Robert II,* no. 20.

67. For a good summary of the political background see Thomas Head, "Letaldus of Micy and the Hagiographic Traditions of Selles-sur-Cher," *Analecta Bollandiana* 107 (1989): 408–411.

68. *Miracula S. Eusicii,* ch. 6; for the identification of the author as Letaldus as well as the latter's parti pris, see Head, "Letaldus of Micy," 393–411. Regarding the military organization and vocabulary see Bachrach, "Angevin Campaign Forces," 75.

69. *Gallia Christ.,* vol. 2, col. 183, provides the reference for Theobald's attack on Selles but confuses the date, giving 1020. This is likely the result of misreading MII or MIII or even MIIII in an old and difficult text. Cf. Head, "Letaldus of Micy," 410, n. 47; see the discussion by Bachrach, "Combat Sculptures," 75.

70. See above, ch. 3, n. 44.

71. Guillot, *Le comte d'Anjou,* 1:25. *Hist. S. Florentii,* 260, 273, for the quotations. Support for the interpretation that Elizabeth died in disgrace may be inferred from the failure of the sources that deal with her family and the health of the souls of its members to mention her at all. See, for example, *Vita Burcardi, passim,* and *Cartul. de l'église de Notre-Dame de Paris,* 1:225, 317.

72. *Cartul. de la Trinité de Vendôme,* no. 44; Fanning, "Les origines familiales de Vulgrin," 245–253.

73. Bachrach, "The Enforcement of *Forma Fidelitatis,*" 796–819.

74. *Chartes de Cluny,* no. 2484; *Cartul. de Saint-Maurice,* no. 130, as dated by Guillot, *Le comte d'Anjou,* 2:33; and Bachrach, "The Accession of Fulk Nerra as Count," 331–342, for an earlier case of association by the Angevin counts.

75. See below, p. 85 ff.

76. *Cartul. de Saint-Maurice,* no. 22.

77. *Cartul, de Saint-Aubin,* no. 25; and Guillot, *Le comte d'Anjou,* 2:30–32.

78. *Chron. S. Sergii,* 134, and the discussion by Bachrach, "Viscount Fulcoius," 1–8.

79. *Cartul. de Saint-Maurice,* no. 23.

80. See the discussion by Bachrach, "Geoffrey Greymantle," 10–11.

81. *Annales Vindocinenses,* 59; Archives de Maine-et-Loire, H 1242; and the discussion by Guillot, *Le comte d'Anjou,* 1:126, 214, n. 81. A comparison of Fulk's relations with Bishop Renaud before and after the Angevin count made his first pilgrimage makes it clear that the prelate's *testamentum* was not made public before Fulk left for the Holy Land during the winter of 1003. For the background see Bachrach, "The Pilgrimages of Fulk Nerra," 205–206.

82. Head, "Letaldus of Micy," 395–396, regarding authorship and parti pris.

83. *Miracula S. Martini,* ch. 7.

84. Bachrach, "Fulk Nerra's Exploitation," 29–49.

85. Ibid., 37–40, for the details of the *divisio.*

86. Maurice Chaume, *Les origines du duché de Bourgogne* (Dijon, 1925), 1:473–478.

87. Le Patourel, *The Norman Empire,* 14–15; *Chron. de Nantes,* ch. 44.

88. Bachrach, "Robert of Blois," 138, n. 1.

89. Lot, *Hugues Capet,* 127–128, n. 2, and the discussion by Bachrach, "Robert of Blois," 133–134.

90. René Merlet, "Dates de la mort d'Eudes 1er et de Thibault II, comtes de Chartres et de Blois," *Procès-verbaux de la Société archéologique d'Eure-et-Loir* 9 (1893): 86–89.

91. Bachrach, "The Pilgrimages of Fulk Nerra," 205–206.

92. Lot, *Derniers Carolingiens,* 358–369; Bachrach, "Robert of Blois," 141–143.

93. Bachrach, "The Pilgrimages of Fulk Nerra," 205–206.

94. Bernard S. Bachrach, "King Henry II and Angevin Claims to the Saintonge," *Medieval Prosopography* 6, no. 1 (1985): 23–45.

95. *Gesta Consulum,* 45–46, and the discussion of this theme by Bachrach, "Geoffrey Greymantle," 38–39.

96. *Gesta Consulum,* 45–46. The focus on Landry is anachronistic as shown by Bachrach, "The Angevin Strategy of Castle Building," 541, n. 25.

97. Archives de Maine-et-Loire, no. 3715 = *Livre rouge,* fols. 29v–30r; *Cartul. blésois de Marmoutier,* no. 5, with the discussion by Bachrach, "Robert of Blois," 135–136.

98. *Hist. Fr.,* 10:583; Bachrach, "The Enforcement of *Forma Fidelitatis,*" 800, n. 24; and *Cartul. de Saint-Maurice,* no. 26.

99. *Gallia Christ.,* vol. 14, col. 556, and the discussion of these taxes by Bachrach, "The Angevin Economy," 7–8.

100. *Gallia Christ.,* vol. 14, col. 556.

101. *Cartul. de la Trinité de Vendôme,* nos. 66, 67, with the discussion by Bachrach, "The Enforcement of *Forma Fidelitatis,*" 810, n. 71.

102. Archives de Maine-et-Loire, no. 3715, *Livre rouge,* fols. 29v–30r.

103. Archives de Maine-et-Loire, H 3038, with the discussion by Bachrach, "Robert of Blois," 136–137.

104. Bib. Nat., n. a. lat. 1930, *Livre noir,* fols. 26v, 27r–v.

105. Bachrach, "Viscount Fulcoius," 4; and also *Cartul. de la Trinité de Vendôme,* no. 73, for the mention of the large viscomital *beneficium* just beyond the walls of Angers itself.

106. Robert's interests in the Mauges region are illustrated by a forged bull and a forged charter. Concerning these see Bachrach, "Robert of Blois," 141–143; but cf. William Ziezulewicz, "A Monastic Forgery in an Age of Reform," *Archivum historiae pontificiae* 36 (1985): 7–42, and "Etude d'un faux monastique à une période de réforme: Une charte de Charles le Chauve pour Saint-Florent de Saumur (8 juin 848)," *Cahiers de civilisation médiévale* 28 (1985): 201–211, who argues for a later date. See Denécheau, "Renaissance et privilèges," 23–35, who does not grasp the difference between logic and fact and develops a circular argument.

107. *Chron. de Nantes,* ch. 44, with the editor's comments, p. 134, n. 2; and Lex, "Eudes, comte de Blois," 209.

108. *Chron. de Nantes,* ch. 44. Cf. Ferdinand Lot, "Hervé évêque de Nantes," *Annales de Bretagne* 13 (1897/8): 45–47.

109. The basic source for Herveus's life is Raoul Glaber, *Hist.,* book 3, ch. 4, paras. 14, 15. See the discussion by the editor, John France, pp. c–ci, and the fine article by Guy-Marie Oury, "L'idéal monastique dans la vie canoniale: Le bienheureux Hervé de Tours (+ 1022)," *Revue Mabillon* 52 (1962): 1–31. Although the traditional date for Herveus's appointment is 1001 (Boussard, "Le trésorier de Saint-Martin," 76, n. 49), there is no evidence to support this dating, as observed by Newman, *Robert II,* no. 30, n. 1. In light of the political circumstances as explained above, late 1003 is a much more likely date.

110. *Chartes de Saint-Julien de Tours,* ed. Denis, no. 5.

111. Bachrach, "The Enforcement of *Forma Fidelitatis,*" 796–819.

112. See the act published by Jean Besly, *Histoire des comtes de Poictou et ducs de Guyenne* (Paris, 1647), 357, and the date discussed by Guillot, *Le comte d'Anjou,* 2:33–34; also Bachrach, "The Pilgrimages of Fulk Nerra," 205–206.

113. Bachrach, "Henry II and Angevin Claims," 28–30.

114. Bachrach, "The Angevin Strategy of Castle Building," 533–560.

Chapter 4: Fulk Nerra's Rapprochement with King Robert II

1. For the altered text of this letter see Raoul Glaber, *Hist.,* book 2, ch. 4, para. 5; and Bachrach, "Pope Sergius IV," 245, for the reconstruction.

2. Concerning Geoffrey's policies see Boussard, "La charte de fondation de Notre-Dame de Loches," 1–10; Bachrach, "Viscount Fulcoius," 1–9; and Bachrach, "Geoffrey Greymantle," 37–38. Useful background on the role of the aristocracy in the rebuilding of the church is provided by John Howe, "The Nobility's Reform of the Medieval Church," *The American Historical Review* 93 (1988): 317–339.

3. Abbo of Fleury, *Epist.,* no. 1.

4. *Cartul. de Saint-Maurice,* no. 25, and the discussion of the arrangement between Geoffrey Greymantle and Viscount Renaud by Bachrach, "Geoffrey Greymantle," 10–11.

5. *Cartul. de Saint-Maurice,* no. 25. For background on ordeals see H. Nottarp, *Gottesurteilstudien* (Munich, 1956), and the more easily accessible work by Bartlett, *Trial by Fire and Water.*

6. *Cartul. de Saint-Maurice,* no. 25.

7. Ibid. Concerning unilateral ordeal see Paul Hyams, "Trial by Ordeal: The Key to Proof in the Early Common Law," in *On the Laws and Customs of England: Essays in Honor of Samuel E. Thorne,* ed. Morris S. Arnold et al. (Chapel Hill, N.C., 1981), 90–126, with particular reference to the Anglo-Saxons.

8. See the interesting observations of Stephen White, "Inheritances and Legal Arguments in Western France, 1050–1150," *Traditio* 43 (1987): 64–70, regarding dispute processing. The case under consideration here, however, falls too early to come into White's net.

9. For the background see *The Settlement of Disputes in Early Medieval Europe,* ed. Wendy Davies and Paul Fouracre; Stephen White, "Feuding and Peace-Making in the Touraine around the Year 1100," *Traditio* 42 (1986): 195–263, and "Inheritances and Legal Arguments," 55–103.

10. *Cartul. de Saint-Maurice,* no. 25. Note the ideas of Colin Morris, "*Judicium Dei*: The Social and Political Significance of the Ordeal in the Eleventh Century," *Studies in Church History* 12 (1975): 95–112; and Bartlett, *Trial by Fire and Water,* 155–156.

11. *Cartul. de Saint-Maurice,* no. 28, with the discussion by Bachrach, "Viscount Fulcoius," 4–5.

12. Hogan, "The *Rainaldi* of Angers," 45–46.

13. *Cartul. de la Trinité de Vendôme,* no. 83.

14. Hogan, "The *Rainaldi* of Angers," 35–62.

15. Bachrach, "Robert of Blois," 138; and Lex, "Eudes, comte de Blois," 211–213, who establishes the chronology. Cf. regarding the date Bates, *Normandy before 1066,* 65.

16. Le Patourel, *The Norman Empire,* 15; Lex, "Eudes, comte de Blois," 211–212; cf. Pfister, *Robert le pieux,* 214.

17. Chaume, *Duché de Bourgogne,* 1:476–479.

18. Boussard, "Les évêques en Neustrie," 174–176, but with the wrong date for his accession. Regarding the date see Newman, *Robert II,* no. 30.

19. *Cartul. de Saint-Maurice,* no. 28.

20. Bachrach, "The Angevin Strategy of Castle Building," 548–549.

21. Bachrach, "The Enforcement of *Forma Fidelitatis,*" 799 (n. 21), 803 (n. 32), 807.

22. Ibid., 807.

23. Bachrach, "The Angevin Strategy of Castle Building," 548.

24. *Chartes de Saint-Julien de Tours,* ed. Denis, no. 5.

25. W. Scott Jessee, "A Missing Capetian Princess: Advisa, Daughter of King Robert II of France," *Medieval Prosopography* 11, no. 2 (1990): 1–16.

26. The basic work on this family is Steven Fanning, "Family and Episcopal

Election, 900–1050, and the Case of Hubert, Bishop of Angers (1006–1047)," *Medieval Prosopography* 7, no. 1 (1983): 39–56.

27. *Cartul. de Cormery*, no. 31. The movements of Fulk Nerra, Theobald, and King Robert as seen in consonance with the politics of the period require this chronology. See Bachrach, "Fortifications and Military Tactics," 542–543; and Chaume, *Duché de Bourgogne*, 1:477–478.

28. Guillot, *Le comte d'Anjou*, 1:225, and in detail Fanning, *A Bishop and His World*, 48–53.

29. *Chron. Turonense magnum*, 117; *Chron. Turonense abbreviatum*, 187; and Halphen, *Le comté d'Anjou*, 31–32, for the chronology.

30. Bachrach, "The Angevin Strategy of Castle Building," 546.

31. Ibid., 542–543, regarding this stronghold and the chronology.

32. *Gesta Consulum*, 48, and *Fondation de Châteaurenault*, 149, with the discussion by Bachrach, "The Angevin Strategy of Castle Building," 541, n. 25.

33. *Gesta Consulum*, 48; Bachrach, "The Angevin Strategy of Castle Building," 536 (n. 7), 541 (n. 23).

34. Bachrach, "Animals and Warfare," 717–718.

35. Bachrach, "Geoffrey Greymantle," 17–20.

36. Bachrach, "The Enforcement of *Forma Fidelitatis*," 800, 803, 806, and Bachrach, "The Angevin Strategy of Castle Building," 544.

37. Bachrach, "The Angevin Strategy of Castle Building," 547.

38. *Cartul. de la Trinité de Vendôme*, no. 44, with the discussion by Bachrach, "The Enforcement of *Forma Fidelitatis*," 810–811.

39. Bachrach, "Robert of Blois," 137–140.

40. Archives de Maine-et-Loire, H 1840, no. 4, for the original which is in poor condition, and Bib. Nat., n. a. lat. 1930, *Livre noir*, fol. 26v, for a later copy.

41. Bib. Nat., n. a. lat. 1930, *Livre noir*, fols. 28r–v, and for a published version from a later manuscript see Halphen, *Le comté d'Anjou*, 346–347.

42. Bib. Nat., n. a. lat. 1930, *Livre noir*, fols. 26v–27v.

43. See above, ch. 4, n. 15.

44. Bachrach, "Robert of Blois," 140.

45. Bib. Nat., n. a. lat. 1930, *Livre noir*, fols. 26v–27v.

46. Lamothe-Dreuzy, "Saint-Florent-le-Vieil," 72–74.

47. Bachrach, "The Enforcement of *Forma Fidelitatis*," 810, n. 71 and n. 72 for Anastasius of la Haye and his brother Roscelinus, who appear to have been tied in friendship, at the least, to the Plastulfi. By contrast, the vicarius Hugh of la Haye appears to have supported Fulk and later entered the Angevin count's newly founded monastery at Belli Locus. See regarding Hugh the charter published by Carré de Busserolle, *Dictionnaire géographique. . .*, vol. 3, no. 6, and the discussion by Bachrach, "Combat Sculptures," 74–75.

48. *Cartul. du Ronceray*, no. 173, provides the documentary evidence for Hildegarde's royal birth. The veracity of this text is unchallenged: e.g., Halphen, *Le comté d'Anjou*, 11, n. 1. Thus far, however, no one has been able to trace her immediate family with any certitude. See the literature cited by Bachrach, "Origins of Countess Gerberga," 14–15, n. 11.

49. *Cartul. de Cormery*, no. 31, as seen in the context of ch. 4, n. 24 above.

50. Newman, *Robert II,* no. 28.

51. Lot, *Hugues Capet,* 174, n. 4, and above, ch. 2, n. 168.

52. Bur, *Comté de Champagne,* 163, n. 36.

53. Bachrach, "The Angevin Strategy of Castle Building," 540, n. 20.

54. Hildegarde's and Fulk's son Geoffrey Martel was born on 14 October 1006 (Halphen, *Le comté d'Anjou,* 10), and thus it is likely that he was conceived in mid-January.

55. See Fulk's letter in Bachrach, "Pope Sergius IV," 246.

56. *Cartul. de Saint-Maurice,* no. 17, with the dating by Guillot, *Le comte d'Anjou,* 2:26.

57. See Bachrach, "Pope Sergius IV," 245, for Fulk's letter.

58. See Bachrach, "Pope Sergius IV," 252–253, concerning the diplomatically complicated texts on this situation. Cf. John Ottaway, "Liberté, ordre, et révolte d'après la charte dite de fondation de l'abbaye de Beaulieu-lès-Loches," in *Violence et contestation au moyen âge: Actes du 114ᵉ congrès national des Sociétés savantes (Paris, 1989): Section d'histoire médiévale et de philologie* (Paris, 1990), 19–46, who makes an effort to rehabilitate the so-called foundation charters and is correct insofar as he sees much of the information found in them to be an accurate representation of Fulk Nerra's acts. Nonetheless, he goes on to try to date some of the material to the reign of Geoffrey Martel and still other material to the mid-twelfth century. His methodology in the latter efforts is unsound. Ottaway apparently is unaware of my rehabilitation of these *acta* in "Pope Sergius IV," 252–253. Part of Ottaway's problem is an excessive reliance on style as a precise indicator of date; e.g., he seems to believe that coinage styles of the middle third of the eleventh century in the west of France can be distinguished so that an exact distinction can be made between what coins may have been struck during the reign of Fulk Nerra ca. 1035 and Geoffrey Martel ca. 1045. Ottaway's major problem, however, stems from his position that the great church at Beaulieu was built by Geoffrey Martel and not by Fulk Nerra and that it was consecrated in 1052. This interpretation is based solely on stylistic grounds. No documents give Geoffrey a role at Belli Locus and there is no reason to believe that Geoffrey had any interest in Belli Locus. The "evidence" Ottaway adduces for the consecration of the church in 1052 is a statement in a letter written in 1869 by G. de Gougny that a local oral tradition has it that the church was consecrated in 1052.

59. Ibid., 66–67.

60. Richer, *Hist.,* book 4, ch. 84; Raoul Glaber, *Hist.,* book 2, ch. 3, para. 4; and *Chron. de Nantes,* ch. 44, with the discussion by Bachrach, "Combat Sculptures," 67–69.

61. Bachrach, "Combat Sculptures," 67–68.

62. Bachrach, "Pope Sergius IV," 245–246, for the letter.

63. *Gallia Christ.,* vol. 14, cols. 64–66, and the related *Privilegium* of Pope John XVIII, with an examination of the diplomatics by Bachrach, "Pope Sergius IV," 252–253, n. 53.

64. Olivier Guillot, "La consécration de l'abbaye de Beaulieu-lès-Loches," *Actes du colloque médiéval de Loches (1973),* in *Mémoires de la Société archéologique de Touraine* 9 (1975): 25, nn. 29, 30. It should not be thought impossible that

Fulk learned about the possible military significance of the cherubim and seraphim while traveling in the Middle East during his first pilgrimage to the Holy Land.

65. Boussard, "La charte de fondation de Notre-Dame de Loches," 1–10, and the discussion by Bachrach, "Geoffrey Greymantle," 17–18, 37–38.

66. *Hist. S. Florentii,* 260, with the discussion by Bachrach, "Pope Sergius IV," 245.

67. The importance attributed to godparents during the Early Middle Ages makes it curious that our sources are silent concerning Geoffrey's sponsors. The identification by Joseph Lynch, *Godparents and Kinship in Early Medieval Europe* (Princeton, 1986), 138–140, of the writings of Dionysius the Areopagite (all discussion of Dionysius, both here and above, refers to the pseudo-Dionysius) as influential in the development of baptism and especially of sponsorship are interesting in light of the putative influence of Dionysius's work in Fulk's entourage. Regarding the latter see Guillot, "La consécration," 25.

68. Bachrach, "Pope Sergius IV," 246.

69. See *Archives d'Anjou,* 2:60, for an early version of this prayer by Fulk.

70. *Gallia Christ.,* vol. 14, col. 65, with the diplomatics discussed in Bachrach, "Pope Sergius IV," 252–253.

71. *Hist. S. Florentii,* 280. Geoffrey's sobriquet, "Martel," may complicate the matter somewhat.

72. The grants are outlined in a text published by Halphen, *Le comté d'Anjou,* 351–352, and *Gallia Christ.,* vol. 14, cols. 64–66. Regarding the diplomatics of the latter see Bachrach, "Pope Sergius IV," 252–253, n. 53; concerning the taxes and licenses, see the discussion by Bachrach, "The Angevin Economy," 5–13.

73. For the letter see Bachrach, "Pope Sergius IV," 245–246.

74. Concerning the archbishop's reply see Bachrach, "Pope Sergius IV," 246, where the reconstruction is made.

75. Raoul Glaber, *Hist.,* book 2, ch. 4, para. 6, and the reconstruction by Bachrach, "Pope Sergius IV," 242, 245–246.

76. See, for example, Bates, *Normandy before 1066,* 191–192.

77. Bachrach, "Fulk Nerra's Exploitation," 29–49, and Bachrach, "Geoffrey Greymantle," 8–9 and *passim.*

78. Boussard, "La charte de fondation de Notre-Dame de Loches," 1–10.

79. Bachrach, "Pope Sergius IV," 248–249. Barbara Rosenwein, Thomas Head, and Sharon Farmer, "Monks and Their Enemies: A Comparative Approach," *Speculum* 66 (1991): 764–796, provide some interesting observations on this problem in general.

80. *Hist.,* book 2, ch. 4, para. 6.

81. Robert Bautier, "L'historiographie en France," *Settimane di Studio de Centro Italiano di Studi sull'alto Medioevo,* 17, no. 1 (Spoleto, 1970): 832–833.

82. Bachrach, "The Angevin Economy," 5–13.

83. Bachrach, "Geoffrey Greymantle," 6–7, 25–28.

84. Bates, *Normandy before 1066,* 105.

85. W. Scott Jessee, "The Angevin Civil War and the Norman Conquest of 1066," in *The Haskins Society Journal: Studies in Medieval History,* ed. Rob-

ert B. Patterson (London, 1991), 3: 101–110, details events between 1066 and 1068 in which many of the variables at issue in Fulk Nerra's reign were recapitulated.

86. Bachrach, "The Angevin Strategy of Castle Building," 554.

87. Ibid., 554–555.

88. Bachrach, "Fulk Nerra's Exploitation," 29–49.

89. Pope John XVIII, *Privilegium,* cols. 1491–1492 (*PL* 139); Guillot, "La consécration," 29–30; and Bachrach, "Pope Sergius IV," 247–249. Cf. Zimmermann, no. 432.

90. Pope John XVIII, *Privilegium,* cols. 1491–1492 (*PL* 139); cf. Zimmermann, no. 432.

91. Raoul Glaber, *Hist.,* book 2, ch. 4, paras. 6, 7, provides the evidence for the episcopal reaction; Guillot, "La consécration," 25–26, discusses the legal situation.

92. "Les débuts du monastère de Beaulieu," 143, provides the local tradition. Bachrach, "Geoffrey Greymantle," 52, n. 62; and see the discussion by Guy-Marie Oury, "Les origines monastique de l'abbaye de Beaulieu-lès-Loches," *Bulletin de la Société archéologique de Touraine* 42 (1988): 169–178.

93. Concerning Herveus see above, ch. 3, n. 109.

94. Earlier in the Middle Ages the connections of Loches with Berry were very close. For example, toward the end of the sixth century Abbot Ursus, who founded many monasteries in Berry, crossed the frontier and established one at Loches. Auguste Longnon, *Géographie de la Gaule au VIᵉ siècle* (Paris, 1878), 275–276. In more recent times, ca. 935, the monks of Saint-Genou fled from l'Estrée because of an invasion by the Magyars and carried the relics of Saint Genou to the nearby castrum of Loches for safety. Devailly, *Le Berry,* 114. See also Bachrach, "Combat Sculptures," 64–65, and Oury, "Les origines," 172–174, who emphasizes monastic strategy rather than external influences.

95. See the discussion by Fanning, *A Bishop and His World,* 77–78; Guillot, *Le comte d'Anjou,* 1:229–233.

96. F. de Fontette, "Evêques de Limoges et comtes de Poitou au XIᵉ siècle," *Etudes d'histoire du droit canonique dédiées à G. le Bras* (Paris, 1965), 533–538.

97. Sharon Farmer, *Communities of Saint-Martin: Legend and Ritual in Medieval Tours* (Ithaca, N.Y., 1991), 38–42, provides some useful background.

98. Devailly, *Le Berry,* 129–142.

99. "Les débuts du monastère de Beaulieu," 143. Oury, "Les origines," 172–173, ably defends the value of this rather late text and perceptively observes that the list likely represents a final accounting.

100. Einhard, *Vita Karoli,* book 3, ch. 26, provides a useful example.

101. Oury, "Les origines," 172, argues convincingly on this point from his analysis of "Les débuts du monastère de Beaulieu," 143.

102. See the discussion of the sources by Bachrach, "Combat Sculptures," 77–78. In principle, there is no reason to reject the report that the monks (believed that they) possessed a piece of wood from the True Cross and a piece of stone from the Holy Sepulchre. What is at issue is the chronology for their acquisition of these relics and from whom they were obtained.

103. See above, ch. 4, n. 101; also for the background H. Silvestri, "Commerce et vol des reliques au moyen âge," *Revue belge de philologie et d'histoire* 30 (1952): 721–739, is useful. Note that the relics brought by Fulk from Rome are not characterized as being stolen while the stone from the Holy Sepulchre is described as stolen by Fulk Nerra. The latter is one of the many examples which eluded the net cast by Patrick Geary, *Furta Sacra: Thefts of Relics in the Central Middle Ages* (Princeton, 1978), concerning which see my review in *The Historian* 41 (1979): 763–764.

104. Lex, "Eudes, comte de Blois," 211–213; cf. Lucien Musset, "Actes inédits du XIe siècle: III: Les plus anciennes chartes normandes de l'abbaye de Bourgueil," *Bulletin de la Société des antiquaires de Normandie* 54 (1959): 43–44, rejects the traditional date, unsuccessfully in my opinion, but is followed by Bates, *Normandy before 1066,* 65.

105. Newman, *Robert II,* nos. 26, 29.

106. Ibid., no. 30.

107. For the date, see above, ch. 4, n. 104, and the discussion by Bates, *Normandy before 1066,* 65.

108. Pfister, *Robert le pieux,* 70–73, regarding Constance's children.

109. Cf. regarding King Robert's relations with both Bertha and Constance, Duby, *Medieval Marriage,* 45–54.

110. Concerning these forgeries see Bachrach, "Robert of Blois," 141–143; but cf. Ziezulewicz, "A Monastic Forgery in an Age of Reform," 7–42, and "Etude d'un faux monastique à une période de réforme," 201–211, who argues for a later date, though unconvincingly in my opinion. Denécheau, "Renaissance et privilèges," 23–35, presents a circular argument.

111. Bachrach, "Robert of Blois," 143–144.

112. See Bachrach, "The Pilgrimages of Fulk Nerra," 214, n. 13, which resolves the chronological problems that have shadowed this matter.

113. Raoul Glaber, *Hist.,* book 3, ch. 2, para. 7; and Fulbert, *Epist.,* no. 13.

114. Fulbert, *Epist.,* no. 13.

115. Ibid.

116. Fulbert, *Epist.,* no. 51, with the discussion of the Roman aspects of such a relationship identified above in my preface, n. 33. In short, from Bishop Fulbert's perspective Roman law and the Roman-influenced context of relations between a dominus and his fidelis were part of an organic whole.

117. Lemarignier, "Apropos de deux textes sur l'histoire du droit romain au moyen âge," 157–168, provides a helpful discussion of Fulbert's letter in the context of Roman law.

118. *Cartul. de Saint-Maurice,* no. 22, with the discussion by Bachrach, "Fulk Nerra's Exploitation," 41.

119. For the chronology see Bachrach, "The Pilgrimages of Fulk Nerra," 207–208.

120. Cf. the perspective of Hubert Guillotel, "Le premier siècle du pouvoir ducal breton (936–1040)," *103rd Congrès national des Sociétés savantes, Nancy–Metz* (1978), 74, 81.

121. Fanning, "Family and Episcopal Election," 41–51.

122. *La légende de la mort de Crescentius,* 146.

123. In general, see Heinrich Fichtenau, "Zum Reliquienwesen im früheren Mittelalter," *Mitteilungen des Institutes für österreichische Geschichtsforschung* 60 (1952): 60–89, and Nicole Herrmann-Mascard, *Les reliques des saints: Formation coutumière d'un droit* (Paris, 1975), 168–189. The power of a saint to thwart being carried off by an unworthy person is made clear in the Angevin tradition with specific reference to the efforts of Fulk Nerra to carry off Saint Florent from Saumur (*Hist. S. Florentii,* 278); this is yet another case missing from the "Handlist of Relic Thefts" published by Geary, *Furta Sacra,* 183–190.

124. *La légende de la mort de Crescentius,* 146. For some background of Fulk's relations with Pope Sergius see Bachrach, "Pope Sergius IV," 249–262; concerning the real Crescentius affair see the studies by P. Fedele, "Richerche per la storia di Roma e del papato nel secolo X," *Archivio della Reale Società Romana di Storia Patria* 34 (1911): 408–423, and O. Gerstenberg, "Studien zur Geschichte des römischen Adels im Ausgange des 10. Jahrhunderts," *Historische Vierteljahrschrift* 31 (1937): 1–26.

125. *La légende de la mort de Crescentius,* 147.

126. In addition to the works cited above in ch. 4, n. 124, see Halphen, *Le comté d'Anjou,* 131, 213, n. 7; but cf. Jules Lair, *Etudes critiques sur divers textes des Xe et XIe siècles* (Paris, 1899), 1:73–88.

127. Pfister, *Robert le pieux,* 68–69.

128. Concerning Adelaide's contacts with Pope Sergius and his support for her position, see J.-P. Poly, *La Provence et la société féodale, 879–1166* (Paris, 1976), 174–176.

129. Bachrach, "Pope Sergius IV," 254–264.

130. *La légende de la mort de Crescentius,* 146. Farmer, *Communities of Saint-Martin,* 78–95, discusses some of the methods and motives used by the Marmoutier writers for legitimizing various aspects of the behavior of the Angevin comital family, but the treatment is selective and limited.

131. *La légende de la mort de Crescentius,* 147.

132. Raoul Glaber, *Hist.,* book 3, ch. 2, para. 7. Cf. the terminology used by Fulbert, *Epist.,* no. 13, who is manifestly hostile to Fulk and echoes the treason terminology found in *Codex Theodosianus,* book 9, title 14, ch. 3, para. 6, when he uses *satellites.* On this point see Lemarignier, "Apropos de deux textes sur l'histoire du droit romain au moyen âge," 157–158.

Chapter 5: The Second Capetian-Blésois Axis

1. *Gesta Consulum,* 45–46; concerning Landry's defection see the discussion by Halphen, *Le comté d'Anjou,* 18–19; for the identification of Landry as being from Dun-sur-Auron in Berry rather than from Châteaudun as argued by Halphen see Bachrach, "The Enforcement of *Forma Fidelitatis,*" 810, n. 70; for the chronology see Bachrach, "Robert of Blois," 246, n. 31.

2. *Gesta Consulum,* 45, with the discussion by Halphen, *Le comté d'Anjou,* 58, concerning Landry's relations with Geoffrey Greymantle; see also Bachrach, "Geoffrey Greymantle," 31.

3. *Gesta Ambaz. dominorum,* 92–93.

4. *Gesta Consulum,* 45–46, with the discussion by Halphen, *Le comté d'Anjou,* 19, 31, as dated by Bachrach, "The Enforcement of *Forma Fidelitatis,*" 813.

5. *Gesta Consulum,* 45–46.

6. Ibid.

7. *Gesta Ambaz. dominorum,* 80, and *Gesta Consulum,* 51, for the time frame that can only fit the period of Fulk's second pilgrimage.

8. For the usual pattern of the inclusion of la Haye, see, for example, *Gesta Consulum,* 33. Regarding Roscelinus's defection and Plastulfus see *Cartul. de la Trinité de Vendôme,* no. 44, with the discussion by Bachrach, "The Enforcement of *Forma Fidelitatis,*" 810–811, n. 72.

9. Hugh of Flavigny, *Chron.,* 207, concerning Passavant; for Montbazon in Fulk's hands in 1006 see *Cartul. de Cormery,* no. 31, but lost by the Angevins sometime before the Angevin retook it in 1015. Fulk's siege of Montbazon in 1015 was the second he undertook; the first was likely ca. 1011 or 1012. See *Gesta Consulum,* 53–54, for the two sieges and for the success of the latter see *Gesta Ambaz. dominorum,* 82, which culminates in the campaigning season prior to the battle of Pontlevoy on 6 July 1016. Langeais fell to Fulk's adversaries sometime between 996, when Fulk successfully held it against Odo I, and 1009, when Landry operated in the middle Loire valley against Maurice (*Gesta Consulum,* 46). Fulk's high level of success between 1005 and 1008 seems to permit the vigorous inference that Langeais was lost during the Angevin count's second pilgrimage rather than during his first journey to the Holy Land.

10. For the pattern of overwhelming loyalty see the evidence presented in Bachrach, "The Enforcement of *Forma Fidelitatis,*" 796–819.

11. *Gesta Consulum,* 45–46; in addition, the authors of the *Gesta* also quote Seneca, *De moribus,* 114, 133.

12. Ibid., 45, n. 2 (this is an as yet unidentified classical text).

13. Fulbert, *Epist.,* no. 51, and the discussion above in my preface, n. 33.

14. Fulbert, *Epist.,* no. 9. This letter and no. 10 are dated by the editor Behrends before 17 February 1008 and before 28 March 1008, respectively. This is far too exact and based ostensibly on the position of these letters in the surviving manuscript collection. All the letters in this group are treated by Behrends, pp. lxxi–lxii, and many require reconsideration with regard to their chronology.

15. Chédeville, *Chartres et ses campagnes,* 264; but cf. Lemarignier, "Politics and Monastic Structures," 109–110. An examination of the documents for the Vendômois makes clear that during the last two decades of his reign as bishop of Chartres, Fulbert exercised no power in the region. See the analysis by Fanning, *A Bishop and His World,* 46–47. Concerning rendability of fortifications see for the background Charles Coulson, "Fortress Policy in Capetian Tradition and Angevin Practice: Aspects of the Conquest of Normandy by Philip II," *Anglo-Norman Studies,* ed. R. Allen Brown (Woodbridge, 1984), 6:13–38.

16. Fulbert, *Epist.,* no. 10, with the comments on chronology in ch. 5, n. 14, above. To try to simplify these rather complicated relationships it is nec-

essary to make clear that a congeries of important resources at Vendôme—including the *castrum* itself—belonged to the bishopric of Chartres and thus the bishop claimed to have particular rights in regard to those who held or possessed these resources. However, the right to appoint the count of Vendôme rested with the king, and thus if the king did not permit the count and others to provide to the bishop what they owed, the latter could ignore the bishop in secular matters. The bishop could always try to coerce these men by excommunicating them. Bouchard the Venerable was count of Vendôme and his immediate heir was Renaud, his son, who was bishop of Paris. The situation was complicated because the count of Blois was also count of Chartres and this gave him something to say in the appointment of the bishop of Chartres, although the king had the last word on this appointment as well. Nevertheless, the count of Chartres usually had considerable influence with the bishop. Within this framework Bishop Fulbert made an effort to enforce his rights at Vendôme and Odo II supported this in order to undermine Angevin influence at Vendôme with the viscount and the count. The counts of Vendôme—Bouchard, Renaud, and Bouchard (son of Adele and grandson of Fulk Nerra) were more rather than less close to the king throughout our story so the king supported them versus the bishop of Chartres and the count of Chartres who was also count of Blois.

17. Adémar of Chabannes, *Chron.*, book 3, ch. 56, and Pierre de Maillezais, *Relatio,* fol. 253v, who do not mention the name of Robert's queen. For Queen Constance's exile at this time see Odorannus, *Chron.*, 100–103. Cf. Pfister, *Robert le pieux,* 287, who believes that the "queen" mentioned by Adémar is Constance and recognizes neither that Odorannus's account telescopes about a decade into this section of his chronicle nor the fact that King Robert traveled to Aquitaine in the company of Odo II, Bertha's son. It is likely that Adémar omitted mention of Bertha's name because she had been excommunicated for her relations with Robert. In addition, it would have been embarrassing to mention Bertha in this context because Adémar made William the Great's piety a major theme of his chronicle. Duby, *Medieval Marriage,* 125, n. 75, follows the traditional chronology.

18. Adémar of Chabannes, *Chron.*, book 3, ch. 56, for those who attended with the exception of Count Hugh of Maine, who is mentioned by Pierre de Maillezais, *Relatio,* fol. 253v. Concerning William of Aquitaine's marriage see Richard, *Histoire des Comtes de Poitou,* 1:169.

19. Adémar de Chabannes, *Chron.*, book 3, chs. 35, 41, 57, 60, 65, 69, and the discussion by Bachrach, "William the Great," 16.

20. "Conventum," ed. Martindale, 542; George Beech, *A Rural Society in Medieval France: The Gâtine of Poitou in the Eleventh and Twelfth Centuries* (Baltimore, 1964), 44.

21. *Gesta Consulum,* 48, 54, and *Gesta Ambaz. dominorum,* 79, 84, both make clear that Lisoius had gained a substantial reputation before ca. 1014. Fulk seems first to have met Lisoius in July 1005, or at least that is the first time they can be documented together (*Chartes de Saint-Julien de Tours,* ed. Denis, no. 5).

22. Fulk's departure from Anjou took place sometime during the first nine

months of 1009, before the end of September. See Bachrach, "The Pilgrimages of Fulk Nerra," 206–207, for the chronology. But Fulk was at Rome during the reign of Pope Sergius IV, which began in July 1009. Fulk was away from home for approximately one and a half years (*Gesta Consulum,* 51), and he is known to have been in Angers by no later than 1 March 1011, as seen from the account of Pierre de Maillezais, *Relatio,* fol. 254r. Regarding Fulk's exploits see Bachrach, "Fulk's Tomb," 16–18.

23. Not only is the question of Fulk's guilt for the murder of Hugh not raised by contemporary and near-contemporary writers after the Angevin count's return from the Holy Land, but Raoul Glaber, *Hist.,* book 3, ch. 2, para. 7, actually praises him. André of Fleury, *Vita Gauzlini,* book 1, ch. 4, when discussing the distribution of Hugh's lands following his death seems consciously to avoid mentioning how he died.

24. The sources are discussed in detail by Bachrach, "Pope Sergius IV," 251–254.

25. *La légende de la mort de Crescentius,* 147.

26. Concerning the tradition of a procession for important dignitaries on their departure from Rome, see the discussion by Fergus Millar, *The Emperor in the Roman World* (Ithaca, N.Y., 1977), 28–29; regarding the *adventus* see Sabine MacCormack, *Art and Ceremony in Late Antiquity* (Berkeley, Los Angeles, London, 1981), 17–89.

27. Concerning these various relics see *Hist. S. Florentii,* 274; *La légende de la mort de Crescentius,* 147; and the discussion of the value of these sources by Oury, "Les origines . . . Beaulieu-lès-Loches," 171–172.

28. *Mirac. S. Nicholai,* 54–56, and *Hist. S. Florentii,* 275.

29. Regarding these persecutions see Hamilton A. R. Gibb, "The Caliphate and the Arab States," in *A History of the Crusades,* ed. Marshall W. Baldwin (Madison, 1969), 1:90–91.

30. See the treatment of these events by Adémar of Chabannes, *Chron.,* book 3, ch. 47, and pp. 205–206; as well as Raoul Glaber, *Hist.,* book 3, ch. 7, paras. 24–25.

31. *Gesta Consulum,* 50–51; *La légende de la mort de Crescentius,* 144–147; *Chron. Turonense magnum,* 118; *Hist. S. Florentii,* 274; and Oury, "Les origines," 172–173.

32. For example, among laymen an effort was made by Adémar of Chabannes to establish William the Great as a holy person. The latter often went to Rome and to Santiago but he never went to Jerusalem. See the discussion by Bachrach, "William the Great," 11–12.

33. Concerning the antiquity of this *adventus* ceremony see MacCormack, *Art and Ceremony in Late Antiquity,* 64–66.

34. *La légende de la mort de Crescentius,* 147, and the brief discussion by Bachrach, "Neo-Roman vs. Feudal," 9–10.

35. See the discussion by Guy-Marie Oury, "Les sculptures de Beaulieu-lès-Loches: Essai d'interprétation," *Historical Reflections/Reflexions historiques* 10 (1983): 56, who deals with Daria and Chrysanthus at Belli Locus.

36. Pierre de Maillezais, *Relatio,* fol. 254r.

37. For a critical edition of the act detailing Abbot Adhebertus's relations with Fulk see Halphen, *Le comté d'Anjou,* 352–354. Abbot Robert died on 8 August 1011 but spent most of the last year of his life at Saint-Mesmin-de-Micy in the Orléanais, where he was also abbot. Adhebertus succeeded shortly after Robert's death but likely ran affairs at Saint-Florent before he actually took office. See *Hist. S. Florentii,* 263–265; and Bachrach, "Robert of Blois," 144.

38. Bachrach, "Fulk Nerra's Exploitation," 29–49.

39. *Gesta Consulum,* 47–48; for the chronology see Bachrach, "The Angevin Strategy of Castle Building," 541, n. 25.

40. Coulson, "Fortress Policy," 24–25, and Bachrach, "The Enforcement of *Forma Fidelitatis,*" 796–799.

41. *Gesta Consulum,* 47–48.

42. See above, ch. 2, n. 83.

43. *Gesta Consulum,* 47–48.

44. Bachrach, "Geoffrey Greymantle," 30–31.

45. *Chron. Turonense magnum,* 119; *Gesta Ambaz. dominorum,* 83; and the discussion by Halphen, *Le comté d'Anjou,* 44, n. 4.

46. *Gesta Consulum,* 48, 59; *Gesta Ambaz. dominorum,* 79, 84; and the discussion by Bachrach, "Enforcement of *Forma Fidelitatis,*" 813.

47. See above, ch. 5, n. 9; regarding the physical characteristics of Montbazon see Bachrach, "Fortifications and Military Tactics," 541–549, where the relevant archaeological studies are discussed and criticized.

48. Bachrach, "The Enforcement of *Forma Fidelitatis,*" 810–811, n. 72.

49. Concerning Hugh see Carré de Busserolle, *Dictionnaire . . . de . . . Touraine,* vol. 3, no. 6 (pp. 319–320).

50. See above, ch. 4, n. 72.

51. *Gallia Christ.,* vol. 14, *instr.* col. 64, with the discussion of its authenticity in Bachrach, "Pope Sergius IV," 252–253.

52. *Gesta Consulum,* 36–37; Bachrach, "The Angevin Economy," 29–30, 53, n. 172.

53. Bachrach, "The Angevin Economy," 30–31.

54. Bryce D. Lyon, "Medieval Real-Estate Development and Freedom," *The American Historical Review* 63 (1957): 47–67, with substantial comparative bibliography.

55. Halphen, *Le comté d'Anjou,* 22–23, provides a useful guide to the early publications on the Loches coinage but unfortunately treats the material in an unsatisfactory manner. For example, he contends that because Belli Locus is not mentioned on the surviving Loches coinage, no coins were minted at Belli Locus. Thus, he concludes that the act under consideration from Belli Locus is inauthentic. In general, Halphen's treatment of documents from Belli Locus is poorly conceived. Additional information is to be found in A. Blanchet and A. Dieudonné, *Manuel de numismatique française,* vol. 4: *Monnaies féodales françaises* (Paris, 1936), Anjou, I, comte d'Anjou, II, Saint-Florent de Saumur, 73–75; Touraine I, Tours, Loches, II, Saint-Martin-de-Tours, III, Chinon, 364–367; and F. Dumas, E. Lorans, and E. Theureau, "Un dépôt monétaire dans

le cimetière de Saint-Mexme de Chinon," *Bulletin de la Société française de numismatique* 43 (1988): 466–468. See for more modern efforts: Guillot, "La consécration," 23–32; Bachrach, "Pope Sergius IV," 240–265; and Oury, "Les origines," 169–178.

56. For the bibliography on these coins see Halphen, *Le comté d'Anjou,* 222–223.

57. Faustin Poey d'Avant, *Monnaies féodales de France,* 1:200–201, for Fulk Nerra's "Gratia Dei, Comes" from Angers; and Bachrach, "Geoffrey Greyman-tle," 38, concerning the relevant charters of the Angevin counts regarding *Gratia Dei*. Cf. Guillot, *Le comte d'Anjou,* 1:394–395, who briefly mentions several written sources that deal with the coinage of the Angevin counts from a constitutional perspective. But Guillot does not deal with the Loches coinage and the implication of numismatic materials for either Fulk's economic policy or his efforts at "propaganda."

58. See above, ch. 5, n. 50.

59. *Gallia Christ.,* vol. 14, *instr.* col. 64; with the discussion of its authenticity in ch. 4, n. 72, above.

60. For the survey of Angevin taxes see Bachrach, "The Angevin Economy," 5–13.

61. Vallery-Radot, "L'ancienne église abbatiale de Beaulieu-lès-Loches," *Congrès archéologique de France* 106 (1958): 131–132.

62. I have quoted here in modified form the observations of Le Patourel, *The Norman Empire,* 362–363, concerning the rationale for William the Conqueror's great effort to build monumental churches. It seems to me that Fulk was thinking along the same lines as his younger contemporary. Of course, William's actions cannot have influenced Fulk, but the Angevin count's activities may have influenced the behavior of the Norman ruler.

63. J. Hardion and R. Michel-Dansec, "Etude archéologique sur l'église du Beaulieu-lès-Loches," *Congrès archéologique de France* 87 (1910): 95; Jacques Mallet, *L'art roman de l'ancient Anjou,* 276, where the innovative nature of the Loches effort is noted and the stone is classified as "le môyen appareil." By contrast, "petit appareil" was the norm at this time. See my review of Mallet's work in *Speculum* 64 (1989): 740–744.

64. For a recent review of the literature on the sculptures of Belli Locus which are regarded as unique for the Romanesque era, see Oury, "Les sculptures de Beaulieu-lès-Loches," 45–58, who has nothing new of substance to add on the particular relief under consideration here.

65. Richer, *Hist.,* book 3, ch. 84.

66. Bachrach, "Combat Sculptures," 67–68.

67. Concerning trial by combat see Bartlett, *Trial by Fire and Water,* 103–126, and the discussion by Bachrach, "Combat Sculptures," 66–67.

68. David Bernstein, *The Mystery of the Bayeux Tapestry* (Chicago, 1987), 126–128, and my review in *Speculum* 65 (1990), 123–124.

69. For roman military monuments see H. Russel Robinson, *The Armour of Imperial Rome,* pls. 238, 298, 301, 305, 460, 472, 475, and figs. 123, 191; and the discussion by Bachrach, "Combat Sculptures," 69.

70. Bachrach, "Combat Sculptures," 69.

71. Concerning Fulk's extensive travels see Bachrach, "The Pilgrimages of Fulk Nerra," 205–217.

72. Bachrach, "Fulk's Tomb," 11, for a discussion of types of sword hilts.

73. Sergius IV, *Privilegium*, cols. 1525–1527 (*PL* 139); with the discussion by Bachrach, "Pope Sergius IV," 249–262. Cf. Zimmermann, no. 462.

74. Sergius IV, *Privilegium*, cols. 1525–1526 (*PL* 139). Cf. Zimmermann, no. 462.

75. Raoul Glaber, *Hist.*, book 2, ch. 4, para. 7, provides the background concerning the compulsion used to assure the presence of the bishops. For the chronology see Bachrach, "The Pilgrimages of Fulk Nerra," 214, n. 13; see also Guillot, "La consécration," 31–32, who clarifies various of the details discussed above. Guillot is followed closely by Oury, "Les origines . . . Beaulieu-lès-Loches," 169–170. Some questions remain concerning when Fulk had the church "reconsecrated" to the Holy Sepulchre. The importance of "Eastern" influences signaled by reference to the Cherubim and Seraphim are noted by both Guillot and Oury.

76. Raoul Glaber, *Hist.*, book 2, ch. 4, para. 7, note that I have followed France's translation here as guided by the historian of architecture, Richard Gem (p. 65, n. 1), who advised France.

77. Raoul Glaber, *Hist.*, book 2, ch. 4, para. 7.

78. Pope Sergius IV, *Epist.*, col. 1527; with the discussion by Bachrach, "Pope Sergius IV," 262–264. Cf. Zimmermann, no. 462.

79. On 11 April 1012 Bishop Hubert of Angers "discovered" the remains of Saint Lupus, a prior bishop of Angers, in the church of Saint-Martin inside a hollow space beneath a large sarcophagus. An official account of the discovery was drawn up by the prelate, and this account was subsequently reburied with the remains of Saint Lupus. For the text of this account see George Forsyth, *The Church of St. Martin at Angers* (Princeton, 1953), 45, n. 80. In light of Fulk Nerra's interest in relics (see, for example, *Cartul. de Saint-Laud*, no. 55) and his close relationship with Bishop Hubert (Fanning, "Family and Episcopal Election," 39–56), it is highly unlikely that the Angevin count was in Angers during the period that began with the discovery of St. Lupus's remains and their subsequent reburial. Had he been in Angers at the time, he surely would have participated in the ceremonies.

80. Forsyth, *The Church of St. Martin at Angers*, 110–112, 212–218.

81. P. Calendeni, "Bernard Iᵉʳ, scholastique d'Angers," in *Dictionnaire d'histoire et de géographie ecclésiastiques*, vol. 8, cols. 578–580, eds. Alfred Baudrillart et al. (Paris, 1935); *Liber Miraculorum Sancte Fidis*, ed. Bouillet, p. xi.

82. *Liber Miraculorum Sancte Fidis*, ed. Bouillet, 2.

83. *Cartul. de Saint-Maurice*, no. 29, and the discussion by Fanning, *A Bishop and His World*, 69–71.

84. Fanning, *A Bishop and His World*, 71–72, calls attention to Fulk's use of the schoolmasters in the comital administration.

85. See the discussion by Bachrach, "The Practical Use of Vegetius' *De re militari*," 253.

86. "Conventum," ed. Martindale, 542; Beech, *A Rural Society in Medieval France,* 44 ff.; Adémar of Chabannes, *Chron.,* book 3, ch. 56; H. Imbert, *Notice sur les vicomtes de Thouars des familles de ce nom* (Niort, 1884), 38–40.

87. "Conventum," ed. Martindale, 242; Coulson, "Fortress Policy," 13–38, regarding rendability.

88. The several *acta* dealing with Vihiers are discussed in detail by Bachrach, "The Enforcement of *Forma Fidelitatis,*" 804–806.

89. Halphen, *Le comté d'Anjou,* 88–96; and Le Patourel, *The Norman Empire,* 317–318.

90. Bachrach, "The Enforcement of *Forma Fidelitatis,*" 804–806.

91. Ibid., 806–807.

92. *Cartul. de Saint-Jouin-de-Marnes,* 22; Bachrach, "Fulk Nerra's Exploitation," 29–49, regarding the *divisio.*

93. *Chron. de Nantes,* chs. 46, 47; *Hist. S. Florentii,* 282.

94. *Hist. S. Florentii,* 264–265; Bachrach, "Geoffrey Greymantle," 46; and *Cartul. de Saint-Aubin,* no. 178.

95. Pfister, *Robert le pieux,* 122, 236–237; cf. Bur, *Comté de Champagne,* 156. See also Fulbert, *Epist.,* no. 27.

96. A Jewish community was already well established at Blois by the last decade of the tenth century and probably a good bit earlier. See Robert Chazen, *Church, State, and Jew in the Middle Ages,* 299–330, who publishes an important document on this situation. For the continued importance of Jews at Blois well into the twelfth century see Robert Chazen, *Medieval Jewry in Northern France: A Political and Social History* (Baltimore, 1973), 40–42, 56–60.

97. Fulbert, *Epist.,* no. 27, and the general account by Bernhard Blumenkranz, *Juifs et Chrétiens dan le monde occidental, 430–1096,* 239–240, who, however, misdates the events by three years.

Chapter 6: Struggle for Mastery in the West: Part 1

1. *Cartul. de Saint-Aubin,* nos. 1, 677, with the discussion by Bachrach, "The Angevin Strategy of Castle Building," 554–555.

2. Concerning Lisoius see *Gesta Consulum,* 46, 48, 54, and *Gesta Ambaz. dominorum,* 75–76, 79, 84, along with the discussion by Bachrach, "The Angevin Strategy of Castle Building," 554–555.

3. For the capture of Mayenne see *Cartul. de Saint-Vincent,* no. 245, with the discussions by Robert Latouche, *Histoire du comté du Maine pendant le Xe et le XIe siècles,* 54, n. 1; and Bachrach, "The Angevin Strategy of Castle Building," 554.

4. *Cartul. de Saint-Maurice,* nos. 22, 27; Bib. Nat., Coll. Dom Housseau, vol. 1, no. 282, with the discussion by Bachrach, "The Angevin Strategy of Castle Building," 554–555, and "The Enforcement of *Forma Fidelitatis,*" 809, regarding Aimo.

5. Orderic Vitalis, *Historia Ecclesiastica,* ed. Chibnall, 2:304.

6. Fulk le Réchin, *Fragmentum historiae Andegavensis,* 233: "Ipse [Fulco] enim adquisivit Cenomannicum pagum."

7. See the discussion by Norgate, *England under the Angevins,* 1:159–160; Halphen, *Le comté d'Anjou,* 66–67; Latouche, *La comté de Maine,* 18, 22; and Guillot, *Le comte d'Anjou,* 1:21.

8. Bachrach, "Geoffrey Greymantle," 25–26.

9. Fanning, *A Bishop and His World,* 30–32.

10. *Cartul. de Saint-Aubin,* no. 85, provides a good example, and see the discussion by Bachrach, "The Angevin Strategy of Castle Building," 555.

11. Fanning, *A Bishop and His World,* 28–29, and Bachrach, "Geoffrey Greymantle," 25–26.

12. *Cartul. de Saint-Aubin,* no. 327, and Bachrach, "The Angevin Strategy of Castle Building," 555.

13. Jacques Boussard, "La seigneurie de Bellême aux Xe et XIe siècles," *Mélanges d'histoire du moyen âge dédiés à la mémoire de Louis Halphen,* 43–54; for a good sample of the frequency of the name Ivo in the Angevin *pagus* and its environs prior to ca. 1015, see *Cartul. de Saint-Aubin,* 3:217; cf. Guillot, *Le comte d'Anjou,* 1:328–330.

14. *Cartul. de la Trinité de Vendôme,* nos. 66 and 67, respectively, with the discussion by Bachrach, "The Enforcement of *Forma Fidelitatis,*" 804.

15. *Cartul. de Saint-Aubin,* no. 85.

16. See Bachrach, "The Angevin Strategy of Castle Building," 55.

17. *Gesta Consulum,* 46, and *Gesta Ambaz. dominorum,* 75–76. The twelfth-century redaction has Sehebrandus but this should not mislead us. Latouche, *Comté de Maine,* 63, n. 1. viz. Geoffrey of Mayenne, the eldest son and successor of Aimo.

18. *Gesta Consulum,* 46, 54; and *Gesta Ambaz. dominorum,* 79, 84. See the discussion by Bachrach, "The Enforcement of *Forma Fidelitatis,*" 807, 812, and Bachrach, "The Angevin Economy," 7–12.

19. *Gesta Consulum,* 48, 54; and *Gesta Ambaz. dominorum,* 79, 84. Additional light is cast on these arrangements for the region of Loches by Boussard, "La charte de fondation de Notre-Dame de Loches," 8–9; by *Cartul. de Saint-Aubin,* no. 178; and by *Bib. Nat.* n.d. 1930, *Livre noir,* fol. 26v. See the general discussion of the remuneration of officials in Bachrach, "The Angevin Economy," 24–27.

20. *Gesta Ambaz. dominorum,* 84, discusses Fulk's grant to Lisoius to take fodder (*segreheria*) beyond the river Cher. Concerning Selles, see above, ch. 3, nn. 67, 68.

21. Pfister, *Robert le pieux,* 11; Newman, *Robert II,* no. 40.

22. Pfister, *Robert le pieux,* 236, 261, 263.

23. Fulbert, *Epist.,* no. 27; *Gesta Ambaz. dominorum,* 82; and Lex, "Eudes, comte de Blois," cat. d'actes, nos. 29, 33.

24. Pfister, *Robert le pieux,* 262; Bur, *Comté de Champagne,* 156.

25. Bachrach, "Robert of Blois," 145; *Gesta Ambaz. dominorum,* 78.

26. See above, ch. 5, n. 9.

27. *Gesta Consulum,* 54; and *Gesta Ambaz. dominorum,* 82, with the discussion by Bachrach, "Fortifications and Military Tactics," 543.

28. Steven Fanning, "La lutte entre Hubert de Vendôme, évêque d'Angers, et l'archevêque de Tours en 1016: Un épisode dans l'histoire de l'Eglise des principautés territoriales," *Bulletin de la Société archéologique, scientifique, et littéraire du Vendômois* (1980), 31–33, and *Rec. des actes des ducs de Normandie,* ed. Fauroux, no. 22, where the absence of Hubert's name from the witness list suggests that he was still under excommunication.

29. *Gesta Ambaz. dominorum,* 82; Lex, "Eudes, comte de Blois," cat. d'actes, nos. 29, 33, and the discussion by Fanning, *A Bishop and His World,* 45–47.

30. Pfister, *Robert le pieux,* 262; *Hist. Fr.,* 10:597; and Newman, *Robert II,* no. 41.

31. Chaume, *Duché de Burgogne,* 1:481, 483, and Pfister, *Robert le pieux,* 237, 262–264.

32. *Gesta Ambaz. dominorum,* 82, for the initial operations, and *Gesta Consulum,* 52, where the action is picked up in the middle of the campaign against Montrichard.

33. *Gesta Ambaz. dominorum,* 82, and *Gesta Consulum,* 52, which complement each other.

34. *Gesta Consulum,* 52.

35. Ibid., and *Gesta Ambaz. dominorum,* 82.

36. *Gesta Consulum,* 52, and *Gesta Ambaz. dominorum,* 82, when read together, provide a reasonably cogent account. By contrast, *Hist. S. Florentii,* 274, grossly distorts the situation in an effort to put Fulk Nerra in the worst light possible. Halphen, *Le comté d'Anjou,* 34, attempts to reconstruct the battle with some success. See Verbruggen, *The Art of Warfare,* 86–89, regarding the lowering of the standard as a signal for retreat.

37. *Gesta Consulum,* 52–53; and *Hist. S. Florentii,* 275.

38. Bachrach, "The Practical Use of Vegetius' *De re militari,*" 245–249.

39. Halphen, *Le comté d'Anjou,* 37–38, n. 2, to which may be added the information found in Fulbert, *Epist.,* no. 71, as now dated by Fanning, "La lutte," 31–33.

40. *Gesta Consulum,* 53, and Halphen, *Le comté d'Anjou,* 37.

41. Bachrach, "The Angevin Strategy of Castle Building," 544–546.

42. Fulk le Réchin, *Fragmentum historiae Andegavensis,* 234; regarding the triumph following Fulk's victory at Conquereuil see above, chapter 2.

43. Mailfert, "Fondation du monastère . . . Saint-Nicholas d'Angers," *p.j.* 4.

44. Lepeletier, *Epitome,* 44.

45. *Recueil des actes de Philippe Ier,* no. 157.

46. Mailfert, "Fondation du monastère . . . Saint-Nicholas d'Angers," *p.j.* 4.

47. Bachrach, "Neo-Roman vs. Feudal," 8–9.

48. Regarding Bernard see *Liber Miraculum,* ed. Bouillet, ix–xiii; Stock, *The Implications of Literacy,* 64–71; and Fanning, *A Bishop and His World,* 69–71. Concerning Roman interest in writing history see, for example, the various issues raised by P. T. Wiseman, "Practice and Theory in Roman Historiography," *History* 66 (1981): 375–393; the discussion by P. A. Brunt, "Cicero and Historiography," *Philias charis: Miscellanea di studi classici in onore di Eugenio Manni* (Rome, 1979), 311–340; and note particularly the interest of

Gregory of Tours, *Hist.*, book 7, ch. 1, where he discusses the notion of credibility based on Sallust, *Catiline*, ch. 3.

49. Fanning, *A Bishop and His World*, 70–72; *Catul. de Saint-Aubin*, no. 106, is particularly worthy of study.

50. For Berenger's work in the comital entourage see Fanning, *A Bishop and His World*, 67–69, 80; regarding Berenger's intellectual range see Stock, *The Implications of Literacy*, 275–281, with the literature cited there.

51. Mailfert, "Fondation du monastère . . . Saint-Nicholas d'Angers," *p.j.* 4.

52. *Gesta Consulum*, 25–27; Bachrach, "Neo-Roman vs. Feudal," 6–7.

53. For these honorifics and several others that likely were thought by eleventh- and twelfth-century writers to have imperial roots see *Cartul. de Saint-Aubin*, nos. 20, 23, 34, 131, 197, 932. Concerning Geoffrey's "Red Cloak" see Bachrach, "Neo-Roman vs. Feudal," 29–30.

54. *Cartul. de Saint-Aubin*, no. 197, with the discussion by Bachrach, "Some Observations on the Origins of the Angevin Dynasty," 3–4, 8.

55. *Cartul. de la Trinité de Vendôme*, no. 6; *Cartul. de Saint-Aubin*, no. 355; and *Cartul. du Ronceray*, nos. 78, 129, 235, provide good examples.

56. *Cartul. de Saint-Aubin*, no. 2, for Geoffrey's recognition of Hugh Capet as his lord. Concerning Fulk see Guillot, *Le comte d'Anjou*, 1:16; but cf. Jacques Boussard, "Le comte d'Anjou au XIe siècle," *Journal des Savants* (1975), 134–135.

57. Bachrach, "The Angevin Economy," 29–32.

58. Halphen, *Le comté d'Anjou*, 95; and most recently Brühl, *Palatium und Civitas*, 1:157.

59. Brühl, *Palatium und Civitas*, 1:157.

60. The fires of 1000 and 1032 obviously provided propitious circumstances for the rebuilding and expansion of the urbs. Regarding the latter see Brühl, *Palatium und Civitas*, 1:157; cf. concerning the former date Halphen, *Le comté d'Anjou*, 62, n. 3. There is no reason to confound the authenticity of the report on the fire with what may perhaps have been a legendary accretion to the story of the death of Fulk's first wife.

61. Bachrach and Aris, "Military Technology and Garrison Organization," 1–17, for the method of calculation. In this framework, as the sophistication of the offensive technology increases, more manpower is required for the defense.

62. Concerning the ages of militia men see Contamine, *War in the Middle Ages*, 155.

63. Halphen, *Le comté d'Anjou*, 93–96, and Forsyth, *St. Martin at Angers*, 141, n. 242. Note that the area under consideration here is that between the 1,900-meter perimeter wall and Saint-Aubin. It should be noted that the space between the two walls was also very crowded.

64. If only able-bodied men between 15 and 55 years of age living within the walls were required to serve in the militia and these men comprised one-third of the population (a worst-case scenario) or one-quarter of the population (a moderate case), then the density of the city would be between 400 and 470 persons per hectare.

65. Fulk le Réchin, *Fragmentum historiae Andegavensis*, 37, and the discus-

sion of the numbers of Angevin fighting forces by Bernard S. Bachrach, "Angevin Campaign Forces in the Reign of Fulk Nerra, Count of the Angevins (987–1040)," *Francia* 17, no. 1 (1990): 67–84, and 77 concerning the value of Fulk le Réchin's numbers.

66. The exceptionally detailed researches of J.-M. Bienvenu, "Pauverté, misères, et charité en Anjou aux XIe et XIIe siècles," *Le moyen âge* 72 (1966): 389–424; 73 (1967): 5–34, 190–216, uncovered very little poverty for the reign of Fulk Nerra.

67. For trade as indicated by the evidence provided by tolls see J.-M. Bienvenu, "Recherches sur les péages angevins aux XIe et XIIIe siècles," *Le moyen âge* 63 (1957): 209–240, 437–467, and the discussion, in general, by Bachrach, "The Angevin Economy," 3–55.

68. Bachrach, "The Angevin Strategy of Castle Building," 533–560.

69. An important text is provided by André of Fleury, *Vita Gauzlini*, ch. 28; for some general background see Bienvenu, "Recherches sur les péages," 212.

70. *Cartul. de Saint-Maurice*, no. 80.

71. Ibid. The author of this account seems to be playing on the double meaning of *magister* here. Had not Michael held this title there would have been no reason to use it in order to tell the story.

72. Ibid. Indeed, as the situation developed, the bishop's interpretation of his exemption prevailed in a hearing before Fulk.

73. *Cartul. de Saint-Aubin*, no. 186.

74. Concerning the praepositus see *Archive d'Anjou*, 2:60; *Cartul. de Saint-Maurice*, no. 22; and Halphen, *Le comté d'Anjou, p.j.* 6. The first identifiable praepositus was likely Gauscelinus, who was followed by Berno. The latter appears to have held the office when the matter of the wash house arose. Cf. Guillot, *Le comte d'Anjou*, 1:410.

75. The basic information is developed by Halphen, *Le comté d'Anjou*, 106–109. For a sense of the complexity of the government not conveyed by Halphen see Bachrach, "Fulk Nerra's Exploitation," 29–49.

76. *Cartul. de Saint-Laud*, no. 55.

77. *Cartul. de Saint-Aubin*, no. 397.

78. For a wide variety of insights regarding the "behavior" of saints see Fichtenau, "Zum Reliquienwesen," 60–89.

79. *Cartul. de la Trinité de Vendôme*, no. 6, which is not greatly distorted regarding the various matters of tenure it describes. Cf. Guillot, *Le comte d'Anjou*, 1:27, n. 139.

80. *Rec. des actes des ducs de Normandie*, ed. Fauroux, no. 22, with the discussion by Halphen, *Le comté d'Anjou*, 36–37, who is followed by Guillot, *Le comte d'Anjou*, 2: 38–39; Lemarignier, *Le gouvernement royal*, 47–50.

81. Bur, *Comté de Champagne*, 156; Bachrach, "William the Great," 16.

82. Jan Dhondt, "Une crise du pouvoir capetien, 1032–1034," *Miscellanea mediaevalia in memoriam Jan Frederik Niermeyer* (Gronigen, 1967), 138–140, for various deals and for Capetian control of the succession to the *comté* of Vendôme. Regarding Fulk Nerra's subsequent control of the *comté* see *Cartul. de la Trinité de Vendôme*, no. 6, and *Livre des serfs de Marmoutier*, no. 52.

83. Boussard, "Services féodaux," 155–156, concerning the garrison and castle guard at Vendôme. Cf. Guillot, *Le comte d'Anjou*, 1:49–51, n. 237, who wants to date the establishment of this military structure to the reign of Bouchard III rather than Bouchard II. The major point at issue for Guillot is the mention of a Count Fulk at Vendôme after Count Bouchard (*Cartul. de la Trinité de Vendôme*, no. 2). Guillot sees this Fulk as the brother and successor of Bouchard III. But the Count Fulk at issue is in fact Fulk Nerra, and the Bouchard mentioned is Bouchard the Venerable, the Angevin count's erstwhile father-in-law. The chronology is established in part from an examination of the men listed in the text as participants. The relevant *acta* are cited below, ch. 6, n. 84.

84. Fulbert, *Epist.*, no. 10; *Cartul. de la Trinité de Vendôme*, nos. 1, 2; and *Livre des serfs de Marmoutier*, no. 52, are the most essential texts.

85. *Cartul. de la Trinité de Vendôme*, no. 1, as discussed concerning authenticity by Halphen, *Le comté d'Anjou*, 64; but cf. Guillot, *Le comte d'Anjou*, 1:27, nn. 137, 139.

86. See the discussion of the relevant texts by Bachrach, "The Angevin Economy," 28.

87. Bib. Nat., n. a. lat. 1930, *Livre noir*, fols. 99r–100r.

88. Bachrach, "The Angevin Economy," 5–13.

89. *Gesta Ambaz. dominorum*, 80.

90. *Hist. S. Florentii*, 264–265, 267.

91. Archives de Maine-et-Loire, H 1840, no. 5; Bib. Nat., n. a. lat. 1930, *Livre noir*, fols. 29v–30v, with the discussion by Bachrach, "The Angevin Economy," 7.

92. Bib. Nat., n. a. lat. 1930, *Livre noir*, fols. 2v–3r, 15r–16v; Archives de Maine-et-Loire, H 3714, fols. 29v–30v; *Hist. S. Florentii*, 265–267; and Bachrach, "The Enforcement of *Forma Fidelitatis*," 805 (n. 87), 812 (n. 82).

93. *Chron. de Nantes*, ch. 47; *Hist. S. Florentii*, 270.

Chapter 7: Struggle for Mastery in the West: Part 2

1. "Conventum," ed. Martindale, 543–547.

2. *Gesta Consulum*, 47–48.

3. See Bachrach, "William the Great," 14–18, with the literature cited there.

4. Bachrach, "Study in Feudal Politics," 116–119.

5. "Chartes poitevines de Saint-Florent," ed. Marchegay, 16; Bachrach, "The Enforcement of *Forma Fidelitatis*," 805–806, n. 48.

6. Bachrach, "The Angevin Tradition of Castle Building," 548.

7. Adémar of Chabannes, *Chron.*, book 3, ch. 56; Bachrach, "The Angevin Strategy of Castle Building," 552.

8. "Conventum," ed. Martindale, 544; Adémar de Chabannes, *Chron.*,

book 3, ch. 56; *Chartes de Cluny,* no. 2716; Besly, *Histoire de Comtes de Poictou,* 307; and Bachrach, "William the Great," 18–19.

9. "Conventum," ed. Martindale, *passim.*

10. Bachrach, "William the Great," 11–21.

11. *Hist. S. Florentii,* 275.

12. Ibid. Charles Jones, *Saint Nicholas of Myra, Bari, Manhattan,* 104, believes that the dove called Fulk to "his duties as a builder." Fulk, however, was constantly building, as we have seen throughout this study. I would hazard an alternative suggestion, namely, that Fulk's observation of the dove building its home recalled the idea of death to the Angevin count because the Latin word for dovecote, *columbarium,* is the same word used for the niche in which the Romans buried the ashes of their dead.

13. *Hist. S. Florentii,* 275.

14. *Miracula S. Nicholai,* in Mailfert, "Fondation du monastère . . . Saint-Nicholas d'Angers," 54–56.

15. Gustav Ainrich, *Hagios Nikolaos: der heiliger Nikolaos in Griechischen Kirche,* vol. 1, in which the texts are collected, and vol. 2, for Ainrich's commentary. See also Jones, *Saint Nicholas,* 1–154.

16. *Hist. S. Florentii,* 275, for the text; for the archaeological evidence with which it should be identified see Brühl, *Palatium und Civitas,* 1:156; the castellum under discussion should be associated with the finds made in rue Kellerman in 1867.

17. Southern, *Making of the Middle Ages,* 87.

18. *Miracula S. Nicolai,* in Mailfert, "Fondation du monastère . . . Saint-Nicholas d'Angers," 54–56.

19. Jones, *Saint Nicholas,* 77, for a list summarizing the attributes discussed.

20. Mailfert, "Fondation du monastère . . . Saint-Nicholas d'Angers," *p.j.* 2.

21. Ibid., *p.j.* 4.

22. Bachrach, "Potius Rex," 15, concerning William the Great; regarding the Normans, Bachrach, "Neo-Roman vs. Feudal," 12.

23. Mailfert, "Fondation du monastère . . . Saint-Nicholas d'Angers," *p.j.* 4.

24. Jones, *Saint Nicholas,* 1–154.

25. Mailfert, "Fondation du monastère . . . Saint-Nicholas d'Angers," *p.j.* 4. Guillot, *Le comte d'Anjou,* 1:177–178.

26. Cf. Farmer, *Communities of Saint Martin,* 71–73.

27. William Ziezulewicz, "From Serf to Abbot: The Role of the 'Familia' in the Career of Frederick of Tours," *The American Benedictine Review* 36 (1985): 285–290.

28. Farmer, *Communities of Saint Martin,* 65–75, provides a brief but useful review of Marmoutier's place in the politics of this period.

29. See, for example, *Livre des serfs de Marmoutier,* nos. 1, 52; *Gallia Christ.,* vol. 14, *instr.* col. 62; and Bib. Nat., Coll. Dom Housseau, vol. 1, nos. 290, 291, along with the discussion by Fanning, "Les origines familiales de Vulgrin," 246–247. Cf. Farmer, *Communities of Saint Martin,* 72–73, who seems to underestimate Angevin influence at Marmoutier during Fulk Nerra's reign.

30. Newman, *Robert II,* no. 55; Lex, "Eudes, comte de Blois," cat. d'actes, nos. 35, 67; Bur, *Comté de Champagne,* 156.

31. Ziezulewicz, "Frederick of Tours," 285–290.

32. *Cartul. de Saint-Aubin,* nos. 275, 952; *Hist. S. Florentii,* 275–280.

33. *Hist. S. Florentii,* 275–276.

34. Ibid.; Halphen, *Le comté d'Anjou,* 39, 162, n. 2.

35. *Hist. S. Florentii,* 275–276, for the sequence of events but with the period from ca. 1021 to 1026 severely telescoped. See also Fulbert, *Epist.,* nos. 45, 46.

36. Bernard S. Bachrach, *"Caballus et Caballarius* in Medieval Warfare," in *The Story of Chivalry,* ed. H. Chickering and T. Seiler (Kalamazoo, Mich., 1988), 173–211. See the brilliant article by John Gillingham, "War and Chivalry in the *History of William the Marshal," Thirteenth-century England,* ed. P. R. Cross and S. D. Lloyd (Woodbridge, 1990), 2:1–13.

37. Lot, *Hugues Capet,* 397–413, and esp. 409–413; Lex, "Eudes, comte de Blois," 221–226; and the useful summary by Behrends in Fulbert, *Epist.,* lxxix–lxxx, with the single exception of misdating Bishop Hubert's attack on Archbishop Hugh. Concerning the date see Fanning, "La lutte," 31–33.

38. For Fulk's meeting with Robert see Archives de Maine-et-Loire, H 3716, fol. 60v.

39. Boussard, "Le trésorier de Saint-Martin," 76–79.

40. Bib. Nat., Coll. Baluze, vol. 76, fol. 256.

41. *Livre des serfs de Marmoutier,* no. 52.

42. Boussard, "Les évêques en Neustrie," 176, 178, n. 103.

43. Halphen, *Le comté d'Anjou,* 63–64; *Cartul. du Ronceray,* no. 391, for Radulfus as viscount, and *Cartul. de Saint-Maurice,* no. 29, for the death of Viscount Hubert before 16 August 1025. For the Vendômois perspective see Fanning, *A Bishop and His World,* 59–60.

44. *Hist. S. Florentii,* 276; *Cartul. de Saint-Maurice,* no. 45. For the basic archaeological work on this stronghold see Michel de Boüard, "De l'aula au donjon: Les fouilles de la motte de La Chapelle à Doué-la-Fontaine (Xᵉ–XIᵉ siècle)," *Archéologie médiévale* 3 and 4 (1973–1974): 5–110.

45. *Cartul. de Saint-Maurice,* no. 45; Bachrach, "The Angevin Economy," 6.

46. Ziezulewicz, "Frederick of Tours," 278–291.

47. See above, ch. 6, n. 38; Bachrach, "The Enforcement of *Forma Fidelitatis,"* 805–806, nn. 48, 49.

48. Fulbert, *Epist.,* no. 86. Cf. Louis Halphen, "La lettre d'Eudes de Blois au roi Robert," *Revue historique* 97 (1908): 287–296.

49. Adémar de Chabannes, *Chron.,* book 3, ch. 64.

50. *Act. Pont.,* 358; also Fulbert, *Epist.,* no. 87.

51. Fulbert, *Epist.,* no. 86.

52. Ibid. Cf. Halphen, "La lettre," 287–296.

53. *Act. Pont.,* 358–359; *Chron. de Nantes,* ch. 47; Fulbert, *Epist.,* no. 86.

54. Latouche, *Comté de Maine,* 14–21.

55. Richard, *Histoire des comtes de Poitou,* 1:182–183.

56. *Chartes de Nouaillé,* no. 104.

57. Fulbert, *Epist.,* no. 104. Behrend's date is about six months off the mark.

58. Ibid.

59. Cf. Bates, *Normandy before 1066,* 69–70.

60. Ibid. Bates does not appear to appreciate that Geoffrey Martel built upon the work of Fulk Nerra.

61. Bachrach, "Geoffrey Greymantle," 32–33, and Bachrach, "The Angevin Strategy of Castle Building," 541–556.

Chapter 8: Master in the West

1. Pfister, *Robert le pieux,* 76, 238–244, 368–381; Bur, *Comté de Champagne,* 169–170; Lewis, *Royal Succession,* 24–25.

2. See two important studies by Jan Dhondt, "Election et hérédité sous les Carolingiens et les premiers Capétiens," *Revue belge d'histoire et de la philologie* 19 (1939): 913–953, and "Sept femmes et un trio de rois (Robert le Pieux, Henri Ier, et Philippe Ier)," *Contributions à l'histoire économique et sociale* 3 (1965): 37–70. See also Lewis, *Royal Succession,* 25.

3. *Annales Vindocinenses,* 60; *Annales . . . Rainaldi,* 86; *Hist. S. Florentii,* 276; and the general discussion by Halphen, *Le comté de Anjou,* 39.

4. *Annales . . . Rainaldi,* 86; *Ann. Vind.,* 60.

5. *Hist. S. Florentii,* 276; *Ann. Vind.,* 60.

6. *Gesta Consulum,* 53; *Hist. S. Florentii,* 276.

7. *Gesta Consulum,* 54; *Gesta Ambaz. dominorum,* 81.

8. *Ann. Vind.,* 60–61; *Annales . . . Rainaldi,* 86; *Gesta Consulum,* 53–54.

9. *Gesta Consulum,* 54; *Gesta Ambaz. dominorum,* 81, "simulans fugam," with the further discussion of these tactics by Bachrach, "Animals and Warfare," 735–740.

10. See for a more detailed discussion Bachrach, "The Angevin Strategy of Castle Building," 556–559.

11. *Hist. S. Florentii,* 280; concerning the use of levies composed of men from the dependent agricultural classes see Bachrach, "The Angevin Economy," 8–10.

12. Fulbert, *Epist.,* nos. 115, 116, and 122; however, Behrends dates no. 122 too late.

13. Adémar of Chabannes, *Chron.,* book 3, ch. 65, regarding William's pilgrimage.

14. *Hist. S. Florentii,* 281, as discussed by Halphen, *Le comté d'Anjou,* 155; *Cartul. du Ronceray,* nos. 125, 126.

15. Adémar of Chabannes, *Chron.,* book 3, ch. 64.

16. *Ann. Vind.,* 61, with the discussion by Halphen, *Le comté d'Anjou,* 69.

17. Pfister, *Robert le pieux,* 78–79; Halphen, *Le comté d'Anjou,* 69.

18. *Chron. de Nantes,* ch. 47, for Alan's conflict with Budic; and *Chron. Kemper.,* 294, for the marriage of Alan to Odo's daughter Bertha, which is dated by Norgate, *Angevin Kings,* 1:159 (n. 4) and 205, to 1027. The marriage certainly took place before 1031.

19. *Act. Pont.*, 61.

20. *Hist. S. Florentii*, 281, and *Cartul. du Ronceray*, nos. 125, 126, along with the observation by Halphen, *Le comté d'Anjou*, 155.

21. *Cartul. du Ronceray*, nos. 125, 126.

22. Fulbert, *Epist.*, no. 120. This letter should be seen to predate no. 122, alluded to above, ch. 8, n. 12.

23. *Gesta Consulum*, 8, and Boussard, "Le trésorier de Saint-Martin," 78.

24. *Gesta Consulum*, 30, 33, for Angevin dominion over these places on the basis of hereditary right, and *Gesta Ambaz. dominorum*, 86, for their later disposition.

25. *Gesta Ambaz. dominorum*, 85–90, and *Gesta Consulum*, 54–57, bear out the soundness of Fulk's judgment in his choice of Lisoius.

26. *Gesta Ambaz. dominorum*, 86.

27. Bachrach, "Geoffrey Greymantle," 45, n. 23, and *Gesta Ambaz. dominorum*, 83–87.

28. *Gesta Ambaz. dominorum*, 85; for the *census* as a land tax within a fortification see Bachrach, "The Angevin Economy," 5–6.

29. Halphen, *Le comté d'Anjou*, 83.

30. Bachrach, "Geoffrey Greymantle," 31.

31. *Gesta Ambaz. dominorum*, 80, 89–90; Bachrach, "The Angevin Economy," 25.

32. See above, ch. 8, n. 18; cf. Norgate, *Angevin Kings*, 1:205, who seems to confuse matters because she failed to see that the *Franci*, from the Breton perspective, were Fulk's men. It is likely that Hugh of Châteaudun tried to kidnap Fulk's daughter at this time. *Cartul. du Ronceray*, no. 125.

33. *Chron. de Nantes*, ch. 47.

34. This is the position taken by Casandra Potts, "Normandy or Brittany? A Conflict of Interests at Mont Saint Michel (966–1035)," in *Anglo-Norman Studies*, ed. Marjorie Chibnall (Woodbridge, 1990), 12:155–156.

35. Bachrach, "The Practical Use of Vegetius' *De re militari*," 246–247, n. 28.

36. *Hist. S. Florentii*, 280; Bachrach, "The Practical Use of Vegetius' *De re militari*," 247; and Bachrach, "Robert of Blois," 143, n. 2.

37. Bachrach, "The Practical Use of Vegetius' *De re militari*," 246–247.

38. Boussard, "Le trésorier de Saint-Martin," 78.

39. *Hist. S. Florentii*, 277–278; for a suggestive interpretation of Abbot Frederick's role see Ziezulewicz, "Frederick of Tours," 279, n. 3.

40. Bachrach, "The Enforcement of *Forma Fidelitatis*," 807.

41. Bachrach, "Robert of Blois," 130–131.

42. For a general treatment of the Angevin tax system as it functioned under Fulk Nerra see Bachrach, "The Angevin Economy," 5–13. Much of what follows is a rather summarized version of the material developed in this study.

43. Bachrach, "The Angevin Economy," 6–7.

44. Ibid.

45. Bib. Nat., n. a. lat. 1930, *Livre noir*, fols. 28v–29r.

46. For the background see Carlrichard Brühl, *Fodrum, Gistum, Servitium*

Regis (Cologne, 1968), 2 vols.; Guillot, *Le comte d'Anjou,* 1:379–381; and Bachrach, "Animals and Warfare," 708–716.

47. For the background see F. L. Ganshof, "La *Tractoria*: Contribution à l'étude des origines du droit de gîte," *Tijdschrift voor rechtsgeschiedenis* 8 (1928): 69–91; regarding areas under Angevin control see the two useful examples provided by *Cartul. de Notre-Dame de Saintes,* no. 1, and *Cartul. de Saint-Maurice,* no. 27.

48. Bachrach, "The Angevin Economy," 8.

49. Bib. Nat., n. a. lat. 1930, *Livre noir,* fols. 29v–30r.

50. Bachrach, "Angevin Economy," 8–9.

51. Bachrach, "Angevin Campaign Forces," 67–84, for the background, esp. p. 82.

52. See Guillot, *Le comte d'Anjou,* 1:391–394, regarding licenses.

53. Bachrach, "The Angevin Economy," 11.

54. Lepeletier, *Breviculum,* 14; Archives de Maine-et-Loire, H 1840, n. 7.

55. Bachrach, "The Angevin Economy," 11.

56. Ibid., 43–44, n. 71.

57. Bienvenu, "Recherches sur les péages," 437–454, provides some useful raw data that has been worked into the general picture by Bachrach, "The Angevin Economy," 19–20.

58. Bachrach, "The Angevin Economy," 17.

59. Ibid., 22–24.

60. Jean Durliat, "Le polyptyque d'Irminon et l'impôt pour l'armée," *Bibliothèque d'Ecole des Chartes* 141 (1983): 183–208.

61. Bachrach, "The Angevin Economy," 19–20.

62. See, for example, *Hist. S. Florentii,* 280; Bib. Nat., n. a. lat. 1930, *Livre noir,* fols. 106r–v, 111r–v; *Cartul. de Saint-Aubin,* no. 236. Jacques Boussard, "L'éviction des tenants de Thibaut de Blois par Geoffrey Martel, comte d'Anjou, en 1044," *Le moyen âge* 69 (1963): 141–149, concerning later Angevin policy. Cf. the few survivors of Fulk's policy at Saint-Florent identified by William Ziezulewicz, "An Argument for Historical Continuity: Low and Middle Vassal Families in the Eleventh-century Saumurois," *Medieval Prosopography* 8, no. 1 (1987): 93–110. Most of these survivors are characterized by Ziezulewicz as minor figures.

63. *Hist. S. Florentii,* 281; *Cartul. de Saint-Maurice,* no. 45; and Archives de Maine-et-Loire, H 3713, fols. 1r–2v. Bachrach, "The Enforcement of *Forma Fidelitatis,*" 813, n. 91.

64. *Hist. S. Florentii,* 281; Halphen, *Le comté d'Anjou,* 183; Bachrach, "The Angevin Strategy of Castle Building," 546.

65. Guillot, *Le comte d'Anjou,* 1:151, n. 91, for Hubert's dates; *Cartul. de Saint-Aubin,* no. 26, but cf. no. 25; concerning Abbot Hubert's service to Fulk Nerra see Fulbert, *Epist.,* no. 13; see for the profits from fines Bachrach, "The Angevin Economy," 11–12.

66. *Cartul. de Saint-Aubin,* nos. 178, 220, 932; Bachrach, "The Angevin Strategy of Castle Building," 545; Bachrach, "Military Administration," 3, n. 5.

67. Bachrach, "Geoffrey Greymantle," 18–19.

68. Bachrach, "The Angevin Strategy of Castle Building," 544–545.

69. *Cartul. de Saint-Aubin,* no. 220, with the discussion of the literature by Bachrach, "Military Administration," 3.

70. The earliest sure use of the title *princeps* by Fulk is in 1032 when he is styled *invictissimus princeps* (Mailfert, "Fondation du monastère . . . Saint-Nicholas d'Angers," *p.j.* 3. An act of 1014, which was redrawn between 1056 and 1059 in order to include Geoffrey Martel, describes both counts together as *Andegavorum principes* (*Cartul. de Saint-Aubin,* no. 178). In the context of the southern frontier, it is important that the monks of Saint-Aubin made clear that Fulk had imposed military duty on them. Thus, when they wanted to reject it in 1056, they said (or at least their abbot-elect is quoted as saying) that he "had not come to guard the *castra* of *principes.*" This act survives in two forms: one is published by Guillot, *Le comte d'Anjou,* 1:469–470, as a *pièce justificative;* the other is in *Cartul. de Saint-Aubin,* no. 6. Cf. Guillot, *Le comte d'Anjou,* 356–358, who believes that Fulk Nerra did not use the title *princeps* but that it was adopted by Geoffrey Martel early in his reign.

71. Bachrach, "The Angevin Strategy of Castle Building," 548–553.

72. Werner, "Kingdom and Principality," 243–290, provides the relevant background regarding principes.

73. Cf. Bachrach, "The Angevin Economy," 21, where after a discussion of the evidence, the imposition of the *consuetudo* is dated to the abbacy of Hubert rather than that of Primaldus.

74. *Cartul. de Saint-Pierre le la Couture,* no. 8; the discussion by Fanning, *A Bishop and His World,* 19–43.

75. Adémar de Chabannes, *Chron.,* book 3, ch. 66; *Historia pontificum et comitum Engolismensium,* chs. 26, 27, 29, 30.

76. Bachrach, "William the Great," 20, n. 2.

77. *Hist. Fr.,* 10:617–619; with Newman, *Robert II,* no. 72.

78. Halphen, *Le comté d'Anjou,* 11 (n. 1) and 12.

79. *Hist. Fr.,* 10:617–619.

80. Bib. Nat., Coll. Baluze, 41:187, along with the discussion by Frédéric Soehnée, *Catalogue des actes d'Henri I", roi de France (1031–1060)* (Paris, 1907), no. 100, and Newman, *Robert II,* no. 54.

81. Abbo of Fleury, *Epist.,* no. 1.

82. For the gifts to Fleury see André of Fleury, *Vita Gauzlini,* book 1, chs. 28, 30, 35.

83. *Gesta Ambaz. dominorum,* 90.

84. *Cartul. du Ronceray,* nos. 1, 2, 15, 125, 126; for comparisons, see the distribution of acts catalogued by Guillot, *Le comte d'Anjou,* vol. 2, nos. 11–78.

85. *Cartul. du Ronceray,* no. 1; see also Bachrach, "Pope Sergius IV," 245.

86. For the quotation see Archives de Maine-et-Loire, H 2117, no. 3; for variations on this wording see also ibid., H 1840, no. 2, and a text published by Marchegay in *Archives d'Anjou,* 1:472. The date is established as prior to May 1030 (*Hist. S. Florentii,* 280), but after (1) the treaty between Fulk and Odo II; (2) the building of at least a part of the church of Saint-Florent outside of the castrum of Saumur was accomplished; and (3) much construction had been done on the monastery buildings outside the castrum. For the information on this chronology see the documents cited above in this note.

87. *Livre des serfs de Marmoutier,* no. 50, and the discussion by Fanning, "Family and Episcopal Election," 39–56.

88. *Hist. S. Florentii,* 270; Bachrach, "Study in Feudal Politics," 117; Fanning, "From *Miles* to *Episcopus*: The Influence of the Family on the Career of Vulgrinus of Vendôme (ca 1000–1065)," *Medieval Prosopography* 7, no. 1 (1986): 10–12; and above, ch. 8, nn. 63, 82, 83.

89. *Hist. S. Florentii,* 287–288; *Chron. de Nantes,* ch. 48; and Halphen, *Le comté d'Anjou,* 52, n. 5.

90. *Chron. de Nantes,* ch. 48; Le Patourel, *Norman Empire,* 14–15; but cf. Bates, *Normandy before 1066,* 70. See Elizabeth van Hoots, "Scandinavian Influence in Norman Literature of the Eleventh Century," *Anglo-Norman Studies,* ed. R. Allen Brown (Woodbridge, 1984), 6:107–121, for a variety of literary perspectives that do not, however, demonstrate continued cooperation between the Norman counts at Rouen and Scandinavia.

91. Richard, *Histoire des Comtes de Poitou,* 1:196, 223, and Guillot, *Le comte d'Anjou,* 1:46.

92. Pfister, *Robert le pieux,* 80–82. At one point during this conflict King Robert took refuge in the stronghold of Fulk Nerra's fidelis Lancellinus of Beaugency (*Miracula S. Benedicti,* 241).

93. Bachrach, "Study in Feudal Politics," 11–22.

94. Bachrach, "The Angevin Strategy of Castle Building," 550.

95. Richard, *Histoire des comtes de Poitou,* 1:223; Bachrach, "Study in Feudal Politics," 119; "Conventum," ed. Martindale, 542, 546.

96. Richard, *Histoire des comtes de Poitou,* 1:223, 228, and *Cartul. de Saint-Hilaire,* no. 113, which incorporates a fragment of an earlier charter, which postdates the accession of William the Fat and predates the battle of Moncoüer, and lists at least some of the resources given to Fulk Nerra.

97. Pfister, *Robert le pieux,* 1.

Chapter 9: The Angevin-Capetian Alliance

1. Dhondt, "Une crise du pouvoir," 137–146; followed by Lewis, *Royal Succession,* 24–25. Dhondt, however, does not develop the diplomatic connections sufficiently.

2. J.-P. Poly, *La Provence,* 186, n. 84, places Adelaide's death in 1026.

3. As Lewis, *Royal Succession,* 25, makes clear, these had already been promised. From a political perspective, however, it was crucial for Henry not only to keep his promise but to act quickly so as to avoid even the impression that he might renege and thus provide his potential adversaries with a grievance.

4. Dhondt, "Sept femmes et un trio de rois," 40–52; Marion Facinger, "A Study of Medieval Queenship: Capetian France, 987–1237," *Studies in Medieval and Renaissance History* 5 (1968): 5–6, 28, 33, 41. For another perspective concerning election see Walther Kienast, *Studien über di französischen Volksstämme des Frühmittelalters* (Stuttgart, 1967), 130–150; Lewis, *Royal Succession,* 25.

5. Dhondt, "Une crise du pouvoir," 138.

6. The key texts are *Cartul. de la Trinité de Vendôme,* nos. 1 and 6, esp. the latter. For a variety of efforts to make sense of these see Dhondt, "Une crise du pouvoir," 138, who seems to see Geoffrey Martel's operation as having been carried out on its own; Guillot, *Le comte d'Anjou,* 1:44–45, who comes closer to the situation; and Bachrach, "Angevin Tradition," 118–125, for an overview of Fulk's relations with Geoffrey which shows a general pattern of close cooperation between Fulk Nerra and his son. Cf. Penelope Johnson, *Prayer, Patronage, and Power: The Abbey of la Trinité, Vendôme, 1032–1187* (New York, 1981), 7, n. 11.

7. Halphen, *Le comté d'Anjou,* 56, n. 3, charts the degrees of relationship.

8. Bachrach, "Angevin Tradition," 118–125.

9. Concerning the respective ages of Geoffrey and Agnes see Halphen, *Le comté d'Anjou,* 40, and Richard, *Histoire des comtes de Poitou,* 1:225.

10. Bachrach, "Geoffrey Greymantle," 10, 47, n. 33.

11. Ibid., 20–21.

12. Bachrach, "King Henry II and Angevin Claims to the Saintonge," 34.

13. Richard, *Histoire des comtes de Poitou,* 1:181–182.

14. Lex, "Eudes, comte de Blois," 231–238, and Bur, *Comté de Champagne,* 171–172.

15. David Douglas, *William the Conqueror* (Berkeley and Los Angeles, 1964), 181–189, with the brilliant understatement (p. 187): "Not only with his own duchy was William concerned at this time. He was also at pains to justify his cause before the public conscience of Europe."

16. *Recueil des actes des ducs de Normandie,* ed. Fauroux, no. <91>. See the compelling argument by Guillot, *Le comte d'Anjou,* vol. 2, no. 49, for the authenticity of this document that Fauroux considered inauthentic. See also Dhondt, "Une crise du pouvoir," 139.

17. *Rec. des actes des ducs de Normandie,* ed. Fauroux, no. <91>. See the citations in Walther Kienast, *Der Herzogstitel in Frankreich und Deutschland (9. bis 12. Jahrhundert* (Munich, Vienna, 1968), 205–217, for the claims made by the king's subjects which Henry did not honor.

18. *Rec. des actes des ducs de Normandie,* ed. Fauroux, no. <91>. Had Queen Constance attended this court, she would have been expected to attest this act since she is known to have taken an interest in the monastery that was benefited. Bachrach, "Robert of Blois," 144. Concerning Constance's normal pattern of participation see Facinger, "Medieval Queenship," 25, 40–41.

19. See Raoul Glaber, *Hist.,* book 3, ch. 9, para. 36; but cf. Dhondt, "Sept femmes et un trio de rois," 51, who seems to make this observation too time-specific, and Lewis, *Royal Succession,* 25, who sees Constance as opposing Duke Robert.

20. Dhondt, "Une crise du pouvoir," 141–142.

21. Clarius, *Chron. S. Petri Vivi Senonensis,* 116–118; Raoul Glaber, *Hist.,* book 3, ch. 9, para. 37. See also the discussion by Dhondt, "Une crise du pouvoir," 141–142.

22. Dhondt, "Sept femmes et un trio de rois," 52, n. 44; Dhondt, "Une crise du pouvoir," 143–145, and the discussion of the date of the treaty,

p. 143, n. 15, where *Miracula S. Benedicti,* book 4, ch. 15, is clarified. Facinger, "Medieval Queenship," 25, sees Constance's power base in much the same terms as does Dhondt.

23. Clarius, *Chron. S. Petri Vivi Senonensis,* 118, and cf. Dhondt, "Une crise du pouvoir," 142, n. 13, who sees this attack on Sens as taking place in August 1032. But Clarius (p. 118) seems to set November, that is, after Gelduin's consecration, for the initiation of hostilities.

24. Clarius, *Chron. S. Petri Vivi Senonensis,* 118.

25. *Annales ... Rainaldi,* 86.

26. Clarius, *Chron. S. Petri Vivi Senonensis,* 118.

27. *Hist. S. Florentii,* 282–283; and cf. *Chron. de Nantes,* ch. 48, which differs from the former and is rejected by Halphen, *Le comté d'Anjou,* 52, n. 5. Dhondt, "Une crise du pouvoir," 142–144, fails to grasp the role that Fulk's problems played in relation to the deterioration of Henry's position.

28. Bachrach, "Study in Feudal Politics," 115–116.

29. *Chartes ... de Saint-Maixent,* no. 91; with the interesting interpretation provided by H. E. J. Cowdry, "The Peace and the Truce of God in the Eleventh Century," *Past and Present* 46 (1970): 58.

30. See *Gesta Consulum,* 59, where with some small confusion, Geoffrey Martel's operations in Aquitaine against William the Fat are linked with the latter's efforts regarding Saintes. For further discussion see below, p. 216. On the entire episode cf. Halphen, *Le comté d'Anjou,* 58.

31. Dhondt, "Une crise du pouvoir," 142; and for the campaigns, Lex, "Eudes, comte de Blois," 232–234, and Bur, *Comté de Champagne,* 171–172. Wipo, *Gesta Chuonradi,* chs. 29, 30, is the best source for these campaigns, but he tries to minimize Odo's accomplishments.

32. Wipo, *Gesta Chuonradi,* chs. 29, 30.

33. *Chron. de Nantes,* ch. 47.

34. Bates, *Normandy before 1066,* 68.

35. Jan Dhondt, "La relation entre la France et la Normandie sous Henri Ier," *Normania* 12 (1939): 465–486; Bates, *Normandy before 1066,* 71, 73.

36. Dhondt, "France et la Normandie," 469–470.

37. See Latouche, *Comté de Maine,* 24–25, for the campaign but without identifying them as Fulk's allies. Potts, "Normandy or Brittany?" 135–156, highlights conflict between Rennes and Rouen with the focus on Mont Saint Michel.

38. Ordericus Vitalis, *Hist. Eccles.,* book 7, ch. 14, with considerable exaggeration as noted by Bates, *Normandy before 1066,* 71.

39. *Miracula S. Benedicti,* book 6, chs. 15–16, and Raoul Glaber, *Hist.,* ch. 9, para. 36. Dhondt, "Une crise du pouvoir," 143, n. 15, indicates Raoul's mistreatment of the chronology.

40. Raoul Glaber, *Hist.,* book 3, ch. 9, para. 36, who gives full credit to Fulk, despite telescoping the time-frame and being hostile to the Angevin count (book 2, ch. 4, para. 7; and book 3, ch. 2, para. 7).

41. Dhondt, "Une crise du pouvoir," 146; Wipo, *Gesta Chuonradi,* ch. 30, with the discussion by Lex, "Eudes, comte de Champagne," 232–234; but cf. Bur, *Comté de Champagne,* 172.

42. *Miracula S. Benedicti*, ch. 17; Clarius, *Chron. S. Petri Vivi Senonensis*, 118.

43. *Gesta Consulum*, 59; four months fits perfectly with the flight of King Henry. Four years makes no sense at all.

44. Ibid.

45. Ibid.

46. Concerning the state of Odo's operations see Wipo, *Gesta Chuonradi*, ch. 31, with the discussion by Lex, "Eudes, comte de Champagne," 232–234, and Dhondt, "Une crise du pouvoir," 146.

47. *Gesta Consulum*, 59–60, along with Halphen, *Le comté d'Anjou*, 58, n. 2.

48. For the problem of deciding with any certainty that Geoffrey Martel was following Vegetian advice see Bachrach, "The Practical Use of Vegetius' *De re militari*," 224–251.

49. Halphen, *Le comté d'Anjou*, 57.

50. Dhondt, "Une crise du pouvoir," 146–147.

51. *Hist. S. Florentii*, 282–283; and Bib. Nat., n. a. lat. 1930, *Livre noir*, fols. 57r–58r, with the discussion of the chronology by Bachrach, "Angevin Tradition," 124, n. 76.

52. *Hist. S. Florentii*, 282–283.

53. Ibid., and the discussion of Angevin military organization by Bachrach, "The Enforcement of *Forma Fidelitatis*," 808–809.

54. Beech, *A Rural Society*, 51, 129–132; "Conventum," ed. Martindale, 542.

55. Bachrach, "Geoffrey Greymantle," 19.

56. Belisaire Ledain, *Dictionnaire topographique des Deux-Sèvres* (Poitiers, 1902), xiii, regarding the road system.

57. Beech, *A Rural Society*, 46–47; Guillot, *Le comté d'Anjou*, 1:52, n. 241; and Bachrach, "The Angevin Strategy of Castle Building," 551, n. 60.

58. Bachrach, "The Angevin Strategy of Castle Building," 550–552.

59. Ibid., and Bachrach, "The Practical Use of Vegetius' *De re militari*," 248–249.

60. Bates, *Normandy before 1066*, 69–70, for the Bellêmes.

61. The best general source for weather and crop conditions is *Miracula S. Benedicti*, book 6, ch. 11, and Raoul Glaber, *Hist.*, book 4, ch. 4, para. 10, is also useful.

62. See Bachrach, "*Caballus and Caballarius*," 173–183, concerning the care and feeding of war horses.

63. The peculiar timing of Robert's pilgrimage has yet to be explained in a satisfactory manner: see, for example, the efforts by Douglas, *William the Conqueror*, 35–36; Bates, *Normandy before 1066*, 147; and Searle, *Predatory Kinship*, 152–153. I am suggesting here that the combination of bad weather and crop failure served as an omen that God was angry, and Robert, who likely felt guilty, could go on pilgrimage at this time when his enemies could have little chance of launching an attack on his lands.

64. Bachrach, "The Pilgrimages of Fulk Nerra," 205–217.

65. Bachrach, "Pope Sergius IV," 245.

66. Concerning Hermengarde's behavior and Geoffrey's response see *Car-*

tul. du Ronceray, no. 64. Earlier she appears to have been involved in an unsuccessful *Raubehe* at the hands of Hugh of Châteaudun.

67. Bachrach, "Pope Sergius IV," 245, for this reconstruction of Fulk's letter.

68. Bib. Nat., Coll. Dom Housseau, vol. 2, pt. 1, no. 407.

69. *Hist. Fr.,* 10:503, with the discussion by Bachrach, "The Enforcement of *Forma Fidelitatis,*" 816, n. 110.

70. *Cartul. du Ronceray,* no. 64.

71. *Hist. S. Florentii,* 279.

72. Guillot, *Le comte d'Anjou,* vol. 2, nos. 1–77, provides fine summaries of a large percentage of acts in which Fulk Nerra played a juridical role; nos. 78–221 do the same with those of Geoffrey Martel.

73. On contemporary scholarly views on the role of genetics in personality formation see Auke Tellegen et al., "Personality Similarity in Twins Reared Apart and Together," *Journal of Personality and Social Psychology* 56 (1988): 1031–1039.

74. Concerning education see the discussion in chapter 1.

75. For Geoffrey's cross see Lepeletier, *Epitome,* 44, and *Gallia Christ.,* vol. 4, col. 823.

76. For Geoffrey's high regard for the written word see, for example, *Rec. des actes de Philippe I*er, ed. Prou, no. 157; *Liber Albus,* no. 177; *Cartul. de la Trinité de Vendôme,* nos. 17, 96; and *Bib. Nat.* n.d. 1930, *Livre noir,* fols. 31r–v.

77. Bachrach, "The Practical Use of Vegetius' *De re militari,*" 244–245.

78. See, for example, Lepeletier, *Epitome,* 7; "Chartes poitevines de Saint-Florent," ed. Marchegay, 16; A. Ledru and L.-J. Denis, *La maison de Maillé* (Paris, 1905), 2:4; *Cartul. de Saint-Jouin-de-Marnes,* 19; and for the dating of these *acta* see Bachrach, "The Enforcement of *Forma Fidelitatis,*" 804–806, nn. 46–49.

79. Bachrach, "The Enforcement of *Forma Fidelitatis,*" 803–806.

80. Ibid., 800, 803, 808.

81. Ibid., 801.

82. See, for example, *Bib. Nat.* n.d. 1930, *Livre noir,* fols. 28v–29r; *Archives d'Anjou,* ed. Marchegay, 2:50; *Cartul. de la Trinité de Vendôme,* no. 62; *Cartul. de Notre-Dame de Saintes,* no. 1; and *Cartul. de Saint-Maurice,* no. 43.

83. *Cartul. de Noyers,* no. 1; Bib. Nat., Coll. Dom Housseau, vol. 1, nos. 290, 291; *Cartul. de la Trinité de Vendôme,* no. 44; Ledru and Denis, *La Maison de Maillé,* 2:4; Halphen, *Le comté d'Anjou, p.j.* 5; *Cartul. de Cormery,* no. 36; Bib. Nat., n. a. lat. 1930, *Livre noir,* fols. 21v–22r, are all good examples depicting the activities of the family. For the dating of several of these *acta* see Bachrach, "Pope Sergius IV," 251–252, and Bachrach, "The Enforcement of *Forma Fidelitatis,*" 817–818.

84. Duby, "Youth in Aristocratic Society," 112–122, exaggerates the problems caused by youthful male heirs by generalizing from a few examples. One of the examples Duby uses is Geoffrey Martel.

85. Bachrach, "The Enforcement of *Forma Fidelitatis,*" 817–818.

86. *Cartul. de la Trinité de Vendôme,* no. 44; Bachrach, "The Enforcement of *Forma Fidelitatis,*" 810 (n. 72), 817–818.

87. Bachrach, "The Angevin Tradition," 118–125; cf. Johnson, *Prayer, Patronage, and Power,* 13, 16.

88. William of Malmesbury, *De gestis regum Anglorum,* vol. 3, ch. 235, with the discussion of the sources by Bachrach, "The Angevin Tradition," 118–119, n. 46.

89. Bachrach, "Fulk Nerra's Pilgrimages," 209–210, and Bachrach, "The Angevin Tradition," 124, n. 78.

Chapter 10: The Last Years

1. Bachrach, "The Pilgrimages of Fulk Nerra," 208–209.

2. *Gesta Consulum,* 50.

3. Adémar of Chabannes, *Chron.,* book 3, ch. 64. It is of heuristic value to note that Adémar, a contemporary of Fulk Nerra's and hostile to him, charges the Angevin count with planning the murders of Count Herbert of Maine and the latter's wife in the very same paragraph; indeed, just before, he points out how Robert of Normandy benefited from the poisoning of his brother Richard.

4. Concerning the battle of Conquereuil see Halphen, *Le comté d'Anjou,* 21–25; *Gesta Consulum,* 48–49; and Bachrach, "The Angevin Tradition," 117.

5. *Gesta Consulum,* 50. In this context, it is important to recall that it was well established that Fulk was saved in Bithynia during his second pilgrimage to the Holy Land through the efforts of Saint Nicholas.

6. Bates, *Normandy before 1066,* 147.

7. *Miracula S. Wulframmi,* 47. The argument by Douglas, *William the Conqueror,* 408–415, that poisoning was not one of the significant ways by which Normans as well as others in the Middle Ages committed murder for political gain is unconvincing.

8. *De gestis regum Anglorum,* 111–112. This poisoner perhaps should be identified with Rodulfus Monin, an obscure member of the ducal entourage, who witnessed an act of Duke Richard at Fécamp in 1025. *Rec. des actes des ducs de Normandie,* no. 35. Likely he should not be confused with the monk Ralph "Moine" who is generally believed to have been William II's schoolmaster (*magister*). Concerning Ralph "Moine" see Searle, *Predatory Kinship,* 55–56.

9. William of Malmesbury, *De gestis regum Anglorum,* 212, indicates that Radulfus poisoned Robert because "spe ducatus animo suo extorserit . . ." The traditional translation of this phrase (e.g., in Douglas, *William the Conqueror,* 409) as "in the hope of obtaining the ducatus . . ." not only omits the words "animo suo" but asks the reader to believe that an inconsequential *minister* harbored thoughts of the impossible, that is, taking over the *ducatus.* Rather, "extorserit" should be understood in the sense of "destabilize" or even more literally "to twist out of joint." For the troubles caused by Robert's murder, which

destabilized the Norman government, and for the Angevin aggression see Bates, *Normandy before 1066,* 50–93.

10. For Avesgaud see Guillot, *Le comte d'Anjou,* 1:55, n. 251; concerning Herbert see Latouche, *Comté du Maine,* 26, n. 4. It is possible that Herbert died as early as 1032, but in light of what is known of subsequent events he probably died while Fulk was on pilgrimage.

11. Douglas, *William the Conqueror,* 37–39, and cf. 39, n. 2, concerning Odo II.

12. Bachrach, "Geoffrey Greymantle," 25–27.

13. Soehenée, *Henri Ier,* no. 40.

14. Note the phrase used by Dhondt, "Une crise du pouvoir," 138: ". . . la rivalité . . . entre les principautés de Champagne et celle d'Anjou . . . permettait aux Capétiens de se maintenir par une politique de bascule."

15. Douglas, *William the Conqueror,* 33–34, discusses the peace-making efforts of Archbishop Robert of Rouen, who brought Duke Robert and Count Alan to terms. In light of this and of Alan's later influence at the Norman court, it is unlikely that he opposed Duke Robert when the latter aided King Henry against Odo II.

16. Norgate, *The Angevin Kings,* 1:170–172, provides a useful assessment of Geoffrey Martel's character, while the brief evaluation by Halphen, *Le comté d'Anjou,* 128, is no less to the point.

17. Halphen, *Le comté d'Anjou,* 69–71; Guillot, *Le comte d'Anjou,* 1:54–55; and Bachrach, "The Angevin Tradition," 122–125. *Act. Pont.,* 363–367, conflates two wars between Geoffrey and Gervasius.

18. *Cartul. de Saint-Aubin,* no. 237.

19. William of Malmesbury, *De gestis regum Anglorum,* 292. See the discussion by Bachrach, "The Angevin Tradition," 118–125.

20. *Cartul. de la Trinité de Vendôme,* nos. 19, 68; and the discussion of these texts by Bachrach, "The Angevin Tradition," 118–125.

21. *Archives d'Anjou,* ed. Marchegay, 1:472.

22. *Chron. S. Maixent,* 116–118, and Richard, *Histoire des comtes de Poitou,* 1:132. Concerning the fact that Geoffrey's contemporaries did not tend to release dangerous prisoners see Bur, *Comté de Champagne,* 197. The release of William may be taken as an index of Geoffrey's difficulties. Cf. Halphen, *Le comté d'Anjou,* 58.

23. *Cartul. de la Trinité de Vendôme,* nos. 62–64.

24. Bachrach, "The Angevin Tradition," 125, n. 80, where the sources are discussed in detail and the chronology is established.

25. *Cartul. de la Trinité de Vendôme,* no. 68.

26. This formulation of a "more than civil war" has its classical roots in Lucan but likely reached the Angevin writers through Isidore. See the discussion of the chronicle evidence by Bachrach, "The Angevin Tradition," 121.

27. Bates, *Normandy before 1066,* 76, 78.

28. H. E. J. Cowdry, "Archbishop Aribert II of Milan," *History* 51 (1966): 9–11; Bur, *Comté de Champagne,* 173; and Lex, "Eudes, comte de Blois," 235–238.

29. *De gestis regum Anglorum,* 292. Fulk Nerra returned from the Holy

Land by December 1036, at which time he is seen "favoring" the appointment of Walter as abbot of Saint-Aubin. See Guillot, *Le comte d'Anjou*, vol. 2, no. 54, who establishes the chronology. Since Fulk was in Asia Minor in July 1035 and from there went on to the Holy Land, he probably did not return home before the beginning of the summer of 1036. See for this chronology, Bachrach, "Fulk's Pilgrimages," 208–210.

30. Bates, *Normandy before 1066,* 163, regarding Norman practice.

31. McCormick, *Eternal Victory,* 57–58, 160–166, 313–314.

32. Ibid.

33. Ibid.

34. *Cartul. de Saint-Aubin,* no. 397.

35. Ibid., no. 186, and the discussion by Bachrach, "The Enforcement of *Forma Fidelitatis,*" 808–809, n. 63.

36. *Cartul. de Saint-Aubin,* no. 397.

37. Ibid., no. 27, along with the discussion of the chronology by Guillot, *Le comte d'Anjou,* vol. 2, no. 54.

38. Guillot, *Le comte d'Anjou,* vol. 2, nos. 54–152, which demonstrate clearly that Walter was not part of the count's inner circle.

39. *Cartul. de Saint-Aubin,* no. 27.

40. Ibid., no. 6; and Guillot, *Le comte d'Anjou,* 1:469, who publishes a second version of this act which shows how the monastery became entangled in Angevin military organization.

41. Halphen, *Le comté d'Anjou,* 58; and Guillot, *Le comte d'Anjou,* 1:53, for the background, with Bachrach, "Study in Feudal Politics," 118–119, for details on Angevin allies.

42. Bachrach, "Study in Feudal Politics," 116–121.

43. Bachrach, "The Angevin Strategy of Castle Building," 551; Bachrach, "The Enforcement of *Forma Fidelitatis,*" 811.

44. Douglas, *William the Conqueror,* 37; and Bur, *Comté de Champagne,* 104.

45. Archives de Maine-et-Loire, 40 H 1, nos. 1, 2 bis; and *Cartul. blésois de Marmoutier,* no. 29. Cf. Farmer, *Communities of Saint Martin,* 71–73, who does not seem to appreciate the extent of Fulk's efforts or perhaps one might say the depth of Marmoutier's interest in the Angevin connection.

46. *Cartul. de Noyers,* no. 1.

47. Fulk le Réchin, *Fragmentum historiae Andegavensis,* 234.

48. Joscelin's earliest appearance in Fulk's following is in 1037, as indicated by *Cartul. de Saint-Aubin,* no. 1, which is to be seen in light of the comments by Bachrach, "The Angevin Economy," 39–40, n. 16. Joscelin's son married the daughter of Berlaius of Montreuil-Bellay and the latter was established in this latter stronghold during the 1030s. Concerning Joscelin's family see Halphen, *Le comté d'Anjou,* 173, 203.

49. Bachrach, "The Angevin Strategy of Castle Building," 46–62.

50. Bachrach, "The Cost of Castle Building," 46–62.

51. Halphen, *Le comté d'Anjou,* 159, n. 1.

52. *Gesta Ambaz. dominorum,* 83, places the recapture of Langeais by Fulk after the death of Odo II, which took place on 15 November 1037.

53. Vegetius, *De re militari,* book 1, ch. 21; book 3, ch. 8; and the discussion by Bachrach, "The Practical use of Vegetius' *De re militari,*" 244–251.

54. *Cartul. de la Trinité de Vendôme,* nos. 16, 17, show Hamelinus in command at Langeais by 1039 at the latest. Cf. Guillot, *Le comte d'Anjou,* vol. 2, no. 126.

55. *Gesta Ambaz. dominorum,* 83, with the lengthy discussion by Bachrach, "The Enforcement of *Forma Fidelitatis,*" 812, n. 85.

56. Regarding Alberic, see the evidence developed by Bachrach, "The Enforcement of *Forma Fidelitatis,*" 812, n. 85.

57. Bachrach, "The Angevin Strategy of Castle Building," 551.

58. *Chron. S. Maixent,* 393.

59. Richard, *Histoire des comtes de Poitou,* 1:235–237.

60. *Chron. S. Maixent,* 393.

61. Richard, *Histoire des comtes de Poitou,* 1:237, establishes the date.

62. *Chron. de Nantes,* chs. 44–48; Douglas, *William the Conqueror,* 37; and La Borderie, *Hist. de Bretagne,* 3:11–12.

63. *Chron. de Nantes,* 141, n. 2; Pfister, *Robert le pieux,* 188.

64. Cf. Bates, *Normandy before 1066,* 112, who seems to accept Robert of Torigny's and Ivo of Chartres' twelfth-century genealogies, which trace "Sainfria" as a sister of Gunnor, the wife of Duke Richard I of Normandy. But Searle, "Fact and Pattern in Heroic History," 133–136, demonstrates that Dudo is to be preferred to the later sources on matters of genealogy. Dudo does not mention "Sainfria" as a sister of Gunnor even though she was one of his patrons. By contrast, the root name Saginfrid- [a], [us] is part of the *Namengut* of the Bellême family, as illustrated by a bishop of that name established at le Mans by Geoffrey Greymantle (Bachrach, "Geoffrey Greymantle," 25–26). This prelate flourished in the generation before "Sainfria." From a political perspective, it certainly made good sense for the Bellêmes to marry one of its offspring to Viscount Roger I of the Hiémois during a period that saw their vigorous effort to dominate the Sées region, which lay between the lands and lordships of both houses.

65. Bates, *Normandy before 1066,* 79, puts the date ca. 1050, but Douglas, *William the Conqueror,* 60, notes it is traditional to associate the marriage with the taking of Domfront. Guillot, *Le comte d'Anjou,* 1:69–72, dates the battle to ca. 1048, but Bates (pp. 255–257) rejects the early date for the battle and prefers Douglas's later dates (pp. 383–390). In short, the dates for both the battle and the marriage remain unsettled.

66. Douglas, *William the Conqueror,* 40, recognizes that the chronicle evidence provides reason to date Alan's death either in 1039 or 1040, and he then follows La Borderie, *Hist. de Bretagne,* 3:13, in accepting the latter. No argument is provided by either scholar.

67. Cf. Douglas, *William the Conqueror,* 409–410, 415, who rejects the allegations that Alan, in particular, was poisoned and that poisoning in general was a tool of political assassination.

68. Halphen, *Le comté d'Anjou,* 78; La Borderie, *Hist. de Bretagne,* 3:114–116; Norgate, *Angevin Kings,* 1:211–212.

69. Bates, *Normandy before 1066,* 79.

70. William of Malmesbury, *De gestis regum Anglorum,* 292.

71. *Gesta Consulum,* 50–51, describes conditions only as they could have existed during Fulk's second pilgrimage, which took place at the height of the persecutions carried out by al Hakim II. See, for example, the account by Jones, *Saint Nicholas,* 102–103.

72. Bachrach, "Pope Sergius IV," 245–246.

73. *Cartul. du Ronceray,* nos. 7, 18, 19, 229, 281, which were made after Geoffrey Martel departed the court at Angers as compared to no. 4, where Geoffrey was still residing in his father's court.

74. Ibid., nos. 5, 6.

75. Mailfert, "Fondation du monastère . . . Saint-Nicholas d'Angers," *p.j.* 4, with Bachrach, "The Pilgrimages of Fulk Nerra," 209–210, for the dating.

76. Bachrach, "The Tomb of Fulk Nerra," 3–29.

77. Oxford, Bodleian Lib., ms. Gough Drawings-Gaignières, 14, fol. 171a.

78. Mallet, *L'art roman,* pl. 54, 241, 1, 61, and 235, respectively, for the churches mentioned.

79. Ibid., pl. 54, 282, and 5, respectively.

80. Ibid., pl. 318, 305, 157, 175, 130, with the discussion by Bachrach, "The Tomb of Fulk Nerra," 6, concerning the columns. For the capitals and bases see Mallet, *L'art roman,* pl. 20, 22, VII.2; *St. Aubin d'Angers du VIe au XXe siècle: Catalogue de l'exposition Saint-Aubin,* ed. Jacques Mallet (Angers, 1985), 57; regarding Belli Locus, see Hardion and Michel-Dansec, "Etude archéologique sur l'église de Beaulieu-lès-Loches," 94.

81. Bachrach, "The Tomb of Fulk Nerra," 8–16; for the sword, Bachrach, "Combat Sculptures," 70.

82. Bachrach, "The Tomb of Fulk Nerra," 16.

83. Richard Krautheimer, *Studies in Early Christian, Medieval, and Renaissance Art* (New York, 1978), 128.

84. Stephen Nichols, *Romanesque Signs: Early Medieval Narrative and Iconography* (New Haven, 1983), 67–94.

85. Bachrach, "Potius Rex," 11–21.

86. Bachrach, "The Tomb of Fulk Nerra," 16.

87. Nichols, *Romanesque Signs,* 67–76.

88. Krautheimer, *Studies,* fig. 50; Nichols, *Romanesque Signs,* 79–80.

89. Bachrach, "The Tomb of Fulk Nerra," 6–7.

90. Nichols, *Romanesque Signs,* 70.

91. Krautheimer, *Studies,* 128.

92. Bachrach, "The Tomb of Fulk Nerra," 17.

93. Bachrach, "The Pilgrimages of Fulk Nerra," 205–217; Bachrach, "Pope Sergius IV," 245.

94. Raoul Glaber, *Hist.,* book 2, ch. 4, para. 5, with the discussion by Bachrach, "Pope Sergius IV," 245–247.

95. The disaster described by Raoul Glaber, *Hist.,* book 2, ch. 4, para. 5 (discussed above in chapter 5) undoubtedly made it necessary to reconsecrate the church as a result of the damage done by the winds and the fallen roof.

96. *Hist. S. Florentii,* 274.

97. *Gesta Consulum,* 51; Bachrach, "The Tomb of Fulk Nerra," 26, n. 117, for a discussion of the text.

98. J. Hardion and L.-A. Bosseboeuf, "L'abbaye de Beaulieu-lès-Loches et quelques monuments de sa dépendance," *Mémoires de la Société archéologique de Touraine* 6 (1914): 31–32.

99. Guillot, *Le comte d'Anjou,* vol. 2, nos. 67–89, lists the relevant *acta* in which Geoffrey makes clear his positive feelings toward his father.

100. Halphen, *Le comté d'Anjou,* 60, n. 4, discusses Fulk's return from the Holy Land; see 11, n. 1, for Hildegarde's pilgrimage and the return of her entourage.

101. *Gesta Consulum,* 54, note e; see also the discussion by Bachrach, "The Tomb of Fulk Nerra," 3–4.

102. Bachrach, "The Tomb of Fulk Nerra," 19, for a discussion of the sources.

Chapter 11: Summing Up

1. Boussard, "La charte de fondation de Notre-Dame de Loches," 8.

2. Le Patourel, *The Norman Empire,* 280. I have quoted from Le Patourel's description of William here not only because it seems to be close to my own appreciation of Fulk but because other scholars have seen many of these same qualities in the Angevin count. See, for example, Norgate, *The Angevin Kings,* 1:144; and Halphen, *Le comté d'Anjou,* 126.

3. Guillot, *Le comte d'Anjou,* 1:376; Bachrach, "The Enforcement of *Forma Fidelitatis,*" 814, n. 102, for a list of examples.

4. Southern, *Making of the Middle Ages,* 87–88.

5. This point is made in a lucid manner by Le Patourel, *The Norman Empire,* 280.

6. Bachrach, "The Enforcement of *Forma Fidelitatis,*" 815, n. 105, for a list of examples.

7. Bachrach, "Some Observations on the Origins of the Angevin Dynasty," 1–23, where some of the missing sources are discussed and some of the still extant texts used by the authors of the *Gesta Consulum* are identified.

8. William of Poitiers, *Hist.,* book 2, chs. 39–40.

9. *Gesta Ambaz. dominorum,* 78.

10. In this list Sallust included "sublevando, ignoscendo" but the authors of the *Gesta* write "sublevando egenis, oppressis ignoscendo." The former addition alters Sallust's meaning somewhat because for him Caesar was dealing with aristocrats while Fulk was relieving the poor. The alteration of the text might well indicate a difference in pardoning aristocratic plotters by Caesar as contrasted to Fulk's pardoning of garrison troops who had surrendered to him.

11. *Cartul. de la Trinité de Vendôme,* nos. 66, 67, provide a good example of Fulk's treatment of exiles.

12. Here Sallust does not modify Caesar's pattern of behavior with "sepe," and thus by the addition of this qualification the Angevin authors realistically represent Fulk's more limited altruism.

13. See Paul Veyne et al., *A History of Private Life from Pagan Rome to Byzantium*, trans. A. Goldhammer (Cambridge, Mass., 1987), 243.

14. Halphen, *Le comté d'Anjou, p.j.* 6.

15. *Hist. S. Florentii*, 260.

16. *Annales . . . Rainaldi*, 86.

17. *Cartul. du Ronceray*, no. 4.

18. For a discussion of Seneca's views on this point see Veyne, *A History of Private Life*, 51.

19. *Fragmentum historiae Andegavensis*, 233.

20. Sullivan, "The Carolingian Age," 267–306, effectively summarizes the contemporary view that the Carolingian empire is a prolongation of the later Roman world and that the new "feudal" Europe emerged in a few crucial decades on either side of the year 1000. The popular view of Fulk Nerra is that developed by Southern, *The Making of the Middle Ages*, 86, where the Angevin count is seen as a pioneer in the art of feudal government.

21. Forsyth, *St. Martin at Angers*; Mallet, *L'art roman*, and the review of the latter by Bachrach, 741–744.

22. *Cartul. du Ronceray*, no. 125.

23. Guillot, *Le comte d'Anjou*, 1:16. South of the Loire there was considerable debate concerning the legitimacy of the Capetian kingship. See the useful examination of this topic by Richard Landes, "L'accession des Capétiens: Une reconsidération selon les sources aquitaines," *Religion et culture autour de l'an mil: Royaume capétien et lotharingie* (Paris, 1989), 151–166.

24. *Ann. Vind.*, 57–58, along with the discussion of the manuscript by Halphen, xxv–xxxi. Clearly the author of this text, which ultimately was copied into the *Vendôme Annals*, wrote in a milieu that not only was comfortable with the idea that both Robert II and Henry I were incompetent but that also saw Robert I, Hugh Capet, and Robert II all as "pseudo-kings" and Henry as a *regulus*, e.g., something less than a true king.

Although the original text cannot be dated exactly, it obviously was written by someone who, as an adult capable of making critical judgments, had seen ("vidimus") enough of the reign of King Robert II (987–1031) to be able confidently to characterize his rule as "inertissime." It is also obvious that King Henry I (1031–1060) was still reigning when the passage was originally written. But, the author was not old enough to remember, if he had even been born yet, that Hugh Capet and his son Robert were not made king at the same time ("simul") but that the former was elected and crowned on 3 July 987 at Noyon while the latter was associated in the kingship only on 30 December of the same year. Concerning the chronology see Lot, *Hugues Capet*, 3–4.

Perhaps we may arrive at greater precision on the date of the original text if we construe the diminutive "regulus" used to describe Henry's position as indicative of his youth, i.e., the little king or young king, rather than simply the pejorative "kinglet," which within the historiographical traditions of the *regnum Francorum* indicates something less than a regular king. Concerning these traditions see J. M. Wallace-Hadrill, *The Longhaired Kings and Other Studies in Frankish History* (London, 1962), 148–163. It is also possible that "regulus" was intended to do double duty, i.e., both youthful and something less than a true king. In this context Henry's incompetence would be seen most glaringly from an Angevin perspective when, early in his reign, he relied on Fulk Nerra to save him from Queen Constance and Odo II.

Bibliography

Only published works cited in the notes are included here. Unpublished sources are fully cited in the notes, with a few common abbreviations, such as Bib. Nat. for Bibliothèque Nationale, Paris.

Abbreviations for Published Sources

Gallia Christ. = *Gallia Christiana in provincias ecclesisticas distributa*. 2d ed. 16 vols. Paris, 1715–1865.

Hist. Fr. = *Recueil des historiens des Gaules et de la France*. 24 vols. Paris, 1734–1904.

Labbe = *Novae bibliothecae manuscriptorum librorum . . . tomi I et II*. Ed. Philippe Labbe. 2 vols. Paris, 1683.

Mansi = *Sacrorum conciliorum nova et amplissima collectio*. Ed. J. D. Mansi. 31 vols. Florence and Venice, 1759–1798.

MGH = *Monumenta Germania Historica*

   SS = *Scriptores*. 30 vols. Hannover, 1824–1924.

   SRM = *Scriptores rerum Merovingicarum*. 7 vols. Hannover, 1884–1951.

PL = *Patrologiae cursus completus . . . series Latina*. Ed. J. P. Migne. 234 vols. Paris, 1844–1903.

Sources

Abbo of Fleury. *Epistolae. PL* 139.

Act. Pont. = *Actus pontificum Cenomannis in urbe degentius*. Eds. G. Busson and A. Ledru. Le Mans, 1902.

Adalbéron de Laon. *Poème au roi Robert*. Ed. and trans. Claude Carozzi. Paris, 1979.

Adémar de Chabannes. *Chronique*. Ed. Jules Chavanon. Paris, 1897.

Aimo. *Vita Abbonis*. In *PL*, vol. 139.

André of Fleury. *Vita Gauzlini = Vie de Gauzlin, Abbé de Fleury*. Ed. and trans. Robert-Henri Bautier and Gillette Labory. Paris, 1969.

Annales . . . Rainaldi = Annales qui dicuntur Rainaldi archidiaconi Sancti Mauricii Andegavensis. In *Recueil d'annales angevines et vendômoises*. Ed. Louis Halphen. Paris, 1903.

Ann. Vind. = Annales Vindocinenses. In *Recueil d'annales angevines et vendômoises*. Ed. Louis Halphen. Paris, 1903.

Archives d'Anjou. Ed. Paul Marchegay. 3 vols. Angers, 1843–1856.

Besly, Jean. *Histoire des comtes de Poictou et ducs de Guyenne*. Paris, 1647.

Brevis historia Sancti Juliani Turonensis. In *Recueil de chroniques de Touraine*. Ed. André Salmon. Tours, 1854.

Carré de Busserolle, J.-X. *Dictionnaire géographique, historique, et biographique d'Indre-et-Loir et de l'ancienne province de Touraine*. 6 vols. Tours, 1878–1884.

Cartulaire blésois de Marmoutier. Ed. Charles Métais. Chartres-Blois, 1891.

Cartulaire de l'abbaye de Noyers. Ed. C. Chevalier. Tours, 1872.

Cartulaire de Cormery. Ed. J. Bourassé. Tours, 1861.

Cartulaire de la Trinité de Vendôme. Ed. Charles Métais. 6 vols. Paris-Vannes, 1893–1897.

Cartulaire de l'église de Notre-Dame de Paris. Ed. B. Guerard. 4 vols. Paris, 1850.

Cartulaire de Notre-Dame de Saintes. Ed. T. Grasilier. Niort, 1871.

Cartulaire de Saint-Aubin d'Angers. Ed. B. de Broussillon. 3 vols. Angers, 1896.

Cartulaire de Saint-Cyprian de Poitiers. Ed. L. Redet. Poitiers, 1874.

Cartulaire de Saint-Hilaire de Poitiers. Ed. L. Redet. Poitiers, 1848.

Cartulaire de Saint-Jean-d'Angely. Ed. G. Musset. 2 vols. Saintes, 1901–1904.

Cartulaire de Saint-Jouin-de-Marnes. Ed. C. de Grandmaison. Niort, 1854.

Cartulaire de Saint-Laud d'Anjou. Ed. A. Planchenault. Angers, 1903.

Cartulaire de Saint-Pierre le la Couture. Ed. Benedictines of Solesmes. Le Mans, 1881.

Cartulaire de Saint-Vincent du Mans. Ed. Charles and S. Menjot d'Albenne. Mamers, 1886.

Cartul. de Saint-Maurice = Cartulaire noir de la cathedrale d'Angers. Ed. C. Urseau. Angers, 1908.

Cartulaire du prieuré de Saint-Marcel-lès-Chalon. Ed. M. and P. Canat de Chizy. Chalon, 1894.

Cartulaire du Ronceray. Ed. Paul Marchegay. Angers, 1856.

Chartes de Cluny = Recueil des chartes de l'abbaye de Cluny. Ed. A. Bernard and A. Bruel. 6 vols. Paris, 1876–1903.

Chartes de l'abbaye de Nouaillé de 678 à 1200. Ed. P. Monsabert. Poitiers, 1936.

Chartes de Saint-Julien de Tours (1002–1300). Ed. L.-J. Denis. 2 vols. Le Mans, 1912–1913.

Chartes et documents pour servir à l'histoire de l'abbaye de Saint-Maixent. Ed. A. Richard. Poitiers, 1886.

"Chartes poitevines de Saint-Florent." Ed. Paul Marchegay. In *Archives historiques du Poitou* 2 (1873): 1–148.

"Chartes tourangelles relatives à la Touraine antérieures à l'an mil." Ed. J. Delaville le Roulx. In *Bulletin de la Société archéologique de Touraine* 4 (1877–1879): 334–374.

Chronicon ecclesiae Beatae Mariae de Loches. In *Recueil de chroniques de Touraine.* Ed. André Salmon. Tours, 1854.

Chron. Kemper. = "Ex Chronico Kemperliegiensi." *Hist. Fr.,* 10:294.

Chronicon Masciacense. Ed. Labbe. Vol. 2.

Chronicon S. Maixent. = *Chronique de Saint-Maixent.* Ed. and trans. Jean Verdon. Paris, 1979.

Chron. S. Petri Aniciensis = *Cartulaire de l'abbaye de Saint-Chaffre du Monastier: Suivi de la chronique de Saint-Pierre du Puy et d'un appendice des chartes.* Ed. Ulysse Chevalier. Paris, 1884.

Chronicon Sancti Sergii Andegavensis = *Recueil d'annales angevines et vendômoises.* Ed. Louis Halphen. Paris, 1903.

Chronicon Turonense abbreviatum. In *Recueil de chroniques de Touraine,* ed. André Salmon. Tours, 1854.

Chronicon Turonense magnum. In *Recueil de chroniques de Touraine,* ed. André Salmon. Tours, 1854.

La Chronique de Nantes (540 environ–1049). Ed. René Merlet. Paris, 1896.

Chronique de Parcé. Ed. H. de Berranger. Le Mans, 1953.

Clarius. *Chronique de Saint-Pierre-le-Vif de Sens, dite de Clarius, Chronicon Sancti Petri Vivi Senonensis.* Ed. and trans. Robert-Henri Bautier and Monique Gilles. Paris, 1970.

Codex Theodosianus = *Theodosiani libri xvi cum constitutionibus Sirmondianis et leges novellae ad Theodosianum pertinentes.* Ed. Th. Mommsen and P. Meyer. 2 vols. Berlin, 1905.

"Conventum." See Martindale.

"Documents inédits pour servir à l'histoire de l'abbaye Sainte-Croix de Poitiers et de ses domaines jusqu'à la fin du XIIIᵉ siècle." Ed. P. Monsabert. In *Revue Mabillon* (1913, 1914), 50–88, 259–395.

Dudo = *De moribus et actis primorum Normanniae ducum auctore Dudone Sancti Quintini deacano.* Ed. J. Lair. Caen, 1865.

Einhard. *Vita Karoli* = *Vie de Charlemagne.* Ed. and trans. Louis Halphen. Paris, 1947.

Flodoard. *Annales* = *Les Annales de Flodoard.* Ed. Ph. Lauer. Paris, 1905.

Fondation de Châteaurenault. In *Chroniques des comtes d'Anjou et des seigneurs d'Amboise,* ed. Louis Halphen and René Poupardin. Paris, 1913.

"Fragments de chartes du Xᵉ siècle provenant de Saint-Julien de Tours." Ed. C. de Grandmaison. In *Bibliothèque d'Ecole de Chartes* 46 (1885): 373–429; 47 (1886): 226–273.

Fulbert, *Epist.* = *The Letters and Poems of Fulbert of Chartres.* Ed. and trans. Frederick Behrends. Oxford, 1976.

Fulk le Réchin. *Fragmentum historiae Andegavensis.* In *Chroniques des comtes d'Anjou et des seigneurs d'Amboise,* ed. Louis Halphen and René Poupardin, 232–238. Paris, 1913.

Gerbert, *Epist.* = Gerbert. *Lettres.* Ed. J. Havet. Paris, 1889.

Gesta Ambaziensium dominorum. In *Chroniques des comtes d'Anjou et des seigneurs d'Amboise,* ed. Louis Halphen and René Poupardin. Paris, 1913.

Gesta Consulum = Chronica de gestis consulum Andegavorum. In *Chroniques des comtes d'Anjou et des seigneurs d'Amboise,* ed. Louis Halphen and René Poupardin. Paris, 1913.

Gesta pontificum Autissiodorensium. Ed. L.-M. Duru. Auxerre, 1850.

Gregory of Tours. *Hist. = Historiarum liber X.* Ed. Bruno Krusch and Wilhelm Levison. In *MGH, SRM,* 2d ed., 1:1.

Helgaud de Fleury. *Vie de Robert le Pieux.* Ed. and trans. Robert-Henri Bautier and Gillette Labory. Paris, 1965.

Historia Gaufredi ducis Normannorum et comitis Andegavorum. In *Chroniques des comtes d'Anjou et des seigneurs d'Amboise,* ed. Louis Halphen and René Poupardin. Paris, 1913.

Historia pontificum et comitum Engolismensium. Ed. Jacques Boussard. Paris, 1957.

Historia Sancti Florentii. In *Chroniques des églises d'Anjou,* ed. Paul Marchegay and Emile Mabille. Paris, 1869.

Hugh de Flavigny. *Chronicon.* In *Hist. Fr.,* vol. 10.

In laudem Iustini Augusti minoris, libri IV. Ed. and trans. with commentary by Avril Cameron. London, 1976.

Isidorus Episcopus Hispalensis. *Etymologiae seu origines.* Ed. W. M. Lindsey. 2 vols. Oxford, 1911.

John of Salerno. *Vita Sancti Odonis.* In *PL,* vol. 133.

John XVIII. *Privilegium.* In *PL,* vol. 139.

La légende de la mort de Crescentius. In *Chroniques des comtes d'Anjou et des seigneurs d'Amboise,* ed. Louis Halphen and René Poupardin. Paris, 1913.

Lepeletier, *Breviculum = Laurent Lepeletier. Breviculum fundationis et series abbatum Sancti Nicholai Andegavensis.* Angers, 1616.

Lepeletier, *Epitome* = Laurent Lepeletier. *Rerum scitu dignissimarum a prima fundatione monasterii S. Nicholai Adegavensis ad hunc usque diem, Epitome, Nec non eiusdem monasterii abbatum series.* Angers, 1635.

Liber Albus. Ed. R. Lottin. Le Mans, 1869.

Liber miraculorum Sancte Fidis. Ed. A. Bouillet. Paris, 1897.

Livre des serfs de Marmoutier. Ed. A. Salmon. Paris, 1885.

Mirac. S. Benedicti = Les miracles de Saint Benoît. Ed. E. de Certain. Paris, 1858.

Miracula Sancti Eusicii. In Labbe, 2:463–466.

Miracula S. Martini. = Miracula Martini abbatis Vertavensis. In *MGH, SRM,* vol. 3.

Miracula S. Nicholai. See Mailfert.

Miracula S. Wulframmi. In *Société de l'histoire de Normandie,* vol. 14. 1938.

"Notices sur les chartes originales relatives à la Touraine antérieures à l'an mil." Ed. J. Delaville le Roulx. Tours, 1879.

Notker. *Gesta Karoli.* Ed. and trans. R. Rau. Berlin, 1960.

Odorannus. *Chron. = Odorannus de Sens, opera omnia.* Ed., trans., and annot. Robert–Henri Bautier and Monique Gilles. Paris, 1972.

Odericus Vitalis = *The Ecclesiastical History of Orderic Vitalis.* Ed. and trans. Marjorie Chibnall. 5 vols. Oxford, 1969–1973.

Petrus "Bechin." *Chronicon = Chronicon Petri filii Bechini.* In *Recueil de chroniques de Touraine,* ed. André Salmon. Tours, 1854.

Pierre de Maillezais. *Relatio.* In *Hist. Fr.,* 10:178–184 (incomplete). See Bib. Nat., ms. lat. 4892.

"Piété de Foulque le Bon." In *Chroniques des comtes d'Anjou et des seigneurs d'Amboise,* ed. Louis Halphen and René Poupardin. Paris, 1913.

Raoul Glaber. *Hist.* = *Rodulfi Glabri historiarum libri quinque.* Ed. and trans. John France. Oxford, 1889.

Recueil des actes de Philippe Ier, roi de France (1058–1108). Ed. M. Prou. Paris, 1908.

Recueil des actes des ducs de Normandie (911–1066). Ed. Marie Fauroux. Caen, 1961.

Rhabanus Maurus. *De procinctu Romanae militae.* Ed. E. Dümmler. In *Zeitschrift für deutsches Alterthum* 15 (1872): 443–451.

Richer. *Histoire de France (888–995).* Ed. and trans. R. Latouche. 2 vols. Paris, 1930, 1937.

St. Aubin d'Angers du VIe au XXe siècle. In *Catalogue de l'exposition Saint-Aubin,* ed. Jacques Mallet. Angers, 1985.

Sergius IV. *Epist.* In *PL,* vol. 139.

———. *Privilegium.* In *PL,* vol. 139.

Syrus. *Miracula Sancti Maioli.* In *Hist. Fr.,* 10:362.

Vegetius, *De re militari* = *Flavi Vegetii Renati epitoma rei militaris.* Ed. C. Lang. Leipzig, 1885.

Vetera analecta sive collectio veterum aliquot operum. 2d ed. Ed. J. Mabillion. Paris, 1723.

V. Domini Burcardi = *Vie de Bouchard le Venerable comte de Vendôme, de Corbeil, de Melun, et de Paris par Odo, moine de Saint-Maure-des-Fosses.* Ed. Charles Bourel de la Roncière. Paris, 1892.

William of Malmesbury. *De gestis regum Anglorum.* Ed. William Stubbs. London, 1889.

William of Poitiers, *Hist.* = *Guillaume de Poitiers, Histoire de Guillaume le Conquérant.* Ed. and trans. Raymonde Foreville. Paris, 1952.

Wipo. *Gesta Chuonradi.* 3d ed. Ed. H. Bresslau. Hannover, 1919.

Zimmermann = *Papsturkunden 896–1046.* 3 vols. Ed. Harald Zimmermann. Vienna, 1984–1986.

Scholarly Works

Ainrich, Gustav. *Hagios Nikolaos: der heiliger Nikolaos in Griechischen Kirche.* 2 vols. Leipzig–Berlin, 1913, 1917.

Arbois de Jubainville, H. *Histoire des ducs et comtes de Champagne depuis le VIe siècle jusqu'au milieu de XIIe siècle.* Vol. 1. Paris, 1859.

Bachrach, Bernard S. "Angevin Campaign Forces in the Reign of Fulk Nerra, Count of the Angevins (987–1040)." *Francia* 16, no. 1 (1989): 67–84.

———. "The Angevin Economy, 960–1060: Ancient or Feudal?" *Studies in Medieval and Renaissance History* n.s., 10 (1988): 3–55.

———. "The Angevin Strategy of Castle Building in the Reign of Fulk Nerra, 987–1040." *The American Historical Review* 88 (1983): 533–560.

———. "Animals and Warfare in Early Medieval Europe." *Settimane di Studio del Centro Italiano di Studi sull'alto Medioevo* 31 (Spoleto, 1985): 1:707–764.

———. "*Caballus et Caballarius* in Medieval Warfare." In *The Story of Chivalry*, ed. H. Chickering and T. Seiler, 173–211. Kalamazoo, Mich., 1988.

———. "The Combat Sculpture at Fulk Nerra's 'Battle Abbey' (1005–1012)." In *The Haskins Society Journal: Studies in Medieval History*, ed. Robert B. Patterson, 3:63–79. London, 1991.

———. "The Cost of Castle Building: The Case of the Tower at Langeais, 992–994." In *The Medieval Castle: Romance and Reality*, ed. K. Reyerson and F. Powe, 46–62 (four plates). Dubuque, Iowa, 1984.

———. "Early Medieval Fortifications in the 'West' of France: A Revised Technical Vocabulary." *Technology and Culture* 16 (1975): 531–569.

———. "Enforcement of the *Forma Fidelitatis*: The Techniques Used by Fulk Nerra, Count of the Angevins (987–1040)." *Speculum* 59 (1984): 796–819.

———. "The Family of Viscount Fulcoius of Angers: Some Methodological Observations at the Nexus of Prosopography and Diplomatics." *Medieval Prosopography* 4, no. 1 (1983): 1–9.

———. "The Feigned Retreat at Hastings." *Mediaeval Studies* 33 (1971): 344–347.

———. "Fortifications and Military Tactics: Fulk Nerra's Strongholds circa 1000." *Technology and Culture* 20 (1979): 531–549.

———. "Fulk Nerra and His Accession as Count of Anjou." In *Saints, Scholars, and Heroes: Studies in Medieval Culture in Honor of Charles W. Jones*, ed. W. Stevens and M. King, 2:331–342. Collegeville, Minn., 1979.

———. "Fulk Nerra's Exploitation of the *facultates monarchorum*, ca. 1000." In *Law, Custom, and the Social Fabric in Medieval Europe: Essays in Honor of Bryce Lyon*, ed. Bernard S. Bachrach and David M. Nicholas, 29–49. Kalamazoo, Mich., 1990.

———. "Geoffrey Greymantle, Count of the Angevins, 960–987: A Study in French Politics." *Studies in Medieval and Renaissance History* 17 (n.s. vol. 7) (1985): 1–67 (two maps).

———. "Gildas, Vortigern, and Constitutionality in Sub-Roman Britain." *Nottingham Medieval Studies* 32 (1988): 126–140.

———. "The Idea of the Angevin Empire." *Albion* 10 (1978): 293–299.

———. "King Henry II and Angevin Claims to the Saintonge." *Medieval Prosopography*, 6, no. 1 (1985): 23–45.

———. "Neo-Roman vs. Feudal: The Heuristic Value of a Construct for the Reign of Fulk Nerra, Count of the Angevins (987–1040)." *Cithara* 30 (1990): 3–30.

————. "The Northern Origins of the Peace Movement at Le Puy in 975." *Historical Reflections/Réflexions Historiques* 14 (1987): 405–421.

————. Observations sur l'importance de la population angevine au temps de Foulque Nerra." In *Le rôle de l'Ouest dans la destinée des Robertiens et des premiers Capetiens,* ed. Olivier Guillot, forthcoming. Paris, 1992.

————. "The Pilgrimages of Fulk Nerra, Count of the Angevins, 987–1040." In *Religion, Culture, and Society in the Early Middle Ages,* 205–217. Kalamazoo, Mich., 1987.

————. "Pope Sergius IV and the Foundation of the Monastery at Beaulieu-lès-Loches." *Revue Bénédictine* 95 (1985): 240–265.

————. "'Potius rex quam esse dux putabatur': Some Observations concerning Adémar of Chabannes' Panegyric on Duke William the Great." In *The Haskins Society Journal: Studies in Medieval History,* ed. Robert B. Patterson, 1:11–21. London, 1989.

————. "The Practical Use of Vegetius' *De re militari* during the Early Middle Ages." *The Historian* 47 (1985): 239–255.

————. Review of David Bernstein, *The Mystery of the Bayeux Tapestry* (Chicago, 1987). *Speculum* 65 (1990): 123–124.

————. Review of Jean Durliat, *Les finances publiques de Diocletien aux Carolingiens (284–889)* (Sigmaringen, 1990). *Francia* 19, no. 1 (1992): forthcoming.

————. Review of Patrick Geary, *Furta Sacra: Thefts of Relics in the Central Middle Ages* (Princeton, 1978). *The Historian* 41 (1979): 763–764.

————. Review article: "Walter Goffart, *The Narrators of Barbarian History (A.D. 550–800): Jordanes, Gregory of Tours, Bede, and Paul the Deacon.*" (Princeton, 1988). *Francia* 17, no. 1 (1990): 250–256.

————. Review of Jacques Mallet, *L'art roman de l'ancien Anjou.*" *Speculum* 64 (1989): 740–744.

————. Review of Rosamund McKitterick, *The Carolingians and the Written Word* (Cambridge, 1989). *Journal of Interdisciplinary History* 21 (1990): 321–323.

————. Review of Alexander Murray, *Germanic Kinship Structure: Studies in Law and Society in Antiquity; and the Early Middle Ages* (Toronto, 1983). *Speculum* 60 (1985): 1003–1004.

————. Review of Eleanor Searle, *Predatory Kinship and the Creation of Norman Power, 840–1066* (Berkeley and Los Angeles, 1988). *Albion* 21 (1989): 609–611.

————. Review of J. M. Wallace-Hadrill, *Early Medieval History* (New York, 1975). *The Historian* 38 (1976): 729–730.

————. "Robert of Blois, Abbot of Saint-Florent de Saumur and Saint-Mesmim-de-Micy (985–1011)." *Revue Bénédictine* 88 (1978): 123–146.

————. "Some Observations on *The Medieval Nobility.*" *Medieval Prosopography* 1, no. 2 (1980): 15–33.

————. "Some Observations on the Military Administration of the Norman Conquest." *Anglo-Norman Studies* 8, ed. R. Allen Brown, 8:1–25. Woodbridge, 1986.

————. "Some Observations on the Origins of Countess Gerberga of the

Angevins: An Essay in the Application of the Tellenbach-Werner Prosopographical Method." *Medieval Prosopography* 7, no. 2 (1986): 1–23.

———. "Some Observations on the Origins of the Angevin Dynasty." *Medieval Prosopography* 10, no. 2 (1989): 1–23.

———. "A Study in Feudal Politics: Relations between Fulk Nerra and William the Great, 995–1030." *Viator* 7 (1976): 111–122.

———. "The Tomb of Fulk Nerra, Count of the Angevins (987–1040)." *Cithara* 29 (1989): 3–29.

———. "Toward a Reappraisal of William the Great, Duke of Aquitaine (995–1030)." *Journal of Medieval History* 4 (1979): 11–21.

———. "Was There Feudalism in Byzantine Egypt?" *Journal of the American Research Center in Egypt* 6 (1967): 163–166.

Bachrach, Bernard S., and Rutherford Aris. "Military Technology and Garrison Organization: Some Observations on Anglo-Saxon Military Thinking in Light of the Burghal Hidage." *Technology and Culture* 31 (1990): 1–17.

Baldwin, John. *The Government of Philip Augustus: Foundations of French Royal Power in the Middle Ages*. Berkeley, Los Angeles, London, 1986.

Balmalle, Marius. "Les comtes de Gévaudan et Brioude." *Almanach de Brioude*, 251–252. Brioude, 1964.

Barlow, Frank. *William Rufus*. Berkeley, Los Angeles, London, 1983.

Bartlett, Robert. *Trial by Fire and Water: The Medieval Judicial Ordeal*. Oxford, 1986.

Bates, David. *Normandy before 1066*. London, 1982.

Bautier, Robert-Henri. "L'historiographie en France." *Settimane di Studio del Centro Italiano di Studi sull'alto Medioevo* 17, no. 1 (Spoleto, 1970): 793–850.

Beech, George. *A Rural Society in Medieval France: The Gâtine of Poitou in the Eleventh and Twelfth Centuries*. Baltimore, 1964.

Belmont, Nicole. "Levana; or, How to Raise Up Children." In *Family and Society: Selections from the Annales: Economies, Sociétés, Civilisations*, eds. Robert Forster and Orest Ranum, trans. Elborg Forster and Patricia M. Ranum, 1–15. Baltimore, 1976.

Bernstein, David. *The Mystery of the Bayeux Tapestry*. Chicago, 1987.

Bienvenu, J.-M. "Pauvreté, misères, et charité en Anjou aux XIᵉ et XIIᵉ siècles." *Le moyen âge* 72 (1966): 389–424; 73 (1967): 5–34, 190–216.

———. "Recherches sur les péages angevins aux XIᵉ et XIIIᵉ siècles." *Le moyen âge* 63 (1957): 209–240, 437–467.

Blanchet, A., and A. Dieudonné. *Manuel de numismatique française*. Vol. 4: *Monnaies féodales françaises*. Paris, 1936.

Bloch, Marc. *Feudal Society*. Trans. L. A. Manyon. Chicago, 1961.

Blumenkranz, Bernhard. *Juifs et Chrétiens dan le monde occidental, 430–1096*. Paris, 1960.

Boüard, Michel. "De l'aula au donjon: Les fouilles de la motte de La Chapelle à Doué-la-Fontaine (Xᵉ–XIᵉ siècle)." *Archéologie Médiévale* 3 and 4 (1973–1974): 5–110.

Bouchard, Constance. "Family Structure and Family Consciousness among the

Aristocracy in the Ninth and Eleventh Century." *Francia* 14 (1986): 639–658.

———. "The Origins of the French Nobility: A Reassessment." *The American Historical Review* 86 (1981): 501–532.

———. *Sword, Mitre, and Cloister: Nobility and Church in Burgundy, 980–1198.* Ithaca, N.Y., 1987.

Bourgeois, Emile. *Hugues l'abbé, margrave de Neustrie et archichapelain de France à la fin du IXe siècle.* Caen, 1885.

Boussard, Jacques. "La charte de fondation de Notre-Dame de Loches." *Actes du colloque médiéval de Loches (1973),* in *Mémoires de la Société archéologique de Touraine* 9 (1975): 133–140.

———. "Le comte d'Anjou au XIe siècle." *Journal des Savants* (1975): 133–140.

———. "Les évêques en Neustrie avant la réforme grégorienne (950–1050 environ)." *Journal des Savants* (1970): 161–196.

———. "L'éviction des tenants de Thibaut de Blois par Geoffrey Martel, comte d'Anjou, en 1044." *Le moyen âge* 69 (1963): 141–149.

———. "L'origine des comtés de Tours, Blois, et Chartres." *Actes du 103e congrès national des Sociétés savantes: 1977,* 85–112. Paris, 1979.

———. "L'origine des familles seigneuriales dans la région de la Loire moyenne." *Cahiers de civilisation médiévale* 5 (1962): 303–322.

———. "La seigneurie de Bellême aux Xe et XIe siècles." *Mélanges d'histoire du moyen âge dédiés à la mémoire de Louis Halphen,* 43–54. Paris, 1951.

———. "Le trésorier de Saint-Martin de Tours." *Revue d'histoire de l'Eglise de France* 47 (1961): 61–68.

———. "Services féodaux, milices, et mercenaires dans les armées, en France, aux Xe et XIe siècles." *Settimane di Studio del Centro Italiano di Studi sull'alto Medioevo* 15 (1968): 131–168.

Boyle, Leonard E. "Diplomatics." In *Medieval Studies: An Introduction,* ed. James M. Powell, 69–101. Syracuse, N.Y., 1976.

Brown, Elizabeth A. R. "The Tyranny of a Construct: Feudalism and Historians of Medieval Europe." *The American Historical Review* 79 (1974): 1063–1088.

Brown, R. Allen. *English Castles.* 3d ed. London, 1976.

Brühl, Carlrichard. *Fodrum, Gistum, Servitium Regis.* 2 vols. Cologne, 1968.

———. *Palatium und Civitas: Studien zur Profantopographie spätantiker Civitates vom 3. bis zum 13. Jahrhundert.* Vol. 1: *Gallien.* Vienna, 1975.

Brunt, P. A. "Cicero and Historiography." *Philias charis: Miscellanea di studi classici in onore di Eugenio Manni,* 311–340. Rome, 1979.

Bullough, Donald A. "Early Medieval Social Groupings: The Terminology of Kinship." *Past and Present* 45 (1981): 3–18.

Bur, Michel. *La formation du comté de Champagne v. 950–v. 1150.* Nancy, 1977.

Calendeni, P. "Bernard Ier, scholastique d'Angers." In *Dictionnaire d'histoire et de géographie écclésiastiques,* vol. 8, ed. Alfred Baudrillart et al. Paris, 1935.

Chatelain, André. *Donjons romans des pays d'Ouest.* Paris, 1973.

Chaume, Maurice. *Les origines du duché de Bourgogne.* Vol. 1. Dijon, 1925.

Chazen, Robert. *Church, State, and Jew in the Middle Ages*. New York, 1980.

———. *Medieval Jewry in Northern France: A Political and Social History*. Baltimore, 1973.

Chèdeville, André. *Chartres et ses campagnes, XIe–XIIIe siècles*. Paris, 1973.

Cheyette, Fredric. "The Invention of the State." In *Essays in Medieval Civilization: The Walter Prescott Webb Memorial Lectures*, ed. B. K. Lackner and K. R. Phillip, 143–176. Austin, Texas, 1979.

———. "Some Notations on Mr. Hollister's Irony." *Journal of British Studies* 5 (1965): 1–14.

Chydenius, J. *Medieval Institutions and the Old Testament*. Helsinki, 1965.

Clanchy, Michael. *From Memory to Written Record: England, 1066–1377*. Cambridge, 1977.

Contamine, Philippe. *War in the Middle Ages*. Trans. Michael Jones. Oxford, 1984.

Coolidge, Robert. "Adalbero, Bishop of Laon." *Studies in Medieval and Renaissance History* 2 (1965): 3–114.

Coulson, Charles. "Fortress Policy in Capetian Tradition and Angevin Practice: Aspects of the Conquest of Normandy by Philip II." *Anglo-Norman Studies*, ed. R. Allen Brown, 6:13–38. Woodbridge, 1984.

Cowdry, H. E. J. "Archbishop Aribert II of Milan." *History* 51 (1966): 1–15.

———. "The Peace and the Truce of God in the Eleventh Century." *Past and Present* 46 (1970): 42–67.

Davies, Wendy, and Paul Fouracre, eds. *The Settlement of Disputes in Early Medieval Europe*. Cambridge, 1986.

Davis, R. H. C. "William of Poitiers and His History of William the Conqueror." In *The Writing of History in the Middle Ages: Essays Presented to Richard William Southern*, ed. R. H. C. Davis and J. M. Wallace-Hadrill, 71–100. Oxford, 1981.

Denécheau, Joseph-Henri. "Renaissance et privilèges d'une abbaye angevine au XIe s.: Étude sur quelques "faux" de Saint-Florent de Saumur." *Cahiers de civilisation médiévale* 34 (1991): 23–35.

Desmaizières, O. *Essai d'inventaire des camps*. Le Mans, 1911.

Devailly, Guy. *Le Berry du Xe siècle au milieu du XIIIe siècle*. Paris, 1973.

———. "L'Eglise médiévale." In *Histoire religieuse de la Bretagne*, ed. Guy-Marie Oury, 45–93. Paris, 1980.

Deyres, Marcel. "Le château de Montbazon au XIe siècle." *Cahiers de civilisation médiévale* 12 (1969): 147–159.

———. "Les Châteaux de Foulque Nerra." *Bulletin Monumental* 132 (1974): 7–28.

Dhondt, Jan. "Une crise du pouvoir capetien, 1032–1034." In *Miscellanea mediaevalia in memoriam Jan Frederik Niermeyer*, 137–148. Gronigen, 1967.

———. "Election et hérédité sous les Carolingiens et les premiers Capétiens." *Revue belge d'histoire et de la philologie* 19 (1939): 913–953.

———. "Quelques aspects du règne d'Henri Ier, roi de France." *Mélanges d'histoire du moyen âge dédiés à la mémoire de Louis Halphen*, 199–208. Paris, 1951.

————. "La relation entre la France et la Normandie sous Henri Ier." *Normania* 12 (1939): 465–486.

————. "Sept femmes et un trio de rois (Robert le Pieux, Henri Ier, et Philippe Ier." *Contributions à l'histoire économique et sociale* 3 (1965): 37–70.

Dillay, Madeleine. "La régime de l'église privée du XIe au XIIIe siècle dans l'Anjou, la Maine, la Touraine." *Revue historique de droit français et étranger,* 4th ser., 5 (1925): 253–294.

Douglas, David. *William the Conqueror.* Berkeley and Los Angeles, 1964.

Duby, Georges. *Medieval Marriage: Two Models from Twelfth-century France.* Trans. Elborg Forster. Baltimore, 1978.

————. *La société aux XIe et XIIe siècles dans la région mâconnaise.* Paris, 1953; reprinted with different pagination, 1971.

————. "Les sociétés médiévales: Une approche d'ensemble." *Annales: Economie, société, civilisation* 26 (January–February 1971): 1–13. Trans. as "Medieval Society," in *The Chivalrous Society,* trans. Cynthia Postan, 1–14. Berkeley, Los Angeles, London, 1977.

————. "Youth in Aristocratic Society: Northwestern France in the Twelfth Century." In *The Chivalrous Society,* trans. Cynthia Postan, 112–122. Berkeley, Los Angeles, London, 1980.

Dumas, F., E. Lorans, and E. Theureau. "Un dépot monétaire dans le cimetière de Saint-Mexme de Chinon." *Bulletin de la Société française de numismatique* 43 (1988): 466–468.

Dunbabin, Jean. *France in the Making: 843–1180.* Oxford, 1985.

Durliat, Jean. *Les finances publiques de Diocletien aux Carolingiens (284–889).* Sigmaringen, 1990.

————. "Le polyptyque d'Irminon et l'impôt pour l'armée." *Bibliothèque de l'Ecole des Chartes* 141 (1983): 183–208.

Easton, C. *Les hivers dans l'Europe occidentale.* Leiden, 1928.

Ehler, Sidney Z. "On Applying the Modern Term 'State' to the Middle Ages." In *Medieval Studies Presented to Aubrey Gwynn, S. J.,* ed. J. A. Watt et al., 492–501. Dublin, 1961.

Facinger, Marion. "A Study of Medieval Queenship: Capetian France, 987–1237." *Studies in Medieval and Renaissance History* 5 (1968): 1–48.

Fanning, Steven. *A Bishop and His World before the Gregorian Reform: Hubert of Angers, 1006–1047.* Philadelphia, 1988.

————. "Family and Episcopal Election, 900–1050, and the Case of Hubert, Bishop of Angers (1006–1047)." *Medieval Prosopography* 7, no. 1 (1983): 39–56.

————. "From *Miles* to *Episcopus*: The Influence of the Family on the Career of Vulgrinus of Vendôme (ca. 1000–1065)." *Medieval Prosopography* 7, no. 1 (1986): 9–30.

————. "La lutte entre Hubert de Vendôme, évêque d'Angers, et l'archevêque de Tours en 1016: Un épisode dans l'histoire de l'Eglise des principautés territoriales." *Bulletin de la Société archéologique, scientifique, et littéraire du Vendômois* (1980): 31–33.

————. "Les origines familiales de Vulgrin, abbé de Saint-Serge d'Angers

(1046–1056) et évêque du Mans (1056–1065), petit-fils du vicomte Fulcrade de Vendôme." *La Province du Maine* 82 (1980): 243–255.

Farmer, Sharon. *Communities of Saint Martin: Legend and Ritual in Medieval Tours.* Ithaca, N.Y., 1991.

Fedele, P. "Richerche per la storia di Roma e del papato nel secolo X." *Archivio della Reale Società Romana di Storia Patria* 34 (1911): 408–423.

Fichtenau, Heinrich. "Zum Reliquienwesen im früheren Mittelalter." *Mitteilungen des Institutes für österreichische Geschichtsforschung* 60 (1952): 60–89.

Finó, J.-F. *Forteresses de la France médiévale: Construction, attaque, défense.* 3d ed. Paris, 1977.

Flandrin, Jean-Louis. *Families in Former Times: Kinship, Household, and Sexuality.* Trans. R. Southern. Cambridge, 1978.

Fontette, F. de. "Evêques de Limoges et comtes de Poitou au XIe siècle." *Etudes d'histoire du droit canonique dédiées à G. le Bras,* 533–538. Paris, 1965.

Forsyth, George. *The Church of St. Martin at Angers.* Princeton, 1953.

Fossier, Robert. *Enfance de l'Europe: Aspects économiques et sociaux.* 2 vols. Paris, 1982.

Fried, M. H. *The Evolution of Political Society.* New York, 1967.

Galbraith, V. H. "The Literacy of the English Medieval Kings." *Proceedings of the British Academy* 21 (1935): 201–238.

Gandilhon, Alfred. *Catalogue des actes des archevêques de Bourges antérieurs à l'an 1200.* Paris-Bourges, 1927.

Ganshof, F. L. "Depuis quand a-t-on pu, en France, être vassal de plusieurs seigneurs." *Mélanges Paul Fournier,* 261–270 (Paris, 1929).

———. *Feudalism.* Trans. Philip Grierson. London, 1953.

———. "La *Tractoria*: Contribution à l'étude des origines du droit de gîte." *Tijdschrift voor rechtsgeschiedenis* 8 (1928): 69–91.

Geary, Patrick. *Furta Sacra: Thefts of Relics in the Central Middle Ages.* Princeton, 1978.

———. "L'humiliation des saints." *Annales* 34 (1979): 27–42. Reprinted as "Humiliation of Saints," in *Saints and Their Cults: Studies in Religious Sociology, Folklore, and History,* ed. Stephen Wilson, 123–140. Cambridge, 1983.

Gerstenberg, O. "Studien zur Geschichte des römischen Adels im Ausgange des 10. Jahrhunderts." *Historische Vierteljahrschrift* 31 (1937): 1–26.

Gibb, Hamilton A. R. "The Caliphate and the Arab States." In *A History of the Crusades,* ed. Marshall W. Baldwin, 1:81–98. Madison, 1969.

Gillingham, John. "War and Chivalry in the *History of William the Marshall.*" In Thirteenth-century England, ed. P. R. Cross and S. D. Lloyd, 2:1–13. Woodbridge, 1990.

Goffart, Walter. *The Narrators of Barbarian History (A.D. 550–800): Jordanes, Gregory of Tours, Bede, and Paul the Deacon.* Princeton, 1988.

Grand, Roger. "Une curieuse appelation de certaines corvées au moyen âge: Le 'bain,' biain,' ou bien.'" In *Mélanges dédiés à la mémoire de Félix Grat,* 1:289–300. Paris, 1946.

Grierson, Philip. "L'origine des comtes d'Amiens, Valois, et Vexin." *Le moyen âge* 49 (1939): 81–125.

Guillot, Olivier. *Le comte d'Anjou et son entourage au XIe siècle*. 2 vols. Paris, 1972.

———. "La consecration de l'abbaye de Beaulieu-lès-Loches." *Actes du colloque médiéval de Loches (1973)*, in *Mémoires de la Société archéologique de Touraine* 9 (1975): 23–32.

———. "La droit romain classique et la lexicographie de termes du latin médiéval impliquant délégation de pouvoir." In *La lexicographie du latin médiéval et ses rapports avec les recherches actuelles sur la civilisation du moyen-âge: Paris 1978*, 153–166. Paris, 1981.

Guillotel, Hubert. "Le premier siècle du pouvoir ducal breton (936–1040)." *103rd Congrès national des Sociétés savantes, Nancy–Metz* (1978), 63–84.

Hackett, W. Mary. "Aspects de la langue vulgaire du Poitou d'après un document latin du onzième siècle." *Mélanges offerts à Rita Lejune*, 1:13–32. Gembloux, 1969.

Hallam, Elizabeth. *Capetian France: 987–1328*. London, 1980.

Halphen, Louis. "Etude sur l'authenticité du fragment de chronique attribué à Foulque le Réchin." *Bibliothèque de la faculté de lettres de Paris* 13 (1901): 7–48.

———. *Le comté d'Anjou au XIe siècle*. Paris, 1906.

———. "La lettre d'Eudes de Blois au roi Robert." *Revue historique* 97 (1908): 287–296.

Hardion, J., and L.-A. Bosseboeuf. "L'abbaye de Beaulieu-lès-Loches et quelques monuments de sa dépendance." *Mémoires de la Société archéologique de Touraine* 6 (1914).

Hardion, J., and R. Michel-Dansec. "Etude archéologique sur l'église du Beaulieu-lès-Loches." *Congrès archéologique de France* 87 (1910): 91–120.

Head, Thomas. "Letaldus of Micy and the Hagiographic Traditions of Selles-sur-Cher." *Analecta Bollandiana* 107 (1989): 393–414.

Herlihy, David. "Family." *The American Historical Review* 96 (1991): 1–16.

Herrmann-Mascard, Nicole. *Les reliques des saints: Formation coutumière d'un droit*. Paris, 1975.

Hogan, Richard. "The *Rainaldi* of Angers: 'New Men' of Descendants of Carolingian *Nobiles*?" *Medieval Prosopography* 2, no. 1 (1981): 32–62.

Howe, John. "The Nobility's Reform of the Medieval Church." *The American Historical Review* 93 (1988): 317–339.

Hyams, Paul. "Trial by Ordeal: The Key to Proof in the Early Common Law." In *On the Laws and Customs of England: Essays in Honor of Samuel E. Thorne*, ed. Morris S. Arnold et al., 90–126. Chapel Hill, N.C., 1981.

Jackson, Stanley W. *Melancholia and Depression from Hippocratic Times to Modern Times*. New Haven, 1986.

Jessee, W. Scott. "The Angevin Civil War and the Norman Conquest of 1066." In *The Haskins Society Journal: Studies in Medieval History*, ed. Robert B. Patterson, 3:101–110. London, 1991.

———. "A Missing Capetian Princess: Advisa, Daughter of King Robert II of France." *Medieval Prosopography* 11, no. 2 (1990): 1–16.

Johnson, Penelope. *Prayer, Patronage, and Power: The Abbey of la Trinité, Vendôme, 1032–1187*. New York, 1981.

Jones, Charles. *Saint-Nicholas of Myra, Bari, Manhattan.* New York, 1978.

Kienast, Walther. *Der Herzogstitel in Frankreich und Deutschland (9. bis 12. Jahrhundert).* Munich-Vienna, 1968.

———. *Studien über di französischen Volksstämme des Frühmittelalters.* Stuttgart, 1967.

Krautheimer, Richard. *Studies in Early Christian, Medieval, and Renaissance Art.* New York, 1978.

Kroll, Jerome, and Bernard S. Bachrach. "Child Care and Child Abuse in Early Medieval Europe." *Journal of the American Academy of Child Psychiatry* 25 (1986): 562–568.

———. "Medieval Dynastic Decisions: Evolutionary Biology and Historical Explanation." *Journal of Interdisciplinary History* 21 (1990): 1–28.

La Borderie, Arthur le Moyne de. *Histoire de Bretagne.* Vol. 2. Rennes–Paris, 1898.

Lair, Jules. *Etudes critiques sur divers textes des Xe et XIe siècles.* Vol. 1. Paris, 1899.

Lamothe-Dreuzy, René de. "Saint-Florent-le-Vieil des origines à 1500." *Bulletin de l'Académie des sciences et belles-lettres d'Angers,* ser. 9, 2 (1968): 69–77.

Landes, Richard. "L'accession des Capétiens: Une reconsidération selon les sources aquitaines." In *Religion et culture autour de l'an mil: Royaume capétien et lotharingie,* 151–166. Paris, 1989.

Landsberger, Josef. *Graf Odo I. von der Champagne (Odo II. v. Blois, Tours u. Chartres), 995–1039.* Berlin, 1878.

Latouche, Robert. *Histoire du comté du Maine pendant le Xe et le XIe siècles.* Paris, 1910.

Lauranson-Rosaz, Christian. *L'Auvergne et ses marges (Velay, Gévaudan) du VIIIe au XIe siècle.* Le Puy-en-Velay, 1987.

Ledain, Belisaire. *Dictionnaire topographique des Deux-Sèvres.* Poitiers, 1902.

Ledru, A., and L.-J. Denis. *La maison de Maillé.* 2 vols. Paris, 1905.

Le Goff, Jacques, et al., eds. *La nouvelle histoire.* Paris, 1978.

Lelong, Charles. "L'enceinte du castrum Sancti Martini (Tours)." In *Comité des travaux historiques et scientifiques: Section d'archéologie,* 43–56. Paris, 1971.

Lemarignier, Jean-François. "Apropos de deux textes sur l'histoire du droit romain au moyen âge (1008 et 1308)." *Bibliothèque d'Ecole de Chartes* 101 (1940): 157–168.

———. "La dislocation du 'pagus' et le problème des 'consuetudines' (X^e–XIe siècles)." In *Mélanges d'histoire du moyen âge dédiés à Louis Halphen,* 401–410. Paris, 1951.

———. "Structures monastiques et structures politiques dans la France de la fin du Xe et des débuts du XIe siècle." *Settimane di Studio del Centro Italiano di Studi sull'alto Medioevo* 4 (1957): 357–400. Revised by the author and reprinted as "Political and Monastic Structures in France at the End of the Tenth and Beginning of the Eleventh Century," in *Lordship and Community in Medieval Europe,* ed. and trans. Fredric Cheyette, 100–127.

Le Patourel, John. "The Norman Conquest, 1066, 1106, 1154?" *Proceedings of the Battle Conference on Anglo-Norman Studies,* ed. R. Allen Brown, 1:103–120, 216–220. Ipswich, 1978.

———. *The Norman Empire.* Oxford, 1976.

———. "The Platagenet Dominions." *History* 50 (1965): 289–308.

Leseur, F. *Thibaud le Tricheur, comte de Blois, de Tours, et de Chartres.* Blois, 1963.

Lewis, Andrew. *Royal Succession in Capetian France: Studies on Familial Order and the State.* Cambridge, Mass., 1981.

Lex, Léonce. "Eudes, comte de Blois, de Tours, de Chartres, de Troyes, et de Meaux (995–1036) et Thibaud, son frère (995–1004)." *Mémoires de la Société des sciences et lettres du Loir-et-Cher* (1891): 192–283.

Longnon, Auguste. *Géographie de la Gaule au VI⁰ siècle.* Paris, 1878.

Lot, Ferdinand. *Les derniers Carolingiens: Lothaire, Louis V, Charles de Lorraine: 954–991.* Paris, 1891.

———. *Etudes sur le règne de Hugues Capet et la fin du X⁰ siècle.* Paris, 1913.

———. "Geoffroi Grisegonelle dans l'épopée." *Romania* 19 (1890): 377–393.

———. "Hervi, évêque de Nantes." *Annales de Bretagne* 13 (1897/1898): 45–47.

———. "Traditions sur Geoffroi Grisegonelle et sur Helgaud de Montreuil." *Romania* 46 (1920): 376–381.

Lynch, Joseph. *Godparents and Kinship in Early Medieval Europe.* Princeton, 1986.

———. *Simoniacal Entry into Religious Life from 1000 to 1260: A Social Economic and Legal Study.* Columbus, Ohio, 1976.

Lyon, Bryce D. "Medieval Real-Estate Development and Freedom." *The American Historical Review* 63 (1957): 47–67.

MacCormack, Sabine. *Art and Ceremony in Late Antiquity.* Berkeley, Los Angeles, London, 1981.

MacKinney, L. *Bishop Fulbert and Education at the School of Chartres.* Notre Dame, Ind., 1957.

Mailfert, Yvonne. "Fondation du monastère bénédictin de Saint-Nicholas d'Angers. *Bibliothèque d'Ecole de Chartes* 92 (1931): 43–61.

Mallet, Jacques. *L'art roman de l'ancien Anjou.* Paris, 1984.

———, ed. *Saint-Aubin d'Angers de VI⁰ au XX⁰ siècle: Catalogue de l'exposition Saint-Aubin.* Angers, 1985.

McCormick, Michael. *Eternal Victory: Triumphal Rulership in Late Antiquity, Byzantium, and the Early Medieval West.* Cambridge, 1986.

McKitterick, Rosamund. *The Carolingians and the Written Word.* Cambridge, 1989.

———. *The Frankish Kingdoms under the Carolingians, 751–987.* London, 1983.

McLaughlin, Mary. "Survivors and Surrogates: Children and Parents from the Ninth to the Thirteenth Century." In *The History of Childhood,* ed. Lloyd de Mause. New York, 1974.

Martindale, Jane. "Conventum inter Guillelmum Aquitanorum comes et Hugonem Chiliarchum." *The English Historical Review* 84 (1969): 528–548.

Merlet, René. "Dates de la mort d'Eudes 1er et de Thibault II, comtes de Chartres et de Blois." *Procès-verbaux de la Société archéologique d'Eure-et-Loir* 9 (1893): 86–89.

———. "Les origines de monastère de Saint-Magloire de Paris." *Bibliothèque d'Ecole de Chartes* 56 (1885): 237–273.

Morris, Colin. "*Judicium Dei*: The Social and Political Significance of the Ordeal in the Eleventh Century." *Studies in Church History* 12 (1975): 95–112.

Murray, Alexander. *Reason and Society in the Middle Ages*. Rev. ed. Oxford, 1985.

Murray, Alexander C. *Germanic Kinship Structure: Studies in Law and Society in Antiquity and the Early Middle Ages*. Toronto, 1983.

Musset, Lucien. "Actes inédits du XIe siècle: III: Les plus anciennes chartes normandes de l'abbaye de Bourgueil." *Bulletin de la Société des antiquaires de Normandie* 54 (1959): 15–54.

Newman, William M. *Catalogue des actes de Robert II, roi de France*. Paris, 1937.

Nichols, Stephen G. *Romanesque Signs: Early Medieval Narrative and Iconography*. New Haven, Conn., 1983.

Niermeyer, J. F. *Mediae Latinitatis lexicon minus*. Leiden, 1959.

Norgate, Kate. *England under the Angevin Kings*. 2 vols. London, 1887.

Nottarp, H. *Gottesurteilstudien*. Munich, 1956.

Ottaway, John. "Liberté, ordre et révolte d'après la charte dite de fondation de l'abbaye de Beaulieu-lès-Loches." In *Violence et contestation au moyen âge: Actes du 114e congrès national des Sociétés savantes (Paris, 1989): Section d'histoire médiévale et de philologie*, 19–46. Paris, 1990.

Oury, Guy-Marie. "La frère de Geoffrey Grisegonelle: Guy II d'Anjou, moine et évêque du Puy (+ av. 998)." *Actes du colloque médiéval de Loches (1973)*, in *Mémoires de la Société archéologique de Touraine* 9 (1975): 61–68.

———. "L'idéal monastique dans la vie canoniale: Le bienheureux Hervé de Tours (+1022)." *Revue Mabillon* 52 (1962): 1–31.

———. Les origines monastique de l'abbaye de Beaulieu-lès-Loches." *Bulletin de la Société archéologique de Touraine* 42 (1988): 169–178.

———. "La reconstruction monastique dans l'Ouest: L'abbé Gauzbert de Saint-Julien de Tours (v. 990–1007)." *Revue Mabillon* 54 (1964): 69–124.

———. "Les sculptures de Beaulieu-lès-Loches: Essai d'interprétation." *Historical Reflections/Reflexions historiques* 10 (1983): 45–58.

———. "La situation juridique des monastères de Cormery et de Villeloin sous l'abbatiat de Guy d'Anjou (v. 964–975)." *Bulletin de la Société archéologique de Touraine* 29 (1975): 551–563.

Peters, Edward. *Europe: The World of the Middle Ages*. Englewood Cliffs, N.J., 1977.

Petit, Ernest. *Histoire des ducs de Bourgogne*. Vol. 1. Paris, 1885.

Pfister, Christian. *Etudes sur le règne de Robert le pieux (996–1031)*. Paris, 1885.

Pocock, J. G. A. *The Ancient Constitution and the Feudal Law: English Historical Thought in the Seventeenth Century*. Cambridge, 1957.

Poey d'Avant, Faustin. *Monnaies féodales de France*. 3 vols. Paris, 1858–1862.

Poly, Jean-Pierre. *La Provence et la société féodale, 879–1166.* Paris, 1976.

Poly, Jean-Pierre, and Éric Bournazel. *La mutation féodale, X^e–XIe siècles.* Paris, 1980.

Port, Célestin. *Dictionnaire historique, géographique, et biographique de Maine-et-Loire.* 3 vols. Angers, 1874.

Potts, Casandra. "Normandy or Brittany? A Conflict of Interests at Mont Saint Michel (966–1035)." In *Anglo-Norman Studies,* ed. Marjorie Chibnall, 12:135–156. Woodbridge, 1990.

Poupardin, René. *Le royaume de Bourgogne (888–1038): Étude sur les origines du royaume d'Arles.* Paris, 1907.

Reynolds, Susan. *Kingdoms and Communities in Western Europe: 900–1300.* Oxford, 1984.

Richard, Alfred. *Histoire des comtes de Poitou, 778–1204.* 2 vols. Paris, 1903.

Riché, Pierre. *Ecoles et enseignement dans le haut moyen âge de la fin du Ve siècle au milieu du XIe siècle.* Paris, 1979.

Robinson, H. Russel. *The Armour of Imperial Rome.* New York, 1975.

Rosenthal, Joel T. "The Education of the Early Capetians." *Traditio* 25 (1969): 366–376.

Rosenwein, Barbara, Thomas Head, and Sharon Farmer. "Monks and Their Enemies: A Comparative Approach." *Speculum* 66 (1991): 764–796.

Salies, A. de. *Histoire de Foulques Nerra.* Angers, 1874.

Searle, Eleanor. "Fact and Pattern in Heroic History: Dudo of Saint-Quentin." *Viator* 15 (1984): 61–67.

———. *Predatory Kinship and the Creation of Norman Power, 840–1066.* Berkeley, Los Angeles, London, 1988.

Silvestri, H. "Commerce et vol des reliques au moyen âge." *Revue belge de philologie et d'histoire* 30 (1952): 721–739.

Soehenée, Frédéric. *Catalogue des actes d'Henri Ier, roi de France (1031–1060).* Paris, 1907.

Southern, Richard. *The Making of the Middle Ages.* New Haven, Conn., 1953.

Stock, Brian. *The Implications of Literacy: Written Language and Models of Interpretation in the Eleventh and Twelfth Centuries.* Princeton, 1983.

Sullivan, Richard. "The Carolingian Age: Reflections on Its Place in the History of the Middle Ages." *Speculum* 64 (1989): 267–306.

Syme, Ronald. *The Roman Revolution.* Rev. 2d ed. Oxford, 1951.

Tellegen, Auke, et al. "Personality Similarity in Twins Reared Apart and Together." *Journal of Personality and Social Psychology* 56 (1988): 1031–1039.

Tellenbach, Gerd. "Zu Erforschung des hochmittelalterlichen Adels (9.–12. Jahrhundert)." In *XXIe Congrès internationale des sciences historiques,* 1:318–336. Vienna, 1965.

Tennant, C., et al. "Parental Death in Childhood and Risk of Adult Depressive Disorders: A Review." *Psychological Medicine* 10 (1980): 289–299.

Uhlirz, Mathilde. *Jahrbücher des deutschen Reiches unter Otto II. und Otto III.* Berlin, 1954.

Vallery-Radot, Jean. "L'ancienne église abbatiale de Beaulieu-lès-Loches." *Congrès archéologique de France* 106 (1958): 126–142.

Van Hoots, Elizabeth. "Scandinavian Influence in Norman Literature of the Eleventh Century." In *Anglo-Norman Studies,* ed. R. Allen Brown, 6:107–121. Woodbridge, 1984.

Verbruggen, J. F. *The Art of Warfare in Western Europe during the Middle Ages.* Trans. Sumner Willard and S. C. M. Southern. Amsterdam, 1977.

Veyne, Paul, et al. *A History of Private Life from Pagan Rome to Byzantium.* Trans. A. Goldhammer. Cambridge, Mass., 1987.

Vogel, Walther. "Die Normannen und das fränkische Reich bis zur Gründung der Normandie (799–911)." *Heidelberger Abhandlungen zur mittleren und neueren Geschichte* 14 (1906).

Wallace-Hadrill, J. M. *The Barbarian West, 400–1000.* 1st ed., 1952; 3d rev. ed., 1967.

———. *Early Medieval History.* Oxford, 1975.

———. *The Longhaired Kings and Other Studies in Frankish History.* London, 1962.

———. "The *Via Regia* of the Carolingian Age." In *Trends in Medieval Political Thought,* ed. Beryl Smalley, 22–41. Oxford, 1965.

Wemple, Suzanne. *Women in Frankish Society: Marriage and the Cloister, 500–900.* Philadelphia, 1981.

Werner, Karl Ferdinand. "Bedeutende Adelsfamilien im Reich Karls des Grossen: Ein personengeschichtlicher Beitrag zum Verhältnis von Königtum und Adel im frühen Mittelalter." In *Karl der Grosse, Lebenswerk und Nachleben: 1 Persönlichkeit und Geschichte,* ed. Helmut Beumann, 83–142. Düsseldorf, 1965. Trans. as "Important Noble Families in the Kingdom of Charlemagne: A Prosopographical Study of the Relationship between King and Nobility in the Early Middle Ages." In *The Medieval Nobility,* ed. and trans. Timothy Reuter, 137–202. Amsterdam, 1978. The translation does not include Werner's appendices, pp. 137–142 of the original.

———. "Königtum und Fürstentum des französischen 12. Jahrhunderts." In *Probleme des 12. Jahrhunderts,* 177–225. Sigmaringen, 1968. Trans. as "Kingdom and Principality in Twelfth-century France." In *The Medieval Nobility,* ed. and trans. Timothy Reuter, 243–290. Amsterdam, 1978.

———. *Les origines (avant l'an mil): Histoire de France.* Vol. 1. Ed. Jean Favier. Paris, 1984.

———. "Untersuchungen zur Frühzeit des französischen Fürstentums (9.–10. Jahrhundert)." *Die Welt als Geschichte* 18 (1958): 256–289; 19 (1959): 146–193; 20 (1960): 87–119.

White, Stephen D. *Custom, Kinship, and Gifts to Saints: The 'Laudatio Parentum' in Western France, 1050–1150.* Chapel Hill, N.C., 1988.

———. "Feuding and Peace-Making in the Touraine around the Year 1100." *Traditio* 42 (1986): 195–263.

———. "Inheritances and Legal Arguments in Western France, 1050–1150." *Traditio* 43 (1987): 55–103.

Wood, Charles T. Review article: "The Return to Medieval Politics." *The American Historical Review* 94 (1989): 391–404.

Zettel, Horst. *Das Bild der Normannen und der Normanneneinfälle in westfränk-*

ischen, ostfränkischen, und angelsächischen Quellen des 8. bis 11. Jarhhunderts. Munich, 1977.

Ziezulewicz, William. "An Argument for Historical Continuity: Low and Middle Vassal Families in the Eleventh-century Saumurois." *Medieval Prosopography* 8, no. 1 (1987): 93–110.

———. "Etude d'un faux monastique à une période de réforme: Une charte de Charles le Chauve pour Saint-Florent de Saumur (8 juin 848)." *Cahiers de civilisation médiévale* 28 (1985): 201–211.

———. "From Serf to Abbot: The Role of the 'Familia' in the Career of Frederick of Tours." *The American Benedictine Review* 36 (1985): 278–291.

———. "A Monastic Forgery in an Age of Reform." *Archivum historiae pontificiae* 36 (1985): 7–42.

———. "'Restored' Churches in the Fisc of St. Florent de Saumur (1021–1118)." *Revue Bénédictine* 96 (1986): 106–117.

Personal Name Index

Items which appear constantly in the text have not been included in the indices: e.g. Fulk Nerra, Anjou, fortifications.

Abbo, abbot of Fleury (Saint-Benoit-sur-Loire), 29, 73, 74, 88, 167, 172, 205
Abbo Drutus, 65
Acfredus, viscount of Châtellerault, 56
Adalardus, archbishop of Tours, 4, 5
Adalbero, bishop of Laon, 50
Adalhard, count, 3
Adalmode, 31, 66–68, 85, 87, 122, 175, 204
Adelaide of Anjou, 6
Adelaide-Blanche, 7, 9, 13, 15, 51, 115, 123, 207
Adelais, 4, 5
Adele, daughter of Fulk Nerra, 72, 73, 77, 92, 158, 208, 218
Adele of Chalon, 13, 14, 30, 31, 73, 210
Adele of Vermandois, 8–12, 23
Adhebertus, abbot of Saint-Florent, 126, 252
Agnes of Burgundy, 164, 204, 205, 209, 217, 221, 225, 226, 240
Aimericus, *fidelis* of Fulk Nerra, 139, 140
Aimericus Pirus, 181
Aimery, viscount of Thouars and count of Nantes, 37, 39, 45, 51, 53, 56, 57, 60, 70, 95, 138

Aimery I of Rancon, 162
Aimery II of Rancon, 162
Aimery of Faye-la-Vineuse, 223
Aimo, archbishop of Bourges, 211
Aimo, viscount of Nantes, 40, 41
Aimo of Mayenne, 143
Alan, count of Nantes, 37, 38
Alan III, count of Rennes, 161, 167, 174, 210, 211–215, 219, 229, 230, 238, 241–243, 253
Alan the Great, count of Nantes, 4, 7, 8
Alberic of Vihiers, 31, 33, 34–36, 57, 61, 85, 95, 98, 139
Albericus of Chinon, 240
Albericus of Montjean, 161, 223
Albericus of Orléans, 35
Albericus of Sainte-Christine, 145
Albert, abbot of Saint-Aubin, 19
Aldebert, count of la Marche and Périgord, 30, 31, 51–52, 56, 58, 62, 65–68, 85, 250
Alfred the Great, 23
Algerius of Bazougers, 145
Al-Hakim, II, 123, 165, 243
Almond, abbot of Mont-Saint-Michel, 188

Place Name Index

Subject Index

Designer: U.C. Press Staff
Compositor: Prestige Typography
Text: 10/13 Galliard
Display: Galliard
Printer: Braun-Brumfield, Inc.
Binder: Braun-Brumfield, Inc.